LOYALTY PROGRAMS

THE COMPLETE GUIDE

First published in 2020 by Loyalty & Reward Co Pty Ltd

© Loyalty & Reward Co Pty Ltd, 2020

The moral rights of the author have been asserted.

All inquiries should be made to the author.

National Library of Australia Cataloguing in-Publication entry:

Creator: Shelper, Philip, author.

Co-creators: Lyons, Stacey; Savransky, Max; Harrison, Scott

Contributors: Hunter, Lincoln; Smith, Michael; Dinnis, Stuart

Title: Loyalty Programs: The Complete Guide (1st edition)/Philip Shelper.

ISBN: 978-0-6483535-6-0 (paperback)

ISBN: 978-0-6483535-8-4 (ebook)

Subjects: loyalty programs

member engagement

lifecycle management

reward programs

Cover design by Scott Harrison.

Editorial services by Stacey Lyons, Max Savransky and Scott Harrison.

Diagrams by Scott Harrison.

Photography by Kate Ireland.

Disclaimer

LOYALTY
PROGRAMS
THE COMPLETE GUIDE

PHILIP SHELPER

CO-CREATED BY
STACEY LYONS - MAX SAVRANSKY - SCOTT HARRISON

WITH CONTRIBUTIONS BY
LINCOLN HUNTER - MICHAEL SMITH - STUART DINNIS

TABLE OF CONTENTS

For Pat and Tony.

For Kate, Erik, Curtis and Litty.

Take the *Loyalty Programs: The Complete Guide* course

Loyalty Programs: The Complete Guide has been developed into an educational course.

Course format

The course provides expert theory gained from decades of combined exposure to all aspects of loyalty. Illustrative case studies and module exercises will ensure you can easily absorb complex concepts. At the end of this course, you will know more about loyalty programs than many loyalty industry professionals.

The lessons cover all aspects of loyalty program strategy, psychology and execution, and include access to over 150 current loyalty program case studies from all over the world.

Fun weekly exercises help students to apply new learnings.

Who is the *Loyalty Programs: The Complete Guide* course for?

- Marketers and brand professionals looking for ways to grow their marketing database, drive repeat purchases, learn more about customers, capture and use data, and build emotional connections with customers.

- Loyalty industry professionals looking to improve their understanding of key loyalty concepts, explore future trends, and access a broad range of global, best-practice case studies.

- Small and medium-sized businesses looking to better understand and reward customers, and differentiate from competitors.

- Corporate employees looking to upskill and develop loyalty expertise within their company.

For more details, visit www.rewardco.com.au/loyalty-programs-course

ABOUT THE AUTHORS

Philip Shelper

Phil has extensive experience within the loyalty industry, including roles at Qantas Frequent Flyer and Vodafone. He is CEO and Founder of leading loyalty consulting agency, Loyalty & Reward Co.

Phil is a member of several hundred loyalty programs, and an obsessive researcher of loyalty psychology and loyalty history, all of which he uses to understand the essential dynamics of what makes a successful loyalty program.

Phil is also the author of Blockchain Loyalty: Disrupting loyalty and reinventing marketing using blockchain and cryptocurrencies.

Connect with Phil: www.linkedin.com/in/philipshelper

Stacey Lyons

Stacey is the Marketing Director for Loyalty & Reward Co.

Stacey has many years' experience as a digital, social media and loyalty marketing expert, working within QSR, retail and online retail companies.

Stacey develops and drives marketing initiatives for clients, including member lifecycle management approaches, ongoing promotional campaign management, digital marketing and social media strategy, market research and investor relations.

Connect with Stacey: www.linkedin.com/in/staceylyons

Max Savransky

Max is the Chief Operating Officer of Loyalty & Reward Co.

Max has many years' experience within the loyalty industry, leading loyalty teams across hospitality, entertainment, financial services and market research.

Max specialises in loyalty program design, commercial modelling, loyalty technology and loyalty operations.

Connect with Max: www.linkedin.com/in/maxsavransky

Scott Harrison

Scott is the Marketing Manager of Loyalty & Reward Co.

Scott has worked in several marketing and design roles across various industries including eHealth, property and financial services.

As Marketing Manager, Scott applies his skills across all aspects of the business, including loyalty program design, member engagement, market research and loyalty strategy development.

Connect with Scott: www.linkedin.com/in/scott-c-harrison

ABOUT THE CONTRIBUTORS

Stuart Dinnis

Stuart is a global expert in Financial Management for Loyalty Programs with IFRS and US-GAAP experience in accounting policies.

Stuart has held CFO roles in Fintech, Transport, Telecommunications and CPG/FMCG. He was the Director of Loyalty for Virgin's Elevate program in North America and Head of Commercial at Virgin Australia's Velocity Frequent Flyer program.

Stuart is a Graduate of the AICD (Australian Institute of Company Directors) and a Fellow of CPA Australia.

www.linkedin.com/in/stuartdinnis

Lincoln Hunter

Lincoln is widely recognised as a leading provider of legal services in the loyalty space and specialises in helping clients get the best out of their customers (in a compliant way) and contracting with or for large coalition loyalty programs.

These days Lincoln is not quite sure whether he is a legal specialist or a loyalty specialist, but for the most part his clients get the benefit of both personalities.

Lincoln has been practising law since 1994 and advising in the loyalty, data and digital space since 2004. He is also the Founder and Principal of Loyalty Legal, where he has been practicing since 2013.

www.linkedin.com/in/lincoln-hunter-4107aa3b

Michael Smith

For the last decade, Michael has been working with loyalty programs to help them manage and prevent fraud.

Prior to co-founding the Loyalty Security Association (LSA), Michael worked for the British Airways Frequent Flyer Program.

In addition to the LSA, Michael is a Board Advisor for Ai Events | Airline Information which operates the leading airline/travel loyalty, co-brand and payments & fraud events.

www.linkedin.com/in/michael-smith-b7250a1

ABOUT LOYALTY & REWARD CO

Loyalty &
Reward Co

Loyalty & Reward Co are a world-leading loyalty consulting agency.

Working with major brands globally across multiple industries and markets including B2C & B2B, their experienced team provides comprehensive insight into all aspects of loyalty including program design, consumer psychology, commercial modelling, marketing strategy, legal and regulatory guidance, technical and platform solutions, data collection and usage, reporting and analytics, and post-launch operations.

Loyalty & Reward Co use their data-driven Deep DIVE© approach to efficiently and cost-effectively design, implement and operate best-practice loyalty programs.

When Loyalty & Reward Co secure a new client for a consulting role, the team join and engage with other loyalty programs in the client's industry in order to research different approaches to loyalty program design, marketing, data collection and usage, and other elements.

This extensive exposure to hundreds of loyalty programs across multiple industries has uniquely equipped Loyalty & Reward Co to provide comprehensive insight into every aspect of the global loyalty market. The team are constantly writing opinion articles about the industry which can be accessed on their blog - www.rewardco.com.au/blog

Connect with Loyalty & Reward Co:

Website: www.rewardco.com.au

Email: hello@rewardco.com.au

LinkedIn: www.linkedin.com/company/loyalty-&-reward-co

GLOSSARY

INDUSTRY AND SHORTENED TERMS

Term	Description
Affiliate revenue	A marketing revenue model by which commission is earned when a company promotes another company's e-commerce offering, leading to a trackable transaction.
Attitudinal commitment	Repeat purchase behaviour driven by an emotional connection.
Behavioural commitment	Repeated purchase behaviour driven by habitual consumption.
Billings	Coalition loyalty programs generate billings when a partner company pays for a member to earn points.
Bot	A software application that runs automated tasks over the internet.
Breakage	Currency (e.g. points) issued which expires due to different rules. This may be because the member has not engaged in account activity, or because the currency has not been redeemed within a specified time period.
Churn	Customers that have ceased using a company's products or services.

Coalition	Where a loyalty program operator develops partnerships with third-party companies (a 'coalition' of partners) to participate in the program by promoting loyalty currency earn to their customers.
Cookie	Text files with small pieces of data used to identify an individual computer and keep track of browsing visits and activity.
Customer centric	A business approach which places the customer as the central focus of all company operations.
Data brokers	Data brokers collect extensive personal data about billions of individuals from all around the world, which they may package up and sell to loyalty programs to help build out and standardise their member profiles.
Deferred liability account	An account which holds the deferred revenue to cover the cost of points that have been issued but not yet redeemed.
Digital EQ	The ability to anticipate and recognise customer sentiment and deliver a digitally enabled response which optimises the customer experience in real time, serving to build a deeper emotional connection.
Efficient rewards	Rewards which are inexpensive for a company to provide compared to the perceived value by the member.
First-party data	Data which is collected via customer interactions which the company owns.
Halo effect	Occurs when positive first impressions positively influence future judgments or ratings of unrelated factors.

Mere-exposure effect	Where people tend to develop a preference for things they are familiar with.
Mileage run/ status run	Where a loyalty program member engaged in additional transaction activity (i.e. unplanned flights) with the sole purpose of earning status credits.
Pareto Principle	An observation which asserts that 80% of outcomes result from 20% of all causes (i.e. 80% of revenues are generated by 20% of members).
Share of wallet	The percentage of total dollar spend a customer regularly devotes to a particular brand.
Zero-party data	Data that is owned by the consumer that they intentionally and proactively share with a brand that they trust.
2FA	Two factor authentication.
AI	Artificial intelligence.
API	Application programming interface.
B2B	Business-to-business.
B2C	Business-to-consumer.
BOPIS	Buy online, pick up in-store.
CDP	Customer data platform.
CRM	Customer relationship management.
CX	Customer experience.
DM	Direct message.
EBITDA	Earnings before interest, taxes, depreciation and amortisation.
EBITDAR	Earnings before interest, taxes, depreciation and amortisation, and rent/restructuring.
eDM	Electronic direct mail.
FOMO	Fear of missing out.
GAAP	Generally accepted accounting principles.
GDP	Gross domestic product.

GDPR	General data protection regulation.
IFRS13	Defines fair value, sets out a framework for measuring fair value, and requires disclosures about fair value measurements.
IP address	Internet protocol address.
MLM	Member lifecycle management.
NBA	Next best action.
OCR	Optical character recognition.
P&L	Profit and loss.
PII	Personally Identifiable Information.
PIN	Personal identification number.
POS	Point of sale.
QR code	Quick response code.
QSR	Quick service restaurant.
RFID	Radio frequency identification.
ROI	Return on investment.
RFM	Recency frequency monetary value.
SDK	Software development kit.
SKU	Stock keeping unit.
SME's	Small-to-medium enterprises.
SMS	Short message service.
UX	User experience.

LOYALTY PROGRAMS

'77 per cent of brands could simply disappear and no-one would care'

Havas Media Group[1]

IT IS BECOMING increasingly important for brands to build a meaningful emotional bond with customers to generate genuine customer loyalty. Generating sustained, meaningful engagement with members requires a deep understanding of consumer behaviour and expectations to effectively respond to their needs at each stage of their journey.

Loyalty programs are structured programs which reward registered members for repeat transactions. A well-designed loyalty program can work to successfully drive engagement between a brand and members, building deeper emotional connections which manifest in increased visits, spend, brand affinity, advocacy, retention and market share.

The overarching goal of this book is to provide the definitive guide for loyalty program theory and practice. Real world case studies from existing loyalty programs globally are used to illustrate the concepts detailed throughout.

Each chapter answers important questions which loyalty professionals can draw on to strategically design, execute, operate and optimise best-practice loyalty programs.

---

1   Havas Group, 2019, 'Meaningful Brands', https://www.meaningful-brands.com/en, accessed 3 July 2020.

Loyalty Programs: The Complete Guide has been organised into 17 chapters which cover all facets of loyalty programs:

- **Chapter 1:** defines what a loyalty program is, and is not, the many benefits and challenges of loyalty programs for consumers, loyalty program operators and merchant partners, as well as consumer expectations from a loyalty program.

- **Chapter 2:** provides a historical review of loyalty programs, detailing the evolution of loyalty program designs, currencies and rewards over time.

- **Chapter 3:** reviews a large body of academic research which both proves and disproves the claim that loyalty programs work to effectively generate genuine customer loyalty.

- **Chapter 4:** accepting that loyalty programs can work, a selection of important academic research studies are presented which identify best-practice principles for loyalty program design. This includes the circumstances under which loyalty programs can best work to effectively establish and maintain meaningful member engagement.

- **Chapter 5:** reviews the extensive body of consumer psychology research which can be directly applied to loyalty program design in an effort to drive desired behavioural changes among consumers.

- **Chapter 6:** defines the loyalty specific biases and heuristics which influence consumer decision making processes and how loyalty programs can be designed to appeal to them.

- **Chapter 7:** outlines the critical importance of desirable rewards in the overall success of a loyalty program, and the types of rewards or reward aggregators available. The types of rewards which are best suited to influencing specific behaviours in different circumstances are also detailed.

- **Chapter 8:** presents a range of loyalty program and member engagement conceptual design frameworks. Each framework, and variations of each model are detailed, together with the associated benefits and challenges. Combining multiple frameworks into a hybrid design is also discussed.

- **Chapter 9:** details how Business-to-Business (B2B) loyalty programs can deliver significant results to companies. The characteristics of a B2B loyalty program are defined, with the differences between B2B and B2C programs distinguished.

- **Chapter 10:** discusses the value of member data and provides insights into how loyalty programs collect and use member data, as well as consumer awareness about the data being collected and traded.

- **Chapter 11:** covers the role technology plays in the execution of a loyalty program, capabilities of a best-practice loyalty platform, and emerging trends and technological innovation in the loyalty industry. Major trends discussed include machine learning and AI, in-store personalisation, subscription memberships, card and bank account linking, digital wallets and payments, third-party aggregators, geolocation tracking, affiliate marketing and blockchain.

- **Chapter 12:** details the approach to member communications across each different stage of the member lifecycle including Acquisition, Onboarding, Growth, Advocacy, Retention and Winback. More complex models are also reviewed.

- **Chapter 13:** analyses ways that both games and gamification can be used as a mechanic to drive deeper member engagement and stimulate desired member behaviours.

- **Chapter 14:** outlines the different ways loyalty programs can generate income for the program operator and defines five commercial models for measuring loyalty program effectiveness and return on investment. The commercial models include Wansink's cost-effectiveness model, lifecycle management model, recency frequency monetary value (RFM) model, coalition program model and member lifetime value model.

- **Chapter 15:** details a general introduction to legal considerations for loyalty programs globally. With different jurisdictions regulating the loyalty industry in various ways, local legal guidance is critical to ensure appropriate compliance.

- **Chapter 16:** presents loyalty specific security and fraud risks which can affect loyalty programs, with details on how each risk should best be mitigated.

- **Chapter 17:** determines the teams, roles and responsibilities involved in operating a loyalty program including all business functions impacted by a loyalty program. Options for insourcing or outsourcing are outlined, with the benefits and challenges associated with outsourcing some, or all, of the loyalty program operations.

- **Conclusion:** considers what the future of loyalty may hold for consumers, loyalty program operators and loyalty solution providers.

CHAPTER 1

LOYALTY PROGRAM BENEFITS AND CHALLENGES

'You don't earn loyalty in a day. You earn loyalty day-by-day.'

- Jeffrey Gitomer

Focus areas

This chapter will address the following questions:

- What is a loyalty program?
- What is the ambition of a company in operating a loyalty program?
- What are the benefits and challenges of loyalty programs for consumers, program operators and third-party partners?
- How are consumer expectations of loyalty programs changing?

LOYALTY PROGRAMS ARE extremely prevalent globally. They are available to consumers across almost every industry, with new programs being launched, or existing programs being relaunched, on a regular basis. Loyalty programs are also increasingly provided to businesses as part of business-to-business (B2B) loyalty strategies.

According to research, on average, each American is active in 8.4 loyalty programs,[2] Canadians belong to an average 8.2 programs, Australians an average of 4.1 programs[3] and South-East Asians an average of 3.5 programs.[4] One article reports Austrians are members of an astonishing average of 14 programs.[5]

To begin the journey into understanding loyalty programs, it is important to define what a loyalty program is. Here are some simple definitions which define what a loyalty program is, as distinct from a customer engagement program and membership program:

- **Loyalty program:** A structured program which rewards registered members for repeat transactions.

- **Membership program:** A structured program which provides registered members with access to benefits not available to non-members.

- **Customer engagement program:** A strategic campaign structure which attempts to stimulate consumers to engage more with a brand or company without the customer needing to register to access benefits.

Loyalty programs and membership programs are the primary focus for this book, although the subject may occasionally extend to customer engagement programs. Engagement itself is discussed extensively, being a primary driver of loyalty. Loyalty programs are about more than just points, miles, discounts and rewards. They involve ideas, processes, interactions and technologies working together to drive meaningful member engagement which strengthens relationships and builds loyalty as an outcome.

For a consumer, the primary intention in engaging with a loyalty program

---

2   Canadian Marketing Association, 2017, 'The 2017 COLLOQUY Loyalty Census', https://www.the-cma.org/Contents/Item/Display/327325, accessed 11 June 2020.

3   The Point of Loyalty, 'For Love or Money 2018'.

4   Vivid Engagement, 'Loyalty Asia Report; 2020 ASEAN Insights', 2020.

5   Ehredt, C., 'Innovators Break The Mould, At The 2020 Loyalty Magazine Awards', Currency Alliance, https://www.linkedin.com/pulse/innovators-break-mould-2020-loyalty-magazine-awards-charles-ehredt/, accessed 18 June 2020.

is to access rewards. Arias-Carrion and Poppel (2007)[6] stated that rewards are experienced as 'making things better' and are therefore liked, desired and pursued. Consumption of rewards produces pleasure. At a base level this pleasure can 'initiate learning processes that consolidate liking the rewarding goal, learning cues that predict its availability and actions that permit its consumption.' Pleasure can also work to assign value, which helps consumers determine what level of effort to put towards obtaining the reward.

There are a range of conflicting studies which both prove and disprove the effectiveness of loyalty programs (which will be explored in Chapter 3). Nevertheless, most industry experts agree on the ambition of a loyalty program; to drive deeper engagement between members and a company or brand, manifesting in increased visits, spend, brand affinity, advocacy, retention and market share.

Consumer benefits and challenges

From a consumer perspective, the benefits a loyalty program can provide, include:

- **Value:** members may be rewarded with points, miles, discounts, value-adds or other tangible benefits which non-members do not receive.

- **Exclusivity:** members may be provided with exclusive benefits such as access to lounges, priority queues and VIP events.

- **Recognition:** members may be shown appreciation through the delivery of surprise gifts or rewards.

- **Relevancy:** members receive tailored communications, offers and rewards specific to their individual preferences, increasing the usefulness and appeal.

Core challenges consumers face when engaging with loyalty programs can include:

- **Value:** the rewards provided by the program are not always adequate, compelling or accessible. For example, the member may not

---

6   Arias-Carrión, O. & Pöppel, E., 2007, 'Dopamine, learning, and reward-seeking behavior', Acta neurobiologiae experimentalis, Vol 67, pp481-8.

spend enough with the brand to earn access to a sufficiently desirable reward, or the reward they can access are not appealing.

- **Program saturation:** consumers may be overwhelmed by the sheer volume of loyalty programs being promoted to them, with most consumer companies offering a program to their customers.

- **Marketing assault:** many loyalty programs send large volumes of marketing materials to members via email, SMS, push notification, banner advertising and mail. For some members, the volume of marketing received may be perceived as excessive, while the content may not be relevant.

- **Data capture and control:** a loyalty program may capture personal data in ways the member is not aware of, or does not approve of, and use it for purposes the member may not deem appropriate. The member may also feel they have a lack of control over how their data is captured and used by the program.

Company benefits and challenges

For a program operator, the potential benefits are numerous:

- **Grow and protect share of wallet:** a loyalty program can grow the recency, frequency and value of member transactions by making the engagement process more rewarding. It can also reduce member churn by developing meaningful relationships and introducing barriers to exit.

- **Better understand members:** a program can play a useful role in better understanding members as individuals and tailoring communications, offers, products and services to meet their needs more accurately.

- **Drive advocacy:** a program can successfully turn members into promoters by delighting and rewarding them above their expectations.

- **Build a marketing database:** a program can be an effective way for a company to build a member database, which in the age of digital marketing is one of the most valuable assets a company can possess, as it increases the effectiveness of marketing while reducing advertising costs.

Core challenges program operators face when executing loyalty programs can include:

- **Expense:** designing, implementing and running a loyalty program can be expensive. Companies generally need to hire expertise to design and operate a program, plus buy, build or lease the required systems and solutions. Additional expenses include marketing, training, legal, accounting and customer service. There is also the cost of rewards. While a small number of large programs generate profits, most programs are considered a cost to the business.

- **Ability to deliver meaningful value:** the key driver of engagement with most loyalty programs is value. Members will join a program because they believe they will access value, and they will continue to engage because they perceive they are accessing value. Some companies do not generate sufficient margin to be able to deliver enough value directly to the majority of the member base to ensure their engagement is maintained.

- **Disengagement:** maintaining consistent member engagement can be incredibly challenging. Many loyalty programs have significant numbers of members on their database who no longer engage with the program at all.

- **Competition:** the loyalty industry is incredibly competitive and growing more so every year. Loyalty program operators need to continually innovate and evolve to ensure they remain attractive and relevant to their members, especially when compared to competitor programs.

Customer retention is a key driver for many companies in introducing a loyalty program. In a study of over 14 industries, Riechheld (1996)[7] reported

---

7   Reichheld, F., 1996, 'The Loyalty Effect: The Hidden Force Behind Growth, Profits, and Lasting Value', Harvard Business School Press, Boston.

that a 5 per cent increase in customer retention can generate a profit increase from between 25 per cent and 95 per cent.

With such a wide range of benefits, it is not surprising that loyalty programs have expanded into most industries and most countries globally. However, many companies struggle to navigate the range of challenges and, as a result, operate at a suboptimal level for both the members and the company.

Coalition loyalty programs

A coalition program is defined as a loyalty program where the program operator develops partnerships with third-party companies (a 'coalition' of partners) to also participate in the program. Third-party companies provide the coalition program operators' branded points/miles to their customers as a reward for transacting with them. The coalition partners pay the loyalty coalition program operator an agreed amount for the points/miles conferred on members, and in return the loyalty coalition program operator may promote the third-party partner to their member base.

In many countries, the loyalty industry is dominated by coalition programs. They are often run by large airlines, hotels, banks and supermarkets, and have the potential to generate massive revenues for their parent companies. Examples of the bigger coalition programs include AAdvantage, Nectar, AirMiles, Asia Miles, Marriott Bonvoy, Hilton Honors, Miles & More and United MileagePlus.

The loyalty coalition program model is detailed further in Chapter 8.

Evolving consumer expectations

The modern digital age has made it more challenging for loyalty program operators (and companies in general) to deliver to consumer expectations. Netflix, Amazon, Uber, Spotify and other companies have redefined what it means to be a service business through the seamless delivery of ultra-convenience, personalisation and value. Sawhney[8] argues that these companies have developed a new customer manifesto:

---

8   Sawhney, M., 'Applications of AI in Marketing and Customer Experience Management', Course 5, https://www.course5i.com/blogs/applications-of-ai-in-marketing-and-customer-experience-management/, accessed 23 May 2020.

- Know me (who I am, what I like)

- Respond quickly (preferably real-time)

- Be where I want to be (I'll choose the channel to engage, not you)

- Tell me what you stand for (your values, mission)

- Speak to my pains and passions (create meaning for me, don't just sell your product)

- Give me value for my privacy (what are you giving me in exchange for my data), and

- Reward me for loyalty (rewards, convenience, etc.)

Sawhney further argues that the only way to keep consumers engaged is to understand the customer journey, and respond to customer expectations and meet their needs at each stage of the journey, a central theme throughout this book.

Key insights

- Loyalty programs are structured programs which reward registered members for repeat purchases.

- The ambition of a company in operating a loyalty program is to drive deeper engagement between members and a company or brand, manifesting in increased visits, spend, brand affinity, advocacy, retention and market share.

- Consumers and companies can enjoy a range of benefits with loyalty programs, but also face many challenges. Program operators should consider these carefully when designing and operating a program to maximise their chances of success.

- Netflix, Amazon, Uber, Spotify and other companies have raised consumer expectations of service standards and have made it more challenging for loyalty program operators (and companies in general) to satisfy member needs. Consumers expect a program to know them, respond quickly, communicate through their preferred channel, create meaning for them, provide valuable rewards and ultra-convenience.

Suggested reading

- Arias-Carrión, Oscar & Pöppel, Ernst, 2007, Dopamine, learning, and reward-seeking behaviour', Acta neurobiologiae experimentalis, *Vol* 67, pp481-8.

- Sawhney, M., 'Applications of AI in Marketing and Customer Experience Management', Course 5, https://www.course5i.com/blogs/applications-of-ai-in-marketing-and-customer-experience-management/

CHAPTER 2

THE HISTORY OF
LOYALTY PROGRAMS

'No Money! And You Need Tea Towels, Bath Towels, Sheets and Pillow Cases? Here's a SECRET! There's MAGIC in GROUP TOKENS. They grow rapidly and CHANGE QUICKLY into "Dri-glo" Bath Towels.'

- Group Tokens advertisement, Merchants Trade Expansion Group Ltd (date unknown).

Focus areas

This chapter will address the following questions:

- When did loyalty programs first appear?
- What are the different types of loyalty currencies which have been used throughout history?
- When did coalition programs first appear?
- How have loyalty programs changed over time?
- How have loyalty programs stayed the same over time?

LOYALTY PROGRAMS HAVE been around for hundreds of years, with approaches becoming more sophisticated over time. This chapter chronologically details the evolution of loyalty currency-based programs used over time.

Beer and Bread Tokens (Ancient Egypt)

In *Ancient Egypt: Anatomy of A Civilisation*[9] Professor Barry Kemp argues that ancient Egyptians practised a type of reward program similar to modern frequent flyer programs, including status tiers and the ability to redeem on a wider variety of rewards.

For much of the pharaoh's thousands of years of rule, they did not have money. It simply was not invented yet. Instead citizens, conscripted workers and slaves alike were all awarded commodity '*tokens*' (similar to loyalty points or miles) for their work and temple time. The most common were beer and bread tokens. The tokens were physical things, made from wood, then plastered over and painted and shaped like a jug of beer or a loaf of bread.

The more senior people in the hierarchy were rewarded with the same tokens but received bonuses. The Rhind Mathematical Papyrus details examples and mathematical equations regarding how higher positions, such as the skipper, crew leader and doorkeeper, received double bread tokens compared to the rest of the crew. This could be construed as a variant of the status tier bonus, where higher tier members earn bonus points for transactions to reward them for their loyalty.

The tokens could also be exchanged for things other than bread and beer. Those high up enough to earn surplus tokens could redeem them on other goods and services, in the same way that frequent flyer members with lots of points can redeem them on flights and on non-flight rewards such as iPads, KitchenAid mixers and Gucci handbags.

While some of the characteristics are quite similar to a modern loyalty program, is this really a loyalty program? Some might argue it is simply a societal exchange system developed in the absence of fiat currency. Others might contend that is exactly what a modern loyalty program design is; a non-fiat exchange system utilising tokenised currencies.

---

9   Kemp, B. J., 2005, 'Ancient Egypt: Anatomy of a Civilization, 2nd Edition'.

Copper Tokens (c. 1700 – 1800s)

The first modern loyalty program, according to a New York Times article by Nagle (1973),[10] commenced in 1793, when a Sudbury, New Hampshire merchant began rewarding customers with *'copper tokens'*. The tokens could be accumulated and used for future purchases, thereby generating repeat visits, the core behavioural objective of loyalty program design. The idea was quickly replicated by other retailers and carried into the 18th century.

Is there evidence to support this claim? While copper loyalty tokens from Sudbury dating back to 1793 could not be found, the authors did identify other merchant-branded copper, brass and aluminium tokens created in the US in the 1800s. For example, the New York Times article by Nagle refers to a brass token created by Robinson & Ballou Grocers, dated 1863, which can be found online for sale by various coin dealers worldwide for as little as US$50.

This would appear to provide support for the existence of merchant loyalty tokens, however further investigation reveals these coins to be more accurately referred to as 'Civil War' tokens, which may not be related to loyalty programs at all.

During the 1861-64 US Civil War, high inflation sparked a frenzy of hoarding, with the focus on gold, silver and copper coins. With few coins left in circulation, merchants began to suffer as small denomination coins were the most commonly tendered at that point in time. To alleviate the situation, merchants began minting their own tokens to fill the void.[11] These were typically one cent in value and made of copper or brass, and were similar in size to government issued coinage.

This was not the first time such an approach has been taken by merchants. Between 1832-1844, 'Hard Times' tokens were created when the United States went through an economic depression over the fate of the Second Bank of the United States and the powers of the Federal Treasury. The climax of that period was the 'Panic of 1837', brought on by President

---

10   Nagle, J., 1971, 'Trading Stamps: A Long History', New York Times, https://www.nytimes.com/1971/12/26/archives/trading-stamps-a-long-history-premiums-said-to-date-back-in-us-to.html, accessed 22 April 2020.

11   Fuld, G. & Fuld, M., 1975, 'U.S. Civil War Store Cards', Quarterman Publishing, Inc.

Andrew Jackson's requirement that banks and receivers of public money only accept gold or silver in payment for public lands as a way to reduce speculation. As a result, gold and silver were hoarded and loans were called in, generating a run on the banks. An insight from an article by the American Numismatic Association (Mudd, 2015)[12] states, 'The immediate reason for the issuance of the tokens was the ongoing shortage of small change in the United States – a situation that had existed ever since the Colonial period despite the best efforts of the United States Mint'.

This provides an important clue for the investigation of the famed Sudbury merchant from 1793. It appears that coinage shortages also existed at that time right across the US. A Quarterly Journal of Economics article (Barnard, 1917)[13] references merchants minting their own coins of brass and tin as early as 1701 after the Massachusetts mint was closed in 1697. Further examples are cited from Virginia as early as 1714, with many more coins created between 1773-74. In Connecticut, copper mine owner John Higley created the first recorded copper tokens between 1737-39, while Chalmers, a goldsmith of Annapolis, Maryland issued tokens in at least three denominations (shillings, sixpence, and threepence) just after the American Revolution in 1783. Barnard states that so many other merchants created silver and copper coins that laws were passed by Pennsylvania, Connecticut and New Jersey prohibiting the circulation of coins not expressly authorised.

Thus, the historical record appears to show the primary driving force for the creation by merchants of branded copper (and other metal) tokens was to address a severe shortage of coinage which was inhibiting commerce.

Did a Sudbury, New Hampshire merchant invent the world's first loyalty program when they began rewarding customers with copper tokens in 1793? It is possible that such a merchant created branded copper tokens, however there is no evidence to support the claim made in the New York Times article (and repeated extensively across numerous books and websites) that they created the tokens in order to reward loyal customers. In fact, the likelihood is

---

12   Mudd, D., 2015, 'Hard Times Tokens', American Numismatic Association, https://www.money.org/ana-blog/TalesHardTimesTokens, accessed 22 April 2020.

13   Barnard, B. W., 1917, 'The Use of Private Tokens for Money in the United States', The Quarterly Journal of Economics, Vol 31, No. 4, pp600-634.

they were created to address a local coin shortage, and this was later misinterpreted as an early form of loyalty program currency.

Irrespective, the Coinage Act of 1864 enacted by Congress made the minting and usage of non-government issued coins illegal, ending this era forever.

Trade Marks (1850s)

Based on the available evidence, the true godfather of the modern loyalty program would appear to be B.T. Babbitt. Born in 1809, Benjamin Talbot Babbitt found his fortune in New York City in his early 30s by designing an original and cheaper process to make *saleratus*, a key base ingredient of baking powder. He soon expanded his product range to include yeast, baking powder and soap powder. He became the first to sell individually wrapped bars of soap, with 'Babbitt's Best Soap' becoming a household name across the US.[14]

To boost repeat sales, in the 1850s[15] B.T. Babbitt, Inc. launched a new (and truly revolutionary) promotional program, where they invited customers to cut-out and collect the '*trade marks*' from product packaging of Best Soap and 1776 Soap Powder. The trade marks could initially be redeemed for coloured lithographs by mailing them to the company. Soon after, the rewards range was expanded into a more comprehensive offering, which was promoted in the company's 'Mailing List of Premiums'.

As an example of the rewards on offer, The 1905 *Mailing List of Premiums* offers a wide range of choices, including a harmonica, felt pencil case or box of school crayons for 25 trade marks; a buckhorn handle pocket knife (2 blades), sterling silver thimble or pair of Uncle Sam suspenders for 50 trade marks; all the way up to a lady's locket chain (14k gold filled), lady's gold ring (12 pearls) or lady's handbag for 225 trade marks.[16] These are not just practical, utilitarian products, but truly aspirational items which would have captivated the member base in a way which history has never seen before.

---

14   Ingam, J.N., 1983, 'Biographical dictionary of American business leaders', Greenwood Press.

15   National Commission on Food Marketing, 1966, 'Organization and competition in food retailing', Technical study No.7, p41

16   B.T. Babbitt, Incorporated, 1905, 'Mailing List of Premiums'.

B.T. Babbitt also introduced the option for customers to visit their premium stores located in major cities across the US, as well as Canada, Porto Rico and Scotland, to redeem trade marks for 'a large number of household articles, dolls, toys, etc.'.

As a new approach to marketing, the company positioned the program as a profit-sharing plan, potentially taking inspiration from dividends paid on shares, or rebates for volume sales. The 1912 *B.T. Babbitt's Profit Sharing List*[17]

---

17   B.T. Babbitt, Incorporated, 1912, 'B.T. Babbitt's Profit Sharing List'.

states 'B.T. Babbitt was the originator of premiums… the firm has continued since that time to give its customers in the form of premiums a very material share of the profits of its immense business.'.

The Profit Share Plan also cautions, 'When you buy all B.T. Babbitt's Products, consisting of Soaps, Cleanser, "1776" Soap Powder, and Pure Lye or Potash, you are entitled to a return in the form of a premium. If you do not save the trade marks from any of the Babbitt articles you are losing just so much. These trade marks are worth fully one-half cent each to you if redeemed from our premiums.'

Checks (c. 1860s)

In the 1860s, the Great Atlantic & Pacific Tea Co. (which was set to become the largest retailer in the world under the A&P brand between 1920 into the 1960s[18]) launched a comparable program to reward their customers for purchasing a selection of their products. When transacting, customers would receive a red coupon known as a *'check'*, detailing the amount it was worth and the terms. One 1890 example states, 'This Check (good for the amount as engraved for presents of Glass ware, China, etc.) is redeemable at any of our 200 Stores. Provided it is Stamped with the Address of the Store that issued it. Managers will be particular and allow no Checks to be given out before they are stamped. This Check is of no value except Stamped as per the foregoing. ALL CHECKS MUST BE PUNCHED AFTER REDEMPTION. PUNCHED CHECKS ARE OF NO VALUE.'[19]

---

18   Levinson, M., 2012, 'Don't Grieve for the Great A&P', Harvard Business Review.

19   The Great Atlantic And Pacific Tea Co, 1890, '1890 Great Atlantic & Pacific Tea Co. Coupon Premium - Handstamp of Big Bleecker'.

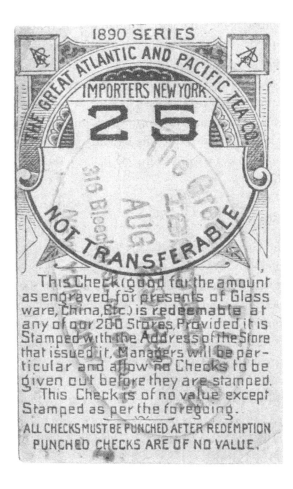

Checks could be accumulated and redeemed in stores for a range of consumer goods. This was incredibly popular with customers and it provided a strategic competitive advantage over smaller merchants who could not afford, and did not have the space, to provide such a sizeable reward range. It also posed some challenges. According to Levinson,[20] 'the premiums not only were costly, but also took up shelf space that could have displayed merchandise for sale. Many stores of the period looked more like gift shops than groceries'.

To address this issue, in the early 1900s the company published The Great

---

20   Levison, M., 2011, 'The Great A&P and the Struggle for Small Business in America,' Hill & Wang, 2011.

Atlantic & Pacific Tea Co. Catalogue. This promoted a range of day-to-day homeware products including saucepans, teapots, knives, ironing boards, sugar tins, wash bowls, spoons, bread trays and more.[21] Once enough checks had been saved, members could send them to a central office and receive the reward by return freight,[22] reducing the need for each store to range the full rewards range.

A few years later, The Great Atlantic & Pacific Tea Co transferred their loyalty program operations to Sperry & Hutchinson, a stamp program covered later in this chapter.

Tickets (1872)

The Grand Union Tea Company was formed in 1872 in Pennsylvania and followed the lead of the Great Atlantic & Pacific Tea Co with their loyalty program design. The owners chose to sidestep retailers and sell their product directly to consumers, starting with door to door sales. They rewarded customers with '*tickets*' which could be collected and redeemed for a wide selection of products from the company's *Catalog of Premiums*.[23] The 1903 version of the *Catalog of Premiums* lists the full product range and prices (coffee, tea, spices, extracts, baking powder soap and sundries), as well as 17 pages of rewards. These include an Oak Roman Chair (100 tickets), lace curtains (120 tickets a pair), Ormolu clock (300 tickets) and dinner set Berlin 1903 (440 tickets). Customers could earn one ticket by buying a pound of coffee at 20 cents, two tickets for premium tea at 40 cents and one ticket for a packet of cloves at 10 cents. The catalogue proudly proclaims, 'We advertise by giving presents with our goods, thus SHARING WITH OUR CUSTOMERS the profits of our business. Remember, you pay less for our goods of same quality than at other stores, and get presents in addition.'

---

21   The Great Atlantic & Pacific Tea Co, 'Great Atlantic & Pacific Tea Co Catalogue,' 1908.

22   Levison, M., 'The Great A&P and the Struggle for Small Business in America,' Hill & Wang.

23   Grand Union Tea Company, 1903, 'Catalogue Of Premiums'.

The 1971 New York Times article by Nagle included an interview with William H. Preis, senior vice president of the Grand Union Tea Company. Preis joined the company in 1933. By the time of the interview, the company had transitioned their tickets program to a coalition-based stamps program run by Stop & Save Trading Corporation. Customers could earn Triple-S Blue Stamps which cost the company 1 ¼ per cent of sales. Preis indicated they had been providing the stamps program for 16 years.[24]

Certificates and Coupons (1890)

This period may have potentially been a boom time for the newly designed loyalty marketing function, with companies big and small adopting the approach. One example from 1890 is a 'People's Trading Coupon' from Hunsicker & Warmkessell Photographers, based in Allentown, Philadelphia. The coupon is

---

24   Nagle, J., 1971, 'Trading Stamps: A Long History', New York Times, https://www.nytimes.com/1971/12/26/archives/trading-stamps-a-long-history-premiums-said-to-date-back-in-us-to.html, accessed 22 April 2020.

a sophisticated punch card which, when completed, provides the member with 'one dozen of our best $4 Cabinet Photographs'. The member is reminded to 'Tell your friends to get a ticket.'[25]

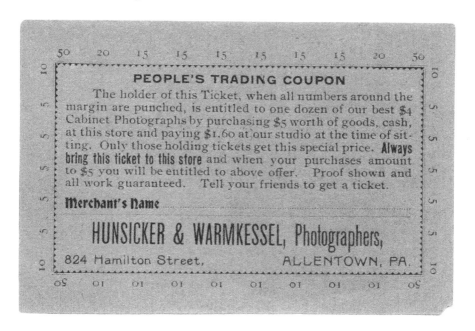

Another example is The United Cigars Store Co., founded in 1901 and sporting over 3,000 retail outlets at its peak in 1926.[26] They ran a successful *'certificates and coupons'* rewards program (where five coupons were equal to one certificate). United built a coalition of partners by making deals with companies including Wrigleys, Swifts, Danish Pride, National, Barkers, Votan and Tootsie, all of which put United coupons within their product packaging. Certificates and coupons were redeemable by mail or at 250 redemption centres around the country. Rewards included a men's gold-filled watch or six place settings of Rogers silver plate flatware (900 coupons), room-size oriental style rug (4,000 coupons), a Remington automatic shotgun (5,000 coupons) and a four-wheel Studebaker carriage (25,000 coupons).

---

25 Hunsicker & Warmkessel, 1890, 'People's Trading Coupon', Allentown, PA.

26 United Cigar Stores, IMASCO, http://www.imascoltd.com/united-cigar-stores/, Accessed 7 April 2020.

The United Cigars Store Co 1924 *Premium Catalog*[27] features a selection of well over one thousand reward items, including clothing, umbrellas, smoking accessories, razors, cutlery, leather goods, toiletries, jewellery, clocks, watches, kitchenware, headphones, cameras, sporting goods, toys, games and silverware.

---

27   United Cigar Stores Company of America, 1924, 'Premium Catalog'.

Stamps (1891)

In the 1890s, companies began using physical '*stamps*' to reward loyal customers. Customers could earn stamps when making purchases and were encouraged to stick them into collecting books. The books could then be exchanged for a wide range of rewards.

The first company to introduce stamps was Schuster's Department Store in Milwaukee in 1891. Customers earned one stamp for every US10c spent. A filled book of 500 stamps was worth US$1 to redeem on rewards (a 2 per cent return on spend). By WWII, it appears the program had expanded into a small coalition, with a stamp book dating from that era promoting 'Valuable Schuster Stamps Are Now Also Given By Many Food Markets.'[28]

In 1896, The Sperry & Hutchinson Company embraced the coalition loyalty program as their central business model. Rather than a company issuing their own loyalty currency, Sperry & Hutchinson created the entire loyalty program apparatus as a service. New England retailers were provided with S&H Green Stamps, books, and catalogues to provide to their customers, and customers could redeem the books directly with Sperry & Hutchinson.

While other companies replicated their model (Gold Bond, Gift House, Top Value and King Korn amongst some of their competitors[29]), Sperry & Hutchison remained the biggest globally. At one point, they claimed they were distributing three times as many Green Stamps as the US Postal Service was distributing postal Stamps.

Every year, Sperry & Hutchinson would release a print version of their catalogue *Ideabook Of Distinguished Merchandise*. The 1966 *70th Anniversary Edition Ideabook Of Distinguished Merchandise*,[30] provides insight into the scale and complexity of their operations when at the height of their popularity. In addition to being able to order rewards via post, members could visit a vast network of redemption centres, with the entire product range priced in books of stamps. The 185-page catalogue contains over 2,000 products across 59 categories, a similar sized range to some frequent flyer program online stores. In the copy possessed by the authors, a young lady has worked her way through the toys' pages, circling the items she desired and writing out the number of books she needed to claim everything on her list. It provides a sense of the process so many households around the world would have followed in deciding which rewards they wanted to aim for, with much discussion and debate ensuing.

---

28   Dahlsad, D., 2013, 'Inherited Values', http://www.inherited-values.com/2013/09/meet-me-down-by-schusters-vintage-department-store-memories-collectibles/, accessed 4 May 2020.

29   Lonto, J. R., 2013, 'The Trading Stamp Story,' StudioZ-7 Publishing, http://www.studioz7.com/stamps.html, accessed 4 May 2020.

30   Sperry & Hutchinson Company, 1966, 'Ideabook Of Distinguished Merchandise 70th Anniversary Edition', S&H Green Stamps.

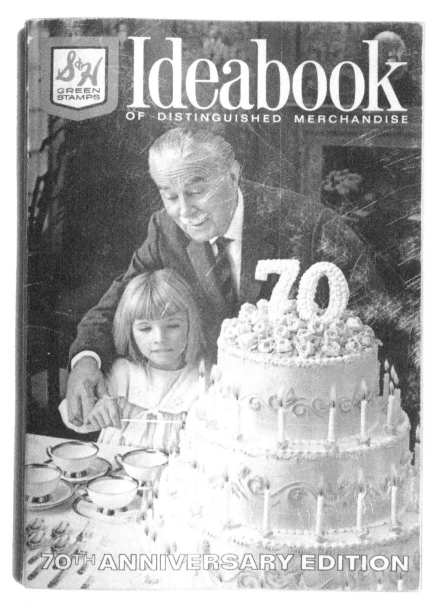

The (pre-computer and internet) logistics for claiming a S&H Green Stamps reward were extensive; the member needed to fill books with stamps, choose the reward products, fill out a separate order form for each reward, then send the books and order forms (plus applicable sales taxes) via first class mail to their nearest distribution centre. Alternatively, the member could visit one of hundreds of retail outlets and spend the stamp books directly. The overheads of running such a massive operation would have been enormous.

The demand for stamps went through several phases during the 1900s. According to the US National Commission on Food Marketing,[31] by 1914 around 7 per cent of retail trade involved the awarding of stamps. This reduced to 2 per cent during World War 1. The Great Atlantic & Pacific Tea Co dropped S&H Green Stamps altogether during the war, which would have been a major blow to Sperry & Hutchison, as they lost the largest grocery chain in the country. Stamp earning stabilised at 2 to 3 per cent of retail trade during the 1920s but fell substantially during the Great Depression and all the way through World War 2.

Post-war, interest in stamps increased substantially. Thirty million US dollars' worth of industry stamps sales were recorded in 1950 in the US, and this grew to US$754 million by 1963, accounting for 16 per cent of total retail trade, and a whopping 47 per cent of grocery trade. Research from the period by Benson and Benson Consumer Studies indicated 83 per cent of all families in the US were saving stamps.[32]

In the US alone there were an estimated 250 to 500 stamp companies operating at the peak of the 'the golden age of stamps'.[33]

Stamps also expanded globally. In the UK, Green Shield and Co-Op Stamps were two popular programs, while in Australia, Green Coupon, Aussie Blue and Group Tokens operated in a competitive market. Other countries also adopted stamps en-masse, including Sweden, Germany, Poland, Switzerland, Canada, Austria, Germany and many more.

Of notable interest is two case studies documented by the US National Commission on Food Marketing which measured whether stamps were successful in helping companies grow revenue.[34] The first related to a business which introduced stamps in a market which did not previously have stamps. The second related to a business which introduced stamps in a market where stamps were already used extensively by their main competitors. While the

---

31 National Commission on Food Marketing, 1966, 'Organization and competition in food retailing', Technical study No.7.

32 Ibid

33 Ibid.

34 Ibid.

circumstances for the two studies were different, in both instances within two years gross margins increased by an amount exceeding the cost of the stamps, demonstrating the programs were a success.

Betty Crocker Coupons (1921)

Stamps were not the only major loyalty currency during this period. In 1921, The Washburn Crosby Company, a flour-milling company and largest predecessor of General Mills, Inc., invented fictional character Betty Crocker to personalise responses to consumer inquiries generated by a promotion for Gold Medal flour.[35] In 1931, the company included a coupon for a silver-plated spoon within Wheaties cereal boxes and bags of Gold Medal flour.[36] The promotion was so successful, the company followed up the next year with a coupon program which allowed customers to access a complete set of flatware. Starting from 1937, the 'Betty Crocker Coupons' were printed on the outside of the box, enabling customers to see how many they could earn with the purchase. In 1962, the Betty Crocker Coupon Catalog was released, an annual publication 'Featuring over 400 items tested and checked for quality in the Betty Crocker kitchens of the world.'[37]

35   Betty Crocker, 2017, 'The story of Betty Crocker', https://www.bettycrocker.com/menus-holidays-parties/mhplibrary/parties-and-get-togethers/vintage-betty/the-story-of-betty-crocker, accessed 2 May 2020.

36   McKinney, M., 2006, 'Betty Crocker closing the book on its catalog sales', Minneapolis Star Tribune, https://www.chron.com/life/article/Betty-Crocker-closing-the-book-on-its-catalog-1506961.php, accessed 2 May 2020.

37   Betty Crocker, 1968, 'Betty Crocker Coupon Catalog', No 6.

A study of the history of Betty Crocker Coupons introduces the concept of emotional engagement generated by a loyalty program. Mark Bergen, marketing department chair at the University of Minnesota's Carlson School of Management, said the Betty Crocker program was remarkable for two characteristics – its longevity and the depth of emotion it inspired among its devotees. It became more than a coupon redemption program, Bergen said, by working its way into the fabric of family life.[38]

---

38   Wilcoxen, W., 2006, 'Betty Crocker retires her catalog', MPR News, https://

*

The mid 1960s marked the beginning of the slow demise of stamps. Some supermarkets dropped stamps and found success by focusing their brand positioning on lowest prices to differentiate against competitors. This approach soon spread to other retail and discount stores.

In the 1970s, a series of recessions and the world oil shock created hardship for most stamp coalition operators, as retail partners sought any way to cut costs. Large-scale rejection of stamps by retailers led to a sudden drop in revenue, and combined with the large cost overheads, ongoing operations became incredibly challenging.

To understand the size of such savings made by supermarkets, in 1977 Tesco in the UK ditched Green Shield Stamps, saving the company an estimated £20m a year[39] (the equivalent of £120m today), which they reinvested in cutting costs.

Miles and Points (1980s)

In 1981, American Airlines launched the world's first currency based frequent flyer program using a new currency (*'miles'*) which corresponded to how many miles a member had flown.[40] Members could earn miles at a set value for free flights allowing them to easily identify what they could redeem their miles for. Brought on by increasing competition with the deregulation of the US airline industry in 1978, the American Airlines AAdvantage program was soon followed by similar schemes from United Airlines, TWA and Delta Airlines.[41]

In 1982, American Airlines upped the ante by introducing a Gold tier to recognise their most loyal members. The same year they launched earn partnerships with Hertz, Holland American Line and British Airways, forming the basis of the first modern coalition program.

Over the next five years, a boom in miles and points-based loyalty programs ensued, including new programs from Holiday Inn (the first hotel

---

www.mprnews.org/story/2006/11/28/bettycrocker, accessed 2 May 2020.

39   Mason, T., 2019, 'Omnichannel Retail,' Kogan Page

40   Everett, M. R., 1995, 'Diffusion of Innovations', The Free Press, 4th Edition.

41   De Boer, E. R., 2018, 'Strategy in Airline Loyalty: Frequent Flyer Programs,' Palgrave Macmillan.

program), Japan Airlines, Marriott, Alaska Airlines, Aeroplan, Korean Air, Pan Am, Diners Club, Northwest Airlines, Continental Airlines (which, in conjunction with the Bank of Main Midland, launched the world's first co-branded credit card program), Hilton, Hyatt, National Car Rental, Holiday Inn, Southwest Airlines (which introduced '*points*' rather than '*miles*' for the first time) and Qantas.

As happened with American Airlines, soon after the launch of these large programs, hotel and car rental companies began partnering with the airlines, and started offering miles and points as a strategy to grow their share of the lucrative business traveller and high-value leisure traveller markets.

With the rapid expansion of the frequent flyer and hotel coalition models and their new currencies, banks and retailers soon replicated their approach. Points and miles loyalty programs quickly became the dominant loyalty program currency globally, ending the ninety-year reign of stamps.

General Mills tried to revitalise the Betty Crocker program by changing coupons to points in 1989.[42] The program was eventually retired in 2006, with Bergen of the Carlson School arguing the decline in engagement was due to shopping pattern changes.[43] Households had given up the habit of saving for a future purchase and started buying on credit, while the idea of cutting out box top coupons and sending them in the mail became old-fashioned in the age of plastic membership cards and ever-evolving reward ranges.

Sperry & Hutchinson also tried to reinvent themselves in 1989, launching a plastic member card which could be swiped at cash registers to earn points. This evolved into S&H Greenpoints in 1999, an attempt to weave the 104-year-old company into the dotcom boom. By 2000, they had attracted 88 participating retailers, including OfficeMax.com, Borders.com and LandsEnd.com.[44] In 2006, the company was purchased by Pay By Touch for over US$100

---

42   McKinney, M., 2006, 'Betty Crocker closing the book on its catalog sales,' Minneapolis Star Tribune, https://www.chron.com/life/article/Betty-Crocker-closing-the-book-on-its-catalog-1506961.php, accessed 2 May 2020.

43   Wilcoxen, W., 2006, 'Betty Crocker retires her catalog', MPR News, https://www.mprnews.org/story/2006/11/28/bettycrocker, accessed 2 May 2020.

44   Slatalla, M., 2000, 'Clicks, Not Licks, as Green Stamps Go Digital', New York Times, https://www.nytimes.com/2000/03/09/technology/online-shopper-clicks-not-licks-as-green-stamps-go-digital.html, accessed 1 May 2020.

million in cash and stock.[45] Their demise should be listed alongside such companies as Kodak, such was the scale of their operation and influence on retail marketing globally, not to mention their penetration of households.

Increasing competition, combined with the birth of the digital age, led to a loyalty program innovation boom from the 1990s onwards. Coalition programs launched online reward stores with thousands of consumer products and gift cards, expanded into insurance products, branded credit cards, financial services, food and wine clubs, massive partner networks and digital marketing agencies. In addition, they developed specialised capabilities in data capture, usage and monetisation, all of which will be explored in later chapters.

Cryptocurrencies and Tokenised Assets

From 2017, several start-ups launched new coalition programs rewarding members with tradeable *'cryptocurrencies'*, such as Bitcoin, Ethereum and branded crypto tokens. The novel variation with cryptocurrencies as a loyalty currency was that the value could increase or decrease based on speculative trading behaviour. The approach taken by start-ups was to establish a coalition program to drive demand for the cryptocurrency, which would subsequently increase in value, benefiting existing members. Most programs failed to deliver the sustained demand necessary to protect the market price of their cryptocurrencies, which instead decreased in value aligning with market sentiment. Programs offering Bitcoin have achieved market traction and continue to build global engagement.

Other programs have evolved to reward members with *'tokenised assets'*. Examples include BrickX (reward members with real estate), Almond (reward members with carbon offsets/tree planting), Bits of Stock (reward members with partner company shares). Shares and real estate allow the member to earn dividends on their tokens (a hark back to B.T. Babbitts). Carbon credits can be offset against tree plantings or even traded. Ostensibly any physical

---

45   The Wise Marketer, 2006, 'Pay By Touch snaps up S&H Solutions & Greenpoints', https://thewisemarketer.com/headlines/pay-by-touch-snaps-up-sh-solutions-greenpoints-2/, accessed 2 June 2020.

asset can be tokenised, opening up an exciting new future in the evolution of loyalty currencies.

*

From a loyalty program design perspective, the most fascinating aspect of the historical review is that the core design of a program has remained consistent throughout time. The currencies have changed constantly (trade marks, checks, tickets, coupons, certificates, stamps, miles, points, cryptocurrencies, tokenised assets and many other variations have all been used), but the program design has not changed. All the companies included in the historical research followed the exact same approach; providing a tokenised currency to a customer when they spent, and allowing the customer to redeem the accumulated currency for a desirable reward.

Currency-based loyalty programs are a consumer-engagement model which has stood the test of time. And this is just one type of loyalty program design. As will be seen in Chapter 8, there are many other types of loyalty program design frameworks which do not involve loyalty currencies at all.

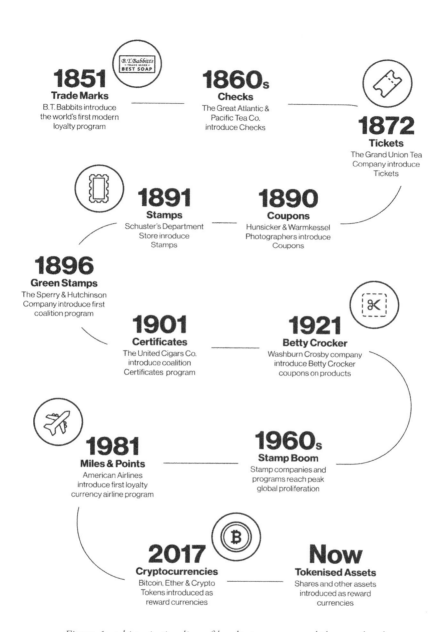

1851
Trade Marks
B.T. Babbits introduce
the world's first modern
loyalty program

1860s
Checks
The Great Atlantic &
Pacific Tea Co.
introduce Checks

1872
Tickets
The Grand Union Tea
Company introduce
Tickets

1891
Stamps
Schuster's Department
Store inroduce
Stamps

1890
Coupons
Hunsicker & Warmkessel
Photographers introduce
Coupons

1896
Green Stamps
The Sperry & Hutchinson
Company introduce first
coalition program

1901
Certificates
The United Cigars Co.
introduce coalition
Certificates program

1921
Betty Crocker
Washburn Crosby company
introduce Betty Crocker
coupons on products

1981
Miles & Points
American Airlines
introduce first loyalty
currency airline program

1960s
Stamp Boom
Stamp companies and
programs reach peak
global proliferation

2017
Cryptocurrencies
Bitcoin, Ether & Crypto
Tokens introduced as
reward currencies

Now
Tokenised Assets
Shares and other assets
introduced as reward
currencies

*Figure 1: a historic timeline of loyalty programs and the new loyalty
currencies utilised within them (copyright Loyalty & Reward Co).*

Go to **rewardco.com.au/the-true-history-of-loyalty-programs/** *to view additional photographs of historic rewards catalogues referenced throughout this chapter.*

Key insights

- A model remarkably similar to modern loyalty programs was utilised in Ancient Egypt, but the first modern loyalty program appeared in New York City in the 1850s, created by B.T. Babbitt, the inventor of the individual bar of soap.

- Trade marks, checks, tickets, coupons, certificates, stamps, miles and points have all been used as loyalty currencies over time, as well as tokenised assets such as cryptocurrencies, real estate and shares.

- The first major coalition loyalty program appeared in 1896 when The Sperry & Hutchinson Company launched their S&H Green Stamps program in New England.

- Over time, loyalty programs have become more prevalent, have grown more sophisticated in the capture and usage of member data, and more complex in their design (such as the introduction of status tiers).

- From their inception, the core design of a loyalty program has remained consistent; companies provide a loyalty currency to a customer when they spend, and the customer can redeem the accumulated currency for a desirable reward. In addition, there are many other types of loyalty program design frameworks which do not involve loyalty currencies at all.

Suggested reading

- Barnard, B. W, 1917, 'The Use of Private Tokens for Money in the United States', The Quarterly Journal of Economics, Vol 31, No. 4, pp600-634.

- Lonto, J. R. 2013, 'The Trading Stamp Story', StudioZ-7 Publishing, http://www.studioz7.com/stamps.html

- National Commission on Food Marketing, 1966, 'Organization and competition in food retailing', Technical study No.7.

- De Boer, E.R, 2018, 'Strategy in Airline Loyalty: Frequent Flyer Programs', Palgrave Macmillan.

CHAPTER 3

DO LOYALTY PROGRAMS GENERATE LOYALTY?

'A study made from 1954 through 1960 by Progressive Grocer indicates that during the early years of the introduction of trading stamps by supermarkets, the supermarkets giving stamps did achieve greater sales gains than those which did not give stamps... Since 1955, however, the surveys made by Progressive Grocer indicate on the average no greater gains by those supermarkets giving stamps than by those supermarkets not giving stamps.'

- National Commission on Food Marketing,
USA, 1966.[46]

Focus Areas

This chapter will address the following questions:

- What academic research is there to indicate that loyalty programs actually work to deliver increased visits, spend, brand affinity, advocacy, retention and market share?

- What academic research is there to indicate that loyalty programs do not work?

---

46   National Commission on Food Marketing, 1966, 'Organization and competition in food retailing', Technical study No.7.

As DETAILED IN Chapter 2, the 1966 US National Commission on Food Marketing report[47] included two case studies which documented where retailers had introduced stamp programs; one into a stamp-free market and one into a saturated market. Within two years, both retailers recorded gross margin increases by an amount exceeding the cost of the stamps, demonstrating the programs were a success. This may be the first published financial study which attempted to test the effectiveness of loyalty programs.

Is this consistent with other loyalty programs over time, and across different industries and geographies? Are loyalty programs always a success? Do loyalty programs actually work to deliver increased visits, spend, brand affinity, advocacy, retention and market share?

The academic and market research is vast and often contradictory. After reviewing the body of research, the main conclusion which can be drawn is that loyalty programs do work, and they do not work.

Evidence that loyalty programs work

Research which indicates loyalty programs generally do work includes a study by Wirtz and Oo Lwin (2007).[48] They investigated credit card reward programs and demonstrated that the more attractive the loyalty program was perceived to be by members, the greater the perception of rewards gained from participation, which in turn was effective in driving share of wallet. This is particularly relevant for a commoditised product such as credit cards, where customers often lack psychological attachment to any particular credit card company. Offering an attractive loyalty program can have the effect of motivating a member to continue buying or using a particular product, service or brand, otherwise known as behavioural commitment.

In an extensive, three-year study of retail programs, Meyer-Waarden (2008)[49] found the impact of loyalty program membership on customer pur-

47   Ibid.

48   Wirtz, J., Mattila, A. S., & Oo Lwin, M., 2007, 'How effective are loyalty reward programs in driving share of wallet?', Journal of Service Research, Vol 9, Issue 4, pp327 -334.

49   Meyer-Waarden, L., 2008, 'The influence of loyalty programme membership on customer purchase behaviour', European Journal of Marketing, Vol 42, Iss 1/2, pp87-114

chase behaviour was significant. They showed that members and non-members demonstrated significantly different purchase behaviours, irrespective of other factors. Member spending behaviour, in terms of total and average shopping baskets, share of purchases, purchase frequency and inter-purchase time, was significantly higher than that of non-members.

Is this due to correlation or causation? In other words, did members increase loyal behaviour because of the program, or were they already more loyal and as a result more pre-disposed to join the program?

Leenheer et al (2007)[50] conducted a study of Dutch households engaging in seven different grocery loyalty programs. They found a small, positive, yet significant effect of loyalty program membership on share-of-wallet, and concluded that creating loyalty program membership was a crucial step to enhance share-of-wallet.

Lederman (2007) reported significant effects of frequent flyer programs on market share in the US.[51] Her study showed that enhancements to an airline's frequent flyer program in the form of improved partner earn and redemption opportunities could be directly associated with an increase in the airline's market share. The effects were demonstrated to be larger on routes that departed from airports at which the airline was more dominant (hubs), which led her to draw the conclusion that frequent flyer programs can serve to reinforce an airlines' market power.

Cairns and Galbraith (1990)[52] went as far as to argue that frequent flyer programs are so effective, they impede competition. Firstly, 'that frequent flyer schemes may generate switching costs for travellers' through the awarding of status tiers which confer benefits on the member which they would lose if

50   Leenheer, J., van Heerde, H. J., Bijmolt, T. H. A., & Smidts, A., 2007, 'Do loyalty programs really enhance behavioral loyalty? An empirical analysis accounting for self-selecting members', International Journal of Research in Marketing, Vol 42, Iss 1, pp31–47.

51   Lederman, M.,2007, 'Do Enhancements to Loyalty Programs Affect Demand? The Impact of International Frequent Flyer Partnerships on Domestic Airline Demand', The RAND Journal of Economics, Vol, 38, Iss, 4, pp1134-1158.

52   Cairns, R. & Galbraith, J., 1990, 'Artificial Compatibility, Barriers to Entry, and Frequent-Flyer Programs', Canadian Journal of Economics, Vol 23, Iss 1/2, pp807-816.

they moved their business to another airline'. Secondly, 'the main strategic barriers to entry in air transport markets are the dominant airport presence by an airline, which might limit access to airport facilities, and the frequent-flyer programs, which are sunk costs that an entrant has to pay to compete with an incumbent. From the point of view of a potential entrant, frequent flyer programs reduce the expected demand on a certain route and therefore may impede a profitable service on that route'.

Lederman, and Cairns and Galbraith's, conclusions are supported by a real-world example which demonstrates just how effective loyalty programs can be. The Norwegian government perceived the frequent flyer program of the incumbent airline, SAS, to be so successful that they banned the earning of loyalty points on domestic routes for a period. In 1994, the government fully-deregulated the airline market to stimulate market competition against the incumbent SAS. The first new entrant, Colour Air, launched in 1998 but failed after just 13 months. According to a note provided by the competition authorities in Norway to the OECD on airline competition, 'an important reason for this was a lack of an attractive frequent flyer program that could compete with SAS' EuroBonus program'.[53] When a new competitor entered the market in 2002, the Norwegian competition authority banned earning points on the SAS frequent flyer program for all domestic routes for a five year period. This was extended indefinitely after the competition authority found it reasonable to assume that a reintroduction of loyalty programs in the Norwegian domestic airline sector would lead to business travellers choosing the airline with the most attractive program. They argued that business travellers constitute the majority of those paying full price for tickets which could have significant consequences for an airline with the least attractive program. The ban was formally lifted in 2013 after it was considered that competition on domestic routes was significantly robust which resulted in lowered overall ticket prices for travellers. A bounce back could be seen on domestic airline seats sold by SAS after the ban was lifted.[54]

---

53   OECD, 2014, 'Airline Competition - Note by Norway,' Directorate For Financial And Enterprise Affairs - Competition Committee, http://www.oecd.org/officialdocuments/publicdisplaydocumentpdf/?cote=DAF/COMP/WD(2014)59&docLanguage=En, accessed 12 July 2020.
54   CAPA Centre For Aviation, 2016, 'SAS, Norwegian and Finnair. The Nordic

Duque (2017)[55] argued that loyalty programs lure consumers with different types of rewards, some of which can make exit costly. He stated, 'delayed rewards, such as points or miles, can trigger a lock-in problem. Once a consumer has started accumulating points with a provider, switching to a different provider implies losing the endowed progress to redeem the first provider's reward'. The loyalty psychology behind the endowed progress effect is discussed further in Chapter 5.

Reichheld (1996) found that loyalty programs can decrease the degree of sensitivity members have towards competing offers or prices,[56] which can prompt them to pay higher average prices for goods they usually purchase, buy them in higher quantity, or choose better quality products and more expensive brands. In a similar study, Nako (1997),[57] and Bolton et al. (2000),[58] argued that a loyalty program can serve to distract members' minds away from price and other negative evaluations of the company. By spending with a specific retailer more often and more frequently, the member may be confronted with competitors' prices less often. Due to being deprived of a comparison, loyalty program members may become less sensitive to higher prices, boosting company revenue and margins.

This was supported by McCaughey and Behrens (2011) who studied actual frequent flyer member flight behaviour in The Netherlands and found that members were willing to pay a price premium of up to six per cent, which could be directly attributable to their frequent flyer program participation.[59]

---

three continue to carve out separate niches', https://centreforaviation.com/analysis/reports/sas-norwegian-and-finnair-the-nordic-three-continue-to-carve-out-separate-niches-267005, accessed 5 May 2020.

55   Duque, O. V., 2017, 'The Costs of Loyalty. On Loyalty Rewards and Consumer Welfare,' Economic Analysis of Law Review, Vol 8, No. 2, pp411-450.

56   Reichheld, F., 1996, 'The Loyalty Effect: The Hidden Force Behind Growth, Profits and Lasting Value', Harvard Business School Press.

57   Nako, S., 1997, 'Frequent flyer programs and business travellers: an empirical investigation', Logistics and Transportation Review, Vol 28, pp395–410.

58   Bolton, R., Kannan, P.K., & Bramlett, M., 2000, 'Implications of loyalty program membership and service experiences for customer retention and value', Journal of the Academy of Marketing Science, Vol 20, pp95-108.

59   McCaughey, N., & Behrens, C., 2011, 'Paying for Status? - The effect of frequent flyer program member status on airfare choice', Monash University

Basso et al (2009) also supported the idea that loyalty programs may reduce price competition, however, this was in the context of employers paying for employee flights. They presented a model which portrayed frequent flyer programs as efforts to exploit the agency relationship between employers (who pay for tickets) and employees (who book travel).[60] They argued that frequent flyer programs 'bribe' employees to book flights at higher prices in exchange for points (and other perks), with the airline program taking advantage of the fact that employees selecting an airline (or hotel, or car rental agency) will not necessarily have the right incentives to find the lowest possible price when the employer is paying the bill. Of interest, their model also indicated that, in a competitive environment, frequent flyer programs can lead to higher prices incurred by employers and lower profits for airlines, with the employees enjoying the benefits of increased value, meaning the program may not work the way the airline intended.

Chaudhuri et al (2019)[61] conducted an exhaustive review of 322 publicly traded firms that introduced a loyalty program between 2000 and 2015. They found that introducing a loyalty program could increase sales and gross profits within the first year, and these positive effects were sustained long term. They also found that programs offering status tiers or earning mechanisms could provide firms with significant increases in sales and gross profits. However, they identified one drawback; the effects on gross profits typically did not become significant until the second quarter after the loyalty program was introduced, and their overall impact on performance lagged substantially behind sales.

Liu (2007)[62] conducted a longitudinal data study of the loyalty program of an undisclosed convenience store franchise. The study demonstrated that

---

Department of Economics.

60   Basso, L. J., Clements, M. T., & Ross, T.W., 2009, 'Moral Hazard and Customer Loyalty Programs,' American Economic Journal: Microeconomics, pp101-123.

61   Chaudhuri, M., Voorhees, C. M. & Beck, J. M., 2019, 'The effects of loyalty program introduction and design on short- and long-term sales and gross profits', Journal of the Academy of Marketing Science, Vol 47, pp640–658.

62   Liu, Y., 2007, 'The Long-Term Impact of Loyalty Programs on Consumer Purchase Behavior and Loyalty', Journal of Marketing, 71 (4), 19-35.

members who were heavy buyers prior to joining a loyalty program were most likely to claim their qualified rewards, but the program did not prompt them to change their purchase behaviour. In contrast, members who were initially low or moderate buyers gradually purchased more and became more loyal to the company. In addition, the loyalty program broadened the light buyers' relationship with the company into other business areas.

A global retail loyalty sentiment report conducted by Nielsen (2006)[63] concluded that, 'Done well, loyalty programs can help drive more frequent visits and heavier purchasing. More than seven in 10 global respondents (72 per cent) agree that, all other factors equal, they'll buy from a retailer with a loyalty program over one without'. The survey also found that '67 per cent (of respondents) agree that they shop more frequently and spend more at retailers with loyalty programs'.

Many other research studies have also concluded that loyalty programs work, demonstrating that:

- There are positive and significant relationships between loyalty programs, customer satisfaction and customer loyalty (Zakaria et al, 2014).[64]

- Loyalty programs enhance customers' psychological bonding with service providers (Mattila, 2006).[65]

- Loyalty programs can cause consumers to engage in recursive purchases, which may lead to the development of habitual consumption, further increasing consumer purchases (Wood & Neal, 2009).[66]

---

63   Nielsen, 2016, 'Global Retail Loyalty Sentiment Report', https://www.nielsen.com/wp-content/uploads/sites/3/2019/04/nielsen-global-retail-loyalty-sentiment-report.pdf, accessed 27 July 2020.

64   Zakaria, I., Ab Rahman, B., Othman, A. K., Yunus, N. A. M., Dzulkipli, M. R. & Osman, M. A. F., 2014, 'The Relationship between Loyalty Program, Customer Satisfaction and Customer Loyalty in Retail Industry: A Case Study', Procedia - Social and Behavioral Sciences, Vol 129, pp23-30.

65   Mattila, A. S, 2006, 'How affective commitment boosts guest loyalty (and promotes frequent-guest programs)', Cornell Hotel and Restaurant Administration Quarterly, Vol 47, Iss 2, pp174 -181.

66   Wood, W., & Neal, D. T., 2007, 'A new look at habits and the habit-goal

- Loyalty programs are effective in increasing customers' perceptions of switching costs and thereby reducing churn (Bendapudi and Berry, 1997).[67]

Evidence that loyalty programs do not work

Research which indicates that loyalty programs typically do not (always) work includes a study by Skogland and Siguaw (2008).[68] They found that business travellers, who constitute a chief target of most hotel loyalty programs, were inclined to switch from one hotel to another even when they had been satisfied with their most recent stays. Furthermore, the results indicated that a strong relationship exists between involvement and loyalty, with the study suggesting that hoteliers should redirect the money spent on loyalty programs to applications that involve the guest emotionally connecting with the hotel, such as better employee training.

Vorhees et al (2015)[69] studied an unnamed major airline's loyalty program and concluded that the effect on share of wallet was significantly stronger for price-seeking customers who are prone to brand switching, but that the loyalty program had no direct effect on share of wallet for brand-loyal customers.

Sharp and Sharp (1997)[70] in a study of coalition loyalty program *flybuys*, identified 'no across the board impact of *flybuys* on loyalty patterns'. Specifically, for the coalition partners, they did find a 'trend towards excess loyalty for *flybuys* brands, though for most it is disappointingly small'.

---

interface', Psychological Review, Vol 114, Iss 4, pp843–863.

67   Bendapudi, Neeli and Berry Leonard L., 1997, 'Customer Receptivity to Relationship Marketing,' Journal of Retailing, Vol 73, Iss 1, pp15-37.

68   Skogland, I., & Siguaw, J. A., 2004, 'Are you satisfied customers loyal? Cornell Hotel and Restaurant Administration Quarterly', Vol 45, Iss 3, pp221 -234.

69   Voorhees, C. M., White, R. C., McCall, M., & Randhawa, P., 2015, 'Fool's gold? Assessing the impact of the value of airline loyalty programs on brand equity perceptions and share of wallet', Cornell Hospitality Quarterly, Vol 56, Iss 2, pp202–212.

70   Sharp, B. & Sharp, A., 1997, 'Loyalty Programs and their Impact on Repeat-purchase Loyalty Patterns', International Journal of Research in Marketing, Vol 14, No. 5, pp473-486.

Ferguson and Hlavinka (2007)[71] analysed data from a 2006 loyalty census by COLLOQUY which identified that while there were 1.3 billion loyalty memberships in the US (12 programs per average household), active participation was just 39.5 per cent. They argued that low participation rates by millions of customer files in a database did not signify a successful loyalty strategy, noting that 'fat membership roles may look good in a press release, but active loyalty program members are the only members who count'. The active participation rate was characterised by COLLOQUY experts as 'dismal'.

Dowling and Uncles (1997)[72] conducted research which concluded that, in the majority of cases, all a customer loyalty program will do is cost a company money to provide more benefits to customers, but it is unlikely to significantly increase the relative proportion of loyal customers and company profitability.

Meyer-Warden and Benavent (2006) found that when all companies in an industry have loyalty programs,[73] the market is characterised by an absence of change of the competitive situation.

A McKinsey study (2014)[74] of 55 publicly traded North American and European companies, showed that overall, companies which spend more on loyalty, or have more visible loyalty programs, grow at about the same rate, or slightly slower, than those that do not (4.4 vs 5.5 per cent per year since 2002). Specific to certain industries, McKinsey identified negative growth impact on airlines, car rentals and food retail, while a focus on loyalty had a positive impact on hotel growth. In terms of overall profitability, companies surveyed

---

71   Ferguson, R., & Hlavinka, K., 2007, 'The colloquy loyalty marketing census: Sizing up the US loyalty marketing industry, Journal of Consumer Marketing, Vol 24, pp313–321.

72   Dowling, G. R., & Uncles, M., 1997, 'Do customer loyalty programs really work?', Sloan Management Review, Vol 38, pp71–82.

73   Meyer-Warden, L., & Benavent, C., 2006, 'The Impact of Loyalty Programmes on Repeat Purchase Behaviour', Journal of Marketing Management, Vol 22, pp 61-88.

74   Nadeau M-C., & Singer, M., 2014, 'Making loyalty pay: Six lessons from the innovators', McKinsey, https://www.mckinsey.com/business-functions/marketing-and-sales/our-insights/making-loyalty-pay-six-lessons-from-the-innovators, accessed 12 June 2020.

that had higher loyalty spend also had EBITDA margins that were about 10 per cent lower than companies in the same sectors that spent less on loyalty.

Caminal and Claici (2006) argued that rather than reinforcing firms' market power and negatively affecting consumer welfare, loyalty programs are 'business stealing' devices that tend to enhance competition by generating lower average transaction prices and higher consumer surplus.[75] They argued against Ledermann's position that the introduction or an enhancement of a frequent flyer program raises the airline's market share by enhancing the airline's market power. Their counterargument was that the use of frequent flyer programs may actually signal fiercer competition among airlines.

A 2015 Roy Morgan study of the Australian supermarket industry found little exclusive loyalty to supermarket brands.[76] When asked how many different major supermarkets they shopped at over the previous four weeks, 37 per cent of grocery-buyers reported shopping at two, 28 per cent said three and 7 per cent said they shopped at all four. Of the respondents who reported shopping typically at Woolworths (the market leader), just 25 per cent shopped exclusively there. For Coles (the main competitor), the comparative number was 24 per cent. This is despite both companies having robust and highly patronised loyalty programs.

A similar study in the US by Zhang et al (2017)[77] showed that 83 per cent of shoppers visited between four and nine grocery stores over the course of a year, with less than 1 per cent remaining loyal to just one store. More than half shopped at an average of five to seven different stores, and 6 per cent shopped at ten or more.

*

With such a vast and contradictory body of research, what conclusions can be drawn? There appears to be substantial evidence to suggest that loyalty

75   Caminal, R. & Claici, A., 2007, 'Are loyalty-rewarding pricing schemes anti-competitive?', International Journal of Industrial Organization, Vol 25, pp657-674.

76   Roy Morgan, 2015, 'Supermarket loyalty: what's that?', http://www.roymorgan.com/findings/6442-supermarket-loyalty-whats-that-201509072312, accessed 20 April 2019.

77   Zhang, Q.,Gangwar, M. & Seetharaman, P., 2017, 'Polygamous Store Loyalties: An Empirical Investigation', Journal of Retailing, Vol 93, Iss 4, pp477-492.

programs can indeed work to generate increased visits, spend, brand affinity, advocacy, retention and market share. There also appears to be evidence that loyalty programs do not always work to deliver the anticipated objectives.

The next chapter will utilise a separate set of questions to further interrogate the available research materials. Accepting there is sufficient evidence to suggest loyalty programs *can* work, under what circumstances *do* they work? And what design elements should loyalty program designers incorporate (and avoid) to increase a program's chance of success?

Key insights

- Academic and market research about loyalty programs is vast and often contradictory.

- There is substantial evidence to suggest that loyalty programs can work to drive a greater share of wallet, increase motivation to buy, create habitual consumption, generate increased visits, spend, brand affinity, advocacy, retention, market power and a competitive advantage. Further studies indicate that loyalty programs can reduce price competition where members become less sensitive to higher prices, boosting revenue and margins whilst reducing churn.

- There is also evidence that loyalty programs do not always work to deliver the anticipated objectives. Research studies have shown that members are inclined to switch brands regardless of the existence of a loyalty program. Some studies also show that loyalty programs may cost a company money without positively impacting company growth.

Suggested reading

- Meyer-Waarden, L., 2008, 'The influence of loyalty programme membership on customer purchase behaviour', European Journal of Marketing, Vol 42, Iss 1/2, pp87-114.

- Lederman, M.,2007, 'Do Enhancements to Loyalty Programs Affect Demand? The Impact of International Frequent Flyer Partnerships on Domestic Airline Demand', The RAND Journal of Economics, Vol, 38, Iss, 4, pp1134-1158.

- OECD, 2014, 'Airline Competition - Note by Norway', Directorate For Financial And Enterprise Affairs - Competition Committee, http://www.oecd.org/officialdocuments/ publicdisplaydocumentpdf/?cote=DAF/COMP/ WD(2014)59&docLanguage=En

- Liu, Y. 2007, "The Long-Term Impact of Loyalty Programs on Consumer Purchase Behavior and Loyalty," Journal of Marketing, 71 (4), 19-35.

- Skogland, I., & Siguaw, J. A., 2004, 'Are your satisfied customers loyal? Cornell Hotel and Restaurant Administration Quarterly', Vol 45, Iss 3, pp221 -234.

- Voorhees, C. M., White, R. C., McCall, M., & Randhawa, P., 2015, 'Fool's gold? Assessing the impact of the value of airline loyalty programs on brand equity perceptions and share of wallet', Cornell Hospitality Quarterly, Vol 56, Iss 2, pp202–212.

CHAPTER 4

UNDER WHAT CIRCUMSTANCES DO LOYALTY PROGRAMS WORK?

'Simplicity is the ultimate sophistication'

- Leonardo da Vinci

Focus areas

This chapter will address the following questions:

- Accepting loyalty programs *can* work, under what circumstances *do* they work?

- What design elements should loyalty program designers incorporate (and avoid) to increase a program's chance of success?

THIS CHAPTER PRESENTS a selection of important academic research studies which have identified best-practice principles for a loyalty program design, including the circumstances under which loyalty programs can best work.

Specific design elements which can be essential in guiding the strategic design and ongoing development of a successful loyalty program have been explored throughout, with supportive industry case studies.

Berman

Berman (2006)[78] argued that the development of an effective loyalty program requires good quality design to set the program on the pathway towards best-practice, organisational infrastructure to optimally run the program, analytics to measure the impacts on customer engagement and an appetite to take corrective action in the event the program is not performing as expected.

He also stated 'marketers need to be aware of several potential pitfalls. These pitfalls include market saturation, low levels of commitment by consumers to loyalty programs, use of the wrong type of program, focusing only on monetary or gift rewards, use of loyalty programs as a cover-up for ineffective marketing, and program privacy issues.'

He indicates the existence of four types:

- **Type 1**: members receive additional discount at register.

- **Type 2**: members receive 1 free when they purchase n units.

- **Type 3**: members receive rebates or points based on cumulative purchases.

- **Type 4**: members receive targeted offers and mailings.

Chapter 8 explores the predominant types of loyalty program framework designs being used in different industries globally, which is well in excess of four. Berman's model, whilst it has merit, if used as the complete program framework consideration set by loyalty program designers, may risk limiting thinking and likely lead to a sub-optimal outcome.

Key take-outs: Invest in ongoing program evolution

A company launching a new loyalty program must recognise that the ongoing operational effort required to make the necessary adjustments to optimise member engagement cannot be overlooked in favour of competing business priorities. It is important to incorporate the future needs of the operational team into project planning and financial modelling to support evolution of the program.

---

78   Berman, B., 2006, 'Developing an effective customer loyalty program', California Management Review, Vol 49, Iss 1, p123.

Two examples of companies who have been able to successfully adjust, fine tune and continuously evolve to suit consumers changing needs and desires over time are outlined below.

Vodafone Voxi Drop

Voxi is the youth brand of Vodafone, aimed at under 30s customers who have very heavy data usage. Voxi provides members with unlimited social media use, unlimited phone calls/texts, and a new monthly Voxi Drop gift to encourage recharging.

Voxi Drop is essentially a rebranding of Vodafone's existing VeryMe program which has been adapted for the youth segment. Inspired by the 'drop culture' which stems from the world of fast fashion, Voxi Drop appeals to the younger consumers desire for spontaneity, excitement, and consistent evolution. Members do not earn points or any recognised loyalty currency (something some younger demographics have negative connotations about), but Vodafone would be covertly measuring and managing customer segments, keeping score behind the scenes.[79]

Not only has the program evolved to speak the language of their members and meet their changing needs, the program gift also continuously evolves each month, maintaining member engagement. Voxi Drop gifts have ranged from restaurant vouchers, concert tickets, festival queue jumps, and other entertaining and contextually relevant surprises which appeal to their consumers.

Sephora Beauty Insider

Sephora's loyalty program is constantly being developed, updated and improved to suit members changing needs, proving that they are truly invested in generating long-term loyalty.

Since Beauty Insider launched in 2007, it has regularly been

79 Ehredt, C., 'Innovators Break The Mould, At The 2020 Loyalty Magazine Awards', Currency Alliance, https://www.linkedin.com/pulse/innovators-break-mould-2020-loyalty-magazine-awards-charles-ehredt/, accessed 18 June 2020.

celebrated by retailers everywhere for its attention to the customer experience, desired rewards, and longevity.[80]

The 2019 New Year brought the biggest overhaul for the rewards program yet with a focus on personalisation and special tier perks (focusing on higher tiers). It cleverly a balanced combination of tangible, instantly gratifying benefits like discounts, as well as many ways for members to build long term emotional connections with Sephora through makeovers, access to beauty inspiration, free gifts and VIB Beauty Event access.

Shortly after the big revamp, in May 2020 (amid the COVID-19 pandemic), Sephora announced the next evolution to their program. Allegra Stanley, Vice President of Loyalty for Sephora, said that the changes were made to match the needs and wants of their customers. She explained how the changes are part of a multi-year journey that seeks to keep shaking things up.

'We've seen that members are craving value more than ever, which speaks to the role that the Beauty Insider program can continue to play in their beauty journey', said Stanley. 'The thing we hear most often from members is that they want to use points in new ways and earn points in new ways.'

'We try to think about our brand holistically, and it's not just about the value-back component. There are different components of the program that customers value more than others. This is just a starting point for us.'

Sephora have since introduced 'Beauty Insider Cash' which allows members to instantly earn US$10 off at the checkout once 500 points are reached, plus two additional member shopping events (one for access to further discounts and one for access to points multipliers on purchases). These enhancements have provided key opportunities for mass program engagement.

---

80   Loyalty Lion, 2019, 'Successful loyalty programs: Sephora gives its loyalty program a makeover', accessed 16 June 2020.

Henderson, Beck and Palmatier

Henderson et al (2011)[81] conducted an exhaustive review of available literature and determined that the theoretical underpinnings of most loyalty programs are psychological mechanisms from three specific domains. They argued that loyalty program-induced change to consumer behaviour typically results from:

1. **Status**: conferring status to consumers which generates favourable comparisons with others.
2. **Habit**: building habits which causes advantageous memory processes.
3. **Relational**: developing relationships which results in more favourable treatment by consumers.

Their first mechanism, the use of *status*, can play a critical role in recognising and rewarding a company's most valuable customers, allowing them to feel a self-esteem boosting sense of superiority and enabling an emotional connection to be built. Conferring *status* on a high-value subset of the member base will generate certain expectations, such as better service, priority access and earn bonuses. In circumstances where insufficient funds and resources are allocated to the program, member expectations may not be met, leading to disengagement, while if too much funding and resources are allocated, the program will not be commercially sustainable. Achieving balance is critical.

Habit would logically appear to be the holy grail for loyalty programs, but it is difficult to manifest, particularly if a change in a member's circumstances no longer reinforces patterns of habitual buying. When a *habit* is reinforced by an emotional connection, the circumstances exist by which the formation of a habit can be a precursor to genuine loyalty (discussed further in Chapter 5).

The third driver, *relational* induced loyalty, can generate many positive outcomes. Developing an emotional connection between a member and a brand can generate a willingness to pay more, stronger commitment, word of mouth promotion and loyalty.[82]

---

81   Henderson, C. M., Beck J. T. & Palmatier, R. W., 2011, 'Review of the theoretical underpinnings of loyalty programs', Journal of Consumer Psychology, Vol 21, pp256–276.

82   Veloutsou, C., 2015, 'Brand evaluation, satisfaction and trust as predictors of brand loyalty: the mediator-moderator effect of brand relationships', Journal of

***Key take-outs: Emotional engagement supports habit and relational
formation***

Structuring a program to boost a member's self-esteem, including conferring
desirable benefits on them, can act to support the development of habitual
engagement behaviour and emotional connections. Relational mechanisms
are very powerful and correlate strongly with attitudinal commitment (discussed in Chapter 5).

> **Subway Subcard**
>
> Subway[83] aim to drive habitual earn activity early in the member
> lifecycle through the application of a Join Bonus.
>
> The Join Bonus enables all new members to unlock a double points
> bonus on every transaction for the first 28 days from join.
>
> Subway use a progress tracker bar within the app to showcase to
> new members how fast they are tracking towards a reward, moti-
> vating them to continue transacting throughout the first month to
> maximise the join bonus.

McCall, Voorhees and Calantone

McCall et al (2010)[84] developed guiding principles for designing an effective
program. They featured the fostering of emotional engagement at the top of
their list. In their report compiled for the hospitality industry, they postulated
that the actual components and structure of most loyalty programs appear to
be driven more by what the competition is offering rather than demonstrated
effectiveness.

Their guiding principles are based on program components that they
believe have been shown to be effective. They include:

Consumer Marketing, Vol 32, Iss 6, pp405-421.

83   Subway, https://www.subway.com/en-US/MyWayRewards, accessed 30 June
2020.

84   McCall, M., Voorhees, C. and Calantone, R., 2010, 'Building Customer
Loyalty: Ten Principles for Designing an Effective. Customer Reward Program',
Cornell Hospitality Report, Vol 10, No 9.

- Evolve the program to foster a deeper emotional connection between the member and brand.

- Capitalise on consumer data and segment the member base to better meet their needs.

- Develop dynamic tier progression and regressions to generate switching barriers.

- Provide a reasonably broad set of rewards, based on consumer desires, to deliver flexibility in their redemption intervals and choices.

- Avoid focusing only on future discounts, as they may inadvertently convert loyal customers to price-sensitive ones.

- Embrace new and innovative technologies.

Key take-outs: Differentiate

Loyalty managers should strive to develop points of differentiation associated with their program to properly position themselves against their competition. This can sometimes be challenging, with limited ways to differentiate a program, hence the need for expert program design.

Ways by which differentiation can be achieved include the development of an exclusive strategic partnership, or the execution of unique member experiences, as demonstrated by the case studies below.

Avis and Budget

The rental car industry is highly homogenised, with the top companies all providing similar products, service, and experiences. One case study provides insight into how a differentiated loyalty program can deliver significant market share gains.

Up until late 2010, Qantas Frequent Flyer Points could be earned at Hertz, Avis and Budget in Australia. In November 2010, an exclusive deal was negotiated between Avis and Budget, and Qantas Frequent Flyer, which meant Hertz could no longer offer their customers Qantas Points, a currency highly desired by business travellers.[85]

This had a significant positive impact on Avis' revenue, which grew in 2012 by 4.6 per cent and in 2013 by a further 8.7 per cent. For the same period, Hertz' revenue declined year-on-year in 2012 by 2.9 per cent, with a further decline in 2013 of 4.3 per cent.

IbisWorld reported 'Avis (and Budget Rent A Car) have benefitted from strategic partnerships with tourism service operators over the past five years, such as the partnership between Avis and the Qantas Frequent Flyer Program. These partnerships have provided the brands with a competitive edge over other passenger car rental companies, particularly in highly competitive positions within airports.'[86]

Naked Wines

Naked Wines[87] have built their brand around the delivery of unique and personalised experiences at scale, helping to differentiate themselves in a crowded market. The central tenet of the Naked Wines proposition is the Angel member. Angels help a network of smaller, talented winemakers to make wines by providing them with guaranteed sales via a distribution channel that delivers a reasonable margin. Angels support the winemakers by depositing as little as A$40 per month into their Naked Wines account towards their next order. The money can be spent on any wine whenever the Angel wants. In return, Angels save at least 25 per cent on each order.

Naked Wines encourage their Angels to download their app, which automatically loads the member's order history. This makes it

85   Qantas, 'News', 2010, https://www.qantas.com/fflyer/dyn/program/news/2010/ aug/changes-to-car-hire, accessed 15th May 2019.

86   Whytcross, D., 2014, 'IBISWorld Industry Report: L6611 Passenger Car Rental and Hiring in Australia,' p23-25.

87   Naked Wines, https://www.nakedwines.com.au/, accessed 26 June 2020.

easy for Angels to rate and review the wines they have tasted and makes them feel part of an exclusive community. After submitting reviews, Angels often receive personal responses from each of the winemakers, thanking them for their feedback.

On their birthday, members can receive an email from Naked Wines with a link to a video of one of their favourite winemakers singing *Happy Birthday*, accompanied by a free bottle of their most highly rated wine as a present. This personalised package works to generate emotional connections with the Naked Wines brand and the winemakers, further fostering loyalty and a willingness to continue to spend with them without the need to provide a discount.

Söderlund and Zheng, Cheung, Lee and Liang

Söderlund (2019)[88] ran an experiment to determine if labelling customers as 'member' versus 'non-member' in the context of a company's loyalty program can influence the customers' evaluations of the brand. He found that evoking member status resulted in a higher level of sense of belonging and higher customer satisfaction. He also confirmed that the customer association with being a member was directly linked to a sense of belonging and satisfaction.

Brands can also build emotional connections via the development of communities. A study by Zheng et al (2015)[89] found that social networking tools (such as Facebook Fan Pages) have enormous potential for enhancing brand loyalty by encouraging engagement behaviours amongst communities. Perceived benefits (value) are crucial in affecting user engagement behaviours, with members demonstrating they are more likely to repeat behaviours that lead to positive rewards and achievements.

---

88   Söderlund, M., 2019, 'Can the label 'member' in a loyalty program context boost customer satisfaction?', The International Review of Retail, Distribution and Consumer Research, Vol 29, Iss 3, pp340-35.

89   Zheng, X., Cheung, C., Lee, M. & Liang, L., 2015, 'Building brand loyalty through user engagement in online brand communities in social networking sites', Information Technology & People, Vol 28, pp90-106.

Key take-out: Develop a sense of belonging

Members who feel a sense of belonging are more likely to want to engage with the program as they are fulfilling an important psychological need which helps them maintain positive self-esteem (discussed further in Chapter 5).

> ### Harley Owners Group
>
> Communities do not need to be online. Harley Davidson turned their business around in the 1980s by focusing on building a brand community of ardent consumers organised around the lifestyle, activities, and ethos of the brand.[90]
>
> This included the development of a company-community relationship strategy through the Harley Owners Group (H.O.G.) membership club, where community-building activities were treated not just as marketing expenses but as company-wide investments in the success of the business model.

Wansink

Wansink (2003)[91] conducted interviews with the managers of forty-one major US loyalty programs deemed 'successful' by business media articles. He identified a range of areas which denote best-practice approaches for a loyalty program. This included an acknowledgement that loyalty programs work best for products and services that have high margins and are difficult to differentiate, as well as products and services that a customer will invest heavily in over an extended period of time. He identified the collection and usage of data as best practice, as well as the continual refinement of benefits to make them relevant for members. He indicated rewards should directly build loyalty in the consumer by supporting the proposition of the brand.

The central focus of Wansink's research was the development of a mathematical model to determine the cost-effectiveness of loyalty programs. His

---

90   Fournier, S. & Lee, L., 2009, 'Getting Brand Communities Right', Harvard Business Review, Vol 87, Iss 4, pp105-111.

91   Wansink, B., 2003, 'Developing a cost-effective brand loyalty program', Journal of Advertising Research, Vol 43, Iss 3, pp301-309.

analysis suggested that a loyalty marketer targeting a specific segment could surprisingly spend less on a program and gain more in return by optimising the rewards (and cost of rewards) provided. For example, programs which prioritise reward budget spend to high-value members may not receive a proportional return, because those members are already loyal and unlikely to increase their spend. This is important for the long-term success of a loyalty program when judged by return-on-investment.

A best-practice program is operated with true clarity on the costs and net gains, and delivers a positive return on investment. Identifying and tracking the true costs associated with a loyalty program can be a challenging task with various accounting, actuarial, and regulatory models (including Wansink's model discussed further in Chapter 14) emerging over time, as well as differing views on recognising and measuring loyalty program benefits and costs.

According to PWC,[92] the costs involved in operating a program include reward redemption and accrued liability, soft benefits (e.g. perks, recognition, member events), program communications (e.g. advertising, mailings, email), technology, enterprise training and support (e.g. call centres), business unit overhead (e.g., staffing payroll and benefits), and research and development. Legal fees, and security and fraud monitoring, can also be added for most large-scale programs.

Key take-out: Ensure the program is cost-effective

Being cost-effective is often specific to the program and the company running it. Some programs can generate positive returns by conferring generous benefits on all members because there is sufficient margin in the business (e.g. candy bar items within cinema programs). Other programs focus on just the top spenders to remain cost-effective, with an understanding that it is unprofitable to confer benefits on lower value, less loyal members (e.g. status tier programs providing generous rewards to high-value members).

Some companies take the opposite approach and allocate most of their loyalty budget to high churn-risk customers to improve their retention rate. This leads to the somewhat ironic situation of ignoring the most loyal customers, with the assumption they will remain loyal without any further investment

---

92   PricewaterhouseCoopers LLP, 2013, 'Loyalty analytics exposed: What every program manager needs to know'.

(e.g. insurance companies who provide better prices to new members while ignoring members who automatically renew every year).

> **British Airways Avios**
>
> In January 2015, British Airways adjusted their Avios loyalty program[93] to provide more valuable rewards to members who buy more premium products and who generally spend more. This approach included reducing the Avios (their loyalty currency) earn rate for economy class tickets by 75 per cent, while boosting business, first-class and flexible-ticket earn by as much as two-thirds.
>
> At the same time, British Airways increased the amount of Avios required for reward seats by as much as 100 per cent.
>
> The move simultaneously reduced the operating costs of the program and tipped the value-equation to provide greater benefit to premium customers. The strategy was designed to lock-in the loyalty of a small percentage of premium customers (who generate a comparably significant percentage of total flight revenues) and do it in a cost-effective way.
>
> A similar strategy has been implemented by multiple frequent flyer programs globally.

Nunes and Drèze

In a Harvard Business Review article, Nunes and Drèze (2006)[94] detailed several components as especially important to an effective loyalty program design:

- **Divisibility of rewards**: the number of discrete reward-redemption opportunities a program provides. Their research showed that in a

---

93   Collinson, P., 2015, 'BA airmiles now offer a worse deal for economy class passengers', The Guardian, https://www.theguardian.com/business/2015/jan/28/british-airways-airmiles-avios-changes, accessed 12 June 2020.

94   Nunes, J. C. & Drèze, X., 2006, 'Your Loyalty Program Is Betraying You', Harvard Business Review, https://hbr.org/2006/04/your-loyalty-program-is-betraying-you, accessed 2 Feb 2020.

grocery store setting (high usage, low differentiation), a $50 reward for every $500 spent engenders greater customer loyalty than either a $10 reward for every $100 spent or a $100 reward for every $1,000 spent (too much and too little divisibility, respectively).

- **Sense of momentum**: providing members with a sense they are progressing towards a reward.

- **Nature of rewards**: providing members with access to rewards they would not normally splurge on with their own money to stimulate excitement about the program and generate pleasant associations with the brand.

- **Expansion of relationship**: utilising the program to introduce members to new products.

- **Combined-currency flexibility**: providing members with the option to access rewards via a combination of loyalty currency and cash, for example 5,000 points + $100.

Nunes and Drèze also identified several mistakes to avoid, including creating a loyalty currency which can be easily replicated by competitors (risking loyalty price wars), providing full benefits to new members of free programs (e.g. instant discount supermarket programs which encourage members to join all available programs, thereby reducing loyalty), providing costly rewards when low cost or costless rewards are available from within the business and, most importantly, conferring benefits on members which cannot be satisfactorily fulfilled.

Key takeouts: The rewards mix is critical to success

Rewards are the reason why consumers join loyalty programs. Ensuring the rewards mix aligns with the core principles outlined by Nunes and Drèze will drive long-term member engagement

Types of reward options are discussed in Chapter 7.

AMC Stubs

AMC Stubs is a program with options for every movie fan.[95] All members earn points when they spend which accumulate towards US$5 rewards vouchers, in addition to ongoing free large popcorn refills, giving all members a sense of value and momentum.

Members can join at three levels; Insider (free), Premiere (US$15 per annum) and A-List (US$19.95-$23.95 per month depending on location), where the relationship between members and AMC products is expanded at every level.

A-List members can enjoy three free movies each week across any format (including IMAX® and Dolby Cinema), free online reservations, 10 per cent back on food and drink purchases (in the form of points), free size upgrades and refills on popcorn and drinks, and priority lanes at the box office and concessions.

Premiere members enjoy all the same perks except for the three free movies per week.

According to Business Insider, in 2019 AMC Stubs had signed up more than 50m moviegoers in the US, penetrating 20m households, a testament to the attractive value provided. This included 800,000 A-List subscribers.

De Wulf, Odekerken, Canniére and Oppen

De Wulf et al (2002)[96] identified five consumer inputs and three program outputs as underlying attributes potentially affecting participation in a loyalty program:

- **Consumer inputs**:

---

95   AMC Theatres, AMC Stubs, https://www.amctheatres.com/amcstubs, accessed 15 July 2020.

96   Dewulf, K., Odekerken, G., Canniére, M. & Oppen, C., 2002, 'What drives consumer participation to loyalty programs? A conjoint analytical approach', Journal of Relationship Marketing, Vol 2.

- ○ Personal data release: member personal data requested at the time of joining the loyalty program.

- ○ Participation cost: a join fee to participate in the loyalty program.

- ○ Purchase frequency: the number of transactions within a specified time period.

- ○ Participation exclusivity: the extent to which membership is restricted to a specific group of consumers.

- ○ Participation efforts: the activities a consumer is expected to undertake to access a desired reward.

- **Program outputs**:

  - ○ Program benefits: what consumers receive in return for their participation in the loyalty program.

  - ○ Number of program providers: the quantity of coalition partners supporting a single loyalty program.

  - ○ Program duration: the period of time during which the program benefits are available to the consumer.

Using conjoint analysis, De Wulf et al identified that participation costs (free) and program benefits (attractive) are the most important attributes determining participation, accounting for 70 per cent of the total consideration weighting. They also found that consumers are more likely to participate in a loyalty program when they reveal a high purchase frequency and when participation in the loyalty program is exclusive to a specific group of consumers. The requirement for a member to only have to provide minimal personal data at launch was also deemed important.

Key take-outs: Engagement will be boosted if the program is free, simple to engage with, and rewarding

Loyalty program operators seeking to scale the size of their member base should consider making the program free to join, while requesting minimal personal information. They should also ensure the pathway to a desirable reward is clear and achievable.

MECCA Beauty Loop

MECCA Beauty Loop[97] is an example of a loyalty program which successfully complements the core focus and value proposition of the brand, whilst economically delivering appropriate benefits to consumers.

Members are only required to provide minimal details when joining (name, email, and password). Date of birth is requested but optional, with a clear justification ('optional – but don't miss your birthday gift!').

Beauty Loop provides members with sample-filled boxes of beauty products four times a year. The higher the status tier, the better the quality of samples provided in the box. Beauty Loop members collect their Beauty Loop boxes in-store, ensuring members visit at least four times a year, providing MECCA with the opportunity to educate and upsell to members.

Higher tier members can also access complimentary makeup applications for when they have a big social event or a date night, plus a free birthday gift each year and surprise periodic bonus gifts. All cosmetics related and all complementary.

The commercial model is also effective for MECCA as the beauty brands stocked by MECCA pay for the samples as a way of reaching highly engaged target customers.

Although the beauty products stocked by MECCA can mostly be bought directly through the individual brands, from large department stores or from lots of other boutique beauty stores, the Beauty Loop boxes keep members purchasing from MECCA, even though MECCA are known not to offer discounts.

The regular rewarding of the member base with samples complements MECCA's promotional advertising, encourages members to trial new products, drives them into store at least four times a year,

---

97   MECCA, Beauty Loop, https://www.mecca.com.au/beauty-loop.html, accessed 26 June 2020.

creates valuable upsell opportunities and stimulates a reciprocating response from members in the form of loyalty to the brand.

Lui and Yang

Lui and Yang (2009)[98] examined the effect of a company's competitive positioning and market saturation on the performance of their loyalty program. They developed a comprehensive model detailing a range of factors affecting loyalty program effectiveness. Their framework highlighted three major factors:

- **Program-related**:

  ○ Convenience and cost of participation.

  ○ Points earn, effort and thresholds, and status tiers.

  ○ Rewards.

  ○ Program management, including utilisation of data and organisational support.

- **Consumer-related**:

  ○ Engagement levels and perceived effort/advantage.

  ○ Consumer traits, including demographics, shopping orientation, price sensitivity and variety seeking.

- **Competition-related**:

  ○ General competition, such as market share, product substitutability (easy/hard to switch to a competitor product), category expandability (extent to which consumption can be grown) and market fragmentation.

  ○ Loyalty program competition, including market saturation, differentiation and order of entry.

Utilising company and individual-level data from the airline industry,

---

98   Liu, Y. and Rong Y. 2009, "Competing Loyalty Programs: Impact of Market Saturation, Market Share, and Category Expandability," Journal of Marketing, Vol. 73 (1), 109-121.

they found evidence which indicated larger airlines tend to benefit more from their loyalty program offerings than smaller ones. Not surprisingly, when the product category demand is rigid, the impact of an individual loyalty program decreases as the marketplace becomes more saturated with competing programs. This reverses when the product category is highly expandable, eliminating the saturation effect. In other words, when the products of one industry can be broadened to satisfy demands in related industries, loyalty program saturation is less of a threat in the principal market.

Key take-outs: Programs can work even in a saturated market

In an industry where overall consumption can be grown (e.g. home delivery of groceries or meals) loyalty programs can help an industry gain competitive advantage over substitute offerings outside the industry. In these circumstances, multiple loyalty programs can effectively coexist, even under a high level of market saturation.

This is not to say that a brand should launch a loyalty program simply because all other competitors are doing so. If the market is already saturated (or in instances where the focus is more on growth), it is up to the brand and program operator to determine the flexibility of market demand, and availability of complementary resources, prior to launching a loyalty program.

> **Quick Service Restaurants (QSR)**
>
> An analysis of the global QSR industry by the authors identified that 80 per cent of the top 150 brands (by revenue) provide a loyalty or member benefits program.
>
> While this would appear to be obvious market saturation, loyalty programs in this industry still drive incremental revenue benefits for their brands.[99]

---

99   Reynolds, P. 2017 '4 Restaurant Loyalty Programs That Really Work,' QSR Magazine, https://www.qsrmagazine.com/outside-insights/4-restaurant-loyalty-programs-really-work accessed 19th August 2020

Bombaij and Dekimpe

Bombaij and Dekimpe (2020)[100] developed a contingency framework designed to determine under what conditions loyalty programs are more, or less effective. They applied the framework across a massive sample of 358 grocery brands from a broad cross-section of 27 western and eastern European countries. Their framework considered five core variables:

- **Reward**:
    - ◦ Timing: immediate or delayed.
    - ◦ Type: direct (rewards that support the value proposition of the brand) vs indirect (other types of reward that have no linkage with the brand).

- **Structure**:
    - ◦ Progressive (accumulation of value over time) vs instant rewards.
    - ◦ Coalition vs sole vendor.

- **Retailer characteristics**:
    - ◦ Price strategy: Hi-Lo (where a firm initially charges a high price for a product and later, when it has become less desirable, sells it at a discount) vs EDLP (everyday low price).
    - ◦ Retailer format: supermarket, hypermarket or discounter.
    - ◦ Country characteristics: retail concentration, competitor loyalty program share and long-term orientation.

- **Retailer performance** (sales productivity).
- **Control** (non-grocery share, private-label share and GDP per capita).

Their results identified a positive revenue effect where the brand was

_____

100 Bombaij, N., & Dekimpe, M., 2020, 'When do loyalty programs work? The moderating role of design, retailer-strategy, and country characteristics'. International Journal of Research in Marketing, Vol 37, Iss 1, pp175-195.

utilising a simpler loyalty program which provided direct and immediate rewards. This positive effect, however, disappeared where the brand was operating a more complex progressive-reward system and when they were part of a coalition program.

They also identified differences in the impact of loyalty programs across retailers and countries. The benefits of the program were positive for both supermarkets and hypermarkets, but lower when operated by discounters. The revenue uplift effects were higher in countries that are more individualistic and long-term oriented. Not surprisingly, the programs were more effective in markets where fewer competitors offered a loyalty program.

Simplicity also appears to be key, with an identified negative effect of program complexity within this industry. Bombaij and Dekimpe did note that studies in the hotel industry have demonstrated progressive reward structures can stimulate consumers to reach a higher spending levels (Kopalle et al, 2012),[101] reinforcing the need to design to fit industry and context.

Key take-out: Programs must be designed for the target audience

A program must be simple to join, understand and engage with. A program must be designed to fit the country, culture, industry and most importantly, the target member base. One size does not fit all when it comes to loyalty program designs.

Albertson's Rewards

The US supermarket Albertson's[102] simplified their rewards program so that members can earn points when they spend across Albertson chains and partners without having to scan their Club Card. Instead, members earn automatically when purchasing through the app or website, or can identify using their phone number.

Members earn 100 points translating into 1 reward. Members can

---

101 Kopalle, P.K., Sun, Y., Neslin, S.A., Sun, B. & Swaminathan, V., 2012, 'The joint sales impact of frequency reward and customer tier components of loyalty programs' Marketing Science, 31 (2), pp. 216-235

102 Albertsons Market, https://www.albertsonsmarket.com/page/savings/shopmore-savemore, accessed 16 June 2020.

accumulate rewards and redeem for a small selection of free everyday grocery items (including eggs (2 rewards), cheese (2 rewards),
24 pack water (2 rewards), milk (3 rewards), salad kit (3 rewards) or
rotisserie chicken (5 rewards)), or they can accumulate rewards and
redeem for a discount off the bill (1 reward = US$1 off, 2 rewards =
US$2 off and so on).

These small but consistent rewards resonate strongly with customers, who perceive they are receiving regular bonuses which can be
redeemed without much effort (making a simple choice whether
to redeem now or on another visit) whilst still offering them choice
and flexibility. This makes it remarkably simple to engage with the
program in a way which best suits them.

Siegel and Gale

Siegel and Gale (2018),[103] in a survey of 15,750 consumers across nine countries, found that 55 per cent of respondents were willing to pay more for simpler
experiences, while 64 per cent of respondents were more likely to recommend
a brand because it provided simpler experiences and communications.

Their research over eight years identified that 'simplicity inspires deeper
trust and strengthens loyalty' and that 'simplicity drives financial gain for
brands willing to embrace it'.

Key take-out: Make it simple, even if it is complex

A loyalty program should be simple for the member to engage with; however, this does not mean it cannot be complex in design. In the current age,
customer experience (CX) together with program communications which
educate new members on the most essential elements as part of the join and
onboarding processes, and use advanced data analytics post-join play a vital
role in maintaining simplicity and delivering a successful program.

---

103 Siegal & Gale, 2018, 'The World's Simplest Brands; 2018-2019', https://sim-
plicityindex.com/2018/region/global/, accessed 8 May 2020.

Southwest Airlines Rapid Rewards

Rapid Rewards[104] members can earn points from hundreds of different earn partners, presenting a challenge to the program when trying to explain how it works in simple terms to new and existing members.

To make it more understandable, Southwest Airlines have divided their earn partners into six major, easily digestible categories (credit cards, travel, shopping & dining, home & lifestyle and special), and have designed icons for each category. This makes it simpler for members to research where they can earn points.

When members receive their monthly statement or visit the website to view their recent rewards activity, the major category icon for which they earned the points is presented as a line item in the report with the number of points earned calculated and totalled.

Members can easily filter and explore categories where they have earned points and where they are missing out, encouraging them to self-educate on ways to access more value from the program.

Stauss, Schmidt and Schoeler

A unique approach taken by Stauss et al (2005)[105] examined loyalty program experiences from the perspective of frustration, a highly negative emotion that occurs when a potentially rewarding act or sequence of behaviour is blocked. An understanding of why members are generally dissatisfied can help determine the underlying principles of why they may disengage at scale (leading to the failure of the program), a useful insight when attempting to design an effective loyalty program. Seven categories of loyalty program frustration were identified:

---

104 Southwest Airlines, Rapid Rewards, https://www.southwest.com/html/rapidrewards/partners/credit-cards/southwest-airlines-rapid-rewards-cards/index.html, accessed 26 June 2020.

105 Stauss, B., Schmidt, M., & Schoeler, A., 2005, 'Customer frustration in loyalty programs', International Journal of Service Industry Management, Vol 16, Iss 3, pp229–252.

- **Qualification barrier**: where the reward is tied to conditions that are difficult or impossible to fulfil.

- **Inaccessibility**: where members fulfil the conditions but are unable to access the reward or program benefit.

- **Worthlessness**: the benefits either prove not to be exclusive or the value of the benefits bears no relationship to the spend required to access them.

- **Redemption costs**: the rewards can only be accessed by investing additional material or mental costs.

- **Discrimination**: less valuable customers are disadvantaged by the company treating the valuable status customers more favourably.

- **Defocusing**: a perception that the company has wrongly focused its priorities on the loyalty program instead of on the core service offering.

- **Economisation**: where the loyalty program quantifies the relationship (e.g. by tying points earn and status tier solely to spend), making the customer feel they are not valued for their emotional commitment to the company.

Key take-out: Focus on what to avoid

Negative experiences may lead to the program not achieving the retention effect aimed for, with an increase in member protests, or even avoidance of the program and the company altogether.

To increase the chances of success, it is equally beneficial to consider the design elements a loyalty program should incorporate, as well as understand the design elements and irritants a program should avoid.

> ### Key insights
>
> - Studies of successful and unsuccessful loyalty programs have identified a range of elements which program designers and operators should include, as well as avoid, to increase the chances of the program delivering to anticipated objectives.
>
> - A best-practice loyalty program should be designed to be agile,

valuable, relevant and cost-effective, with the aim to stimulate meaningful engagement and develop an emotional connection between a member and a company.

- Generating member engagement with a loyalty program can deliver a number of positive outcomes including increases in value, trust, attitudinal commitment, word of mouth, loyalty and brand community involvement.

Suggested reading

- Berman, B., 2006, 'Developing an effective customer loyalty program', California Management Review, Vol 49, Iss 1, p123.

- McCall, M., Voorhees, C., Calantone, R. 2010, 'Building Customer Loyalty: Ten Principles for Designing an Effective Customer Reward Program', Cornell Hospitality Report, Vol 10, No. 9.

- Nunes, J. C. and Drèze, X., 2006, 'Your Loyalty Program Is Betraying You', Harvard Business Review, https://hbr.org/2006/04/your-loyalty-program-is-betraying-you, accessed 2 Feb 2020.

- Liu, Y. and Rong Y. 2009, 'Competing Loyalty Programs: Impact of Market Saturation, Market Share, and Category Expandability', Journal of Marketing, Vol. 73 (1), 109-121.

- Bombaij, N., & Dekimpe, M., 2020, 'When do loyalty programs work? The moderating role of design, retailer-strategy, and country characteristics', International Journal of Research in Marketing, Vol 37, Iss 1, pp175-195.

- Stauss, B., Schmidt, M., & Schoeler, A., 2005, 'Customer frustration in loyalty programs', International Journal of Service Industry Management, Vol 16, Iss 3, pp229–252.

CHAPTER 5

LOYALTY PSYCHOLOGY

'… people provided with artificial advancement toward a
goal exhibit greater persistence toward reaching the goal.'

- Joseph Nunes & Xavier Drèze, 2006 [106]

Focus Areas

This chapter will address the following questions:

- What are the main consumer psychology theories and studies relevant for loyalty programs?

- How is consumer psychology used to guide loyalty program design and operation?

CONSUMER PSYCHOLOGY HAS heavily influenced the design of loyalty programs.

Feldman[107] stated, 'The real currency of any loyalty program lies in its ability to drive changes in consumer behaviour'. Consumer psychology provides a solid, research-based foundation to guide the program design in a way which will maximise its chances of successfully influencing the desired behavioural changes.

---

106 Nunes, J. & Drèze, X., 2006, 'The Endowed Progress Effect: How Artificial Advancement increases Effort', Journal of Consumer Research, Vol 32, Iss 4, pp504-512.

107 Feldman, D., 2016, 'The psychology of loyalty programs,' https://www.linkedin.com/pulse/psychology-loyalty-programs-david-feldman-gaicd?trk=v-feed, accessed 10 April 2019.

This chapter reviews a wide body of consumer psychology academic research and theory, illustrating its practical application within loyalty programs.

The Law of Effect and the Law of Exercise

Edward Thorndike was a prominent psychology professor at Colombia University. He was elected president of the American Psychological Association in 1912 and became one of the very first psychologists to be admitted to the National Academy of Sciences in 1917.

Thorndike is famous in psychology for his work on learning theory. He experimented with cats by placing them in puzzle boxes. The cats were encouraged to escape to claim a piece of fish placed outside, while Thorndike timed how long the escape took.

Thorndike observed that the cats would experiment with different ways to escape the puzzle box, and eventually trigger a lever which opened the cage. In successive trials, the cats would adapt their behaviour and become increasingly faster at pressing the lever.

Figure 2: Thorndike Puzzle Box. Thorndike would record how long it would take for a cat to escape by using the lever to open the cage. Adapted from 'Animal intelligence: an experimental study of the associative processes in animals' by E.L Thorndike, 1898, Figure 1, p 8[108].

---

108 Thorndike, E. L., 1898, 'Animal intelligence: an experimental study of the associative processes in animals', New York, Macmillan, Figure 1, p8, https://archive.org/

The study led to 'Animal Intelligence' (1911),[109] a publication which detailed two important laws relevant to loyalty programs; the *law of effect* and the *law of exercise*.

The law of effect stated: '*Of several responses made to the same situation, those which are accompanied or closely followed by satisfaction to the animal will, other things being equal, be more firmly connected with the situation, so that, when it recurs, they will be more likely to recur; those which are accompanied or closely followed by discomfort to the animal will, other things being equal, have their connections with that situation weakened, so that, when it recurs, they will be less likely to occur. The greater the satisfaction or discomfort, the greater the strengthening or weakening of the bond.*'

The law of exercise stated: '*Any response to a situation will, other things being equal, be more strongly connected with the situation in proportion to the number of times it has been connected with that situation and to the average vigor and duration of the connections.*'

Thorndike demonstrated that behaviour that resulted in a pleasant outcome was likely to be repeated, while behaviour that resulted in an unpleasant outcome was not likely to be repeated. And behaviour that is repeated may develop a habitual attachment to the situation.

For a loyalty program operator providing rewards to members to stimulate repeat purchase behaviour, Thorndike's research should be regarded as the foundation of loyalty psychology.

Ritual Rewards

Originally launching in Toronto, and now in more than 50 cities and 7 countries globally, Ritual Rewards[110] is a restaurant based rewards app which enables members to order through any restaurant or café in the Ritual network and earn points for their spend.

---

details/animalintelligen00thoruoft/page/8/mode/2up, accessed 16 July 2020.

109 Thorndike, E. L., 1911, 'Animal Intelligence', Laws and hypotheses for behavior laws of behavior in general,' Chapter 5, https://psychclassics.yorku.ca/Thorndike/Animal/chap5.htm, accessed 12 June 2020.

110 Ritual, https://help.ritual.co/hc/en-au, accessed 29 June 2020.

Points can be redeemed at any restaurant or café within the Ritual network.

Ritual Rewards focuses on rewarding repeat behaviour with the aim to build intrinsic member habits. Some of the ways Ritual Rewards encourages the formation of habits include:

- Attaching rewards to known habits like daily coffees and lunches.
- Bonus rewards for visiting the same place twice.
- Bonus rewards for transacting for dinner as well as lunch.
- Personalised points challenges which reward consecutive daily transactions with incremental bonuses.

Operant Conditioning

B.F. Skinner was a psychology professor at Harvard University who was ranked by the American Psychological Association as the 20th century's most eminent psychologist. He built on the work of Thorndike to develop a theory of *operant conditioning* (1948).[111]

Skinner introduced two new terms into the law of effect; *reinforcement* and *punishment*. He used these to identify three key insights which expanded on Thorndike's work:

- Behaviour can be increased or maintained by the addition of pleasant stimuli or the removal of aversive stimuli (Reinforcement).
- Behaviour can be decreased by the removal of pleasant stimuli or the addition of aversive stimuli (Punishment).
- Behaviour which is reinforced tends to be repeated (i.e. strengthened), while reinforced behaviour which is no longer reinforced tends to extinguish (i.e. weaken).

Skinner's first experiment studied the behaviour of pigeons provided with access to food at regular intervals. The study identified that the pigeons tended to learn whatever response they were making when the food appeared (e.g.

---

111 Skinner, B. F, 1948, '"Superstition" in the pigeon, Journal of Experimental Psychology, Vol 38, Iss 2, pp168–172.

coincidentally flapping its wings at the time food appeared influenced the pigeon to start flapping its wings whenever it wanted food to appear). Skinner suggested that 'the experiment might be said to demonstrate a sort of superstition. The bird behaves as if there were a causal relation between its behaviour and the presentation of food, although such a relation is lacking.' The pigeon made an illogical association between its behaviour and the consequence of being provided with food.

Inspired by Thorndike's puzzle boxes, Skinner invented a box which contained a lever (for rats) or a key (for pigeons) that the animal could operate to either obtain food or water (as a positive reinforcer) or stop a small electric shock (as a negative reinforcer). The box was connected to electronic equipment that recorded the animal's actions, thus allowing for the precise quantification of the behaviour. A simple experiment involved the animal pushing the lever and receiving a pellet of food, thereby reinforcing the behaviour that pushing the lever would result in a reward.

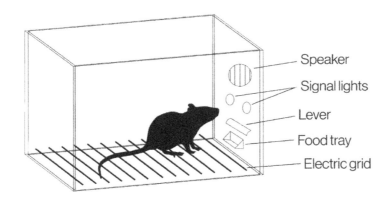

Figure 3: Skinner Box. Several stimuli including lights, images and sounds were used to measure responses. Adapted from 'The Behaviour of Organisms: An Experimental Analysis' by B.F Skinner, 1938, Figure 1, p 49[112].

112 Skinner, B. F., 1938, 'The Behaviour of Organisms: An Experimental Analysis', Cambridge, Massachusetts, Figure 1, p49, http://s-f-walker.org.uk/pubsebooks/pdfs/The%20Behavior%20of%20Organisms%20-%20BF%20Skinner.pdf, accessed 16 July 2020.

Substituting a rat or pigeon with a consumer, if the purchase of a product or service earns points, and the points are redeemed for a desirable reward, the consumer may be more likely to repeat the behaviour, as it has been reinforced with a positive consequence. This effect can be reinforced further with good-quality CX design and marketing which informs and reminds the member of the benefits they have accessed, similar to a slot machine ringing bells and flashing lights each time a gambler wins.

Similarly, threatening the removal of rewarding stimulus (such as removing access to status tier benefits for not earning sufficient status credits) can motivate the member to reduce their stagnant engagement behaviour.

Finally, by removing the reward altogether, program operators can expect a weakening (extinction) of the purchase behaviour.

Hilton Honors

Hilton Honors[113] members unlock benefits for reaching 'nights stayed' thresholds. i.e. a member will reach silver status and unlock a range of additional benefits after they stay 10+ nights. This is an example of 'fixed ratio reinforcement' whereby a reward is offered when a behaviour is performed a certain number of times.

Members are encouraged to continue engaging in this behaviour to unlock an even more desirable set of rewards. This includes free breakfast, bonus points and access to potential room upgrades after 40+ nights stayed when Gold status is unlocked.

Hilton also reinforce behaviour through the application of punishment. That is, members who do not stay enough nights to maintain their status tier will be relegated to a lower tier. With that reduction in status comes the loss of tier privileges, signalling to the member that they must maintain their higher visitation levels to avoid these negative consequences.

---

113 Hilton, Hilton Honors, https://www.hilton.com/en/hilton-honors/guest/my-account/, accessed 29 June 2020.

Social Identity Theory

Psychology has demonstrated that consumers do not just feel emotional connections to preferred brands, but they adopt them as part of their identity.

Tajfel (1978)[114] proposed *social identity theory*, whereby a person's sense of who they are is based on their membership of different groups. Tajfel theorised that groups which people belonged to as social classes (such as sporting teams, families, groups of friends, workplaces, etc.) were an important source of pride and self-esteem. He determined that groups give individuals a sense of social identity and a sense of belonging to the social world.

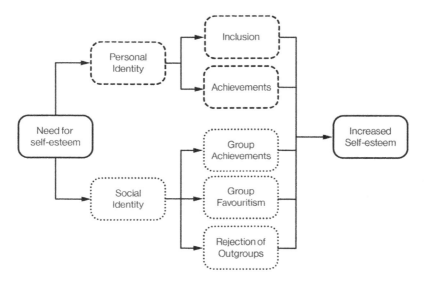

Figure 4: Under social identity theory, the sense of self is based on both personal identity and a collective social identity. Adapted from 'Group Dynamics 3c Identity and Inclusion: Social Identity (Part 3)' by D.R Forsyth, 2014.[115]

---

114 Tajfel, H. & Turner, J. C., 1978, 'An Integrative Theory of Intergroup Conflict', The social psychology of intergroup relations, pp33-47.

115 Forsyth, D. R., 2014, 'Group Dynamics 3c Identity and Inclusion: Social Identity (Part 3)' from the book 'Group Dynamics', https://www.youtube.com/watch?v=XPIJjcJUw7w, accessed 14 October 2019.

Bhattacharya and Sen (2003)[116] expanded this further by exploring social identity theory as it related to brands. They proposed that 'strong consumer-company relationships often result from consumers identification with those companies, which helps them satisfy one or more important self-definitional needs'. In other words, consumers connect with brands in much the same way they connect with their social class, sporting teams and friendship groups, and the brand plays a critical role in making them feel better about themselves by increasing their self-esteem.

As detailed in Chapter 4, a program which serves to make members feel a sense of exclusivity and belonging can play a central role in the member adopting the brand (sub-consciously or otherwise) as an element of their own self-definition.

Many loyalty programs incorporate status tiers in an attempt to tap into the power of social identity theory. For example, many major beauty brands and high-end retailers provide their VIP members with custom makeovers, personal styling sessions and private store access to make them look and feel confident and beautiful, blurring the lines between brand and self.

As detailed in Chapter 4, Söderlund (2019)[117] identified that simply labelling customers as 'member' versus 'non-member' was sufficient to stimulate a higher level of sense of belonging and customer satisfaction.

Ivanic (2015)[118] identified that high status tier members engage in status-reinforcing behaviours, even if doing so offers no material or social signalling benefit, and even if it incurs costs, as engaging in these behaviours generates elevated feelings of prestige. When high status is noticeable, members demonstrate a greater propensity to engage in status-reinforcing behaviours. By contrast, members who reported as already having a reinforced sense of status were less likely to engage in status-reinforcing behaviours. Ivanic concluded

---

116 Bhattacharya, C. B. & Sen, S., 2003, 'Consumer-Company Identification: A Framework for Understanding Consumers' Relationships with Companies', Vol 67, pp76-88.

117 Söderlund, M., 2019, 'Can the label 'member' in a loyalty program context boost customer satisfaction?', The International Review of Retail, Distribution and Consumer Research, Vol 29, Iss 3, pp340-35.

118 Ivanic, A., 2015, 'Status Has Its Privileges: The Psychological Benefit of Status-Reinforcing Behaviors', Psychology & Marketing, Vol 32, pp697-708.

that this suggests that utilising status privileges serves as a reinforcing behaviour, even in the absence of a status threat.

The most common application of this theory can be seen within airline, hotel and bank programs where tier benefits are a formidable driver of member stickiness and retention.

> **Thai Airways Royal Orchid Plus**
>
> A Platinum Royal Orchid member (or an equivalent frequent flyer status level within the Star Alliance partner network) is provided with a range of benefits when flying with Thai Airways including free lounge access, priority boarding / check-in / baggage handling and complimentary upgrades. By recognising and rewarding members, while making them feel they belong to something meaningful, Thai Airways help their members enjoy a boost in self-esteem which can lead to the establishment of an emotional connection with the company.
>
> Cairns and Galbraith (1990) suggested that, 'frequent flyer schemes may generate switching costs for travellers' through the awarding of status tiers which confer benefits on the member which they would lose if they moved their business to another airline'. According to Social Identity Theory, the loss for some would also include a loss of self-esteem, feeling of importance and sense of belonging. This makes the stickiness effect of Royal Orchid and similar frequent flyer programs particularly powerful.

Endowed Progress Effect

Many loyalty programs tap into a psychological phenomenon known as the *endowed progress effect*. This was demonstrated by Nunes and Drèze (2006) [119] in a research study which involved a stamp card loyalty program at a car wash. Members could earn a free wash by collecting stamps.

---

119 Nunes, J. & Drèze, X., 2006, 'The Endowed Progress Effect: How Artificial Advancement increases Effort', Journal of Consumer Research, Vol 32, Iss 4, pp504-512.

Nunes and Drèze divided participants into two groups; for the first group, members needed to collect ten stamps, but the card already had two 'free' stamps on it. The second group were only required to collect eight stamps but did not receive any free stamps. Thus, both groups required eight stamps to claim their free wash.

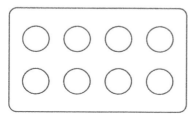 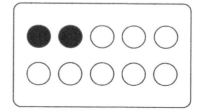

Figure 5: the two stamp card models used within the car wash program experiment by Nunes and Drèze. The right side exhibits two 'free' stamps. Adapted from the research paper 'The Endowed Progress Effect: How Artificial Advancement increases Effort' by J. C Nunes and X Drèze, 2006.[120]

The first group with two 'free' stamps recorded a reward redemption rate of 34 per cent and transacted more often. The second group saw a redemption rate of just 19 per cent. The conclusion — members provided with artificial advancement toward a goal exhibit greater persistence toward reaching the goal. In other words, when consumers feel like they have started on the journey towards a reward, they feel compelled to complete the journey to claim the reward.

Nunes and Drèze[121] wrote: '*Research has proven that the further along members are in a loyalty program, the more they use it. By contrast, at the outset of their membership, their involvement is irresolute. Because they have not yet made any progress, the rewards seem far away. Worse, they have little sense of how easy it will be to achieve the goals. Rather than lose a customer's interest right out of the gate, the best designed programs provide what we've termed "endowed progress", a little push to get things moving.*'

120 Ibid.

121 Nunes, J. C. and Drèze, X., 2006, 'Your Loyalty Program Is Betraying You,' Harvard Business Review, https://hbr.org/2006/04/your-loyalty-program-is-betraying-you, accessed 2 Feb 2020.

Miles, points and stamps serve to drive repeat purchase because the member is accumulating with each transaction, giving them a sense they are progressing towards a goal. Loyalty program operators take advantage of this drive in a variety of ways: by providing bonus points to new members to get them started on the journey, by communicating to members their progress towards their goal (via progress trackers) and by promoting the desirable reward they will earn if they complete the journey.

Jamba Rewards

Jamba Rewards[122] members earn 1 banana point for every US$1 spent at Jamba Juice with a US$3 voucher automatically redeemed when 35 banana points are reached. In the rewards tab within the app, members can clearly see how many banana points they have earned which is communicated via a visual progress tracker and supportive messaging. i.e. '20 / 35 banana points' and 'You're 15 banana points away from $3 off'.

When signing up for Jamba Rewards, members are also provided with their first US$3 off voucher so they become immediately familiar with the process of earning, redeeming and enjoying rewards.

Goal Gradient Effect

First reported by Hull (1934),[123] the *goal gradient effect* states that the tendency to approach a goal increases with proximity to the goal. Hull found that rats in a straight alley ran progressively faster as they proceeded from the starting box to food.

Kivetz et al (2006)[124] demonstrated the presence of this phenomenon in loyalty programs. They utilised a coffee card reward program experiment to

122 Jamba, https://www.jamba.com/rewards, accessed 29 June 2020.

123 Hull, C. L., 1934, 'The rats' speed of locomotion gradient in approach to food', Journal of comparative psychology, Vol 17, pp393-422.

124 Kivetz, R., Urminsky, O., & Zheng, Y., 2006, 'The Goal-Gradient Hypothesis Resurrected: Purchase Acceleration, Illusionary Goal Progress, and Customer Retention', Journal of Marketing Research, Vol 43, pp39-58.

measure the effect on consumers, and reported that members of the program were prone to purchase coffee more frequently the closer they were to earning a free coffee.

The same phenomenon can be observed in loyalty program status points earn, where members have been seen to increase their consumption (more flights, more stays, more rentals) as they approach the next status tier in order to achieve it sooner (so called 'status runs' or 'mileage runs').[125] Loyalty programs have been observed to capitalise on this insight by promoting bonus status points or miles offers to members as they approach a tier threshold in order to stimulate a boost in discretionary purchase behaviour.

Dollard and Miller (1950)[126] built on Hull's research, identifying gradients of approach (which become steeper the nearer the desired object) and gradients of avoidance (where the tendency to avoid a feared stimulus is stronger the nearer the subject is to it). The found that the gradient of avoidance is steeper than that of approach, indicating the desire to avoid something is greater than the desire to obtain something. This may help explain the effectiveness of status tier programs in generating member stickiness.

Drèze & Nunes (2011)[127] used data from a major frequent flyer program to demonstrate that success in achieving a goal contributes to an increase in effort by the member in consecutive attempts to reach the next goal. They replicated the effects in a laboratory study that showed that the impact of success is significant only when the goal is challenging. Importantly, they identified that progress enhanced perceptions of self-efficacy, with successful completion of the tasks provided an added boost.

Gutt et al (2020)[128] explored whether the phenomenon of self-efficacy

---

125 Graham, M., 2018, 'Five Qantas Status Runs', The Australian Frequent Flyer, https://www.australianfrequentflyer.com.au/qantas-status-runs/, accessed 9 April 2019.

126 Dollard, J., & Miller, N. E., 1950, 'Personality and psychotherapy; an analysis in terms of learning, thinking, and culture', McGraw-Hill.

127 Drèze, X & Nunes, J., 2011, 'Recurring Goals and Learning: The Impact of Successful Reward Attainment on Purchase Behavior', Journal of Marketing Research, Vol 48, pp268-281.

128 Gutt, D., Rechenberg, T.V., & Kundisch, D., 2018, 'Goal Achievement, Subsequent User Effort and the Moderating Role of Goal Difficulty'. Journal of

associated with goal progression also extended to status tiers. They found evidence to suggest that members would increase their base level of effort after achieving a tier as long as the difficulty of obtaining a tier kept increasing. If the difficulty to reach the next tier was lower than or equal to the previous level, members were observed to hold their base level of effort constant. This indicated the existence of a positive effect of tier achievement on subsequent member contribution levels through increased self-efficacy, but only as long as the achievement of tiers remained challenging.

> **Starbucks Rewards**
>
> The Starbucks Rewards[129] app uses a combination of visual progress communications (how far a member has come) and Goal Gradient communications (how far the member has to go), to motivate members to increase their frequency of transactions to unlock more rewards.
>
> Members are informed within the app how many more stars they need to earn to access a reward. For example, '1 Star Until Next Reward'. This maintains the members' focus on the goal to stimulate transaction momentum.
>
> Starbucks capitalise on the goal gradient effect by providing members with additional opportunities to earn starts so they can reach their goal faster. Examples include allowing stars to be earned on Starbucks products (packaged coffee, pods, syrups, cookies, etc.) bought at petrol stations and grocery stores.

Customer Delight and Decision Affect Theory

Customer delight is a powerful technique for driving deeper member engagement. Psychological studies suggest that when a customer's expectations are met, they will be satisfied and when a customer's expectations are exceeded, they will be slightly more satisfied, but when a customer is unexpectedly

Business Research, Vol 106, pp277-287.

129 Starbucks, Starbucks Rewards, https://www.starbucks.com/rewards/, accessed 29 June 2020.

delighted (commonly referred to as 'surprise and delight' in the loyalty industry) their satisfaction levels will be substantial.

Schwarz (1987)[130] ran a study to test the impact of a positive event occurring on a subject's overall life satisfaction. He placed a small coin on a photocopier for the next user to find. He then conducted an interview with those who found the small coin about their life perspective. 'Those who found the coin were happier, more satisfied and wanted to change their lives less than those who didn't find a coin', reported Schwarz.[131] The value of the coin appeared to be irrelevant; it was significant that something positive and surprising happened to them.

There is evidence to suggest surprise and delight activity can improve a person's liking towards another. Regan (1971)[132] ran a study where a participant provided an unexpected bottle of Coca-Cola to the subject. Subjects reported liking the person giving the free Coke more than when no Coke was provided.

Mellers et al (1997)[133] explored the power of surprise and delight by looking at the difference between expected and unexpected positive outcomes. Their *decision affect theory* demonstrated that unexpected outcomes have a greater emotional impact than expected outcomes, even when the reward was of lower value. Their study required students to complete a task. The students were either told how much they would be rewarded prior to undertaking the task, or were surprised with a reward after completing the task. Smaller, surprising wins were shown to be more elating than larger, expected wins. For example, the researchers found a surprise $5 reward was rated as more enjoyable by subjects than an expected $9 reward.

---

130 Schwartz, N., 1987, 'Stimmung als Information (Mood as information)'.

131 Ager, S., 1999, 'A dime can make a difference,' The Baltimore Sun, https://www.baltimoresun.com/news/bs-xpm-1999-08-22-9908240363-story.html, accessed 11 June 2020.

132 Regan, R., 1971, 'Effects of a favor and liking on compliance', Journal of Experimental Social Psychology, Vol 7, Iss 6, pp627-639.

133 Mellers, B.A., Schwartz, A., Ho, K. & Ritov, I., 1997, 'Decision Affect Theory: Emotional Reactions to the Outcomes of Risky Options', Psychological Science, Vol 8, No 6, pp423-429.

Oliver et al (1997)[134] developed a *customer delight model* which hypothesised the loyalty psychology underpinning this effect. They found evidence that positive surprise and delight experiences elicit pleasure, joy and elation. They also proved that delight is a positively valanced state reflecting high levels of consumption-based affect, and the experience of delight creates a desire for future recurrences of the sensation via the repetition of consumption, which creates loyalty.

Most importantly, delighted customers have been proven to demonstrate higher loyalty to a company. Berman (2005)[135] reported significantly higher levels of loyalty from delighted versus satisfied customers. The findings also noted other potential positive consequences of delight to 'include lower costs due to increased word-of-mouth promotion, lower selling and advertising costs, lower customer acquisition costs, higher revenues due to higher initial and repeat sales, and long-term strategic advantages due to increased brand equity and increased ability to withstand new entrants.' Berman cites one study where 'Mercedes-Benz USA found that the likelihood that a client who is dissatisfied with the service at a retailer will buy or lease from the same retailer is only 10 per cent. Mere satisfaction produces a 29 per cent likelihood of rebuy or re-lease. However, the likelihood of a delighted client rebuying or re-leasing is 86 per cent.'

Turning to neuropsychology, Pagnoni et al (2002)[136] found evidence that an unexpected event (such as surprise and delight) can powerfully stimulate the *nucleus accumbens* (the 'pleasure centre' of the brain), releasing dopamine into the blood stream, a hormone related to addiction. Subjects underwent MRI scans while having fruit juice or water squirted into their mouths through a tube either in a predictable or unpredictable pattern. The study found the *nucleus accumbens* responded much more strongly when the liquid was unanticipated, even with water. 'The region lights up like a Christmas tree on the

134 Oliver, R. L., Rust, R. & Varki, S., 1997, 'Customer Delight: Foundations, Findings, and Managerial Insight', Journal of Retailing, Vol 73, Iss 3, pp311-336.

135 Berman, B., 2005, 'How to delight your customers,' California Management Review, Vol 48, Iss 1, pp129-151.

136 Pagnoni G., Zink C. F., Montague P. R. & Berns G. S., 2002, 'Activity in human ventral striatum locked to errors of reward prediction', Nat Neuroscience, Vol 5, pp97-98.

MRI', said study co-author Dr Montague. 'That suggests people are designed to crave the unexpected.'[137]

Applications of surprise and delight campaigns within loyalty programs are extensive. They may include airline, hotel, rental car and banking programs sending premium members surprise gifts, telecommunications customers being invited to select from a range of unexpected rewards or meal kit delivery customers receiving something extra in their box.

As the research shows, if executed correctly, surprise and delight can be an extremely powerful tool used to generate an emotional connection with a company or brand, to drive purchase behaviour and to create genuine member loyalty. In order to execute surprise and delight effectively it should be unexpected (i.e. telling a member they will receive a $10 voucher on their birthday is not surprise and delight), be viewed as a gift, hold a perceived value and focus on the customer, making them feel truly special and recognised in that moment.

Mastercard Priceless Surprises

Mastercard US have been running a long-term advertising campaign which drives their social media presence called 'Priceless Surprises'.[138] The campaign surprises cardholders with spontaneous gifts ranging from specialty cupcake deliveries, concert tickets and seat upgrades to celebrity meetings.

The #PricelessSurprises campaign has surprised almost 100,000 cardholders spanning 25 countries, with Mastercard enjoying the benefits of masses of user-generated social media content which they also use to connect with potential cardholders.[139]

---

137 Sommerfield, J., 2002, 'Human brain gets a kick out of surprises', MSNBC, http://www.ccnl.emory.edu/Publicity/MSNBC.HTM, accessed 11 June 2020.

138 Mastercard, Priceless Surprises, https://pricelesssurprises.com/, accessed 29 June 2020.

139 Ad Age, 'Best Practices: How Brands Can Build Loyalty With 'Surprise-and-Delight' Efforts', https://adage.com/article/digitalnext/brands-build-loyalty-surprise-delight-strategies/298425, accessed 29 June 2020.

They have even inspired existing members to gift their own surprises to family and friends, further expanding their reach and advocacy.

Norm of Reciprocity

The *norm of reciprocity* refers to an expectation that people will help those who helped them (Gouldner, 1960). [140] For example, one person buys another lunch, and the other person feels a compulsion to return the favour.

Regan's (1971)[141] study (where subjects reported liking a person giving them a free Coke more than when no Coke was provided) also studied the effects of reciprocity. It found that providing a subject with a free Coke made them more willing to comply with a request from the provider to buy a raffle ticket. Subjects reported that it was not because they liked the provider more, but because they felt obligated to return the favour.

Regan's experiment built on the earlier study of Goranson and Berkowitz (1966),[142] who found evidence that conferred favours generate feelings of obligation and the desire to reciprocate. They provided a large group of female students with a dull task, and informed them the successful completion of the task would win a cash prize for their supervisor. Subjects who received voluntary help from the supervisor were observed to work harder that those who did not.

Studying the power of reciprocity, Kunz and Woolcott (1976)[143] examined whether people would send a Christmas card to a complete stranger who sent them one. For Christmas 1974, they sent 578 Christmas cards to strangers, and received an overall response rate of an astonishing 20 per cent. A follow-up study by Kunz (2000)[144] found the same 20 per cent response rate.

---

140 Gouldner, A. W., 1960, 'The norm of reciprocity: A preliminary statement', American Sociological Review, Vol 25, pp161–178.

141 Regan, R., 1971, 'Effects of a favor and liking on compliance', Journal of Experimental Social Science Research, Vol 5, pp627-639

142 Goranson, R. E., & Berkowitz, L., 1966, 'Reciprocity and responsibility reactions to prior help', Journal of Personality and Social Psychology, Vol 3, Iss 2, pp227–232.

143 Kunz, P. R. & Woolcott, M., 1976, 'Season's greetings: From my status to yours', Social Science Research, Vol 5, Iss 3, pp269–278

144 Kunz, J., 2000, 'Social Class Difference in Response to Christmas Cards', Perceptual and Motor Skills, Vol 90, Iss 2, pp573–576.

Fifteen years later, a similar study by Meier (2015)[145] received just a 2 per cent response rate. A second study by Meier indicated two potential reasons for the low response rate; perceived threat/suspicion and high e-mail use (something which was not mainstream during the Kunz study period).

Reciprocity does have its limits. Although a person may feel obligated to return a favour, they do not always carry through with the intent. Brehm and Cole (1966)[146] found that the desire to reciprocate does not always correlate with the actual behaviour.

There is evidence that reciprocity translates to customer loyalty. Morias et al (2004)[147] studied tourism operators and found that that if customers perceived that a provider was making an investment in them, they in turn made a similar investment in the provider, and those investments led to measurable loyalty. This suggests that investments of love, status, information and time are more closely associated with loyalty than investments of money (e.g. points and miles earn). They concluded that their findings explain how well-designed loyalty programs may lead to increased psychological attachment to the brand and company.

Hertz Gold Plus Rewards

Hertz Gold Plus Rewards[148] capitalise on the norm of reciprocity by giving their members free vehicle upgrades when better vehicles within their fleet are available. This gesture generates very little incremental cost to Hertz, however having happy customers drive away in a vehicle that is more valuable, advanced, spacious and stylish than what they originally booked can generate incremental benefits for Hertz thanks to the norm of reciprocity.

---

145 Meier, B., 2015, 'Bah Humbug: Unexpected Christmas Cards and the Reciprocity Norm', The Journal of Social Psychology, p156.

146 Brehm, J. W. & Cole, A. H., 1966, 'Effect of a favor which reduces freedom', Journal of Personality and Social Psychology, Vol 3, Iss 4, pp420–426.

147 Morais, D. B., Dorsch, M. J. & Backman, S. J., 2004, 'Can Tourism Providers Buy their Customers' Loyalty? Examining the Influence of Customer-Provider Investments on Loyalty', Journal of Travel Research, Vol 42, Iss 3, pp235–243.

148 Hertz, Hertz Gold Plus Rewards program Benefits, https://www.hertz.com.au/rentacar/misc/index.jsp?targetPage=membership_benefits.jsp, accessed 29 June 2020.

> The member is likely to feel positively about the relationship and may feel inclined to find ways to give back in the form of purchasing additional add-ons (GPS, full insurance or an extra day), repeat business, social sharing, a positive review or persuading a friend to join, even when there may be cheaper alternatives available.

> Free upgrades can provide a fantastic return on investment (ROI) for Hertz as they can be conferred at little or no incremental cost and lay the foundations for future business, referrals and long-term loyalty.

Behavioural and Attitudinal Commitment Theory

Day (1969)[149] identified that methods used to gauge loyalty in the 1960s were flawed because they only measured purchase behaviour, and neglected to consider whether the behaviour may be due to lack of choice, long-term offers or better product positioning rather than true loyalty. He argued that many consumers who identified as 'loyal' lacked any attachment to the brand, and could easily be captured by competitors offering better deals or product promotion. Day hypothesised that loyalty should be measured by both *behavioural commitment* (where a customer repeatedly purchases a product or brand) and *attitudinal commitment* (when a customer chooses to be loyal because of a positive brand preference).

Beatty and Kahle (1988)[150] argued that *brand commitment* is conceptually similar to brand loyalty. Brand commitment is an emotional or psychological attachment to a brand within a product class, and appears to result from felt concern or ego involvement with the product or purchase decision (in other words, an attitudinal attachment). They attempted to predict the type of decision-making process subjects would make about soft drink purchases based on whether they had low or high commitment to specific brands. They concluded that commitment is the emotional or psychological attachment to

---

149 Day, G. S., 1969, 'A Two-Dimensional Concept of Brand Loyalty', Journal of Advertising Research, Vol 9, Iss 3, pp29-35.

150 Beatty, S. E., Homer, P. M. & Kahle, L. R., 1988, 'The involvement--commitment model: Theory and implications', Journal of Business Research, Vol 16, Iss 2, pp149-167.

a brand that develops before a customer would be able to determine that their repeat purchase behaviour was derived from a sense of loyalty. In other words, commitment to a brand is a precursor to genuine loyalty.

A core feature of commitment is resistance to change. As discussed in Chapter 4, loyal members that have formed an emotional connection (or attitudinal commitment) to a brand are more resistant to discounts and promotions from competitors. Pritchard et al (1999)[151] built a model which measured resistance to change as primary evidence of commitment. The model allowed for the measurement of loyalty, which accounted for both consumers' purchase behaviour and attitudinal commitment toward the brand. It indicated that resistance to change (and therefore commitment) is maximised when consumers identify with the values and images embodied by a particular brand, and have a need for consistency and confidence in their decisions.

One technique brands use to build loyalty is to invite members to declare their level of commitment, ideally in a public space. Encouraging a public 'commitment statement' is a powerful technique for generating customer loyalty as people have a bias towards maintaining consistency which what they have done or have said they will do, thus avoiding inconsistency, an undesirable trait. A common example is 25 words or less competitions, where the entrant must write something positive about the brand or product. This is also widely used within the fitness industry to encourage members to continue engaging and ultimately derive satisfying transformative results.

> **Soul Cycle**
>
> Many gym programs, including Soul Cycle in the US, have designed 'challenges' for their members. These challenges encourage members to set and commit to goals which ultimately increase visitation frequency, create upsell opportunities, drive advocacy and deliver member satisfaction.
>
> Soul Cycle have applied commitment theory in two ways:
>
> • 30 Day Challenge: where members set challenge goals, join a

---

151 Pritchard, M., Havitz, M. & Howard, D., 1999, 'Analyzing the Commitment-Loyalty Link in Service Contexts', Journal of the Academy of Marketing Science, Vol 27, pp333-348.

> team (or invite friends to start a new team) and then ride like crazy – 'The more you clip in as a community the more donations you unlock to a charity of choice'.[152] When the team reaches the shared goal, they unlock a bonus donation of US$100.
>
> - Warrior Week: a 4 week challenge where 'we push ourselves to ride four times in one week'.[153] Together, members push themselves to meet their Warrior Week commitment, with those who complete it unlocking a 20 per cent discount on their next retail purchase.
>
> The public declaration of commitment to other members acts to reinforce the member's loyalty to Soul Cycle.

Mattila (2006)[154] explored commitment theory as it related to loyalty programs in the hospitality industry. Her analysis suggested that the accumulation of points and accessing of rewards at major hotel programs such as Hilton Honors, Hyatt's Gold Pass and Marriott Rewards were not sufficient to create loyalty. She argued that what was needed instead was to foster an emotional bond between the member and the brand, which is driven by both affective (attitudinal) commitment and calculative commitment (a sense of being locked into a service provider due to the economic costs of leaving). Calculative commitment may be confused with resistance to change, but scrutiny indicates it is more related to boosting resistance by introducing switching costs.

These are important insights for loyalty program operators to consider when analysing their base of 'loyal' members. Behavioural commitment may be perceived as true loyalty, but without attitudinal commitment (ideally

---

152 Soul Cycle, 'Everything you need to know about SoulCup – our first ever team challenge', 2019, https://www.soul-cycle.com/community/inside/soulcupfaq/3163/, accessed 11 May 2020.

153 Soul Cycle, 'Warrior Week March 2020: everything you need to know', 2020, https://www.soul-cycle.com/community/inside/warriorweek2020/3188/, accessed 11 May 2020.

154 Mattila, A. S, 2006, 'How affective commitment boosts guest loyalty (and promotes frequent-guest programs)', Cornell Hotel and Restaurant Administration Quarterly, Vol 47, Iss 2, pp174 -181.

reinforced by calculative commitment), the program is at risk of rapidly losing members if a better product or service offering makes itself available.

Blockbuster and Netflix

In 2000, Blockbuster led the video rental industry globally, with thousands of retail locations, millions of customers and substantial marketing budgets. According to Holmgren (2006),[155] engagement with their loyalty program Movie Pass was one measure of store productivity, alongside revenue and active members. Movie Pass was designed to offer benefits and enhance customer loyalty by encouraging customers to rent movies only from Blockbuster stores. Blockbuster utilised a customer relationship management (CRM) strategy to segment their customer base as a way to build relationships with new members and preserve higher-value member relationships.

From a loyalty measurement perspective, Blockbuster senior management may have been led to believe they had been successful in developing a vast, highly loyal member base. In retrospect, it can be argued that the majority of the base was primarily demonstrating behavioural commitment (such as consistent rental behaviour week after week) but not attitudinal commitment. This meant that Blockbuster's business model was at risk of significant disruption from potential competitors if a better customer experience could be successfully offered.

Famously, Netflix provided that disruption by solving a range of inherent problems with Blockbuster's offering; they did not charge late fees (Blockbuster's late fees had become such an important part of their revenue model that the company's profits were highly dependent on them),[156] their movies were always available

155 Holmgren, L., 2006, 'An Inside Look at Blockbuster, Inc.', The University of Michigan.

156 Satell, G., 2014, 'A Look Back At Why Blockbuster Really Failed And Why It Didn't Have To,' Forbes, https://www.forbes.com/sites/gregsatell/2014/09/05/a-look-back-at-why-blockbuster-really-failed-and-why-it-didnt-have-to/#34e8927b1d64

> (according to the company's own figures, members could not get popular movies at Blockbuster stores up to 75 per cent of the time)[157] and they did not require two trips to a store to watch a movie (pick-up and drop-off).
>
> Could attitudinal commitment have saved Blockbuster? It is unlikely it could have saved their business model, however if Blockbuster had been more successful in generating true emotional loyalty from their members, it may have slowed their demise, allowing them to transition to a new business model, such as their own streaming service. They would have been in a position to promote it to an engaged audience and grow more rapidly than Netflix, thereby offering genuine competition in an emerging market.

Expectancy Theory of Motivation

Expectancy theory of motivation (Vroom, 1964)[158] proposes that people are motivated to behave because they believe their actions will lead to their desired outcome. This can provide loyalty program operators with a foundation on which to build a better understanding of ways to motivate members to engage.

The theory states that individuals will be motivated if they believe that there is a positive correlation between efforts and performance, and that favourable performance will result in a desirable reward. This makes the desire to satisfy the need strong enough to make the effort worthwhile.

Vroom outlined three core variables in his theory; *expectancy, instrumentality* and *valence*.

accessed 21 June 2020.

157 Nash, K. S., 2009, 'How Blockbuster Plans to Beat Netflix,' CIO, https://www.cio.com/article/2430765/how-blockbuster-plans-to-beat-netflix.html accessed 21 June 2020

158 Vroom, V.H., 1964, 'Work and motivation', New York: Wiley.

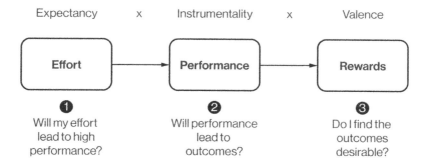

Figure 6: three components of expectancy theory by V.H Vroom, 1964. Reprinted from iEdunote[159] with permission.

Expectancy involves the belief that increases in effort leads to increases in performance. Instrumentality involves the belief that an appropriate reward will be received for the right performance. Valence is the importance a person places on the outcome that is expected.

Specific to a loyalty program, a member will be motivated to engage if they have the expectancy that their efforts will move them forward on a pathway towards accessing a reward (instrumentality) that satisfies an important need (valence).

For loyalty program design, expectancy theory is a useful tool for empathising with the members point of view. Focusing on the three core areas critical for motivation can help to clarify important and non-essential features, supporting the development of a simple yet sophisticated design. It is equally valuable when auditing existing programs, by directing the attention of the program operator to deficient aspects of the program which either block motivation, or do not motivate sufficiently.

Sharma and Verma (2014)[160] examined the application of motivation

159 iEdunote, 'Expectancy Theory of Motivation', https://www.iedunote.com/expectancey-theory, accessed 16 July 2020.

160 Sharma, D. & Verma, V., 2014, 'Psychological and economic considerations of rewards programs', Journal of Retailing and Consumer Services, Vol 21, Iss 6,

theory to influence a consumer's intention to enrol in a loyalty program. They identified several motivational factors relevant to program design:

- **Goal proximity**: how near the goal is from joining, which is positively related to intent to enrol in a rewards program.

- **Perceived effort**: how much work will be required to achieve the goal, which is negatively related to intent to enrol.

- **Reward valence**: how much the member values the reward, which is positively related to intent to enrol.

- **Customer reactance**: resistance to attempts to control behaviour or limit freedom of choice, which is negatively related to the intent to enrol.

Sharma and Verma argued a balance between all four factors is needed for a loyalty program to be successful, noting that their research suggested reward valence has the strongest positive effect and perceived effort has the strongest negative effect.

Sharma and Verma provide two examples to illustrate the application of their model; Delta Airlines and Citibank:

Delta Airlines Skymiles

In 2004, Delta Airlines revamped their Skymiles program after identifying they were rewarding members who were not even covering the costs of delivering the transportation. They readjusted the Goal Proximity for discount economy passengers by providing only one quarter of the mileage reward that was being given to higher paying members. This adjustment ensured they stopped rewarding members for behaviour that was detrimental to the company's goal of profitability and instead rewarded those members which increased revenue and profits.

pp924-932.

Citibank

Citibank launched a credit card where members could earn American Airlines AAdvantage miles. To boost enrolments, Citibank offered 10,000 free miles just for opening a new account (equivalent to US$10,000 in purchases). Detrimentally, a significant percentage of customers signed up for the card, earned the free miles, and defected to the next deal being offered from a similar bank. This is an example of members being enticed by too high a level of reward valence and too low a level of perceived effort, with the unfortunate outcome being no measurable loyalty.

Cognitive Dissonance Theory

Festinger (1957)[161] proposed that human beings strive for internal psychological consistency to function mentally in the real world. A person who experiences internal inconsistency tends to become psychologically uncomfortable and is motivated to reduce their *cognitive dissonance*.

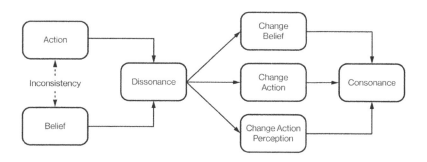

Figure 7: the development of cognitive dissonance. Adapted from 'A Theory of Cognitive Dissonance' by L Festinger, 1957.[162]

From a consumer perspective, cognitive dissonance may arise post-purchase, where buyer's remorse (or post-purchase regret) is experienced. A study

---

161 Festinger, L., 1957, 'A theory of cognitive dissonance', Stanford University Press.
162 Ibid.

by Skelton and Atwood (2017)[163] found 82 per cent of adults in Great Britain have regretted a purchase in the past. This was shown to be particularly prevalent for takeaway food, clothing and footwear. They estimated the annual expenditure on regretted purchases to be £5-25bn, equivalent to 2-10 per cent of annual consumer spending on goods in Great Britain.

Sharifi and Esfidani (2014)[164] conducted a study on mobile phone customers to test whether it was possible to mitigate cognitive dissonance in the post-purchase stage through relationship marketing activities. They identified that post-purchase cognitive dissonance discouraged satisfaction and loyalty, therefore addressing it was important for customer retention. Relationship marketing activities included direct marketing, database marketing, quality management and services marketing, which aimed to communicate messages of trust, commitment, co-operation and shared values. They found that targeting customers with relationship marketing activities after a high-involvement purchase reduced severe cognitive dissonance.

Customers tend to try to reduce dissonance on their own, and marketing managers can accompany such inherent efforts after the purchase to support the customer. Such personalised marketing efforts should be a standard campaign approach for companies focused on building customer loyalty.

There is a clear role for loyalty programs to play in reducing cognitive dissonance, and thereby building customer satisfaction and encouraging loyalty. This may include rewards tied to the transaction ('I spent all this money, but look how many points I earned!'), post-purchase communications efforts which strive to make the member feel they have made the right decision, and invitations to join clubs and communities which provide the customer with a sense of belonging and exclusivity, while connecting them to other like-minded customers.

---

163 Skelton, A. C. H. & Allwood, J. M., 2017, 'Questioning demand: A study of regretted purchases in Great Britain', Ecological Economics, Vol 131, pp499-509

164 Sharifi, S. & Esfidani, M., 2014, 'The impacts of relationship marketing on cognitive dissonance, satisfaction, and loyalty: The mediating role of trust and cognitive dissonance', International Journal of Retail & Distribution Management, Vol 42.

Bentley Continental Club

A loyalty program by British heritage car brand Bentley likely acts to reduce the cognitive dissonance which may be associated with investing in such a high value purchase.

The Continental Club offers a range of rolling benefits which 'kick in as the car leaves the comfort zone of the manufacturer's warranty',[165] reducing the feeling of uncertainty which may arise at this key time.

Members of the Continental Club are entitled to substantial discounts on their car services and maintenance work, free 'while you wait' oil top-up, car wash and tyre pressure checks, as well as additional aspirational benefits like access to exclusive launch events for new models.[166]

Key insights

- Consumer psychology provides a solid, research-based foundation to guide loyalty program design in a way which will maximise chances of successfully driving the desired behavioural changes.

- An extensive body of consumer psychology theories and studies exist which are immediately relevant for loyalty programs. These include the law of effect and the law of exercise, operant conditioning, social identity theory, endowed progress effect, goal gradient effect, customer delight and decision affect theory, norm of reciprocity, commitment theory, expectation theory of motivation and cognitive dissonance theory.

Suggested reading

- Skinner, B. F, 1948, 'Superstition' in the pigeon', Journal of Experimental Psychology, Vol 38, Iss 2, pp168–172.

---

165 Chilli Pepper, Top Marques, https://chillipepper.ie/top-marques/, accessed 29 June 2020.

166 Ibid.

- Ivanic, Aarti, 2015, 'Status Has Its Privileges: The Psychological Benefit of Status-Reinforcing Behaviors', Psychology & Marketing, Vol 32, pp697-708.

- Nunes, J. & Drèze, X., 2006, 'The Endowed Progress Effect: How Artificial Advancement increases Effort', Journal of Consumer Research, Vol 32, Iss 4, pp504-512.

- Kivetz, R., Urminsky, O., & Zheng, Y., 2006, 'The Goal-Gradient Hypothesis Resurrected: Purchase Acceleration, Illusionary Goal Progress, and Customer Retention', Journal of Marketing Research, Vol 43, pp39-58.

- Schwartz, N., 1987, 'Stimmung als Information (Mood as information)'.

- Regan, R., 1971, 'Effects of a favor and liking on compliance', Journal of Experimental Social Psychology, Vol 7, Iss 6, pp627-639.

- Mellers, B.A., Schwartz, A., Ho, K. & Ritov, I., 1997, 'Decision Affect Theory: Emotional Reactions to the Outcomes of Risky Options', Psychological Science, Vol 8, No 6, pp423-429.

- Oliver, R.L., Rust, R. & Varki, S., 1997, 'Customer Delight: Foundations, Findings, and Managerial Insight', Journal of Retailing, Vol 73, Iss 3, pp311-336.

- Sharma, D., & Verma, V., 2014, 'Psychological and economic considerations of rewards programs', Journal of Retailing and Consumer Services, Vol 21, Iss 6, pp924-932.

- Festinger, L., 1957, 'A theory of cognitive dissonance', Stanford University Press.

CHAPTER 6

BIASES AND HEURISTICS

'… people rely on a limited number of heuristic principles which reduce the complex tasks of assessing probabilities and predicting values to simpler judgmental operations. In general, these heuristics are quite useful, but sometimes they lead to severe and systematic errors.'

- Tversky, A. and Kahneman, D, 1974[167]

Focus areas

This chapter will address the following questions:

- What are heuristics and biases?

- How are heuristics and biases relevant for loyalty programs?

- Which heuristics and biases are utilised by loyalty programs to influence member behaviours?

LOYALTY PROGRAMS AIM to influence consumer behaviour. Therefore, understanding how consumers make decisions and the factors that influence decision making is an important area of research for loyalty program designers and operators.

One area of psychology which warrants more comprehensive review is the

---

167 Tversky, A. & Kahneman, D., 1974, 'Judgment under Uncertainty: Heuristics and Biases', Science, Vol 185, Iss 4157, pp1124–1131.

effect of *heuristics* and *behavioural biases* which underpin the way consumers inherently behave.

A heuristic is defined as a mental shortcut that allows people to solve problems and make judgments quickly and efficiently. Heuristics form because consumers do not have the capacity, time or motivation to recognise and evaluate all the available information in their complex environment.[168]

Psychological biases, or cognitive biases, are defined as thinking patterns based on observations and generalisations that may lead to memory errors, inaccurate judgments, and faulty logic (Evans et al,[169]), causing consumers to make decisions without looking at the bigger picture.

While the influence of biases and heuristics can introduce information asymmetries and inaccuracies, and may lead to irrational decisions, they are deemed necessary to reduce the complexity of everyday decision-making processes by reducing the effort associated with cognitive tasks. Shah and Oppenheimer (2008)[170] stated that effort reduction relies on at least one of the following principles; examining fewer cues, reducing the difficulty associated with retrieving and storing cue values, simplifying the weighting principles for cues, integrating less information and examining fewer alternatives.

In the early 1970s, Kahneman & Tversky[171] introduced their foundational studies on biases and heuristics. They identified the concept of heuristics, and how cognitive biases stem from the reliance on judgemental heuristics. They proposed a number of heuristic principles which explain the ways in which people assess probabilities and predict values to arrive at their choices.

Three primary heuristics were identified:

- **Representativeness heuristic**: occurs when people compare and categorise objects based on a limited number of similarities, rather

---

168 Changing Minds, The Size Heuristic, http://changingminds.org/explanations/decision/size_heuristic.htm, accessed 29 May 2019.

169 Evans, J. St. B. T., Barston, J. L. & Pollard, P., 1983, 'On the conflict between logic and belief in syllogistic reasoning. Memory & Cognition, Vol 11, Iss 3, pp295-306.

170 *Shah*, A. K., *Oppenheimer*, D.M., 2008, '*Heuristics made easy: An effort-reduction framework*', Psychological Bulletin, Vol 134, pp207–222.

171 Tversky, A. & Kahneman, D., 1974, 'Judgment under Uncertainty: Heuristics and Biases', Science, Vol 185, Iss 4157, pp1124–1131.

than using objective statistics or knowledge.[172] One example of the representativeness heuristic relates to the judgement of value and size, where consumers misjudge the relationship between the two, thinking one directly resembles the other. To calculate how big something is, consumers may categorise this as 'lots', mistaking 'lots' for 'big'. For example, a pile of one thousand 1c coins can somehow seem more than a ten dollar note.

- **Availability heuristic**: states that people are inclined to retrieve information that is most readily available when making a decision (Redelmeier, 2005).[173] Tversky and Kahneman[174] offered the availability heuristic as an explanation for 'illusory correlations' in which people wrongly judge two events to be associated with each other, explaining that people judge correlation on the basis of the ease of imagining or recalling the two events together. If information comes to mind easily then consumers may overestimate the likelihood of an experience occurring. For example, if people have a vivid memory of being in a car accident or missing a flight, they are more likely to rate the odds of it happening again much higher than base rates would indicate.

- **Anchoring & adjustment heuristic**: occurs when people are estimating quantities. It states that they will arrive at an initial judgement based on an estimate (anchor) and then adjust this number based on additional information obtained. In Tversky and Kahneman's[175] experiments, subjects did not shift sufficiently far away from the anchor number to make a large enough adjustment to accurately reflect the real value. For example, a real estate agent may provide an opening bid well above the fair value price as a way

---

172 Kahneman, D. &Tversky, A., 1972, 'Subjective probability: A judgment of representativeness', Cognitive Psychology, Vol 3, Iss 3, pp430–454.

173 Redelmeier, D. A., 2005, 'The cognitive psychology of missed diagnosis', *Annals of Internal Medicine, Vol 142, Iss* 2, pp115-120.

174 Tversky, A. & Kahneman, D., 1973, 'Availability: A Heuristic for Judging Frequency and Probability', Cognitive Psychology, Vol 5, Iss 2, pp207–232.

175 Ibid.

of providing an anchor for negotiations. With a higher anchor, the final price will tend to be higher.

These concepts identified by Kahneman & Tversky have been refined and built upon over time, with huge bodies of research and hundreds of different behavioural biases identified since. Some are immediately relevant to specific loyalty programs, some are more closely related to general marketing functions and others do not apply to loyalty programs at all.

Loyalty programs can be designed to appeal to consumer reliance on specific biases and heuristics. The following theories are discussed in relation to practical applications within loyalty programs to influence member decisions and behaviours.

Representativeness heuristic

The *representativeness heuristic* identified by Kahneman and Tversky is utilised by points and miles programs. Program operators appeal to this heuristic by attempting to make the value of a reward appear bigger than it really is. For example, if a member spends $100 with a retailer and that retailer rewards them with 1 per cent of the total spend, then the member will receive $1 of value back, which may not sound very rewarding to the member. But if it is part of a loyalty program, the member can earn one hundred points (at 1c per point, which is equal to $1). By applying the representativeness heuristic, 'one hundred' points may be perceived as significantly bigger than 'one' dollar, making the member feel that the reward they have received is bigger than in reality.

The reverse is also true. Research on consumer processing of pricing information by Coulter and Coulter (2005)[176] determined that consumers are frequently unaware of how their price and value inferences are derived. They may typically be unable to articulate the exact reasons why some aspect of the way price is presented translates into lower (or higher) perceived value. Their research determined that consumers could perceive product prices to be smaller simply by displaying the price in a smaller font size.

---

176 Coulter, K. & Coulter, R., 2005. 'Size Does Matter: The Effects of Magnitude Representation Congruency on Price Perceptions and Purchase Likelihood', Journal of Consumer Psychology, Vol 15, pp64-76.

Accor Hotels Le Club

For Le Club members, Accor Hotels ran a four-week 'Million Points Giveaway'[177] promotion in 2019 where any member who stayed at a participating Accor Hotel gained an entry into the draw.

The draw stated that 'Ten members will each win 100,000 Rewards points'.

While one million points sounds like a lot to giveaway (it almost sounds like €1 million), the cost to Accor was likely to be in the order of €10,000 euros or less. These types of promotions are an effective way for programs to drive strong engagement for a very low cost.

Time (hyperbolic) Discounting bias

Frederick et al (2002)[178] coined *time discounting* (otherwise referred to as *hyperbolic discounting*) to refer to differences in the relative valuation placed on rewards by comparing value at different points in time. Their research suggested present rewards are weighted more heavily than future ones. If reward availability is very distant in time, it ceases to be valuable. In their study, subjects chose a $100 reward they could receive immediately over a $120 reward they could access in one month.

Building on time discounting is *present-biased preference*, where consumers have the inclination to prefer a smaller present reward to a larger later reward, but reverse their preference when both rewards are equally delayed. Chakraborty (2017)[179] provided the following example to illustrate:

---

177 Accor, Million Points Giveaway, 2019, https://all.accor.com/loyalty-program/promotions-offers/added-value/owm010724-001-millionpointsgiveaway.en.shtml, accessed 5th May 2020.

178 Frederick, S., Loewenstein, G. & O'Donoghue, T., 2002, 'Time discounting and time preference: A critical review', Journal of Economic Literature, Vol 40, pp351-401.

179 Chakraborty, A, 2019, 'Present Bias,' University of California, Davis.

Figure 8: the example options provided within 'present-biased preference' research by A Chakraborty, 2019, p1.[180]

Most subjects chose A over B, but D over C, despite the time differences being the same.

These biases provide direction for loyalty program operators to structure their program to deliver to specific objectives:

- **To encourage points redemption**: offer lower value rewards which can be instantly accessed via website or app redemptions.

- **To encourage points accumulation**: set higher minimum points requirements for product redemptions and delay access to the reward.

Chipotle Rewards

Chipotle[181] have designed their rewards program to encourage more frequent visits from members looking to unlock instant, lower value rewards. Small amounts of points can be redeemed for free entrees, while program communications are focused on encouraging members to buy a meal in order to access their free entrée before it expires within 60 days.

---

180 Ibid.

181 Chipotle, https://www.chipotle.com/order/rewards, accessed 29 June 2020.

> ## Choice Privileges
>
> The Choice Privileges rewards program offers different options for members to redeem points, however the program encourages the accumulation of points through setting a minimum points requirement for redemption. Members must redeem a minimum of 8,000 points within the hotel network or transfer a minimum of 5,000 points when exchanging for airline miles.[182]

Endowment Effect bias

An *endowment effect bias* occurs when people irrationally overvalue an object they own, regardless of its objective market value, whereby 'people often demand much more to give up an object than they would be willing to pay to acquire it' (Thaler, 1980).[183]

Kahneman et al (1991)[184] ran a series of experiments to test the endowment effect. In one experiment, 77 students were randomly assigned roles as buyers or sellers, with sellers provided with university-branded coffee mugs. Few trades ensued, with sellers asking for an average $7.12 for a mug, while buyers only wanted to pay an average $2.87. The experience suggested that the low volume of trade was primarily produced by the seller's reluctance to give up their endowment, rather than by buyers' unwillingness to spend their cash.

182 Choice Hotels, Terms and Conditions, https://www.choicehotels.com/en-au/choice-privileges/rules-regulations#general, accessed 18 June 2020.

183 Thaler, R., 1980, 'Toward a Positive Theory of Consumer Choice,' Journal of Economic Behavior and Organization, Vol 1, pp39-60.

184 Kahneman, D., Knetsch, J. L. & Thaler, R. H., 1991, 'Anomalies: The endowment effect, loss aversion, and status quo bias', Journal of Economic Perspectives, Vol 5, Iss 1, pp193-206.

Figure 9: the results derived by Kahneman et al in their experiment, with the right side exhibiting the impact of the endowment effect bias on subjects overvaluing an object they own. Adapted from findings within research paper 'Anomalies: The endowment effect, loss aversion, and status quo bias' by D Kahneman et al, 1991.[185]

Qatar Airways Privilege Club

Qatar Airways utilised the endowment effect bias to attract and retain high-value customers from competitors. They provided non-members with instant access to a premium tier, hoping to make the new members feel a sense of ownership over their status, and hence value it more than if they were simply aspiring to achieve it.

In May 2020, Qatar Airways launched their first ever status match campaign.[186] Status matching allows loyal members of one program to access equivalent benefits with another program for a set period.

Qatar Airways offered silver, gold and platinum frequent flyers from Emirates, Etihad, Singapore Airlines, South African Airways, Turkish Airlines and Virgin Australia the corresponding status within their Privilege Club, without having to build up status credits.

By bestowing instant premium status on a new Privilege Club

185 Ibid.

186 Ollila, J., 2020, 'Qatar Airways Privilege Club Status Match Campaign May 2020', https://loyaltylobby.com/2020/05/18/qatar-airways-privilege-club-status-match-campaign-may-2020/, accessed 1 July 2020.

member for a full year, and creating a feeling of ownership, Qatar Airways hoped members would be motivate to fly more with Qatar (and less with competitors) in order to retain their status.

Loss Aversion bias

Loss aversion suggests that the pain of losing something feels twice as powerful as the pleasure of gaining the same thing.

Kahneman and Tversky (1979)[187] conducted a series of experiments where subjects were asked to choose between more or less risky propositions which provided the potential to win or lose money (e.g. an equal chance of winning or losing $100). They found 'the aggravation that one experiences in losing a sum of money appears to be greater than the pleasure associated with gaining the same amount', and that most people find symmetric bets of that form to be distinctly unattractive.

---

187 Kahneman, D. & Tversky, A., 1979, 'Prospect Theory: An Analysis of Decision under Risk', Econometrica, Vol. 47, Iss 2, pp263-9.

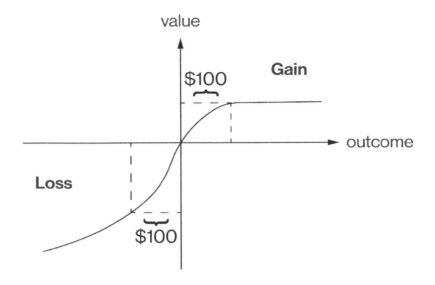

Figure 10: the findings by Kahneman and Tversky, showing the fear of losing $100 is twice as powerful as the prospect of gaining $100. Adapted from 'Prospect Theory: An Analysis of Decision under Risk', D Kahneman and A Tversky 1979.[188]

These findings have led to the development of strategies whereby workers and students have been motivated by penalties rather than rewards. Hossain & List (2012)[189] determined that framing outcomes as penalties resulted in improved performance in a Chinese production factory. Fryer et al (2012)[190] demonstrated that exploiting the power of loss aversion, where teachers were paid in advance and asked to give back the money if their students did not improve sufficiently, increased math test scores by more than one standard deviation.

People appear to be more willing to take risks or behave dishonestly to

188 Ibid.

189 Hossain, T. & List, J., 2009, 'The Behavioralist Visits the Factory: Increasing Productivity Using Simple Framing Manipulations', National Bureau of Economic Research, Inc, NBER Working Papers, Vol 58, Iss 12, pp2151-2167.

190 Fryer, R. G., Levitt, S. D., List, J. & Sadoff, S., 2012. 'Enhancing the Efficacy of Teacher Incentives through Loss Aversion: A Field Experiment,' NBER Working Papers 18237, National Bureau of Economic Research, Inc.

avoid a loss than to make a gain. A study by Schindler & Pfattheicher (2016)[191] used a die-under-the-cup game and a coin-toss task, with the opportunity for participants to engage in dishonest behaviour either to avoid a loss or to approach an equivalent gain. Their results found that people showed more dishonest behaviour to avoid a loss.

Loss aversion is used extensively in loyalty programs (and marketing strategies more widely) to stimulate member engagement. Programs can provide members with something which they feel ownership for and value, and then establish conditions whereby they might have ownership removed. This can act as a motivational force to compel the member to continue transacting. This includes:

- The threat of status tier members losing their benefits if they fail to earn enough status credits.

- Members facing the risk of their points expiring if they do not engage with the program on a regular enough basis (or redeem them in time).

- Members not being able to access desirable rewards (reward seats, hotel rooms, etc.).

- Members having to spend a greater amount of points if they do not book early enough.

According to Ries (2012),[192] some private fitness centres allow people to invest their own money in weight-loss incentives (e.g. by putting in $200 and receiving a portion back as they achieve incremental weight-loss goals). Websites like www.stickK.com operate on the same basis in the online environment. They help people achieve goals via a 'commitment contract'; a binding agreement which involves putting money on the table to ensure the user follows through with their intentions using loss aversion.

Loyalty programs also build in benefits which minimise the risk of loss

---

191 Schindler, S. & Pfattheicher, S., 2017, 'The frame of the game: Loss-framing increases dishonest behavior', Journal of Experimental Social Psychology, Vol 69, pp172-177.

192 Ries, N. M., 2012, 'Financial incentives for weight loss and healthy behaviours. Healthcare policy = Politiques de sante', Vol 7, Iss 3, pp23–28.

aversion. For example, offering members money back guarantees, extended returns, free returns or automatic refunds if prices reduce on purchased items. These program benefits can provide the member with an extra sense of security by lowering the perceived risk of losing money.

Mileage Runs

A 'mileage run' or 'status run' involves members of a frequent flyer program taking a flight with the sole purpose of earning enough status credits to ensure their status tier is maintained. The destination or the number of frequent flyer points earned for the trip can be secondary considerations.

If a member has not flown enough in a calendar year to qualify or re-qualify for a premium status, sometimes they will engage in a mileage or status run due to the high value placed on the benefits they stand to lose.

Many websites and forums exist for frequent flyer members to research or discuss how a member can book a flight with the necessary status credits for the lowest cost. For example, one forum, Flyertalk, has 13,508 threads related to mileage run discussions.[193]

After recognising the patterns of mileage runners, airlines may adjust their promotions by offering more frequent status credit promotions on certain routes rather than offering sale prices (i.e. double status credits).

Framing of Attribute Information bias

The *framing of attribute information bias* (Levin and Gaeth, 1988)[194] states people will react to a particular choice in different ways depending on whether it is presented as a loss or a gain. More specifically, people tend to avoid risks

---

193 Flyertalk, https://www.flyertalk.com/forum/mileage-run-discussion-627/, accessed 18 June 2020.

194 Levin, I. & Gaeth, G., 1988', 'How Consumers Are Affected by the Framing of Attribute Information Before and After Consuming the Product', Journal of Consumer Research, Vol 15, pp374-78.

when a positive frame is presented but seek risks when a negative frame is presented, a bias which has links to loss aversion.

Levin and Gaeth asked subjects to rate several qualitative attributes of ground beef that framed the beef as either 75 per cent lean or 25 per cent fat. Subjects provided more favourable evaluations of the beef labelled 75 per cent lean.

 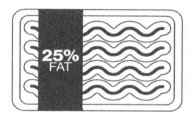

Figure 11: the experiment run by Levin and Gaeth, showing the effects of framing of ground beef attributes on subjects. Adapted from 'How Consumers Are Affected by the Framing of Attribute Information Before and After Consuming the Product', Levin, I and Gaeth, G, 1988.[195]

Diamond and Campbell (1988) tested subjects in a laboratory simulation which compared monetary promotions (such as discounts) with non-monetary promotions (such as free goods or extra amounts of the product) using the same referenced price value. Subjects rated non-monetary promotions as making them feel that they are 'gaining something extra'. In contrast, subjects rated monetary promotions as making them feel that they were 'losing less than usual'.[196] In short, non-monetary promotions were framed as gains and monetary promotions were framed as reduced losses, indicating non-monetary promotions are viewed more favourably.

This hypothesis was again tested in an experiment specifically involving

---

195 Ibid.

196 Diamond, W. D. & Campbell, L., 1988, 'The Framing of Sales Promotions: Effects on Reference Price Change', https://www.acrwebsite.org/volumes/6862/volumes/v16/NA-16, accessed 29 June 2020.

supermarket coupons.[197] The test demonstrated that supermarket shoppers presented with redeemable coupons were significantly more likely to choose a test promotion if it were framed as a gain (buy a spaghetti sauce and get a free soup valued at 49c) than if it were framed as a reduced loss (buy a spaghetti sauce and a soup and get 49c off the bill).

Framing provides important direction for communication positioning within a loyalty program. Program operators can utilise framing in a variety of ways:

- Position rewards as additional perks that are provided to loyal customers at the company's expense (O'Malley and Prothero, 2002).[198]

- Use progress trackers, which highlight the progress made towards the completion of a goal and unlocking of a reward. Despite the need for a member to make further transactions, the progress tracker enables communications to be framed as a gain (e.g. earn just 200 points more to unlock a free flight) rather than a loss (e.g. $200 spend is required to unlock a free flight). The goal may be access to a reward product or the achievement of a status tier.

- Tailor messages to loyalty program members to emphasise their special status and acknowledge the importance of the relationship with the brand (Shugan, 2005).[199]

- Implement a points plus pay option as part of the standard purchase flow, allowing members to reduce the amount of cash they spend by subsidising the cost with points. Examples include airlines which allow members to reduce the total cost of the fare by paying with a combination of cash and frequent flyer points (a positive

197 Diamond, W. D. & Sanyal, A., 1990, 'The Effect of Framing on the Choice of Supermarket Coupons', http://www.communicationcache.com/uploads/1/0/8/8/10887248/the_effect_of_framing_on_the_choice_of_supermarket_coupons.pdf, accessed 29 June 2020.

198 O'Malley, L., & Prothero, A., 2002, 'Beyond the frills of relationship marketing', Journal of Business Research, Vol 57, Iss 11, pp1286-1294.

199 Shugan, S. M., 2005, 'Brand loyalty programs: Are they shams?', Marketing Science, Vol 24, pp185-93.

frame). Drèze & Nunes (2004)[200] conducted research which delivered a mathematical proof that a combination of cash and points can be superior to a standard, single-currency price by lowering the psychological or perceived cost.

Returning to Levin and Gaeth's study on lean vs fat beef, they reported that the magnitude of the framing effect lessened when subjects actually tasted the meat, suggesting a diagnostic product experience dilutes the impact of framing. This is an important consideration which cautions that while consumers may be influenced by framing, they will be influenced more by the actual experience of consumption. A focus on delivering a customer experience that is consistent with, or exceeds, expectations must be a priority in the pursuit of genuine member loyalty.

Dosh

Dosh[201] is a card linked cashback program based in the US with over 1,000 affiliate partner stores and restaurants. Members can link their credit or debit card to the Dosh app, and when they make a purchase at a partner store with the linked credit card, 'Dosh' (a cashback percentage of the purchase) is automatically applied.

By magnifying the gain (cashback), rather than the loss (financial), Dosh are framing the program as positive (i.e. their website states it as 'the easiest money you've ever made').

Watching the Dosh add up on the cashback counter in the app over time, members are constantly presented with the positive effects of their amplified 'gains'.

---

200 Drèze, J. & Nunes, J., 2004 'Using Combined-Currency Prices to Lower Consumers' Perceived Cost.' Journal of Marketing Research, Vol. 59, pp. 59-72

201 Dosh, https://www.dosh.com/, accessed 29 June 2020.

Informational Social Influence (social proof) bias

Sherif (1935) ran a famous study using optical illusions to test the influence of social conformity. When looking at a stationary point of light in a dark room, the light appears to move back and forth. Sherif found that when subjects were tested alone, they established their own range for judging the distance the light was perceived to move and used this as an anchor to guide future judgements. When subjects were tested in a group, there was clear convergence on the range with group norms being established. Even when later tested alone, group norms persisted. When subjects within this study were asked if they were influenced by the judgements of other people in the group, only 25 per cent of subjects reported they were, showing that social conformity occurs sub-consciously.

In an equally famous study, Asch (1951)[202] conducted a series of experiments which utilised a similarly clever approach to explore the effects of social conformity. Asch placed a subject in a room with seven actors who had been instructed to provide specific answers. A line length judgement test was used, where a target line was presented, followed by three other lines (labelled A, B and C). Each participant took turns to state which line was most like the target line in length across 18 different tests. The actors deliberately said the wrong answer for 12 of the 18 tests. On average, subjects conformed to the incorrect answers on 32 per cent of the tests, with 74 per cent of subjects conforming on at least one obvious test. This is an astonishing result considering the correct answer was generally obvious.

Cialdini (1984)[203] built on this insight with the concept of *social proof*, where individuals mimic the actions of others in ambiguous social situations, irrespective of whether that behaviour is appropriate and logical. Cialdini hypothesised that 'one means we use to determine what is correct is to find out what other people think is correct'. This is based on the bias that when a lot of people are doing something, it is likely the correct thing to do.

Specific to loyalty programs (and the wider field of marketing), the digital

---

202 Asch, S. E., 1951, 'Effects of Group Pressure on the Modification and Distortion of Judgments', In Guetzknow, H., Ed., Groups, Leadership and Men, Pittsburgh, PA, Carnegie Press, pp177-190.
203 Cialdini, R. B., 1993, 'Influence: The Psychology of Persuasion'.

age has made it easier to observe what others are doing, at scale and over vast geographies. Social media, review websites and word of mouth have all been identified as powerful influencers of consumer behaviour and attitudes towards brands and products. They establish group norms and stimulate mass conformity in ways not previously possible.

A loyalty program can play a role in building a positive brand presence across these promotional channels in four ways:

- Building the member base and developing a positive relationship with members to increase their propensity to become advocates. This is best supported via a comprehensive lifecycle management strategy, which is covered in Chapter 12.

- Utilising gamification techniques to encourage members to engage with the channels (e.g. awarding bonus points for following a brand on social media). Gamification is covered in Chapter 13.

- Prompting members who have recently transacted to provide their feedback via review, and responding to that review, whether it is positive or negative (studies have shown that nearly 95 per cent of shoppers read online reviews before making a purchase[204] and 97 per cent of shoppers say reviews influence buying decisions[205]).

- Providing members with access to a referral program (as covered in Chapter 8), where both the member and their family members or friends can earn a bonus reward for joining the loyalty program.

This approach of gamifying social media engagement can deliver additional benefits. Rehnen et al (2017)[206] ran a field study where subjects earned loyalty points for social media engagement. The results showed significantly

---

204 Spiegal Research Centre, 2017, 'How Online Reviews Influence Sales', https://spiegel.medill.northwestern.edu/online-reviews/, accessed 12 May 2020.

205 Fan and Fuel, 2016, 'No online customer reviews means BIG problems in 2017', https://fanandfuel.com/no-online-customer-reviews-means-big-prob-lems-2017/, accessed 12 May 2020.

206 Rehnen, L., Bartsch, S., Kull, M. & Meyer, A., 2017, 'Exploring the impact of rewarded social media engagement in loyalty programs, Journal of Service Management, Vol 28, pp305 – 328.

higher attitudinal commitment to the program and the brand than that of members who earned points solely through transactions. They concluded that rewarding customers for social media engagement can be a beneficial way of boosting active participation in loyalty programs, however they cautioned that the experience needs to be enjoyable and self-determined.

There is also a large movement towards social responsibility which aligns with social proof, as people want to be seen to be doing the right thing, with social media the enabler. The market has long been full of programs providing the option for members to donate their points to charity (e.g. Amex, Singapore Airlines and *flybuys* to name a few), and while this premise usually tests well among consumers in market research, it rarely materialises into consumer action. So, when there is no social pressure or social gain attached to doing the right thing, there is far less incentive to attract consumers to continue engaging in this way.

However, if loyalty programs can leverage the power of social media to support social movements, then the results can be powerful. For example, some brands are designing programs around the wellness social movement. Nike Training Club, Lorna Jane Active Living and Reebok Unlocked not only sell activewear but also incorporate rewards for fitness, nutrition, training and wellness, with results able to be shared on social media as a form of social proof.

> **Reebok Unlocked**
>
> By revamping their loyalty program in 2019 to focus on rewarding engagement, and in-particular public engagement, Reebok continues to build on its mission to attract a younger audience. At launch, their global head of digital stated 'We'll be rewarding consumers for their loyalty and consistent brand interaction, with experiences that we know resonate with them and speak to their passions.'[207]
>
> The program structure places a focus on rewarding customers for

---

207 The Drum, News, 2019, 'Reebok's hunt for a younger consumer continues with first foray into customer loyalty', https://www.thedrum.com/news/2019/04/02/reebok-s-hunt-younger-consumer-continues-with-first-foray-customer-loyalty, accessed 12 May 2020.

social media interactions and for attending Reebok social events. Reebok also leverage the social networks of well-known health and wellness leaders who unlock access to training programs as rewards to members, creating a social community.

The program also rewards members with bonus points for rating and reviewing a product. Attaching bonus points in exchange for ratings/reviews on social media or a website also taps into the norm of reciprocity where consumers who receive something free (points) feel compelled to provide something in return (a positive review).

Moral Self-Licensing bias

A *self-licensing effect* occurs when past good deeds 'liberate individuals to engage in behaviours that are immoral, unethical, or otherwise problematic, behaviours that they would otherwise avoid for fear of feeling or appearing immoral' (Merritt et al, 2010).[208] That is, if a person performs a behaviour which they perceive to be moral, they allocate themselves a 'moral surplus' which they justify as licence to subsequently behave immorally, bringing them back to a state of moral equilibrium. A simple example would be a dieter rewarding themselves with a 'naughty treat' for sticking to their meal plan.

Effron et al (2009)[209] tested the impact that voicing support for Barack Obama just before the 2008 election would have on subjects making ambiguously racist statements. Subjects were asked to play the role of a sheriff recruiting either a black or white officer to a police department. On average, subjects said that a police force job was equally well suited for both white and black candidates. By contrast, subjects who were provided with an opportunity to express their support for Obama prior to conducting the main part of the experiment were more likely to say the job was better suited for a white candidate. The self-licensing effect is said to have occurred because the subjects

208 Merritt, A. C., Effron, D. A. & Monin, B., 2010, 'Moral Self-Licensing: When Being Good Frees Us to Be Bad', Social and Personality Psychology Compass, Vol 4, pp344-357.

209 Effron, D. A., Cameron, J. S. & Monin, B., 2009, 'Endorsing Obama Licenses Favoring Whites', Journal of Experimental Social Psychology, Vol 45 pp590-593.

who expressed support for Obama made them feel that they no longer needed to prove their lack of prejudice.

This study replicated an original study by Monin & Miller (2001),[210] who tested the self-licensing effect on racist attitudes as well as sexist attitudes, finding subjects who were provided with the opportunity to demonstrate they were not racist or sexist were more inclined to demonstrate racist or sexist decisions.

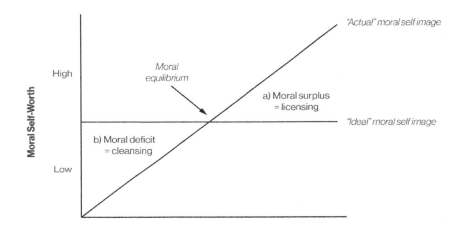

Figure 12: the process of moral self-regulation, demonstrating that when people engage in moral or immoral actions, this may lead to a surplus or deficit from their ideal state which licenses them to engage in subsequent immoral or moral behaviour respectively to re-establish equilibrium. Adapted from 'The limits of Moral Licensing' by Y Hertzman and D Stolle, 2013, Figure 1, p 4.[211]

Kivetz and Simonson (2002)[212] identified a self-licensing effect in loyalty programs. They conducted research on the effort members invested to obtain different types of rewards. They found that a higher level of effort tended to

210 Monin, B. & Miller, D. T., 2001, 'Moral credentials and the expression of prejudice', Journal of Personality and Social Psychology, Vol 81, pp33–43.

211 Hertzman, Y. & Stolle, D., 2013, 'The limits of Moral Licensing', https://ruben-son.org/wp-content/uploads/2013/11/TPBW_StolleHertzman.pdf, accessed 16 July 2020

212 Kivetz, R. & Simonson, I., 2002, 'Earning the Right to Indulge: Effort as a Determinant of Customer Preferences Toward Frequency Program Rewards', Journal of Marketing Research - J MARKET RES-CHICAGO, Vol 39, pp155-170.

shift member preferences from necessity to luxury rewards. They hypothesised this was the result of a self-licensing effect where the higher efforts required to earn enough points acted to reduce the guilt often associated with choosing luxuries over necessities. Providing further evidence for the self-licensing in loyalty programs, they also identified that the effect was stronger on members who tended to feel guilty about luxury consumption. For example, many frequent flyer program members refuse to pay for business class seats but are comfortable redeeming points for business class upgrades. Members may justify or give themselves moral license to indulge on a business class seat by detaching loyalty currencies from money, or mentally accounting a reward as being 'free', whereby guilt is also mentally detached.

This is reflective of Nunes and Drèze (2006),[213] who argued the more successful loyalty programs feature less functional and more pleasure-providing rewards as 'consumers love to be given a treat they would not splurge on with their own money.'

Mastercard Pay With Rewards

Rather than offering rewards which a member could easily buy themselves, Mastercard have moved towards experiential rewards to align with the changing desires of their members. Pay With Rewards gives cardholders the flexibility to use their points however they desire.[214]

They have focused on providing rewards options which add an extra level of service across a member's lifestyle to deliver a complete end-to-end experience. For example, a member can use Pay With Rewards to splurge on a night out which can include everything from the ride there, the restaurant, the movies and the ride home, making the entire experience rewarding at every touchpoint. This

---

213 Nunes, J. C. & Drèze, X., 2006, 'Your Loyalty Program Is Betraying You', Harvard Business Review, https://hbr.org/2006/04/your-loyalty-program-is-betraying-you, accessed 2 Feb 2020.

214 Mastercard, https://www.mastercard.com.au/en-au/issuers/products-and-solutions/grow-manage-your-business/loyalty-solutions/pay-with-rewards.html, accessed 29 June 2020.

structure gives members the chance to enjoy indulging in luxuries, holidays, or even groceries they may not have given themselves license to buy otherwise.

Priming bias

Priming is a psychological technique whereby exposure to a certain stimulus may influence the response to a subsequent stimulus. North et al (1999)[215] investigated the extent to which stereotypically French and German music could influence supermarket customers selecting of French and German wines. Over a two-week period, French and German music was played on alternate days from an in-store display of French and German wines. French music led to French wines outselling German wines, whereas German music led to German wines outselling French wines. Responses to a questionnaire suggested that customers were unaware of these effects of music on their product choices.

---

215 North, A. C., Hargreaves, D. J. & McKendrick, J., 1999, 'The influence of in-store music on wine selections.' Journal of Applied Psychology, Vol 84, Iss 2, pp271-276.

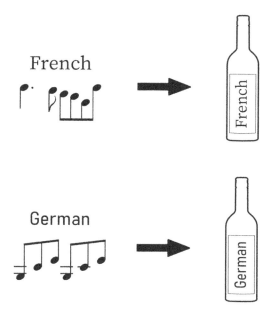

Figure 13: the results derived by North et al, with French music positively impacting the purchase of French wine and German music positively impacting the purchase of German wine. Adapted from findings within 'The influence of in-store music on wine selections' by A.C North et al, 1999.[216]

Priming can have different effects on different people. A study by Rick et al (2008)[217] tested the effect of priming on subjects who experienced different levels of anticipatory mental pain when paying for products ('Spendthrifts', who experience low pain vs 'Tightwads', who experience high pain). When primed with sad music, the Spendthrifts indicated they would spend more, while the Tightwads indicated they would spend less. Both strategies aimed to make them feel better: Spendthrifts cheered themselves up by going shopping, while Tightwads made themselves feel more in control by managing their

216 North, A. C., Hargreaves, D. J. & McKendrick, J., 1999, 'The influence of in-store music on wine selections.' Journal of Applied Psychology, Vol 84, Iss 2, pp271-276.
217 Rick, S. I., Cryder, C. E. & Loewenstein, G., 2008, 'Tightwads and spendthrifts', Journal of Consumer Research, Vol 34, Iss 6, pp767–782.

budget. This provides some evidence for the need for segmentation strategies when utilising these types of approaches.

For loyalty programs, understanding whether members respond better to bonus earn promotions, bonus redemption promotions or discount offers will increase the effectiveness of priming members to take a desired action. For example, informing the member they will earn bonus points for a transaction may act to reduce the mental pain of the member spending money.

Another application of priming is the use of status tier labels invoking value (e.g. Gold, Platinum, Emerald and Diamond). Drèze and Nunes (2009)[218] found that using status-laden colours (Gold and Silver) primed members to form a perception of a pyramid-shaped hierarchy without them needing to specify the percentage of customers in each tier. This was not the case when the colours Blue and Yellow were used.

Woolworths Everyday Rewards

Product placement within physical supermarkets is a primary driver for influencing purchase behaviours, and Everyday Rewards have found a way to deliver the same effects digitally by priming their member base.

Woolworths prime their program members to try new products that they usually would not purchase by strategically placing them alongside commonly purchased products within personalised emails. In this way, members become familiar with products that they have never even considered.

As an example of the type of insight they have learned and applied to grow member spend, Everyday Rewards identified that 'new products sandwiched between familiar products or brands are more likely to be bought and tried by consumers'.[219]

---

218 Drèze, X. & Nunes, J., 2009, 'Feeling Superior: The Impact of Loyalty Program Structure on Consumers' Perceptions of Status', Journal of Consumer Research, Vol 35, pp890-905.

219 Maes, I., cited in Croft, L., 2018, 'We must treat data as a precious gift', says Woolies Exec', http://www.bandt.com.au/marketing/must-treat-data-precious-gift-says-woolies-exec, accessed 10th April 2019.

Sunk Cost Effect bias

Arkes and Blumer (1985)[220] identified the *sunk cost effect* as greater tendency to continue an endeavour once an investment in money, effort, or time has been made. They conducted a field study where customers who had initially paid more for a season subscription to a theatre series attended more plays during the next six months, presumably because of their higher sunk cost in the season tickets.

Sunk costs are deemed a fallacy because they are irrecoverable investments that should not influence decisions, which should be made on the basis of expected future consequences.

Sweis et al (2018)[221] identified that rats, mice and humans are all sensitive to sunk costs after they have made the decision to pursue a reward. They suggested this indicates the sensitivity to temporal sunk costs lies in a vulnerability distinct from deliberation processes, and that this distinction is present across species.

Ashley et at (2015)[222] identified a sunk cost effect in subscription loyalty programs by running a study which demonstrated consumers who pay a fee to participate in a loyalty program have more favourable attitudes, and more positive evaluations of value for the money and benefits than non-paying members.

Whilst the sunk cost effect can provide benefits for subscription-based loyalty program operators, it is important for them to also manage the issue of 'subscription guilt'. For Love or Money 2019[223] explores the reality of 'subscription guilt', revealing that 30 per cent of members who participate in

220 Arkes, H. R. & Blumer, C., 1985, 'The psychology of sunk cost', Organizational Behavior and Human Decision Processes, Vol 35, pp124-140.

221 Sweis, B. M., Abram, S. V.,Schmidt, B. J., Seeland, K. D., MacDonald III, A.W., Thomas, M. J. & Redish, A. D., 2018, 'Sensitivity to "sunk costs" in mice, rats, and humans', Science (New York, N.Y.), pp178-181.

222 Ashley, C., Gillespie, E. A. & Noble, S. M., 2015, 'The effect of loyalty program fees on program perceptions and engagement', Journal of Business Research, Vol 69, Iss 2, https://digitalcommons.uri.edu/cgi/viewcontent. cgi?article=1051&context=cba_facpubs, accessed 26 April 2020.

223 The Point of Loyalty, 'For Love Or Money 2019', https://thepointofloyalty. au/subscription-guilt-myth-or-reality/, accessed 5 May 2020.

loyalty programs with a subscription have *felt guilty for not using or accessing enough of the benefits offered through that subscription'*. This effect increases to 46 per cent of women aged between 18-45, indicating different generational and gender cohort impacts.

> **BahnCard**
>
> The BahnCard is a successful German customer loyalty approach that Deutsche Bahn, the German national railway company, introduced in 1992.
>
> The BahnCard follows a subscription model where travellers purchase an annual BahnCard and subsequently unlock a discount on the regular travel fare price for that year. The original option, the BahnCard 50, costs €255 and unlocks 50 per cent off standard fares for a year. The product range also has additional options unlocking different discount levels up to 100 per cent.
>
> BahnCard members have been shown to behave as if they received a straight discount, ignoring the cost of the BahnCard and regarding it as sunk.[224] As a result, demand for railway travel has increased as members perceive they are obtaining more favourable out-of-pocket expenses through the program, and there is a strong incentive to 'maximise the use of the program as a means of saving more money'.[225]

224 FAZ, 2014, ⊠Warum die BahnCard das Ticket nicht um die Hälfte billiger macht⊠, Retrieved from http://www.faz.net/aktuell/wirtschaft/wirtschaftspoliti k/ deutsche-bahn-bahncard-50-gibt-gar-nicht-50- prozent-rabatt-13302187.html, cited by Kramer, A., 2017, 'Demystifying the "Sunk Cost Fallacy": When Considering Fixed Cost in Decision-Making is Reasonable', Journal of Research in Marketing, Vol 7, Iss 1.

225 Butscher, S. A., 1999, 'Using pricing to increase customer loyalty', Journal of the Professional Pricing Society, pp29-32, cited by Kramer, A., 2017, 'Demystifying the "Sunk Cost Fallacy": When Considering Fixed Cost in Decision-Making is Reasonable', Journal of Research in Marketing, Vol 7, Iss 1.

Scarcity bias

Worchel et al (1975) stated the *scarcity effect* as when an item is more difficult to acquire, it will be valued more highly. They conducted experiments where students were asked to rate the value and attractiveness of cookies that were either in abundant or scarce supply. They found that when the same cookies were labelled as in scarce supply, subjects rated them as more desirable than cookies labelled as in abundant supply. In addition, cookies were rated as more valuable when their supply changed from abundant to scarce, than when they were constantly scarce.

In economics, the scarcity effect is reflected in the water-diamond paradox; water is cheap, but necessary for survival, while diamonds are expensive, but not required for survival. This indicates that object value is not merely determined by usefulness, but also by availability.

Song et al (2019)[226] conducted research on credit card loyalty programs using the scarcity effect as part of their marketing strategy. They studied how different messages motivated engagement of the associated reward referral program and found limited-quantity messages had the highest positive impact on consumers' behavioural intentions.

Airline and hotel loyalty programs utilise scarcity to drive desire for reward products. Airlines only have a limited number of available reward seats, and hotels only have a limited number of available reward rooms. In addition to members feeling fortunate when they manage to access such a reward, programs also allocate a proportion of their inventory to status tier members, making them feel a heightened sense of exclusivity by being able to secure rewards that lower or non-status members cannot.

From 2017-2019, a number of companies launched cryptocurrency loyalty programs (Shelper, 2019).[227] The essence of the programs was to reward members with a loyalty currency which had a finite supply, denoting scarcity. Thus, as more and more members joined the program and earned, the currency would increase in value. The majority of these programs collapsed

---

226 Song, C., Wang, T. & Hu, M., 2019, 'Referral reward programs with scarcity messages on bank credit card adoption', International Journal of Bank Marketing, Vol 37.

227 Shelper, P., 2019, 'Blockchain Loyalty: Disrupting Loyalty and reinventing marketing using blockchain and cryptocurrencies - 2nd Edition'.

relatively quickly, primarily due to the fact that they were unsuccessful in generating sufficient member engagement to stimulate enough demand to drive the value of the cryptocurrency higher. However, some programs rewarding members with major cryptocurrencies, such as Bitcoin, are succeeding and growing.[228]

Wyndham Rewards

Members of Wyndham Rewards[229] earn points and status credits when they spend with Wyndham hotel brands across 22 countries, with partner brands or with their Wyndham Rewards Visa card. Members can redeem points within the Wyndham hotel network, as well as on gift cards, merchandise and airline miles.

Another way for members to redeem points is at a Wyndham Auction. Typical auction items include experiences such as a chance to see Jennifer Lopez's show in Las Vegas, family passes to Legoland or a two-night getaway at a luxury Wyndham hotel. Like eBay, members may bid on multiple auctions simultaneously, and track the history of their bids to assess the effectiveness of their bidding strategy. Auctions run for 2-3 weeks and winners are notified via email.[230]

The auction feature places a fresh spin on redemption, capitalising on the scarcity bias due to the limited nature of auction items. The scarcity element has helped Wyndham Rewards to generate sustained engagement with the program, motivating members to continue earning points for more chances to win desired auction items.

228 Kahatri, Y., 2020 'Bitcoin rewards startup Lolli raises $3 million in new funding,' Yahoo! Finance, https://finance.yahoo.com/news/bitcoin-rewards-startup-lolli-raises-133312938.html accessed 17 July 2020

229 Wyndham Rewards, https://www.wyndhamhotels.com/en-ap/wyndham-rewards, accessed 1 July 2020.

230 O'Neill, S., 2017, 'Wyndham Hotels Debuts Online Auctions for Loyalty Program Redemption', Skift, https://skift.com/2017/07/26/wyndham-hotels-debuts-online-auctions-for-loyalty-program-redemption/, accessed 1 July 2020.

Key insights

- Heuristics are mental shortcuts that allow people to solve problems and make judgments quickly and efficiently.

- Biases are thinking patterns based on observations and generalisations that may lead to memory errors, inaccurate judgments, and faulty logic, causing consumers to make decisions without looking at the bigger picture.

- Loyalty programs can be designed to appeal to consumer reliance on heuristics and the prevalence of biases.

- An extensive body of heuristics and biases theories and studies exist which are immediately relevant for loyalty programs. These include the representativeness heuristic, elimination-by-aspects heuristic, commitment bias, time (hyperbolic) discounting bias, endowment effect and loss aversion bias, framing bias, social proof bias, moral self-licensing bias, priming bias, sunk cost effect bias and scarcity bias.

Suggested reading

- Tversky, A.; Kahneman, D., 1974, 'Judgment under Uncertainty: Heuristics and Biases', Science, Vol 185, Iss 4157, pp1124–1131.

- Shah, A.K., Oppenheimer, D.M., 2008, 'Heuristics made easy: An effort-reduction framework', Psychological Bulletin, Vol 134, pp207–222.

- Tversky, A., 1972, 'Elimination by aspects: A theory of choice', Psychological Review, Vol 79, Iss 4, pp281–299.

- Jacoby, J. and Kyner, D. B., 1973, 'Brand Loyalty vs Repeat Purchasing Behavior', Journal of Marketing Research, Vol 10, Iss 1, pp1-9.

- Thaler, Richard, 1980, 'Toward a Positive Theory of Consumer Choice', Journal of Economic Behavior and Organization, Vol 1, pp39-60.

- Schindler, S., & Pfattheicher, S., 2017, 'The frame of the game: Loss-framing increases dishonest behavior', Journal of Experimental Social Psychology, Vol 69, pp172-177.

- Levin, Irwin & Gaeth, Gary, 1988, 'How Consumers Are Affected by the Framing of Attribute Information Before and After Consuming the Product', Journal of Consumer Research, Vol 15, pp374-78.

- Thorndike, E. L., 1920, 'A constant error in psychological ratings', Journal of Applied Psychology, Vol 4, pp25-29.

- Asch, S. E, 1946, 'Forming impressions of personality', The Journal of Abnormal and Social Psychology, Vol 41, Iss 3, pp258–290.

- Cialdini, R.B., 1993, 'Influence: The Psychology of Persuasion'.

- Merritt, A.C., Effron, D.A. and Monin, B, 2010, 'Moral Self-Licensing: When Being Good Frees Us to Be Bad', Social and Personality Psychology Compass, Vol 4, pp344-357.

- North, A. C., Hargreaves, D. J. & McKendrick, J., 1999, 'The influence of in-store music on wine selections', Journal of Applied Psychology, Vol 84, Iss 2, pp271-276.

CHAPTER 7

REWARDS

'Recent investigations suggest that the firing of dopamine neurons is a motivational substance as a consequence of reward-anticipation. This hypothesis is based on the evidence that, when a reward is greater than expected, the firing of certain dopamine neurons increases, which consequently increases desire or motivation towards the reward.'

- Oscar Arias-Carrión and Ernst Pöppel, 2007 [231]

Focus areas

This chapter will address the following questions:

- Why are consumers motivated to join a loyalty program?

- What are the different classifications of rewards used in loyalty programs?

- Which types of rewards are best suited for different circumstances and situations?

- Which industries are best able to provide efficient rewards?

- How are rewards supplied and fulfilled within large loyalty programs?

---

231 Arias-Carrión, O. & Pöppel, E., 2007, 'Dopamine, learning, and reward-seeking behavior', Acta neurobiologiae experimentalis, Vol 67, pp481-8.

The critical importance of rewards

Academic literature emphasises the critical role rewards play in driving member acquisition and engagement with loyalty programs.

Sharma and Verma (2014)[232] hypothesised that members are motivated to join loyalty programs in order to access desirable rewards, therefore 'the nature of reward offered can influence the outcomes of the loyalty program'.

Mauri (2003)[233] identified that customers become members of a loyalty program if the expected rewards are higher than the expected costs. This was reinforced by Reinares and Garcia-Madariaga (2007)[234] who found that the main cause of non-members' refusal to join a program was because they perceived the rewards to be inadequate in comparison to the effort required.

Johnson et al (2003)[235] determined that rewards and benefits provide the foundation for the development of switching costs, which create a certain degree of calculative commitment or stickiness in customer relations with the company.

Roem et al (2002)[236] found that the reward that is offered in a loyalty program is important to whether the program succeeds or fails at building brand loyalty.

Reward type classifications

Loyalty program rewards can be classified in several different ways:

232 Sharma, D. & Verma, V., 2014, 'Psychological and economic considerations of rewards programs', Journal of Retailing and Consumer Services, Vol 21, pp924–932.

233 Mauri, C., 2003, 'Card loyalty. A new emerging issue in grocery retailing', Journal of Retailing and Consumer Services, Vol 10, Iss 1, pp13–25.

234 Reinares, P. & Garcia-Madariaga, J., 2007, 'The importance of rewards in the management of multisponsor loyalty programmes', The Journal of Database Marketing & Customer Strategy Management, Vol 15.

235 Johnson, M. D., Gustafsson, A., Andreassen, T.W., Lervik, L. & Cha, J., 2001, 'The evolution and future of national customer satisfaction index models', Journal of Economic Psychology, Vol 22, Iss 2, pp217–245.

236 Roehm, M., Pullins, E. & Roehm, H., 2002, 'Designing Loyalty-Building Programs for Packaged Goods Brands', Journal of Marketing Research - J MARKET RES-CHICAGO, Vol 39, pp202-213.

- **Tangible vs intangible**: tangible rewards are concrete, visible, and easily measurable (such as a consumer product), while intangible rewards are relatively less observable and measurable (such as a status tier or recognition).

- **Immediate vs deferred**: an immediate reward is accessed instantly (such as a discount or bonus product), while a deferred reward may require the accumulation of value over time to redeem for a reward (such as building up a points balance to unlock a consumer product or a free flight).

- **Direct vs indirect**: direct rewards support the value proposition of the brand (such as free product samples), while indirect rewards have no obvious linkage with the brand (such as a third-party product discount).

- **Efficient vs inefficient**: efficient rewards are inexpensive compared to the perceived value by the member (such as a free flight which costs the airline little but is valued highly by the member), while inefficient rewards are worth the same to the member and the company (such as cashback which costs the company the same amount as the perceived value by the member).

- **Monetary vs non-monetary**: a monetary reward might be a cash or a cash-equivalent reward (such as an account credit), while a non-monetary reward is not a cash reward (such as a consumer good or an experience).

- **Visible vs invisible**: a visible reward might be something which people can present to others, sometimes with attached trophy value and self-esteem boost (such as priority boarding), while an invisible reward is generally not seen by others (such as a discount or cashback credit).

- **Utilitarian vs hedonic**: utilitarian rewards are useful or practical rewards (such as a toaster), while hedonic rewards are pleasure-producing rewards (such as a luxury spa experience).

Research has shown different reward types may be better suited to generating engagement in different circumstances.

Yi and Jeon (2003)[237] found that in high-involvement situations (where the customer invests time in researching options), direct rewards are preferable to indirect rewards, while in low-involvement situations (where the product is not of utmost concern to the member), immediate rewards are more effective in building value-perception than deferred rewards.

As detailed in Chapter 6, Kivetz and Simonson (2002)[238] identified that a higher level of effort invested in earning a reward tends to shift member preferences from necessity (utilitarian) to luxury (hedonic) rewards. They argued this self-licensing effect occurs when the higher efforts required to access the reward acted to reduce the guilt often associated with choosing luxuries over necessities.

Ruzeviciute and Kamleitner (2017)[239] conducted research which suggested that monetary rewards are more attractive than non-monetary rewards. They found that 'across different industries, the monetary loyalty program was consistently perceived as more attractive, and it was more likely to inspire intentions to join the program. Even in light of variations in consumption goals (hedonic vs. utilitarian), the effect persisted.'

Despite this, non-monetary rewards, such as achieving status tiers, appear to play a critical role in generating brand engagement. Braesher et al (2016)[240] found that non-monetary benefits from loyalty programs can promote brand engagement by inducing customers' feelings of status and belonging in a company-initiated community. Ivanic (2015)[241] identified that members who hold high status in a loyalty program engage in status-reinforcing behaviours, even

---

237 Yi, Y. & Jeon, H., 2003, 'Effects of Loyalty Programs on Value Perception, Program Loyalty, and Brand Loyalty', Journal of The Academy of Marketing Science - J ACAD MARK SCI, Vol 31.

238 Kivetz, R. & Simonson, I., 2002, 'Earning the Right to Indulge: Effort as a Determinant of Customer Preferences Toward Frequency Program Rewards', Journal of Marketing Research - J MARKET RES-CHICAGO. Vol 39, pp155-170.

239 Ruzeviciute, R. & Kamleitner, B., 2017, 'Attracting new customers to loyalty programs: The effectiveness of monetary versus nonmonetary loyalty programs', Journal of Consumer Behaviour, Vol 16, Iss 6, pp113-124.

240 Brashear, T., Kang, J. & Groza, M., 2015, 'Leveraging loyalty programs to build customer–company identification', Journal of Business Research. Vol 69.

241 Ivanic, A., 2015, 'Status Has Its Privileges: The Psychological Benefit of Status-Reinforcing Behaviors', Psychology & Marketing, Vol 32, pp697-708.

when doing so offers no material or conspicuous social signalling benefit, and in fact causes them to incur some costs.

In a study of employee benefits programs, Jeffrey (2004)[242] argued that cash is not always the best extrinsic incentive to use and that tangible non-monetary incentives may accomplish a firm's objectives better than a cash award of equal market value. One of the reasons provided by Jeffrey included that a tangible non-monetary incentive enhances social utility because it is a visible prize that others will know about, making it unnecessary for the employee to advertise that they earned the prize. In other words, a visible, desirable reward delivers 'trophy' value which a monetary payment fails to deliver.

Subconsciously, people may blend the cash reward with their everyday cash and use it to make utilitarian purchases (Kelly et al, 2017),[243] which consequently derive little meaning or appreciation (Dunn et al, 2014).[244] As these are unmemorable and unemotional transactions, any positive associations between the member and the brand that provided the benefit are lost quickly (Allen et al, 2003;[245] Eisenberger et al, 2001[246]). This is a particularly large risk

242 Jeffrey, S., 2004, 'The Benefits of Tangible Non-Monetary Incentives', Incentive Research Foundation, https://theirf.org/research/the-benefits-of-tangible-non-monetary-incentives/205/, accessed 15 June 2020.

243 Kelly, K., Presslee, A. & Webb, A., 2017, 'The Effects of Tangible Rewards Versus Cash in Consecutive Sales Tournaments: A Field Experiment, Accounting Review, Vol 92, Iss 6, cited by Incentive Research Foundation in 'Award Program Value & Evidence White Paper, 2018, https://theirf.org/research/award-program-value-evidence-white-paper/2455/, accessed 29 March 2020.

244 Dunn, E., Aknin, R. & Norton, M., 2014, 'Prosocial Spending and Happiness Using Money to Benefit Others Pays off', Current Directions in Psychological Science, Vol 23, Iss 1, pp41-47, cited by Incentive Research Foundation in 'Award Program Value & Evidence White Paper, 2018, https://theirf.org/research/award-program-value-evidence-white-paper/2455/, accessed 29 March 2020.

245 Allen, D., Shore, L. & Griffeth, R., 2003, The Role of Perceived Organizational Support and Supportive Human Resource Practices in the Turnover Process, Journal of Management Vol 29, Iss 1, pp99-188, cited by Incentive Research Foundation in 'Award Program Value & Evidence White Paper, 2018, https://theirf.org/research/award-program-value-evidence-white-paper/2455/, accessed 29 March 2020.

246 Eisenberger, R., Armeli, S., Rexwinkel, B., Lynch, P. & Rhoades, L., 2001, Reciprocation of Perceived Organizational Support, Journal Applied Psychology , cited by Incentive Research Foundation in 'Award Program Value & Evidence

associated with cashback, credit and discount loyalty program design frameworks (reviewed in Chapter 8).

Fun, enjoyable experiences stimulate a part of the brain that cash does not.[247] Within this area, there has been an uplift in loyalty programs offering experience-based rewards such as holidays, tickets to live sporting events or music concerts, theatre and cinema tickets as well as 'money can't buy' experiences, such as celebrity meet-and-greets. These go beyond standard rewards to build lasting memories and positive emotional connections, acting to develop attitudinal commitment.

Friends of Laphroaig

Laphroaig say that 'our acres of peat fields are not only essential to produce the most richly flavoured of all Scotch whiskies, they are a tangible reward for our global community.'[248] When a customer purchases a Laphroaig Whisky, they are invited to become a Friend of Laphroaig.

A Friend of Laphroaig is given their own honorary square foot of land from the Laphroaig fields. All members who wish to visit their land are welcome whenever they wish and are each given a map to direct them to their plot of land. Those who make the pilgrimage can collect 'rent' from their plot of land during their visit, which is a dram of Laphroaig from the distillery. Friends of Laphroaig can also contact their 'neighbour' online, which serves to strengthen the Laphroaig Whisky community.

By attaching the reward (which is highly efficient and inexpensive to deliver) to a unique and positive experience, Laphroaig are creating lasting memories from visitors who feel attitudinal commitment to

---

White Paper, 2018, https://theirf.org/research/award-program-value-evidence-white-paper/2455/, accessed 29 March 2020.

247 Kelly, K., cited by Incentive Research Foundation, 2018, 'Award Program Value & Evidence White Paper', https://theirf.org/research/award-program-value-evidence-white-paper/2455/, accessed 15 June 2020.

248 Laphroaig, https://www.laphroaig.com/en/islay/our-plots#joinfol, accessed 29 June 2020.

the brand through ownership of their piece of the land. As shown by the endowment effect (reviewed in Chapter 6) people over-value the things they feel ownership for.

Roehm et al (2002)[249] conducted a series of experiments to investigate the effects of loyalty programs on generating loyalty towards packaged goods brands. They identified that:

- Tangible rewards are more appropriate than intangible when influencing short-term buying behaviour.

- Intangible rewards are more effective in reinforcing relations between the company and the member soon after joining.

- Immediate rewards are better suited to changing short-term behaviour.

- Deferred rewards are better suited to establishing a long-term relationship and stable modification of consumer behaviour.

In a study of coalition programs, Reinares and Garcia-Madariaga (2007)[250] identified that there are significant differences in the evaluation of rewards between members and non-members, indicating a risk that not offering certain rewards in the catalogue may condition non-members to avoid participation.

O'Brien and Jones (1995)[251] argued that a rewards range should include five characteristics: cash value, choice, aspirational value, relevance, and convenience. Cash value relates to how much the member perceives its cash equivalent to be, while choice means ensuring a wide enough range of options to inspire the member. Aspirational value refers to rewards that motivate a customer to change their behaviour over a longer period of time, while relevance

249 Roehm, M., Pullins, E. & Roehm, H., 2002, 'Designing Loyalty-Building Programs for Packaged Goods Brands', Journal of Marketing Research - J MARKET RES-CHICAGO, Vol 39, pp202-213.

250 Reinares, P. & Garcia-Madariaga, J., 2007, 'The importance of rewards in the management of multisponsor loyalty programmes', The Journal of Database Marketing & Customer Strategy Management, Vol 15.

251 O'Brien, L. & Jones, C., 1995, 'Do Rewards Really Create Loyalty?', Harvard Business Review, May–June 1995 Issue.

and convenience focus on ensuring the member can access something meaningful in a way that is adequately accessible.

Efficient vs inefficient rewards

Certain companies and industries are better positioned to provide rewards aligned with O'Brien and Jones' criteria than others. The ability for a company to access low-cost, high-perceived value rewards (efficient rewards) and provide these to their members has a material bearing on the program design which will best suit their business.

Efficient rewards (vs inefficient rewards) are clearly a preferred option in delivering cash value and aspirational value in particular. Few industries provide the opportunity for companies to establish the appropriate business structure to deliver truly efficient rewards. The industries which can deliver them tend to dominate the loyalty industry, reinforcing the critical role rewards play in an overall program's attractiveness. For example:

- Frequent flyer programs can access empty seats on flights and provide them to members in exchange for points, at a cost to the program of 5-10 per cent of the ticket price. Free upgrades to business class can also be provided at very low additional cost to the airline.

- Hotels can provide members with empty rooms in exchange for points, costing them little more than cleaning and toiletry expenses. Free room upgrades can also be provided with little cost impact.

- Car rental firms can provide members with a free rental of an unrented car, paid with points, with no cost other than wear and tear. Car upgrades can also be provided at a relatively small cost.

- Cinemas can provide members with free tickets (no cost) and candy bar items (with around 90 per cent margin on most products).

- QSR's can provide members with free food or drink, or a size upgrade, at very low cost to their business.

A challenge faced by some of these businesses, particularly in travel and hospitality, is limited reward inventory. While free flights and hotel rooms are highly desirable, they rely on accessing supply which the company cannot sell directly (which would generate a more profitable outcome). Thus, high-demand travel periods, and popular routes and locations, tend to offer the least amount of reward inventory, causing member dissatisfaction.

Oneworld alliance

Oneworld Alliance is a partnership network of 30 affiliated airlines operating across over 160 countries, carrying over 500 million passengers a year.[252] While the alliance was set up to serve international travellers by allowing frequent flyer points and miles to be redeemed for reward seats with any partner airline, it is also the cause of some member disappointment.

The disappointment stems from the sheer volume of members wishing to redeem for the limited available reward seats, which are subject to capacity controls and route restrictions.

Some programs apply different restrictions to manage the needs of their more valuable members. For example, Finnair only make business class award seats available to members of partner frequent flyer programs 60 days in advance at most, prioritising Finnair Plus members over Oneworld alliance members.[253]

Other industries do not provide such opportunities for efficient rewards and are often required to source rewards from third parties (e.g. gift cards which cost the operator almost as much as their face value). Many consumer goods retailers operate on small margins, making it exceedingly difficult for them to provide members with access to free products. Utilities such as gas, electricity, and telecommunications, are similarly challenged in providing members with efficient rewards as part of a formal loyalty program. Banks have limited opportunities, as do companies operating in the insurance, superannuation, health, and real estate industries.

---

252 Oneworld, 'Oneworld receives sixth best airline alliance of the year', https://www.oneworld.com/news/oneworld-receives-sixth-best-airline-alliance-of-the-year, accessed 29 June 2020.

253 One Mile At A Time, 2020, https://onemileatatime.com/finnair-blocking-business-class-awards/, accessed 18 June 2020.

> ### Telstra Plus
>
> Telstra,[254] a major telecommunications company, have negotiated an exclusive deal for their members to access best in market offers from Event Cinemas.
>
> Telstra pay Event Cinemas a lump-sum to provide all their program members with unlimited access to discounted movie tickets, regardless of how many tickets are purchased.
>
> This 'Always On' benefit for Telstra Plus members provides attractive value in a form which Telstra could never afford to fund as a direct discount.

Reward aggregators

Loyalty program members globally earn hundreds of billions of points, miles and other loyalty currencies each year. These are redeemed on flights, hotel rooms, cash discounts on supermarket shopping, experiences, consumer goods, gift cards, movie tickets and more. As the loyalty programs have expanded their reward ranges, a parallel industry has developed to service the demand.

Loyalty program operators tend to avoid directly sourcing and warehousing thousands of consumer goods and hundreds of gift cards for their members. This is not their core capability and would involve significant incremental cost to the business, both from a logistics perspective, but also for warehousing and stock management. For example, Lufthansa' Miles & More World Shop offers over 3,000 consumer goods and gift cards which members can access by redeeming points. For Miles & More to purchase and warehouse all those products would not be feasible, particularly when some of the products will see little or no redemption activity, while others will be superseded by new versions. It is safe to say that modern loyalty programs are not structured to operate in the same way that the big stamps programs of old were run.

Instead, most programs have developed relationships with large product and gift card aggregators whose core business is to source and warehouse stock which they can deliver on demand via a drop-ship model, or provide digital goods such as gift cards to order. For example, if a member redeems points

---

254 Telstra, https://www.telstra.com.au/plus, accessed 29 June 2020.

for a case of wine on an online store hosted by the loyalty program, an order will be sent to a third-party wine supplier that will pick, pack and dispatch the wine to the member. On completion of the order, the wine supplier will invoice the loyalty program for the wholesale cost of the wine. One additional advantage of this partnership is the loyalty program does not need to hold a liquor license, as this is covered by the wine supplier.

There are many reward product suppliers operating around the world that have grown their businesses to specifically support loyalty programs by offering large consumer product or gift card ranges, while other businesses have developed new divisions within their existing company to support the reward demand.

In rare instances, a larger loyalty program may request exclusivity for a particular product in order to attempt to gain a competitive advantage. In other instances, the brand or product supplier may insist they only want to have their product ranged with a specific loyalty program or a small selection of loyalty programs which they feel are aligned to their brands positioning in the market.

These aggregators tend to support competition in the loyalty program industry. A program can very quickly develop a large and attractive range of consumer goods and gift cards to offer to their member base as rewards.

RewardOps

RewardOps[255] are a rewards supply aggregator that have networked with dozens of reward suppliers offering millions of reward products across multiple categories (gift cards, merchandise, discounts, donations, music, movies, magazines, events, travel and more).

A loyalty program can connect to the RewardOps platform, curate their own rewards catalogue, manage their reward store, distribute rewards, and track redemptions and browsing activity. Invoicing is also all managed by RewardOps, so the company only needs to pay one single monthly invoice to RewardOps for their entire reward store, allowing them to focus on their core business.

---

255 RewardOps, https://rewardops.com/, accessed 29 June 2020.

> **PointCheckout**
>
> Point Checkout[256] is a payment gateway for loyalty points. They have relationships with thousands of merchant partners. This allows program members to pool their loyalty points from existing programs (or points + card) and spend them through participating merchant apps and online stores in real time.

Concierge services

In instances where a member may not be able to find a reward that appeals to them, some loyalty programs offer basic concierge services. This allows the member to request the sourcing of a specific product or service they desire. The concierge will calculate a price in points for procurement, and if the member chooses to progress with the redemption, the concierge will process the points transaction and organise fulfilment of the order.

Other programs have expanded the concierge concept to provide additional services. This may include a dedicated phone number, website and app which allows members to request travel bookings, restaurant bookings, event and show tickets, private shopping events, golf course bookings and rental car bookings. Members can also access additional perks, including flight, car and room upgrades, access to sold-out events, exclusive restaurants and airport lounges, and priority discounts.

Alternatively, a company with an existing call centre can potentially train their team accordingly and in turn divert some internal resources to managing the concierge service at a lower cost than outsourcing may deliver. The benefits and challenges associated with insourcing and outsourcing are detailed in Chapter 17.

> **Aspire Lifestyles**
>
> Aspire Lifestyles[257] is a concierge management service designed for prestigious brands to offer this service to their affluent high-value members. Rather than each brand creating and managing their

---

256 PointCheckout https://www.pointcheckout.com/en/ accessed 17 July 2020.

257 Aspire Lifestyles, https://www.aspirelifestyles.com/services/concierge/, accessed

own concierge services, they can engage Aspire Lifestyles to act on behalf of their brand as a white label solution with pre-negotiated benefits and experienced staff.

The Aspire Lifestyles concierge team provide members with a high-touch, 24/7, benefits fulfilment service which may include anything from accessing dining reservations at exclusive restaurants, booking a holiday, sending a gift, pet sitting or finding a personal trainer in the area.

With the existence of a multitude of reward options, loyalty program operators need to select the type of reward which fits the specific behaviour they are seeking to influence. Different reward types tend to correlate to specific loyalty program design frameworks. For example, monetary rewards may be suited to discount and credit frameworks, whilst non-monetary rewards may be better suited to status tier, member benefits, and surprise and delight frameworks. Achieving the optimal balance between valuable and cost-effective rewards is also critical.

Key insights

- Consumers are motivated to join loyalty programs to access desirable rewards, and therefore the nature of rewards offered can influence the effectiveness of the loyalty program. Consumers will be more likely to become members of a loyalty program if the perceived rewards are higher than the perceived costs.

- Rewards that are offered in a loyalty program are important to whether the program succeeds or fails at building behavioural and attitudinal commitment. A reward range should include five characteristics: cash value, choice, aspirational value, relevance, and convenience.

- Rewards can be tangible vs intangible, immediate vs deferred, direct vs indirect, efficient vs inefficient, monetary vs non-monetary, visible vs invisible and utilitarian vs hedonic.

29 June 2020.

- Some rewards types are better suited to influencing certain behaviours. Research suggests that tangible rewards are more appropriate than intangible when influencing short-term buying behaviour; intangible and visible incentives are more effective in reinforcing relations between the company and the member soon after joining; immediate rewards are better suited to changing short-term behaviour, while deferred incentives are better suited to establishing a long-term relationship and stable modification of consumer behaviour.

- Industries which can provide members with efficient rewards have a natural advantage in delivering value and tend to dominate the loyalty industry. This includes airlines, hotels, car rental companies and quick service restaurants.

- Product and gift card aggregators source and warehouse stock which they can deliver on demand via a drop ship model, or provide digital goods such as gift cards to order. Reward aggregators have grown their businesses to specifically support loyalty programs by offering large consumer product or gift card ranges, while other businesses have developed new divisions within their existing company to support demand.

Suggested reading

- Sharma, D. & Verma, V, 2014, 'Psychological and economic considerations of rewards programs', Journal of Retailing and Consumer Services, Vol 21, pp924–932.

- Mauri, C., 2003, 'Card loyalty. A new emerging issue in grocery retailing', Journal of Retailing and Consumer Services, Vol 10, Iss 1, pp13–25.

- Roehm, Michelle & Pullins, Ellen & Roehm, Harper, 2002, 'Designing Loyalty-Building Programs for Packaged Goods Brands', Journal of Marketing Research - J MARKET RES-CHICAGO, Vol 39, pp202-213.

- Kivetz, Ran & Simonson, Itamar., 2002, 'Earning the Right to

Indulge: Effort as a Determinant of Customer Preferences Toward Frequency Program Rewards', Journal of Marketing Research, Vol 39, pp155-170.

- Ruzeviciute, Ruta & Kamleitner, Bernadette, 2017, 'Attracting new customers to loyalty programs: The effectiveness of monetary versus nonmonetary loyalty programs', Journal of Consumer Behaviour, Vol 16, Issue 6, pp113-124.

- Jeffrey, Scott., 2004, 'The Benefits of Tangible Non-Monetary Incentives', Incentive Research Foundation, https://theirf.org/research/the-benefits-of-tangible-non-monetary-incentives/205/

- O'Brien, L. and Jones, C., 1995, 'Do Rewards Really Create Loyalty?', Harvard Business Review, May–June 1995 Issue.

CHAPTER 8

LOYALTY PROGRAM DESIGN FRAMEWORKS

'Good design is good business.'

- Thomas Watson Jr, second president of IBM, 1973

Focus areas

This chapter will address the following questions:

- What are the different types of design frameworks utilised in loyalty programs?

- What are the benefits and challenges of each design framework type?

- How are different design frameworks combined to create a more comprehensive loyalty program?

THIS CHAPTER PRESENTS a range of loyalty program (and member engagement program) design frameworks. While companies may utilise a single design, it is common practise to combine elements from a number of frameworks to create a more comprehensive program design.

The conceptual frameworks and variations presented throughout this chapter aim to provide guidance in considering different design approaches. Certain designs may not be suitable in delivering to a specific company's needs and objectives. Strategically working through a range of design options will help ensure the framework adopted by a company is well considered and appropriate.

As discussed in Chapter 7, specific rewards will influence and motivate members in varying ways and will generate engagement in different circumstances. Certain rewards are also more appropriately suited to specific loyalty design frameworks.

Punch and stamp cards

<u>Model</u>

The most pervasive loyalty program design in the world is the punch/stamp card. A member collects punches/stamps for purchases, and after earning enough to complete the card, a reward is unlocked, which is usually a free product, such as a coffee.

Paper cards are low cost to produce and the reward provided is generally high margin, making the program low cost to implement and run. The commercial model is a smart design. For example, a café wanting to sell more coffee can decide to offer a 10 per cent discount, but loyal and non-loyal customers will access it equally. The punch/stamp card essentially gives loyal customers a 10 per cent cumulative delayed discount (buying ten coffees and getting one free is worth roughly the same as a 10 per cent discount on each of 10 cups), while one-off and irregular customers will pay full-price, protecting the café from unnecessary discounting.

Over the past decade, the introduction of digital punch/stamp cards has provided convenience for customers (one less card in their wallet) and a better ability for cafes to track usage, including the ability to collect some customer data (a key limitation of a paper card).

In exploring punch/stamp card programs, three design variations are considered; basic, complex and multi.

1. Basic punch/stamp cards:

The basic model involves the member earning a stamp/punch for each transaction to unlock a set reward. It is effective when the price of the product being purchased is relatively consistent, such as a cup of coffee or a car wash. Each time a specific item is purchased, the punch/stamp card is marked, and the customer is one step closer to accessing that item for free once the card is completed.

> ### McDonald's
>
> McDonald's have incorporated a digital stamp card into their mobile app to reward members for purchasing coffee from McCafe.[258] Members purchasing five coffees get the sixth free, with the progress tracked visually through digital stamps.
>
> Stamps can be earned by members when purchasing from the counter, kiosk or 'Drive-Thru' by scanning their unique QR code in the app, or by ordering and paying directly through the app.

2. Complex punch/stamp cards:

A more complex punch/stamp card model allows members to be rewarded for purchases which have a wider variability in cost. When the member has earned the required number of stamps for their transactions, the total amount spent is calculated, and a percentage of the total is provided as the reward.

> ### Hotels.com
>
> For every ten nights booked via Hotels.com, members of Hotels.com Rewards earn one night free.[259]
>
> Hotels.com utilise a digital stamp card to allow members to track progress towards the reward, which is communicated on their

---

258 McDonalds, https://www.mcdonalds.com/us/en-us/mccafe/rewards.html, accessed 29 June 2020.

259 Hotels.com, https://au.hotels.com/hotel-rewards-pillar/hotelscomrewards.html, accessed 29 June 2020.

website and via email communications. Hotels.com average the total spent over the ten nights and return 10 per cent of the total spent as a reward.

If the member books a room for less than the value available, their booking is free (with Booking.com earning some margin on this transaction). If the room costs more than the available reward, the value is applied as a discount.

The reward excludes fees and taxes, helping to reduce program costs.

Hotels.com place an expiry rule on stamps, where members must collect a stamp or redeem for a free night at least once every 12 months to ensure stamps are retained.

3.   Multi-punch/stamp cards:

When a program incorporates multiple punch cards within a single program framework. Members can track progress towards unlocking rewards from each individual punch card simultaneously.

This model is commonly used when a company has multiple products at differing price points, or when a company has multiple partners offering different reward values. Both case studies below reflect each of these scenarios respectively.

Krispy Kreme Rewards

Krispy Kreme Rewards allows members to track their progress around a number of doughnut shaped trackers, with the reward featuring in the middle of each tracker.

Members earn a stamp each time a dozen doughnuts are purchased. When a member accumulates 12 stamps for purchasing 12 dozen, they unlock a free dozen.

Simultaneously, when a member purchases a single doughnut, they earn a stamp on their single doughnut tracker. When a member purchases 12 single doughnuts and earns 12 stamps, a free single doughnut reward is unlocked.

Uber Eats

Uber Eats have many different restaurant, café and QSR partners, each with different levels of value which they can afford to provide back to customers in the form of a reward.

Uber Eats list different stamp cards with varying stamps required to unlock varying value rewards for each partner. For example, some restaurants have an Uber Eats stamp card which allows members to unlock a $10 reward after making just 3 orders, while others may require 5 orders to unlock a $10 reward or 10 orders to unlock a $15 reward with that restaurant and so on.

When a new restaurant joins, they have the option to include their own individual stamp card for repeat purchases at their individual restaurant, with spend also tracking towards the wider Uber Rewards points based program.

Loyalty currencies

Model

The evolution of loyalty currencies over several centuries was detailed in Chapter 2, where it was shown that trade marks, checks, tickets, coupons, certificates, stamps, miles, points, cryptocurrencies and tokenised assets have all been used throughout the ages. In the current age, the dominant loyalty currencies globally are points and miles. Other variations include Stars (Starbucks), Tokens (Subway), Deli Dollars (Jason's Deli), Beefsteak Bucks (Beefsteak), as well as Bitcoin (Lolli), tokenised shares (Bits of Stock) and tokenised real estate (BrickX).

Loyalty currency frameworks are flexible, allowing them to be used across many different company types and industries to reward members. To earn the currency, members are required to identify at each transaction, enabling valuable data capture opportunities.

Loyalty currency programs are more complex than punch/stamp cards, and typically require a technology system to manage, but are still sufficiently simple.

To simplify illustrating loyalty currency design frameworks and their benefits, loyalty currencies will be referred to as 'Points', with the understanding that this can be substituted for any alternative currency name.

In exploring loyalty currency programs, two design variations are considered: basic and coalition. There are many sub-variations of the two main models.

1. Basic loyalty currency program:

This basic model involves a single brand providing the ability for members to earn points by transacting with them. Commonly, the points are redeemable on the company's products. The program may also provide the option for members to redeem points for third-party products, although this is less common because it can result in higher program costs.

An attractive feature of this design is the ability for a company to control the associated costs. For example, if a member earns one point for every dollar they spend, and 1,000 points is equal to a $10 reward, the retailer is contributing 1 per cent return on each dollar spent. Irrespective of whether the member spends more, or less, the 1 per cent cost remains constant, allowing the company to manage their program spend to budget.

> **PetSmart Treats**
>
> Members of PetSmart earn eight points for every US$1 spent on PetSmart products and services in-store and online.[260] Members can redeem points on any product or pet service for up to 12 months with no exclusions. Treats start at 1,000 points for a redemption.

---

260 Petsmart, https://www.petsmart.com/treats-rewards.html, accessed 20 July 2020.

> Additional *Treats* built into the program include special bonus points offers.

> Allowing points to be redeemed only on PetSmart products and services makes the program operation more cost-effective, as PetSmart only pay wholesale cost for a product which the member values at the retail price.

2. Coalition loyalty currency program:

As referenced in Chapter 1, a coalition loyalty program allows members to earn points across multiple partners, such as airlines, banks, supermarkets, utilities, retailers and hotels. These programs are primarily controlled by a single company, which is responsible for distribution of points as well as management of member accounts, marketing and program rules. Many coalition programs generate sizeable profits, utilising sophisticated commercial models which will be explored in Chapter 14.

Rather than starting their own points program, a company may instead choose to join a coalition as a program partner, allowing them to offer coalition points as a reward to their customers. This can deliver a range of benefits, including access to an effective marketing database, attracting new customers and retaining existing customers by rewarding with an already desirable loyalty currency, and using the coalition to turbocharge member acquisition. They may also face challenges, such as insufficient marketing support, excessive costs for purchasing points, and a lack of tangible results and exclusivity.

> ### Alaska Airlines Mileage Plan

> Alaska Airlines' Mileage Plan program allows members to earn when they spend with Alaskan Airlines, but also across thousands of everyday retail partners online and in-store. Retail partners include the likes of Disney, Sephora, Adidas, Macy's, Costco, FedEx and Jimmy Choo.

> Partners leverage the Mileage Plan platform to market promotions to the large Mileage Plan member base as an effective advertising channel.

Status tiers

<u>Model</u>

As detailed in Chapter 2, the first modern status tier structure appears to have been introduced by AAdvantage in 1982, when they launched Gold status to recognise their most loyal members. Many programs now segment members based on spend via overt or covert tiers that deliver a range of exclusive tangible and intangible benefits.

The tiering approach is loosely aligned to the Pareto Principle, whereby a small number of customers can account for a sizeable amount of a company's revenue (the so called 80/20 rule). While this does not occur across all companies (e.g. utilities, subscription companies and insurance companies do not appear to have such a pronounced effect within their consumer bases), it does manifest elsewhere (such as airlines, hotels and car rental companies) providing the conditions by which a status tier program can be usefully applied.

Pareto Principle conditions are favourable for the success of status tier programs, as tiering is most effective when a relatively small number of high-value customers are concentrated into elite hierarchies and provided with disproportionate attention and benefits. This is only cost-effective when the number of elites is small, because if the tier population is too big, the program operator will not be able to afford to bestow the generous benefits which make status

---

261 Alaska Mileage Plan, https://www.mileageplanshopping.com/b.htm, accessed 19 June 2020.

tiers successful. Furthermore, research shows larger tier populations appear to make existing tier members feel less special (Drèze and Nunes, 2009).[262]

In exploring status programs, two design variations are considered: stand-alone and within program.

1. Stand-alone status tier programs:

This model involves status tiers with set benefits provided to members at each tier level.

Members can progress tiers in two ways:

- Member engagement: when a certain amount of currency is accumulated (based on spend or other activities), a new tier is unlocked for the member. The currencies (i.e. status credits) themselves cannot be redeemed on any rewards, but are specifically designed to track progress towards the next tier.

- Purchasing a tier subscription: allow members to pay a monthly or annual fee to instantly access one or a selection of tiers, with accompanying benefits.

This model can deliver the same engagement benefits as a points program; members are motivated to identify at each transaction to ensure they continue to progress towards the next tier, utilising the endowed progress effect and goal gradient effect. More valuable members are automatically recognised and rewarded with elite benefits and status titles, helping to develop their brand loyalty via social identity theory.

Subscription tier members are also likely to experience the sunk cost effect bias, where they will feel compelled to engage more with the program to realise a return on their spend.

---

262 Drèze, X. & Nunes,J., 2009, 'Feeling Superior: The Impact of Loyalty Program Structure on Consumers' Perceptions of Status', Journal of Consumer Research, Vol 35, pp890-905.

Swarovski Club

Swarovski have embraced a status tier design for their loyalty program, Swarovski Club.[263] Member spend is tracked, with automatic progression to higher tiers when spend thresholds have been reached.

Swarovski Club encompasses four status tiers:

- Bronze: (A$0 spend)
- Silver: (from A$350 spend)
- Gold: (from A$900 spend)
- Platinum: (from A$1,800 spend)

This structure makes it relatively easy to access the higher tiers, with A$1,800 spend unlikely to be perceived as excessive for a Swarovski obsessive.

Benefits improve by tier, and include exclusive pre-sales, 15 per cent discount birthday voucher, free shipping, VIP events, and extra Gold/Platinum discounts and gifts.

2.   Within program status tiers:

A more common application of status tiers is within a broader loyalty currency program, such as an airline, hotel, car rental or bank program. The design segments members by their value to the business, and provides them with incremental benefits to recognise their loyalty. It reinforces the endowed progress effect and goal gradient effect, whereby members can track their progress towards a reward (with points or miles) and track a parallel pathway to a status tier (with a different loyalty currency, such as status credits).

The most common structure is four tiers (e.g. Bronze, Silver, Gold and Platinum), although some major coalitions have extended to five (a super elite tier above the previous top tier). Drèze and Nunes' (2009)[264] study found that

---

263 Swarovski Club https://www.swarovski.com/en_GB-AU/club/ accessed 20th August 2020

264 Drèze, X. & Nunes, J., 2009, 'Feeling Superior: The Impact of Loyalty Program Structure on Consumers' Perceptions of Status', Journal of Consumer Research, Vol

a three-tier program is more satisfying to all members of a program than a two-tier program (Gold and no-status), even to those who do not qualify for elite status. It is unusual that they did not extend their study to four-tier programs.

IHG Rewards Club

The IHG Rewards Club is the hotel loyalty program of The Intercontinental Hotel Group (IHG). Members earn points which can be redeemed during stays at more than 4,600 of their hotels and resorts globally, on merchandise or experiences from partners, for frequent flyer points from over 40 airline partners or for car rentals, and other rewards.

Alongside points, IHG Rewards Club has four membership tiers which unlock valuable benefits based on nights stayed:

- Club: ten points for every US$1 spent plus late checkout, free newspaper and free Wi-Fi.

- Gold: Club benefits plus additional 10 per cent bonus on base points earn rate and priority check in.

- Platinum: Gold benefits plus additional 50 per cent bonus on base points earn rate, rollover nights to help maintain status, guaranteed room availability and complimentary room upgrades.

- Spire Elite: Platinum benefits plus additional 100 per cent bonus on base points earn rate and a choice of either a 25,000 annual points bonus or ability to gift Platinum to a family member or friend.

Member benefits

35, pp890-905.

<u>Model</u>

Many companies do not earn sufficient margin, or do not have customers spending enough at an individual level, to support a loyalty currency program or status tier program that delivers adequate value to drive consistent member engagement. A popular alternative is a member benefits program, which provides members with access to a range of benefits simply by joining. These may be provided by the company, but primarily tend to be sourced from third-party partners.

Members may access benefits by presenting a membership card or voucher, by calling a dedicated phone number, or by accessing a website or app.

Member benefits programs are particularly prevalent across specific industries, such as utilities, telecommunications, insurance and pension funds/superannuation, where large member bases spend relatively small amounts at an individual level, but the companies are wealthy enough to invest in quality partnerships to access desirable benefits. These are companies where customers tend to make regular periodic payments and where there is a dedicated focus on reducing customer churn.

Membership may be provided as complimentary as a way to reward members for being a customer. Alternatively, program access may be provided as part of a subscription model.

In exploring member benefits programs, three design variations are considered: company-provided, supplier-provided and third-party provided.

1. Company-provided member benefits program:

Under the company-provided member benefits design, members are provided with access to desirable benefits which are products or services of the company.

The strategic imperative is to offer members a bundle of benefits which they value highly, but cost the company little to deliver. This may include free samples, extended warranties, charity donations and other benefits that make it worthwhile enough for the member to identify when transacting, or sticky enough to reduce their propensity to churn.

The challenge for companies is being able to deliver program benefits of significant appeal to their wider population of customers.

IKEA Family

Members of IKEA Family[265] are encouraged to swipe their card at the checkout each time they transact to access a bundle of benefits. This differs by country, but can include free insurance to cover the transport of the product from store to home, an extended returns policy, entry into a draw to win IKEA gift cards and a small donation to a local charity.

The bundle is perceived by members as good value, stimulating membership card swipe behaviour, and allowing IKEA to capture important member transaction data, while the cost of running the program equates to a fraction of a per cent of revenue per member.

In reality, members are unlikely to return a product if they have not already done so under the standard non-member 3 months returns policy. The claims associated with store-to-home insurance are estimated to be exceedingly small. The gift card prizes cost each store a few thousand dollars per year, and likely stimulate incremental revenue by persuading the member to spend more than the value of the card. The small charity donation is capped, allowing IKEA to manage the cost because once the limit has been reached, member card swipes no longer generate a donation until it resets at the end of the year.

While the cost to IKEA is likely incredibly low, when presented as a carefully constructed stack of contextually relevant benefits, the value to the member feels greater.

2. Supplier-provided member benefits program:

Certain companies are fortunate enough to access product samples or rewards from suppliers, which they can incorporate into loyalty programs. Accessing free samples is a fantastic way for members to try new products without having to commit to a purchase. Under this model, members receive access to a selection of regular samples, combining the delivery of relevant rewards with surprise and delight, as members do not know what specifically they

---

265 IKEA, https://www.ikea.com/au/en/ikea-family/, accessed 29 June 2020.

will receive. This enables a dynamic where the member places a high value on a reward which costs the company little, an approach which is particularly prevalent in the beauty and cosmetics industries.

> **Priceline Sister Club**
>
> Priceline Sister Club program is the rewards program of Priceline, with over 7 million members.[266] Priceline Sister Club is primarily a points-based program; however they have introduced tiers which unlock a number of benefits including access to secret sales, VIP events and competitions. The most valuable reward advertised, to which all members are encouraged to strive for, is the Pink Diamond Gift which is available to their highest tier Pink Diamond Members.[267]
>
> The Pink Diamond Gift is a complimentary gift box provided every quarter and containing 3-4 sample products. The samples are provided by Priceline suppliers who use this as an opportunity to get their brand and product lines in front of the company's most engaged and loyal shoppers.

3. Third party-provided member benefits program:

Where benefits cannot be sourced internally, or provided via supplier samples, a company may develop relationships with a range of third-party partners to provide member benefits. This is the most prevalent member benefits design in market.

While company and supplier provided member benefits programs (such as IKEA Family and Priceline Sister Club) stand-out for their cost-efficiency, third-party provided member benefits programs can be more expensive to run, particularly if the company is seeking exclusive, best-in-market offers. These types of offers can require annual licensing fees, reciprocal marketing support and other concessions. For example, a company wishing to provide their

---

266 Australian Pharmaceutical Industries Limited, Annual report 2017, p11. No membership figures were listed in the Annual report 2018.

267 Priceline, https://www.priceline.com.au/sister-club, accessed 29 June 2020.

customers with access to discount event tickets may need to pay an annual fee to the ticketing partner for the rights, as well as promoting certain events to their member base.

> ## O2 Priority
>
> O2 Priority,[268] the loyalty program of UK telecommunications company O2, provide rotating benefits to members across over thirty exclusive categories, including discount event tickets, discounts at major brands such as The Body Shop, free cookies and crisps, free Uber rides and generous discounts on new technology.
>
> The rotation of the offers keeps them fresh, compelling members to continually check-in to ensure they do not miss a bargain.

Discounts

Model

Discounting is used extensively in loyalty and member engagement programs by providing members with offers which are not accessible to non-members (exclusivity).

In exploring discount programs, five design variations are considered: basic, delayed, tiered, bundled, and third-party.

Access to discount programs is normally free, however some companies may charge a subscription fee.

---

268 O2 Priority, https://priority.o2.co.uk/, accessed 29 June 2020.

1. Basic discount program:

This is one of the simplest program designs, whereby members who join are entitled to a set discount off every purchase for in-store and online transactions. This type of design is simple to understand and engage with, and can drive high participation rates (with members not wanting to miss out on their discount), ensuring substantial member data is captured.

While useful in generating behavioural commitment, it is questionable whether discounting can drive attitudinal commitment. Anyone can access the discount (one-time and truly loyal members), making it expensive to operate. If a member can access a better price or discount at a competitor, there are no exit costs if they switch, meaning the design may be limited in its ability to generate stickiness.

Baby Bunting

Baby Bunting VIP Membership gives members who register an immediate 5 per cent discount across a range of items in-store.[269] The member retains the 5 per cent discount ongoing for all qualifying future purchases with Baby Bunting.

Beyond+

The Beyond+ program from Bed Bath & Beyond is a paid yearly membership program (US$29 per year) which gives all members access to 20 per cent off their entire purchase made at any Bed Bath & Beyond store in the US or online during the year of membership, plus members also receive free shipping.[270]

Incorporating the ongoing member discount and benefit within a yearly subscription is a sound strategy to leverage the sunk cost effect bias and generate stickiness from members looking to make the most of their US$29 membership.

---

269 Baby Bunting, https://www.babybunting.com.au/vip-membership, accessed 20 July 2020.

270 Bed Bath & Beyond, Beyond+, https://www.bedbathandbeyond.com/store/loyalty/beyondplus, accessed 29 June 2020.

The membership fee is also another revenue stream for the program.

2. Delayed discount program:

Delayed discounts are a more sophisticated version of a basic discount program, where a member transacting above a certain amount earns a discount to use on a future purchase. For example, 'spend $50 and save 10 per cent on your next visit'.

This design is simple to understand and engage with, and has the added advantage of locking the customer into a future purchase to access the discount. An expiry date can be applied to the discount to stimulate FOMO (fear of missing out) and encourage the member to transact more quickly than they may have been intending. One-time customers will not access the discount, helping to manage program costs.

My Cub Rewards

My Cub Rewards[271] offers a delayed discount on fuel for all members who refuel at participating Holiday Station stores.

For every US$100 a member spends at Cub, they get ten cents off per gallon of fuel the next time they fill up at any participating location. Frequent shoppers can redeem up to US$1.50 per gallon which would save them US$24 on a 16-gallon tank.

This strategy takes advantage of the loss aversion bias where members are motivated to avoid losing their benefit before it expires, resulting in repeat purchases.

3. Tiered discount program:

With a tiered discount, the level of discount provided increases based on the cumulative value of spend. For example, a member may start by receiving a 2 per cent discount, which increases to 4 per cent when they spend a cumulative

---

271 Cub, https://www.cub.com/savings/fuel-rewards.html, accessed 29 June 2020.

$2,000 over a one-year period, and further increases to 6 per cent for $5,000 cumulative spend.

It can be argued this is a simple version of a status tier program, with status resetting at the end of the period. This approach is unique amongst the discount program designs in supporting the endowed progress effect and goal gradient effect.

Home Depot Pro Xtra Rewards

Pro Xtra Rewards[272] by Home Depot is a tiered discount program. Cumulative spend with Home Depot accrues and once certain spend thresholds are reached, the discount off purchases increases thereafter. Members who reach Bronze level (after spending US$2,000) get 10 per cent off everything, members who reach Silver level (after spending US$4,000) get 15 per cent off everything, and members who reach Gold level (after spending US$7,500) get 20 per cent off everything.

Since all purchases are counted towards the total spend, members are reluctant to give up the progress they have made towards unlocking higher discounts by shopping at a competitor.

4. Bundled discount program:

Bundled discounts involve members being provided with a set discount off all products or services when a minimum number of products or services are purchased. For example, a member takes out three different insurance products with a single insurance company, earning them a 10 per cent discount off all insurance products.

Like a basic discount program, this design is simple to understand and engage with, however it also has some additional advantages. The discount is only provided to members who have a minimum amount of product or service consumption (indicating some level of brand loyalty), and program stickiness is built-in, because if a member reduces the number of product or

---

272 Home Depot, Pro Xtra, https://www.homedepot.com/c/Pro_Xtra, accessed 29 June 2020.

services they access, they will lose their discount across all products (a clear exit cost). For example, if the member reduces their insurance products from three to two, they will lose the 10 per cent discount on the remaining two products.

> **NRMA**
>
> NRMA is an insurance provider offering a loyalty discount[273] to members. Members can use the loyalty discount calculator on the NRMA website to determine the amount they could save across all policies based on the below inputs:
>
> - How many eligible policies the member has taken out with NRMA
>
> - How many consecutive years the member has been with NRMA
>
> The loyalty discount is re-calculated at each renewal and is adjusted based on how many active policies the member has at that time.

5. Third-party discount program:

Under the third-party discounting model, brands provide discounts which can be used at third-party companies. For example, 'spend $50 and earn a 10 per cent discount voucher to use at brand X'. This may be because the company does not have sufficient margin to offer its own discounts. It may also be because it is an independent program which relies on sourcing third-party offers for its reward pool.

This program design faces some challenges. It is more complicated to understand. It assumes members transacting with them will also be interested in transacting with the company honouring the discount. It involves the company promoting another brand, which may be positive (a halo effect could eventuate) or negative (marketing efforts focus on promoting another brand). There may be costs to access the third-party partner's discounts.

---

273 NRMA, https://www.nrma.com.au/loyalty-discount, accessed 29 June 2020.

AIA Vitality

AIA Vitality[274] is a third-party rewards program aimed at improving the health of members by rewarding them for meeting health goals. The cost of rewards to members aims to be offset by a reduction in AIA insurance claims on the premise that members will have reduced their health risks and thus their liability to the company.

Members earn AIA Vitality Points for committing (commitment bias) to making healthy choices like healthy eating, going to the gym, going for a health check or completing a set number of steps. Members can redeem points for third-party rewards like discounted movie tickets, spa vouchers or shopping vouchers.

The AIA Vitality program is offered as the rewards program for members of a range of companies across banking, insurance, healthcare and other industries.

Credits

Model

Closely related to the discount program design is the credit program; where members earn a credit amount for future spend on the company's products. This may be in the form of a voucher or be held in their account.

The program is typically structured such that the margin required to cover the cost of the credit is built into the price of the product. Thus, the member perceives they are receiving incremental value, while the company can control the costs of the program.

One advantage credits have over discounting is they may be more likely to be perceived as something tangible (a specific dollar amount visible in the

---

274 AIA Vitality, https://www.aiavitality.com.au/vmp-au/, accessed 29 June 2020.

member's account vs an unallocated percentage). A credit which the member has earned and feels ownership over may be more likely to tap into the endowment effect and loss aversion biases, meaning the member may be more reluctant to lose access to their credit compared to a discount.

An additional advantage is that credits avoid creating a negative precedent (i.e. members expect to see the same thing next time and hold off purchasing until another discount becomes available) or lower perceived value in the same way that discounts can generate.

A challenge with a credit program is the cost of the credit may need to be a greater value than a loyalty currency to excite the member (i.e. offering 1 per cent return on $100 spend in the form of 100 points can work, but a cash equivalent credit of $1 may not sound valuable enough to motivate the member). In addition, the credit may be mentally combined with the price, neutralising the feeling of goodwill that a loyalty program should engender, although this is less likely to be the case than with discounts.

In exploring credit programs, three design variations are considered: delayed credit, interest payments and lowest price guarantee.

1. Delayed credit program:

This is an identical model to the Delayed discount program, however instead of being provided with a discount, the member is awarded an account credit which they can apply to their next purchase.

> **Modern Market Rewards**
>
> As a join bonus, customers who sign up to Modern Market Rewards[275] receive US$2 credit into their account aimed at immediately encouraging them to spend at Modern Market to take advantage of their credit.
>
> Every time the member dines at Modern Market they progress towards earning their next US$10 credit. A US$10 credit is triggered ready for redemption each time a US$100 spend threshold is

---

275 Modern Market, https://modernmarket.com/rewards, accessed 29 June 2020.

reached, encouraging continuous earn activity to progress towards more credits.

Accumulated value can be redeemed simply by activating the credit and presenting it to the cashier at checkout.

2. Interest payments credit program:

This model involves inviting members to pay money into a holding account to apply against future purchases. Members are rewarded with 'interest' on their deposits, which acts as an account credit.

The program design may appear complex, but the core proposition messaging is simple, and when compared to the low rates of interest provided by banks, can be quite compelling. The credit is typically applied against high margin products which can support generous discounts, making it cost-effective. One advantage is members may feel they are being provided with additional spending power, which can act to stimulate their desire to transact, particularly when this builds over time.

The approach requires investment in technology systems to manage member accounts, organise direct debit transactions, present clear transaction records and provide robust security to protect against breaches.

Virgin Wines UK

Virgin Wines UK have created a wine credit service called WineBank[276] which allows members to save a chosen amount within their WineBank account each month (from £15 to £100) to spread the cost of buying wine and maintain consistent wine bills.

For every £5 a member saves in their WineBank account, an extra £1 interest is added to the account by Virgin Wines. This acts as a 20 per cent discount when the member chooses to spend their WineBank credits.

---

276 Virgin Wines, https://www.virginwines.co.uk/winebank, accessed 29 June 2020.

3. Lowest price guarantee credit program:

Lowest price guarantee credits are a structure which provides an automatic credit to members in the event they purchase a product which later reduces in price. This is typically confined to a fixed period of time post-purchase, with the difference between what the member paid and the new price credited to their account. For example, 'if the price reduces within two weeks of purchase, you will receive the difference as an account credit'[277]. The member can access the credit on their next transaction.

This strategy is based on a similar premise to a lowest price guarantee company committing to matching or beating competitor prices in order to give customers confidence they are always accessing the cheapest price available. Best price guarantee companies constantly study the competition and adjust prices to remain the low-cost leader. In the instance that a customer finds a better price from a competitor, they will honour and potentially even beat it with a committed discount. This strategy aims to reduce comparison shopping by customers, representing a form of loyalty.

The systems required to operate a lowest price guarantee company are already relatively sophisticated. Extending these systems to support a price guarantee credit program will require investment in platform development. For companies with large product ranges and constantly changing prices, the operational complexities of such a program may be too onerous. Customer service support requirements to provide adequate responses to member enquiries may also require investment.

> **Super Cheap Auto Club Plus**
>
> The Super Cheap Auto Club Plus Membership[278] offers members several benefits including a 'Get Credit Back' promise. That is, 'if an item you just purchased goes on sale, we'll automatically credit you the difference!'.
>
> The join fee to sign up to Club Plus is A$5 per member with members receiving an automated A$10 credit into their online account

---

277 Supercheap Auto, https://www.supercheapauto.com.au/p-supercheap-auto-club-plus-membership/900440.html, accessed 10 September 2020.
278 Ibid.

once it is activated. This program design helps create a lock-in effect for members who have paid (sunk cost bias), provides instant gratification whilst familiarising members with using credits and gives them confidence they will always be accessing the cheapest promotional discount.

If a member buys a catalogue item and the price is reduced within two weeks, the difference is credited to their account, and they have 30 days to spend the credit.

Referrals

Model

A referral program is a structured framework which makes it simple and rewarding for a customer to refer a brand or product to someone they know. Berman (2016)[279] indicates referral programs rely on 'motivating satisfied/delighted customers as a referral base, seeking current customers that can provide referrals with a high lifetime value, using referral-based marketing programs to augment traditional promotions, and developing a compensation system for referrals based on either direct payment or increased visibility'.

In exploring referral programs, two design variations are considered: within program and standalone.

279 Berman, B., 2015, 'Referral marketing: Harnessing the power of your customers', Business Horizons, Vol 59.

1. Referrals within an existing program:

Referrals can be a feature within an overarching program. As an option to earn bonus rewards, members can invite friends to participate in or engage with the program. This is a common component built within many best-practice loyalty programs.

> ### DiDi
>
> Chinese rideshare giant DiDi[280] leverage their member network to further grow their member database through a referral program within their app and email communications.
>
> Members can easily share their unique referral link with as many friends as they desire in order to give their friends A$20 worth of DiDi ride value and receive A$20 of DiDi ride value in return when they take their first trip.
>
> The referral feature is prominently positioned on the homepage of the member app and within the onboarding email and push notification series.

2. Referrals as a standalone program:

If operating as a standalone program, members are rewarded for referring family and friends with product credits, discounts, vouchers or third-party rewards. This approach is particularly useful for B2B programs, where a referral for a loyal client can lead to a substantial revenue boost from new clients.

> ### Tesla
>
> Tesla created a successful referral program to capitalise on the loyal sentiment of Tesla owners with 97 per cent reporting that their next motor purchase will also be a Tesla.[281]

---

280 Didi, https://australia.didiglobal.com/, accessed 10 September 2020.

281 Luckerson, V., 2015, 'Tesla's Elon Musk responds to Consumer Reports Model S criticism', Fortune, https://fortune.com/2015/10/22/tesla-musk-consumer-reports/, accessed 2 June 2020.

The program was originally designed in a way which ranked refer-rers (gamification) by the amount of successful referrals they cre-ated, with those at the top of the leader board able to obtain exclu-sive invites to the Tesla factory, attend the launch of new models and receive early access to purchase new models (social identity theory). The first referrer to achieve 10x referrals in North America, Europe and Asia would receive a free Tesla SUV. The referrer was also able to give up to 10x friends a US$1000 discount as a reward for the referee.

One referrer was responsible for selling 188 Tesla cars in just two months (at an average of US$85,000 per car) equating to almost US$16 million in revenue from one referrer, and costing Tesla US$188,000 in referrer rewards and US$188 million in referee rewards (representing an ROI of 42x on every dollar spent).[282] It has been claimed that all referrers combined were responsible for selling about 5,000 new Model S cars during this iteration of the referral program with a total value of US$425 million assuming an average sale price of US$85,000.[283]

Tesla are now up to their eighth iteration of their evolving referral program. While Tesla leveraged their loyal customers to grow sales to new heights, including best-selling luxury car in the US and the best-selling electric car in the world, the company has decided to redirect referral program dollars towards minimising the cost of the product. They stated that although the previous program was suc-cessful, it came at significant costs.

Now the referral program rewards both the referrer and referee with 1,000 free miles of Supercharging plus the chance to win a Founder's Series Model Y every month and a Founder's series

282 Toledano, E., 2016, 'How Tesla's Magnetic Referral program Delivered Over 40x ROI in Q4 2015', Business 2 Community, https://www.business2community. com/loyalty-marketing/teslas-magnetic-referral-program-delivered-40x-roi-q4-2015-01450250#BLybFfug4kCUkp0K.97, accessed 2 June 2020.
283 Ibid.

> Roadstar supercar quarterly, both signed by Tesla owners Elon
> Musk and Franz von Holzhausen.
>
> It is likely the program design will continue to evolve.

Merchant funded

<u>Model</u>

A merchant funded program involves a third-party partner (or merchant) covering the cost of the benefits provided to the member. This is generally because of the loyalty program promoting the third-party partner to the member, leading to the member transacting with that partner.

A number of programs have built their entire strategy around affiliate, recruiting members to spend online via advertisers to earn cashback. Most major coalition programs, particularly frequent flyer programs, have adopted affiliate earn as part of their wider program offering.

In exploring merchant funded programs, three design variations are considered: affiliate, card-linked and gift card-linked.

1. Affiliate merchant funded program:

Affiliate is a digital business model connecting thousands of advertiser and promoter businesses globally. The promoter business publicises the advertiser to their marketing database. The members click through to the advertiser's online store and transact. The advertiser pays a percentage of the total amount spent by the member to the promoter, known as affiliate marketing revenue. The promoter rewards the member with cashback or points funded by the affiliate marketing revenue.

The percentage return provided in the form of affiliate marketing revenue can range from 1 per cent up to 20 per cent and even more, making it an attractive extension for points programs where the average earn rate may only be a 1 or 2 per cent return. Advertisers often run short-term promotional campaigns which increase the percentage return, making it increasingly attractive.

Two challenges faced by program operators utilising this affiliate marketing framework include payment delays (to avoid situations where members return items after affiliate marketing revenue is paid, many advertisers align the affiliate marketing payment with the official refund period, which can be up to 90 days) and onerous member processes (members must remember to follow a certain process to ensure they earn their cashback or points which commonly requires the member to sign into their program account, find the logo of the relevant brand and click through to their online store to transact).

ShopBack

Shopback[284] have partnerships with over 1,300 large brands which pay a commission for any purchases made on their ecommerce stores which are linked to Shopback members. Shopback shares the commission with the member that made the purchase in the form of a cashback. Cashback accumulated in a member's ShopBack account can be withdrawn into member's bank accounts via Paypal.

Shopback also have a 'Toolkit' for members to install so they 'Never miss a Shopback opportunity' and do not have to remember to go to the Shopback website and click through to the brands site to gain the cashback. The toolkit includes either a Google Chrome or Firefox browser extension which enables an automated pop-up when a member visits the online store of a participating advertiser. Members click an 'activate' button to link their Shopback account prior to transacting to access the cashback on their purchase.

The browser extension approach used by Shopback has been instrumental in boosting member engagement with affiliate programs. However, there is mixed feedback among the advertisers, with some opting out as they believe they would have gained the

---

284 Shopback, https://www.shopback.com.au/how-we-work, accessed 29 June 2020.

member sale (with the member already on their website when the browser extension pop-up notifies them to activate) without the need to pay commission to Shopback, thus unnecessarily eating into profits.

2. Card-linked or bank account-linked merchant funded program:

This approach involves the linking of a credit/debit card or bank account to a member account.

For card-linking, when the member uses the registered card to transact with a participating merchant, the transaction data is routed from Mastercard, Visa or Amex to the program operator, and an agreed percentage of the total transaction is retained (similar to affiliate marketing revenue). The program operator can use the retained revenue to reward the member with points, cashback or credits etc.

For bank account-linking, any transaction made via the member's bank account is redirected to the program operator, allowing them to identify transactions made with participating retailers, and apply the relevant reward. The participating merchant can then be invoiced for the cost of the reward at some time in the future.

This approach provides some advantages over affiliate marketing. The benefit is provided to the member real-time (or at the latest within 24 hours) instead of having to wait up to 90 days. The member can spend online, but more importantly in-store, expanding the flexibility of shopping options. The member does not need to follow specific processes to earn, but simply pays with the registered card or bank account.

Hooch Rewards

Hooch[285] is a hospitality perks app with over 250,000 global partners spanning hotels, restaurants and bars. Members download the Hooch app and link their credit card, then when members travel and dine with a partner as they normally would, they earn TAP Dollars instantly. Rewards are instantaneous and secure due

---

285 Hooch, https://hoochrewards.com/, accessed 29 June 2020.

to Hooch using blockchain technology to facilitate and encrypt the transactions.

Members receive up to 10 per cent back on purchases in TAP Dollars which is funded by the merchant partners.

Liquor brands like Bacardi and Paramount use the Hooch app as an advertising platform to connect with relevant target customers.

3. Gift card-linked merchant funded program:

Gift cards are typically sold to loyalty programs (and other retailers such as supermarkets) at a discount to the face value amount. Loyalty programs have developed app solutions which allow members to register a credit or debit card and purchase a variable value gift card for a specific brand in real-time. The gift card barcode displays in the app and can be scanned at the checkout, completing the sale. The gift card discount is used to reward the member with points or miles. Discounts can range from 1 per cent up to 15 per cent for different brands.

United MileagePlus

United MileagePlus offers MileagePlus X,[286] a payments app which allows members to earn miles across hundreds of retailers across the US.

Members register their credit/debit card in the app. When they are transacting, they search for the participating retailer and enter the amount they wish to spend. In the back end, the system purchases a digital gift card of the same variable amount, and presents a QR code in the app for the member to scan to complete the purchase.

MileagePlus buy the gift cards at a discount. They use the discount to cover the cost of the miles they award to the member, making the rewards cost neutral.

The model is clever in two ways; firstly, the discounts provided on

286 United, https://www.united.com/ual/en/us/fly/mileageplus/earn-miles/mileage-plus-x.html, accessed 29 June 2020.

gift cards are often quite generous (5-10 per cent or more can be common), meaning the member receives a healthy miles bonus, and secondly, gift card affiliate suppliers have already negotiated the relationships with the gift card providers, making it easy for MileagePlus to build out a rapid expansion of their coalition without having to negotiate individual agreements.

MileagePlus X offer over 270 popular brands, such as Panera Bread (earn 5 miles), Krispy Kreme (earn 4 miles), Sephora (earn 3 miles), Apple iTunes (earn 2 miles), and Walmart (earn 0.5 miles).

Surprise and delight

Model

The surprise and delight model focuses on providing members with periodic surprise gifts to elicit positive emotional responses and build attitudinal commitment. Reciprocity also plays a role in the effectiveness of this design approach.

Extensive consumer psychology research indicates unexpected delight can develop an emotional connection between members and a brand and can be cost-effective (as detailed in Chapter 5). However, maintaining the element of surprise over a long period of time and measuring the direct effects of surprise and delight can be challenging.

In exploring surprise and delight programs, three design variations are considered: basic, member journey and touchpoint.

1. Basic surprise and delight program:

A basic model involves providing the member with an unexpected reward as part of their purchase and consumption journey in the hope it will trigger an emotional response which stimulates the member to seek a repetition of the experience.

This may be provided when the member transacts, when they receive their product or independent to a specific consumer action.

Marley Spoon

Marley Spoon[287] attempt to surprise and delight their customers by providing a small gift in meal kit boxes. This may be a wooden spoon, an apron or a tea towel, ensuring members feel extra delighted when they receive and open their box.

Having Marley Spoon branding on these items which are utilised within their member's kitchens reinforces the generosity of Marley Spoon.

:86 400

:86 400 is a smartbank with capability for members to connect accounts from over 100 financial institutions, as well as view upcoming expenses and predictions based on regular payments, bills and subscriptions, providing a full view of their financial picture.

Each week, :86 400 randomly select over 100 customers via their #payitforward campaign and pay one of their predicted bills. On one occasion the authors received a credit to cover their upcoming Netflix subscription, and on another, their next Spotify payment.

2. Member journey surprise and delight program:

Some customer purchase journeys are complex and involve a series of steps. This creates an opportunity for a company to provide their customers with unexpected treats at each step.

---

287 Marley Spoon, https://marleyspoon.com.au/, accessed 29 June 2020.

This approach reinforces the customer service focus of the company and increases the likelihood that the customer will proceed to the next step. It also increases the propensity for a customer to wish to repeat the journey in the future, as well as promote the company to family and friends.

> **Direct Property Network Merci Program**
>
> This property and financial services consulting agency places critical importance on owning the emotional connection with customers. To reinforce their decision and reduce any uncomfortable feelings which can often be attached to making such a large investment like purchasing a property, they have developed their 'Merci Program'. This program provides gifts to customers at strategic times throughout the customer journey to help them proceed to the next step and reflect on their decision favourably and with certainty.[288]
>
> The major gifting milestones for customers include when they purchases a property, when their loan is approved, when they sign the papers, when the settlement period ends, when they get the keys, when they move in and on their first anniversary since moving in.
>
> Attaching these key moments to gifts accompanied by messages of encouragement work to reduce any incidence of cognitive dissonance associated with the purchase while simultaneously building attitudinal commitment.

3. Touchpoint surprise and delight:

The touchpoint model ensures the customer is delighted at each interaction with the company. It is more relevant for service organisations, and requires heavy investment in staff training, quality management, systems and processes.

The desired outcome is a service culture which makes customers feel as if they are the centre of the company's universe. This approach is less of a

---

288 Breen, M., MPA Magazine, https://www.mpamagazine.com.au/sections/features/innovation-at-direct-property-network-242222.aspx, accessed 29 June 2020.

formalised program design and more of a brand actualisation. It is arguably the most sophisticated application of surprise and delight.

> **Waldorf Astoria**
>
> This luxury hotel corporation executes surprise and delight at an extremely advanced level with the aim to make every interaction unique, personalised, unforgettable and delightful.
>
> The hotel famously allocates two staff members for each guest. Staff members are encouraged to learn small amounts of information about each guest, from the coffee they drink, the type of sheets they prefer, the flowers they love, the newspaper they read and the activities they like which can be drawn upon to deliver delightful experiences which deepen connections with members.
>
> Examples of the lengths Waldorf Astoria go to make members feel like they are the centre of the universe, are showcased through thousands of positive member reviews online, most of which refer to these special moments.[289] Many of these guests also mention that the thoughtful surprises, amazing service and personal gifts are the reason they felt compelled to provide a positive review online and will be returning for another stay.

Gamification

---

289 Reviews published on TripAdvisor, https://www.tripadvisor.com.au/Search?q=waldorf%20astoria&searchSessionId=652F5BE9932CC9714793C827891B82BB1593407950594ssid&searchNearby=false&geo=295424&sid=8446226E978364D404979EFB359608171593407971976&blockRedirect=true, accessed 29 June 2020.

<u>Model</u>

Gamification is the use of elements of gameplay in non-game contexts to stimulate specific behaviours. Gamification can play a key role in loyalty programs because of its ability to make a mundane task less boring and can stimulate members to engage in extremely specific, desirable behaviours.

The potential of gamification, the consumer psychology supporting it and the applications in real-world loyalty programs are extensive. Chapter 13, dedicated specifically to gamification and gaming, provides a detailed overview of gamification within different program design variations.

> **Volkswagen Group BONEO**
>
> The Volkswagen Group built the BONEO program with the aim to encourage weekly interaction with customers, a particularly challenging task due to the frequency in which consumers buy cars.
>
> The gamified BONEO app immediately provides members with their own car avatar during onboarding. Members can overcome challenges or interact digitally with other members to improve or upgrade their avatar as well as earn other awards such as a free drive in a Porsche or Audi, or to occupy virtual sectors of territory on the in-app map.
>
> Members can also win virtual Lootboxes which are distributed periodically to encourage habitual engagement with the app. These prizes may be tangible rewards like a free car wash, a free coffee at a petrol station or a free weekend with a Porsche.
>
> The BONEO app has been successful through the use of several gamified mechanisms like avatars, challenges, status levels, territory trackers and rewards to achieve weekly engagement and form a stronger connection between customers and their cars.[290]

---

290 The Octalysis Group, Case Studies, https://octalysisgroup.com/case-studies/, accessed 19 June 2020.

Combining frameworks / hybrid models

There are clear benefits and challenges associated with each design framework, however, brands do not need to commit to just one framework. Many loyalty programs are a combination of multiple frameworks, creating a hybrid model that is better suited to delivering to the business objectives. These programs are more difficult to operate and communicate, but provide a much richer pool of assets from which to incentivise members, a more meaningful way to communicate with members ongoing, more opportunities and flexibility to deliver value to members, and more opportunities to collect and apply data insights to drive incremental visits and spend.

e.l.f Beauty Squad

e.l.f[291] integrate a combined total of seven different design frameworks within their Beauty Squad program.

These include:

- Points: members receive 25 points as a join bonus and continue to earn points with every purchase. Points can be redeemed for dollars off e.l.f products.

- Tiers: the amount of points a member has accumulated directly determines the members tier. 'Extra' is the base tier level, 'Epic' tier requires 101+ points and 'Icon' tier requires 401+ points to qualify.

- Member benefits: different tiers unlock access to different member benefits such as access to a birthday gift, bonus points offers, double points events, early access to sales, new product launches and bonus vouchers and discounts.

- Credits: one of the benefits enjoyed by members of the Epic tier is a US$5 credit applied to orders of US$20 or more.

- Discounts: one of the benefits enjoyed by members of the Icon tier is a 25% discount off purchases.

- Referrals: members can refer their friends by giving them a US$5

---

291 E.l.f, https://www.elfcosmetics.com/e.l.f.-beauty-squad/, accessed 21 July 2020.

credit voucher. When the friend joins and spends, the referrer gets 150 points.

- Surprise and Delight: e.l.f send their valued members periodic surprise gifts (i.e. samples within their orders), bonus offers and discounts to recognise, reward and delight them.

As part of the design, e.l.f also have native receipt scanning functionality within the app where members are encouraged to submit receipts from purchases made at Walmart, Target and Amazon, allowing members to earn bonus points. In return, e.l.f receive valuable insights about members, such as other products they are buying and where they are shopping.

Ekta Chopra, VP of Digital at e.l.f has stated 'If I think about 2020, my single goal is take that data, harness it in a way that we can make every single loyalty consumer experience very, very relevant.'[292]

While complex in design, the Beauty Squad program is simple for members to understand and engage with. The value of points, status levels and member benefits are all clear.

Through a hybrid of frameworks and rewards, e.l.f benefit from being able to deliver instant gratification through immediate tangible rewards, whilst building attitudinal commitment through status tiers and carefully curated experiential, visual and delightful rewards.

Most importantly, they harness rich member data collected from multiple touchpoints to support the delivery of hyper-personalised member experiences and relevant communications and rewards.

---

292 Serna, I., 'Loyalty Designed For Authentic And Brand Driven Experience Commerce With Insights From E.L.F. Cosmetics', Annex Cloud, https://www.annexcloud.com/blog/annex-cloud-elf-cosmetics-glossy-summit/, accessed 21 July 2020.

Key insights

- There are many distinct types and sub-types of design frameworks utilised in loyalty programs.

- The overarching design framework models are loyalty currencies, status tiers, member benefits, discounts, credits, referral, merchant funded, surprise and delight, and gamification.

- Certain designs may be better suited to delivering to a specific company's needs and objectives, with each model providing different benefits and challenges, and some models dictating the rewards which are offered. Working through a range of design options and conducting thorough market research will help ensure the framework adopted is appropriate.

- Many programs use a combination of multiple frameworks, creating a hybrid model which is better suited to delivering to the short term and long-term business objectives.

Suggested reading

- Drèze, Xavier & Nunes, Joseph., 2009, 'Feeling Superior: The Impact of Loyalty Program Structure on Consumers' Perceptions of Status', Journal of Consumer Research, Vol 35, pp890-905.

- Berman, B., 2015, 'Referral marketing: Harnessing the power of your customers', Business Horizons, Vol 59.

CHAPTER 9

BUSINESS-TO-BUSINESS (B2B) PROGRAMS

'Once we receive your application for the Nufarm Priority Partnership programme, your application is processed and a Welcome email (complete with membership number and login details) is sent to you. Using your Rural Supplier information provided, our Team match the relevant supplier's details, with your Nufarm Priority Partnership membership number to provide points. As a member you earn Nufarm Priority Partnership points for purchases on all qualifying Nufarm products. As points are accumulated, they can be redeemed from over 5,000 quality rewards within the Nufarm Priority Partnership website, or by contacting the Priority Partnership Team.'

- Nufarm Priority Partnership information page[293]

Focus areas

This chapter will address the following questions:

- How are B2B loyalty programs different to B2C programs?
- Does loyalty play as important a role in B2B industries as B2C industries?

---

293 Nufarm, Priority Partnership, http://www.prioritypartnership.co.nz/pp_app/page_public.php?page=about_priority_partnership accessed 10 June 2020.

- Who within a company should the B2B loyalty program attempt to engage?
- What are the main design frameworks utilised within B2B loyalty programs?

The importance of loyalty within B2B industries

Most of the academic focus and societal awareness around loyalty programs relates to consumer-focused programs (B2C). Business-to-business (B2B) programs can also work to drive desirable behaviours from business customers; increased spend, repeat purchase, data capture, relationship development and advocacy.

This chapter provides a focus on B2B programs; academic research, similarities and differences compared to consumer programs, and framework designs supported by case studies.

Research supports the importance of customer loyalty as part of a B2B relationship.

Haghkhah (2013)[294] stated that retaining an organisation's current customers and making them loyal is a critical component for a company to be successful. 'With loyal customers, companies can maximise their profit because loyal customers are willing to purchase more frequently; spend money on trying new products or services; recommend products and services to others; and give companies sincere suggestions. Thus, loyalty links the success and profitability of a company.'

Asgarpour (2013)[295] argued that customer loyalty is essential if a company is going to retain its current customers and that client loyalty is one of the most sought-after objectives of B2B companies today.

Eakuru and Mat (2008)[296] indicated that the ultimate goal of companies

294 Haghkhah, A., 2013, 'Commitment and Customer Loyalty in Business-To-Business Context', European Journal of Business and Management, Vol 5, Iss 19, pp156-164.
295 Asgarpour, R., Abdul Hamid, A. B., Mousavi, B. & Jamshidy, M., 2013, 'A Review on Customer Loyalty as a Main Goal of Customer Relationship Management', Jurnal Teknologi (Sciences and Engineering), Vol 64, pp109-113.
296 Eakuru, N. & Mat, N. K. N., 2008, 'The Application of Structural Equation

is to build customer loyalty, which is achieved via the mediating influence of customer trust. This acts to enhance the impact of corporate identity, corporate image, and the reputation of the company.

B2B loyalty program characteristics

There are a range of options for companies to develop loyalty amongst B2B customers which do not include a formal loyalty program. This includes providing superior products and services, attractive pricing and exclusive discounts, quality account management, supportive post-sales customer service, events and conferences, and education courses.

That being said, companies are increasingly embracing formal B2B loyalty programs as a method to build customer loyalty. Krafft et al (2017)[297] identified that in recent years more B2B companies have implemented customer relationship management (CRM) practices and, increasingly more B2B companies are introducing loyalty programs to build stronger relationships with their best customers.

Examples of companies that have introduced B2B loyalty programs globally include MailChimp, HP, American Express, Schneider Electric, Ingram Micro, Trend Micro, WeWork, Lenovo, IBM, Thomas Cook, Fujitsu, Countrywide, Cisco, Nufarm, Uber, The Iconic and Mercedes-Benz.

The characteristics of B2B programs tend to be different to B2C programs in six fundamental ways.

- **Member base size**: B2B programs generally have smaller member bases than B2C programs. Not surprisingly, this is because B2B companies have access to a smaller pool of customers from which to draw members. This provides B2B program operators with an advantage; a smaller member base makes personalisation of communications and services much more achievable. B2B relationships tend to involve a greater level of intimacy than B2C models, with face-to-face meetings, social events, tailored services and

Modeling (SEM) in Determining the Antecedents of Customer Loyalty in Banks in South Thailand', The Business Review, Vol 10, No 2, pp. 129-139.

297 Viswanathan, V., Sese, F. J. & Krafft, M., 2017, 'Social Influence in the Adoption of a B2B Loyalty Program: The Role of Elite Status Members', International Journal of Research in Marketing, Vol 34, Iss 4, pp 901-918.

post-purchase support. This provides a good opportunity to build a positive brand connection and attitudinal commitment.

- **Member base spend**: on average B2B programs generally provide greater value to members than B2C programs. This is because B2B customers tend to spend more than B2C customers, allowing the company to return more value to the business customers as rewards. For example, a program providing 1 per cent return on one million dollars of business spend will be able to provide a much more generous reward that a program where a consumer spends one thousand dollars. This is an important distinction; as value is a key principle in generating program engagement, B2B programs have a natural advantage over B2C programs.

- **Purchasing drivers**: businesses have different purchasing approaches to consumers, which necessitates variations in program design. According to Kaushik (2019),[298] consumers buy based on family needs, fashion and social necessity, they make fast and simple decisions, receive relevant marketing primarily via mass market channels (internet, social media, radio, TV, newspaper ads, etc.) and are reasonably sensitive to technological changes. By comparison, businesses buy to enhance profitability, productivity, payback, and operational ease and maintenance, make slow and complex decisions, receive relevant marketing primarily via direct one-to-one presentations and discussions, and are overly sensitive to technological changes. Thus, the factors which influence a consumer to be positively influenced by a loyalty program are distinct to the factors which will influence a business decision. Adequate client research is essential to identify those factors and tailor the design accordingly.

- **Relationships**: the complexity of the buying relationship is greater for B2B than B2C, meaning the program needs to cater for multiple member relationships within a single account. Kaushik (2019)[299] highlighted that while a B2C relationship is generally one-to-one, a

298 Kaushik, P., 2019, 'B2B Marketing,' Lecture series, Atharva Institute of Management Studies.

299 Kaushik, P., 2019, 'B2B Marketing,' Lecture series, Atharva Institute of Management Studies.

B2B relationship may be between multiple participants, including owners, initiators, influencers, deciders, users, buyers and gatekeepers. This can make it incredibly challenging to design an effective program. For example, a B2B program which rewards the business owner or leader may fail to influence purchase behaviour if procurement decisions are made by buyers. A program which rewards buyers may not be effective if they are following the product-selection direction of the users. A program which rewards users may not be effective if their decisions are often overruled by the gatekeepers. Research of individual businesses is required to ascertain which participants the program is best targeted towards. Flexibility within the program design to adjust the targeting for different businesses is also important, as is understanding that different stakeholders will have different agendas and objectives which they believe a loyalty program should deliver to.

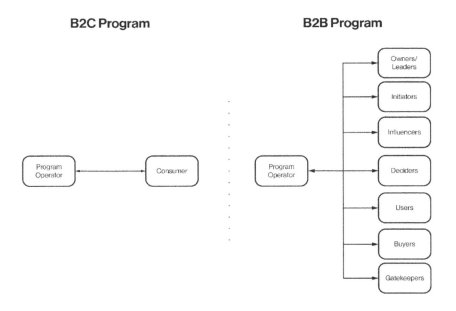

Figure 14: the different relationships between program operators and stakeholders/members within both B2C and B2B loyalty programs.

A side-effect of this dynamic is that B2B programs which deliver rewards based on spend tend to be better suited to targeting smaller businesses (small-to-medium enterprises or SMEs) than large businesses. SME's are more likely to be able to receive and distribute rewards within the business, while this is more challenging within large companies due to the greater number of engaged stakeholders.

- **Fundamental challenges**: the design of a B2B program needs to accommodate three fundamental challenges; ethical, communications and employee longevity. For *ethical*, a program needs to ensure it is not influencing decision-making in a way which delivers a poorer outcome for the business or their customers. For example, if a buyer decides to purchase a service from one business over another because they will receive a loyalty program reward, ethical challenges arise if the service is more expensive or delivered at a lower quality. In this instance, the loyalty program could be viewed as a form of bribery. For *communications*, the program design needs to identify which participants within the customer business should receive program information, and the nature of that information. For *employee longevity*, the program operator needs to quickly identify when a participant leaves the business and update the membership status to accommodate new participants. This can be particularly challenging for larger member programs.

- **Reward variations**: B2B programs tend to have different reward ranges than B2C programs. While they may incorporate consumer goods and gift cards, they also tend to include the businesses own products, direct discounts, free education courses, access to events and conferences, and other benefits more suited to the needs of particular customers.

B2B customer commitment

In the same way that commitment (measured as resistance to change) leads to loyalty within B2C programs, B2B programs should strive to build customer commitment to the brand. Gilliland and Bello (2002) identified that attitudinal commitment by a client towards another business motivates specific actions to manage and advance ongoing relationships. This includes a greater willingness to use relational, over contract-based mechanisms to keep behaviours consistent with the contractual agreements. They hypothesised that attitudinal commitment for B2B relationships consists of two components: a rational, economic calculation (calculative commitment) and an emotional, social sentiment (loyalty commitment).

Gilliland and Bello identified three important characteristics specific to loyalty commitment within B2B relationships; it makes it difficult to exit the relationship, partially because loyalty sentiments motivate participants to work out problems rather than leave; it suggests a preference for one company over their competitors when making supply decisions; and, it maintains the relationship even if the decision may be economically irrational. These are clearly desirable and valuable relationship characteristics for a business to generate with a customer.

A well-designed B2B loyalty program can help develop loyalty commitment in order to support the realisation of these benefits.

B2B program design frameworks

B2B loyalty program designs are diverse, although less so than B2C programs. They often mimic B2C designs, but with some variations. The remainder of this chapter presents a range of program design frameworks used by B2B loyalty programs. As with B2C, it is common for a B2B program to combine elements from a number of frameworks to create a more comprehensive design.

Loyalty currencies and status tiers

Members earn points for transactions, which can be redeemed on a set reward range. Members can also achieve status tiers to unlock greater benefits.

Schneider Electric Club Clipsal

Schneider Electric is a multinational company providing energy and automation digital solutions, and Clipsal is a subsidiary brand providing electrical accessories.

Club Clipsal is Australia's largest loyalty club for the electrical industry with over 8,000 members in the rewards program.[300] Operating on a three-tiered membership basis, the program offers members the ability to earn points by purchasing Clipsal products from their selected wholesalers. The program features an earn accelerator, where the higher the tier, the higher the earn rate per dollar spent. Points can then be redeemed via a rewards store for a variety of gift cards and consumer goods.

Members of Club Clipsal also access exclusive functions for networking, social gatherings, and getaways. In addition to the earn accelerator, higher tiers have access to some additional member perks such as discounts on insurance, business management services, and fleet purchases.

Member benefits and discounts

Members can access a bundle of desirable benefits, which may include some form of preferred discounting structure, preferred payment terms, credit lines or invitations to exclusive conferences and events.

Uber Pro Partner Rewards

Uber Pro Partner Rewards[301] program was designed to recognise and reward Uber drivers. Like their B2C program, points and status tiers provide drivers with the ability to reach higher tiers and unlock more desirable member benefits.

Provided by Uber and partner third-party companies, member benefits include economic rewards such as fuel discounts, free coffees, and discounts for business support services, as well as more functional and experiential rewards such as providing drivers with the ability to view trip duration and direction before accepting a

---

300 Schneider Electric, Clipsal, https://www.clipsal.com/club-clipsal, accessed 29 June 2020.

301 Uber, Uber Pro, https://www.uber.com/au/en/drive/uber-pro/, accessed 29 June 2020.

job, receive priority airport rematches, 24/7 support and accident replacement vehicles.

An interesting element of the B2B program is that points are earned during a fixed three-month period, with points determining the status tier. Drivers earn points for each trip completed with a significant multiplier during peak times and points reset at the end of the three-month period. Members can continue enjoying their rewards (and achieved status) until the end of the following three-month period as long as they keep their star rating above 4.7 and cancellation rate below 3 per cent.

Ultimately, the design of the program incentivises Uber drivers to behave in ways which deliver benefits to Uber such as completing more trips, ensuring drivers are available during peak times and ensuring passengers receive a high level of customer service.

Allianz Blue Eagle Program

Allianz is a German multinational financial services company with core businesses insurance and asset management. The Allianz Blue Eagle Program[302] exists to engage and reward their broker network, primarily through networking, educational and celebratory events.

The program offers one point of call for all the information brokers require, such as program news, policy and claims information, online training, and product quoting and binding. An important aspect of the program is to build a sense of community between brokers and the brand, and Allianz do so by organising a variety of initiatives to get members involved.

These networking initiatives include:

- Annual Allianz Blue Eagle Awards: an exclusive celebratory event rewarding highly distinguished Blue Eagles for their achievements, while offering an opportunity to network with fellow members.

---

302 Allianz, https://www.einsure.com.au/wb/blueeagle-welcome.html, accessed 29 June 2020.

- Young Eagle program: designed to educate insurance brokers on how to operate an effective insurance company. Young brokers are regularly brought together to learn and compete in team-based scenarios, coached by members of the Allianz board.

- Blue Eagle Ladies Day: celebrating female brokers and Allianz staff, providing an opportunity to network and build broker-staff relationships.

- Tipping competitions: the Blue Eagle community can compete in annual tipping competitions for grand prizes such as overseas holidays.

Merchant funded

Members can accumulate value by transacting with third-party partners, with the cost of the reward covered by the third-party partner.

Nufarm Priority Partnerships

Nufarm is an agricultural chemical company which provides an extensive range of agricultural and crop protection products around the globe.

Nufarm's B2B loyalty program[303] allows members to accumulate points when purchasing eligible Nufarm products and transacting with relevant Nufarm suppliers. Points can be redeemed via the Priority Partnerships reward store which hosts over 5,000 rewards including a selection of consumer goods, travel, sporting equipment, events and more.

Rewarding members for ordering through verified third-party suppliers and partners provides an additional purchase incentive to build the feedback loop and reinforce client commitment both with Nufarm and its suppliers.

---

303 Nufarm, Priority Partnership, http://www.prioritypartnership.co.nz/pp_app/page_public.php?page=about_priority_partnership, accessed 29 June 2020.

Surprise and delight

Members receive unexpected delights to recognise and reward them for their business and to build an emotional connection.

> ### Influitive
>
> Influitive is a SaaS product and professional services company which specialises in providing customer marketing platforms and tools to drive customer advocacy and engagement.
>
> In December 2016, Influitive created a personalised video messaging tool which allowed their customers to deliver a surprise 1:1 holiday season message to their customers and business partners via one of three fun characters.
>
> The videograms were delivered to each recipient via Twitter, personally addressing both the sender and receiver, designed to 'pack a bigger emotional punch with them'[304] and show customers they care.
>
> This surprise and delight initiative cost 'a few hundred dollars in costumes, décor and a few new video cards',[305] but the effort and personalisation is what made the most impact, strengthening the relationship and increasing retention by making both Influitive customers and their customers feel special.

Education, training and mentoring

Members may be able to access online and classroom courses relevant to their industry and career progression. They may also be able to access mentoring support from leaders in the industry.

---

304 Influitive, 2016, 'The Secret to Delighting B2B Customers in 30 Seconds This Holiday Season', https://influitive.com/secret-delighting-b2b-customers-30-seconds-holiday-season/, accessed 29 June 2020.
305 Ibid.

Know Your IBM (KYI)

IBM's primary B2B loyalty program, KYI[306] targets resellers in its distribution channel with rewards structured around two key components:

- Learn & Earn: provides points to members who undertake educational activities and modules, learning about various IBM products and solutions, including skill enhancement courses and certifications.

- Sell & Earn: allows members to earn points for selling eligible IBM products, services, or solutions.

Members can redeem their points for products and gifts from participating merchants.

Periodically, IBM drives member engagement and retention by integrating gamification into e-learning. An example of this is KYI Badge Bingo, which involves members completing specific e-learning modules to be given the opportunity to share in a KYI points pot, as well as compete on leaderboards for bonus points.

Results published by Moviforce[307] indicate that KYI's 2018 results broke all previous year's records. In addition, the 15 per cent of IMB's B2B channel that participated in KYI generated 62 per cent of IBM's overall revenue for all products and services that were incentivised in KYI. They also state that KYI participants outperformed similar profiled non-participants (same geography, similar size and turnover) by a record 800 per cent. Due to these impressive results, further IBM divisions such as IBM Watson and IBM Security asked to join the program in 2019.[308]

---

306 IBM, https://www.ibm.com/partnerworld/resources/manage/incentives-promotions, accessed 30 June 2020.

307 Motivforce, 2019, 'Motivforce wins best B2B Loyalty Program with IBM for second year running at Loyalty Magazine Awards', https://www.motivforce.com/blog/back-to-back-award-winning-b2b-loyalty-program#:~:text=Know%20Your%20IBM%20(KYI)%20is,as%20sales%20of%20eligible%20solutions., accessed 29 June 2020.

308 Ibid.

Referrals

Members may be able to unlock benefits by referring other businesses.

> **American Express Partner Plus**
>
> Partner Plus[309] is a referral-based partnership program with American Express. Akin to most referral programs, members are rewarded if they successfully refer a business contact to American Express' Global Commercial Services.
>
> Partners can track the status of submitted leads at any time through a partner portal and receive support from an appointed sales representative. When successful, members reap the benefits as a percentage of the new account volume. Simple and straightforward for members to understand, the program creates a win-win situation for existing and new members.

Corporate social responsibility initiatives

Members may be able to participate in activities which contribute to social causes.

> **HP Planet Partner Rewards**
>
> HP Planet Partner Rewards[310] is available in over 76 countries and territories worldwide, with the objective to reward companies for returning used HP print cartridges, supporting HP's recycling initiative. The program goes beyond rewards, enabling organisations to contribute towards social and environmentally responsible actions, and earn HP points in the process.
>
> The design is simple, with HP leveraging their partnerships with collection agencies to make the pick-up and recycling processes

309 American Express, Partner Plus, https://corporateforms.americanexpress.com/PartnerPlusCompetitionAU, accessed 29 June 2020.

310 HP Planet Partners Return and Recycling Program, http://www.hp.com/hpinfo/newsroom/press_kits/2010/ecoachievement/HP_PP_Recycling_Program.pdfm, accessed 29 June 2020.

seamless and convenient. Points are awarded based on the quantity of returns, with more points awarded per item for scale. Points can be redeemed by partners for HP gift vouchers which can be used to purchase HP products from selected channel partners.

The program has a threefold impact, where partners save resources and get rid of empty cartridges for free, partners earn points to save money on future purchases, and they contribute to a cleaner environment by opting for safe and responsible recycling.

Key insights

- B2B loyalty programs are similar to B2C programs, however there are a number of characteristics which differ; smaller member bases, higher spend, different purchasing approaches, more complex buying relationships, reward range variations, and ethical, communication and employment longevity challenges.

- Loyalty is a critical component for the success and profitability of a company. The ultimate goal of companies is to build customer loyalty, which is achieved via the mediating influence of customer trust. This acts to enhance the impact of corporate identity, corporate image and the reputation of the company.

- In recent years more B2B companies have implemented customer relationship management (CRM) practices and, increasingly more B2B companies are introducing loyalty programs to build strong relationships with their best customers.

- A B2B relationship may be between multiple participants, including owners, initiators, influencers, deciders, users, buyers and gatekeepers, which can make it incredibly challenging to design and operate an effective loyalty program with appropriate rewards.

- The main B2B design framework categories are loyalty currencies, status tiers, member benefits, discounts, merchant funded, surprise and delight, education, training and mentoring, and corporate social responsibility initiatives.

Suggested reading

- Haghkhah, A., 2013, 'Commitment and Customer Loyalty in Business-To-Business Context', European Journal of Business and Management, Vol 5, Iss 19, pp156-164.

- Asgarpour, R., Abdul Hamid, A. B., Mousavi, B. and Jamshidy, M., 2013, 'A Review on Customer Loyalty as a Main Goal of Customer Relationship Management', Jurnal Teknologi (Sciences and Engineering), Vol 64, pp109-113.

- N. Eakuru and N. K. N. Mat, 2008, 'The Application of Structural Equation Modelling (SEM) in Determining the Antecedents of Customer Loyalty in Banks in South Thailand', The Business Review, Vol 10, No 2, pp. 129-139.

- Krafft, Manfred & Viswanathan, Vijay & Sese, F. Javier., 2017, 'Social Influence in the Adoption of a B2B Loyalty Program: The Role of Elite Status Members', International Journal of Research in Marketing, Vol 34, Iss 4, pp 901-918.

CHAPTER 10

DATA CAPTURE, ANALYSIS, AND USAGE

'McKinsey's DataMatics 2013 survey shows that companies that are receptive, i.e. use customer analytics extensively, are more than twice as likely to generate above-average profits as those that don't. They also outperform their peers across the entire customer lifecycle, are nine times more likely to enjoy superior customer loyalty, and a whopping 23 times more likely to outperform less analytical peers on new-customer acquisition.'

- McKinsey & Company, 2015[311]

Focus areas

This chapter will address the following questions:

- What value can member data deliver to a loyalty program?

- How is data collected directly and indirectly by loyalty programs?

- How is data analysed and used by loyalty programs?

- How aware are consumers about the data being collected about them?

---

311 McKinsey & Company, 2015, 'Marketing & Sales: Big Data, Analytics, and the Future of Marketing & Sales', https://www.mckinsey.com/~/media/McKinsey/Business%20Functions/Marketing%20and%20Sales/Our%20Insights/EBook%20Big%20data%20analytics%20and%20the%20future%20of%20marketing%20sales/Big-Data-eBook.ashx, accessed 15 June 2020.

Loyalty programs can play a key role in the entire data value chain; facilitating the collection of member personal data, utilising loyalty platforms to analyse the data (detailed in Chapter 11) and harnessing the insights generated to stimulate deeper member engagement by using sophisticated segmentation and lifecycle management models. This allows loyalty program operators to determine when, why and how members are engaging with the program.

Today, there is more data available than ever, but not all companies are structured to make best use of it. Types of data collected by loyalty programs include personally identifiable information (meaning any data that could potentially identify a specific individual) and more general data related to demographic and psychographic insights, and behavioural actions.

The amount of data collected by loyalty programs globally is best viewed through the lens of Big Data. The term Big Data was coined in 2005 by Roger Mougalas,[312] and refers to a large set of data that is almost impossible to manage and process using traditional business intelligence tools.

In 2011, McKinsey Global Institute (MGI)[313] calculated that a retailer using Big Data could increase its operating margin by more than 60 per cent, while the US healthcare sector could create more than US$300 billion in value every year, of which two-thirds would be in the form of reducing US healthcare expenditure by about 8 per cent.

Four years later, a McKinsey & Company report[314] acknowledged that the level of impact MGI foresaw had proved difficult to realise. While certain companies such as Google and Apple had made data analytics the foundation of their enterprise, most companies had failed to unlock the full benefits that Big Data promised. They identified a range of reasons; management not

---

312 Van Rijmenam, M., 2013, 'A Short History Of Big Data', Datafloq, https://datafloq.com/read/big-data-history/239, accessed 25 May 2020.

313 McKinsey Global Institute, 2011, 'Big data: The next frontier for innovation, competition, and productivity', https://www.mckinsey.com/business-functions/mckinsey-digital/our-insights/big-data-the-next-frontier-for-innovation, accessed 15 June 2020.

314 McKinsey & Company, 2015, 'Marketing & Sales: Big Data, Analytics, and the Future of Marketing & Sales', https://www.mckinsey.com/~/media/McKinsey/Business%20Functions/Marketing%20and%20Sales/Our%20Insights/EBook%20Big%20data%20analytics%20and%20the%20future%20of%20marketing%20sales/Big-Data-eBook.ashx, accessed 15 June 2020.

perceiving enough immediate financial impact to justify additional invest-ments; frontline managers lacking understanding and hesitating to employ insights; existing organisational processes unable to accommodate advance-ments in analytics and automation; and a lack of organisational adaptation required to take advantage of opportunities.

While companies are increasingly making the required investments and organisational adjustment to take advantage of Big Data, many companies still struggle. Loyalty program approaches can help companies to address these issues and unlock the value which data provides. This includes the use of plat-form technology which incorporates dashboard reporting, machine learning/AI (Artificial Intelligence) and automated marketing capabilities.

This chapter details methods by which member data can be collected (both directly by the loyalty program, and indirectly via third parties), to build a rich data profile of each member's demographic, geographic and psychographic state. It then details the many ways in which data can be applied, and provides some insight into consumer attitudes towards data collection and usage.

Direct member data collection

Member personal data can be collected directly by loyalty programs via many touchpoints.

Join process

When a member registers to join a loyalty program they are required to pro-vide personal details (e.g. their name, date of birth, email address and mobile phone number) which forms the basis of their member profile.

While it can be tempting for the loyalty program to ask for copious amounts of data as part of the join process, this can significantly reduce regis-tration completion rates. Best-practice approaches utilise balance. This means having the marketing discipline to request the minimal amount of infor-mation required to operate the program. Companies should identify what information is essential (e.g. does the program really need the member's mail-ing address?) and what can be accessed post registration (e.g. transaction data which can be used to identify the member's preferred products). It can also be useful to clarify to the member why the information is being requested (e.g. 'your date of birth will allow us to send you a birthday gift'). Information should principally be captured for the purpose of enhancing the member's experience as a pathway to driving deeper engagement.

Once the join process is complete, there may be a section or preference centre within the new account where the member is invited to share their likes and interests.

> ### *flybuys*
>
> Once the registration process is completed, *flybuys*[315] loyalty program invites new members to fill in a profile section. This includes fields for home and work phone, residential and postage address, number of people living in the household, including number of people under 18 years old and any pets, number of cars, whether the member owns their own business, the month of the year when they intend to review their home insurance, car insurance and mobile phone contract, how often they take flights for personal travel, which loyalty programs they are a member of, mobile phone, pay TV and internet products they use, internet shopping habits, and alcohol purchase behaviour.
>
> This is all highly valuable information for *flybuys* to build a comprehensive member profile, while for the member it is entirely voluntary.

Interactions

When and how an individual member interacts with a brand and their marketing material can be tracked at a micro level. This includes click maps or real-time user recordings across websites and electronic direct mail, and heat maps for in-store visits.

Digital assets are a particularly rich source of customer insights. This may include where a member's cursor gravitates to on a website, where in the sales funnel they take an action, what products they leave in their basket, which colour buttons they are more likely to click, what elements are confusing or missing, and which banner ad messaging resonates most. Interactions with

---

315 Flybuys, https://join.flybuys.com.au/desktop/fullname, accessed 29 June 2020.

a brand's customer service team may also be tracked and stored against the member's profile, including the nature of the call.

Using cookies, loyalty programs can track different websites which a member visits to better understand what brands and products they are interested in. However, the use of cookies is set to be disrupted extensively which will likely present a future challenge for the loyalty industry (and digital marketing more broadly). From 2022, cookies will no longer be allowed in Google's Chrome browser, while tracking cookies are already blocked in Safari, Firefox and Brave Browser. This shift away from collecting cookies will affect current digital marketing and retargeting practices, and hand Facebook and Google more market power than they have today.[316] This will increase the importance of collecting actual authenticated member data, and thus the usefulness of loyalty programs accordingly. Companies will be more likely to incentivise user sign-ins and the capture of zero-party data (data that is owned by the consumer that they intentionally and proactively share with a brand that they trust) and first-party data (data which is collected via customer interactions which the company owns).

Browser extension installations are becoming increasingly popular among loyalty program members. Members install these free toolbars because they can be helpful in notifying them when loyalty points, cashback or coupons are available, and to access price comparisons. They are a valuable source of member data, providing information about the user's device, IP address, geolocation, browsing history, mouse movements and logins.

316 McIntyre, P., 2020, Mi3, 'ACCC's Sims: adtech inquiry eye on cookie collapse, privacy regs as risks to more Google, Facebook as market power', https://www.mi-3.com.au/28-05-2020/acccs-sims-adtech-inquiry-looks-cookie-collapse-privacy-regs-risks-more-google-facebooks?utm_medium=email&utm_campaign=Top%205%20%20podcast%20-%20Monday%2018th%20May&utm_content=Top%205%20%20podcast%20-%20Monday%2018th%20May+CID_fa8356ab61b6494f12d51d a4481e4ff1&utm_source=Weekly%20newsletter&utm_term=ACCCs%20Sims%20adtech%20inquiry%20eye%20on%20cookie%20collapse%20privacy%20regs%20as%20risks%20to%20more%20Google%20Facebook%20ad%20market%2-0power&_lrsc=83833ec4-bf13-459e-b43f-4168bac97f3a, accessed 15 June 2020.

Shopkick, Swagbucks, Honey and Cashrewards

These companies are just a few examples of the range of affiliate marketing programs which allow members to collect points or cashback for online shopping via partner sites (the merchant funded framework detailed in Chapter 8). They each have browser extensions which run across Chrome, Firefox and Safari which, when installed, allow members to shop online as normal whilst receiving pop-up notifications when they are on an affiliate partner's website.

While these programs make it very easy for their members to earn and save points/cash, members are also opening themselves up to extensive tracking of personal information, banking details, browsing activity and online shopping patterns and interactions.

For example, Cashrewards state within their privacy policy that they 'collect, use and share aggregated data such as statistical or demographic data for any purpose'.[317]

As detailed earlier, members connecting to free Wi-Fi can be tracked, even without them needing to sign-in to an account. If the member accesses Wi-Fi once and signs-in, each time they visit the same location, the Wi-Fi may automatically connect and track their activity.

This provides loyalty programs with important data on how different segments of members utilise online and locational data. For example, a retail loyalty program operator could track behaviour inside store locations in different ways; learning how they move, where they reside and how long they stay, which can all be mapped and processed to gain better member insights.

---

317 Cashrewards, privacy, https://www.cashrewards.com.au/privacy, accessed 27 May 2020.

Skyfii

Skyfii state that they 'scale and customize the guest Wi-Fi user experience across multiple locations' and 'consolidate data from Wi-Fi, people counters, and other sources in a single view'.[318]

This type of technology is used extensively in shopping centre loyalty programs to track the movements of members and non-members around stores. The insights inform business decisions and marketing strategies which aim to stimulate member engagement and increased buying behaviour.

Consumers can virtually try on clothes, shoes, cosmetics, glasses, and other goods using augmented reality technology. The experience, available online and via apps, as well as in-store, allows brands to collect valuable member data which can be used to better understand members likes and preferences.

The data includes what a member looks like, what items they try and reject, what items they place in their wishlist or shopping basket, and which items they finally purchase.

L'Oréal Paris

L'Oréal Paris[319] launched a virtual try-on feature within their app using ModiFace[320] augmented reality technology. The tool allows L'Oréal members to easily try on hundreds of different cosmetics products or change their hair colour virtually.

The patented technology uses a face-tracking algorithm that can detect 63 landmarks on a member's face, providing the member with a realistic result when trying on L'Oréal products without any cost or commitment to purchase. L'Oréal benefit from increased engagement with the app and their products, as well as detailed

318 Skyfii, https://skyfii.io/, accessed 15 May 2019.

319 L'Oréal Paris , https://www.lorealparisusa.com/virtual-try-on/makeup.aspx, accessed 22 July 2020.

320 ModiFace, https://modiface.com/, accessed 22 July 2020.

> product preference data captured, which can then be used for hyper-personalised marketing and retargeting purposes.
>
> This is a clear trend among the beauty industry with Maybelline, Sephora, *bareMinerals*, MAC, Bobbi Brown, Redken and others, all integrating virtual tools within their apps for members to find and easily compare different foundation, lipstick, blush or hair colour hues.

Transactions

When, where and how often a member transacts, and how much they spend, provides valuable data about the member's lifestyle, habits, interests, motivations and goals. This data is collected by loyalty programs in a variety of ways.

The most common way is the member purposefully identifying when they transact by scanning their membership card or app in-store, signing into their account online or via an app, or providing verification to a call centre agent.

For loyalty programs that offer credit cards which earn points, when the member spends with the credit card, the loyalty program may receive the transaction data, such as time and date, retailer and amount spent. For example, a bank loyalty program which provides members with a credit card will receive all the member's transaction data. Other loyalty programs, such as frequent flyer programs, may not receive this data if the bank chooses not to (or is not able to) pass it on to them. Instead, they are likely to just receive the total amount the member spent for the month to facilitate the points earn calculations.

Some loyalty programs require the member to link a credit-card or their bank-account when they join, with points earn or cashback automatically processed when they spend at participating retailers. This provides the program operator with a significant amount of transaction data. In the case of bank account-linking, the program operators receive details of all transactions made through the member's bank account. This approach is covered in more detail in Chapter 11.

Some retailers have implemented a process where they automatically link any credit or debit card used by the member to their profile, enabling them to capture transactions, even when the member does not scan their membership card.[321] To illustrate, a member of a supermarket loyalty program scans their membership card at the checkout, then pays using a specific credit card. The loyalty program platform automatically matches the credit card against the member's profile. If the member spends with that card at the supermarket but does not scan their loyalty card, the loyalty platform will still collect the transaction data by recognising the credit card. While cost effective for the program operator because they collect valuable member data without having to reward the member with loyalty points, this practice is being scrutinised by governments with some going so far as to demand that the practice cease.[322]

Some programs require the member to scan receipts to prove they have made a valid transaction. The loyalty platform identifies relevant data (time, date, store location, SKU, amount spent, etc.) and calculates the points earn, discount or cashback applicable. While this approach requires the member to take extra steps in the earn process (friction which inevitably leads to lower engagement rates), the platform also captures other items on the receipt, helping to build a more complete profile of the member's spend habits.

Snap My Eats

NPD Group, one of the world's biggest market research agencies, runs a reward program called Snap My Eats[323] in the UK.

Members can download the app and register, then earn up to £5 of credit per month just for taking surveys and snapping pictures of receipts from their food and drink purchases. This includes things like a snack or coffee on the go, fast food, restaurant meals, or even an impulse candy purchase.

Snap My Eats requires the member to accumulate £10 of value before they can process a redemption, ensuring the program takes advantage of the endowed progress effect to drive ongoing member engagement, while simultaneously reducing costs.

---

321 Australian Competition and Consumer Commission, 2019 'Customer loyalty schemes: Final report,' pg 65 https://www.accc.gov.au/publications/customer-loyalty-schemes-final-report accesses 20th August 2020.

322 Ibid

323 Snap My Eats, https://www.snapmyeats.uk/, accessed 19 July 2020

Surveys

Loyalty programs often invite members to participate in surveys. These can be used for two purposes: to capture attitudes and opinions about the loyalty program, and, to collect additional data about the member.

> **Qantas Frequent Flyer**
>
> Qantas Frequent Flyer released a survey in March 2019 asking participating members a wide range of questions including:
>
> - Whether the member would recommend the Qantas Frequent Flyer loyalty program to family and friends.
> - Which competitor loyalty programs members belong to (from a list of 17 local and international programs) and the NPS rating and ranking for each.
> - How the member generally redeems points with the competitor programs.
> - A comparison of aspects of the Qantas Frequent Flyer program and the member's favourite competitor program across customer service, ease of use of scheme benefits, value accessed by the member, the credibility of the program, ease of accessing information, ease of accessing flight reward bookings and perceptions of the programs website.
> - Household income figures including how much the member spends on groceries each week, how much is spent on credit cards, how many dependent children live in the household and their ages, work status and number of employees in the member's company and whether the member flies mainly for work or business.
>
> Qantas Frequent Flyer also requested permission to store the survey answers against the member's profile 'to be used for program development (including delivering program benefits to our members)'. Such data would provide the program with rich insights about that member, including attitudinal views, which can often be hard to obtain.

Apps

When a member downloads a loyalty program app, they are generally requested to provide permission for the loyalty program to gain access to certain features and data, plus the ability to track location (either all the time, or only when the app is being used). This approval can provide extensive access including precise user location, access to the member's contacts, access to phone call logs, access to the camera and microphone, ability to read contents of storage, and ability to read phone status and identity.[324]

As a result of these permissions, smartphones have grown to become a major source of member data for loyalty program operators by allowing the loyalty program to extensively track member activity even when they are not engaging with the loyalty program or parent company.

The number of app control settings for users have increased, however, apps still bundle a number of permissions together, making it difficult for users to make decisions. For example, it is necessary for a food delivery company to access location information to function optimally, however this permission may be bundled together with permission to share information with advertisers, something not critical for operations.

> **Air New Zealand Airpoints**
>
> The Air New Zealand website terms of use state the ways by which they collect, combine, use and share Airpoints member data. Privacy policies and data practices of this nature are common among loyalty programs:
>
> '...where you are an Airpoints member, Koru member, have a myairnz login or subscribed to our grabaseat or Special Offers database, we combine the information we collect from your computer, mobile or other devices with the other information we collect about you, for example your booking history with us, your Airpoints or Koru membership information, information we collect from third parties in accordance with our Privacy Statement and

---

324 Cleary, G., 2018, 'Mobile Privacy: What Do Your Apps Know About You?', Symantec Corporation, https://www.symantec.com/blogs/threat-intelligence/mobile-privacy-apps, accessed 11 April 2019.

information that is publicly available (for example, information in public directories and publicly available social media information). We use this combined information to learn about your interests and preferences so that we can provide you with an improved and personalised online experience, improve our products and services, and identify suitable offers and promotions that you might be interested in.

We may disclose your personal information to the range of third parties identified in our Privacy Statement. For example, to our third-party business partners including marketing and advertising companies, data processing companies and data analysis companies to conduct sales, marketing and advertising research and analysis on our behalf so that we can better understand your preferences, carry out business improvement analysis, present you with suitable offers that you might be interested in, and for any of the other purpose described in the Privacy Statement.'[325]

Virtual home assistants

Some companies are experimenting with the use of virtual home assistants (such as Google Assistant, Alexa, or Siri) to support new ways for customers to interact.[326]

While there is some nervousness among members of the public about the conceivably invasive nature and eavesdropping potential of these devices, their household penetration is forecast to grow exponentially over the next five years.[327] As the capability evolves to better maintain and interpret reasonable

---

325 Air New Zealand, https://www.airnewzealand.com.au/website-terms-of-use, accessed 30 June 2020.

326 Crozier, R., 2019, 'Woolworths looks to large-scale conversational AI', IT News, https://www.itnews.com.au/news/woolworths-looks-to-large-scale-conversational-ai-518016, accessed 11 April 2019.

327 Hargreaves, I., 2018, 'Voice Assistant use to grow 1000% to reach 275 million by 2023, Juniper says', PC World, https://www.pcworld.idg.com.au/article/642969/voice-assistants-use-grow-1000-reach-275-million-by-2023-juniper-says/, accessed 11 April, 2019.

levels of conversation, they have the potential to become a valuable personal data source for loyalty programs.

> **Marriott**
>
> Marriott partnered with Amazon to offer an Amazon Echo device (equipped with microphones and speakers, and connected to a network) within hotel rooms allowing the services of Alexa to bring simplicity and convenience to guests. Guests can ask Alexa for hotel information (like pool or gym open times), request guest services (like room service or a wakeup call), play music from their hotel room and more.[328]
>
> This conversational AI can help build a bond between the AI assistant and user (Shulevitz, 2018)[329] and also helps strengthen the Marriott brand through the ability to collect data, personalise experiences, influence decisions and predict future behaviour.

Social media

Tools like Facebook Connect and Google+ can be used by loyalty programs to allow members to login with their existing credentials, with the primary benefit to the consumer being the convenience of not having to create a separate login each time they want to interact with a different loyalty program.

Facebook Connect allows sharing of data between the website and Facebook. This includes the member's name, email, birthday, relationships, friends list, education history, work history, interests, friend interactions, wall posts and comment frequency. Much of this data would be complex or arduous to collect via a loyalty program's own registration form.

---

328 Jones, V. K., 2019, 'Experiencing Voice-Activated Artificial Intelligence Assistants in the Home: A Phenomenological Approach', Public Access Theses and Dissertations from the College of Education and Human Sciences, Vol 348, accessed via https://digitalcommons.unl.edu/cehsdiss/348, 3 June 2020.

329 Shulevitz, J., 2018, 'Alexa, should we trust you?', The Atlantic, accessed via https://www.theatlantic.com/magazine/archive/2018/11/alexa-how-will-you-change-us/570844/, 3 June 2020.

Facebook also allows loyalty programs to build and target 'look-a-like audiences' based on this data to run targeted advertising.

> **Asics Runkeeper**
>
> When logging into the Asics Runkeeper[330] mobile app for tracking running activity, social sign-in is prompted and encouraged. Users are given the option to connect their accounts via Facebook and Google+ networks. There are both benefits to the user (faster, easier and more familiar sign-in process with a single password, single account to manage and fewer clicks) and to Asics (increase sign-ups and leverage existing social data which can improve app personalisation and marketing ability).
>
> Loyalty psychology and behavioural biases studies show that connecting social networks can facilitate stronger levels of social motivation and engagement with the app and the brand (appealing to the social proof and commitment biases).

Households

Loyalty programs may link multiple members to a specific mailing address, allowing them to build out their data profile by matching members living in the same household. This may be spouses, children, parents or housemates.

Some loyalty programs, such as supermarket, bank and hotel programs in particular, allow members to apply for companion cards, where the member can nominate another individual to receive a secondary card of the same account to enable both card-carriers to earn points.

This household profile approach allows for the loyalty program to view a much broader consumption profile than for an individual member, providing new and relevant insights.

---

330 ASICS, https://runkeeper.com/, accessed 29 June 2020.

My Cold Stone Club Rewards

My Cold Stone Club Rewards awards members with 1 point per dollar spent at Cold Stone Creamery, with 25 bonus points for joining. Every time the account reaches 50 points, the points are automatically redeemed for a US$5 voucher.

The program allows up to seven family members to be added to the same account to help accumulate points. Each family member has their own profile and will receive individual birthday offers. The terms and conditions warn that while household pooling allows points to be earned faster with no limits to the amount of US$5 vouchers members can accumulate, this also means family members 'can redeem your rewards'.[331]

Indirect member data collection

Member personal data can also be indirectly sourced by multiple third parties, with the data fed into the loyalty program's systems and matched against individual member profiles. This is primarily facilitated via data brokers, data exchanges and database generators.

Data Brokers

In the digital age, individual consumers are sharing unprecedented amounts of personal data — sometimes overtly and sometimes without being aware. Numerous research articles detail what Google,[332] Facebook,[333] Apple,[334]

---

331 Cold Stone Creamery, FAQ's, https://www.coldstonecreamery.com/faqs/eclub/index.html, accessed 29 May 2020

332 Desjardins, J., 2018, 'What Does Google Know About You', Visual Capitalist, https://www.visualcapitalist.com/what-does-google-know-about-you/, accessed 15 April 2019.

333 Fried, I., 2019, 'What Facebook knows about you', Axios, https://www.axios.com/facebook-personal-data-scope-suer-privacy-de15c860-9153-45b6-95e8-ddac8cd47c34.html, accessed 15 April 2019.

334 Murphy, D., 2018, 'I Asked Apple For Everything It Knows About Me, And Here's What I Found', Life Hacker, https://www.lifehacker.com.au/2018/12/i-asked-apple-for-everything-it-knows-about-me-and-heres-what-i-found/, accessed 15 April

Amazon[335] and many other companies know about individuals, including who they are, where they go, who their friends are, what they like and dislike, their future plans, their online life and much more.

Often member personal data is publicly accessible, such as social media posts. Additional data can come from tracking software in website and apps,[336] plus Wi-Fi. More data to understand members can be sourced from consumer surveys and census data.

Data brokers accumulate masses of information about consumers. They may provide database tools for loyalty programs to help them improve their member profiling, or even provide the data directly to the loyalty program to be matched against existing member profiles. Globally, data brokers 'have highly detailed profiles on billions of individuals, comprising age, race, sex, weight, height, marital status, education level, politics, shopping habits, health issues, holiday plans, social media posts, income and more'.[337]

Data brokers can match the individual member's data against the loyalty programs' existing databases using common denominators such as name, email address and mobile number. Such a service can build a profile for an individual member from tens to hundreds of datasets overnight, making this a valuable service for loyalty programs which use machine learning/AI analytics to generate member insights and power hyper-personalised marketing campaigns.

Data brokers match data to members in three basic ways:

- **User account integration**: a personal identifier in a member's profile (primarily an email, or name and email combination) is matched to the same identifier in the database of the data broker.

2019.

335 Haselton, T., 2018, 'Here's how to find what Amazon knows about you', CNBC, https://www.cnbc.com/2018/04/05/what-does-amazon-know-about-me. html, accessed 15 April 2019.

336 Couts, A., 2019, 'Top 100 websites: How they track your every move online', Digital Trends, https://www.digitaltrends.com/web/top-100-websites-how-are-they-tracking-you/, accessed 16 April 2019.

337 Molitorisz, S., 2018, 'It's time for data brokers to emerge from the shadows', IT News, https://www.itnews.com.au/news/its-time-for-data-brokers-to-emerge-from-the-shadows-488450, accessed 16 April 2019.

- **Mobile ID tracking**: identifiers such as email addresses can be matched to a specific mobile device ID such as Apple's IDFA (Identifier for advertisers),[338] or Google's AAID (Google advertising Identifier),[339] which are shared by partners which also collect this information. Third-party data platform companies may also embed code within their client's apps to track the mobile phone usage of the user, further building out their unified customer data pools.

- **Cookie syncing**: data brokers rely on partners freely sharing their individual member's cookie data which they tag and match with cookies from other independent company data to create matches within their ecosystem of individual devices.

Experian

Experian, a global data broking company, state on their website that 'Consumers are creating large amounts of data every day, and you're capturing it at every moment through your brand, product and service touch points. While this information can be leveraged and used to your advantage, often it doesn't provide you with some of the most important insights you need – going beyond the customer journey to actually get to know the customer.'

They inform potential clients that their platform, 'layers comprehensive information about every household on top of your existing data, giving you unprecedented insights into who your customers are, how they operate, and how best to reach them. Next-level segmentation brings your customers to life with pen portraits, word

---

338 Nichols, J., 2017, 'Mobile Tutorial Series – What is an IDFA or Apple Identifier for Advertisers?', Singular, https://www.singular.net/mobile-tutorial-series-idfa-apple-identifier-advertisers/, accessed 9 April 2019.

339 Google Support, 2019, 'Target mobile apps with IDFA or AAID', Authorized Buyers Help, https://support.google.com/authorizedbuyers/answer/3221407?hl=en, accessed 9 April 2019.

clouds, infographics, animations, interactive maps, bar charts and crosstabs.'[340]

As detailed earlier in this chapter, one challenge many loyalty programs struggle with is utilising the data available to them. Data brokers deliver additional value by not only providing extensive additional data but formatting it in ways that are accessible and user-friendly for programs, enabling them to be better positioned to extract value from their investment.

How trustworthy is broker data? Due to the secretive nature in which data brokers acquire information and create segmented audience data, loyalty program operators should be aware of the issue of potential inaccuracies in the information supplied. Researchers from the Harvard Business Review conducted a review of popular audience segments supplied by a range of brokers and found consumer information sold by brokers varies greatly in quality.[341] For example, demographic data such as age tiers or gender had very low levels of accuracy, whereas other target lists such as interest-based segments had an accuracy of 80 per cent. The findings indicate prospective buyers of data broker lists and audience profiles should be cautious, especially when seeking information for broad segments, which appear to be the least cost-effective.

Acxiom

Acxiom is one of the largest data brokers in the world with 'over 23,000 servers collecting and analysing consumer data, collecting up to 3,000 data points per person'.[342] They track consumers digital footprints online using invisible tracking pixels and combine this with offline information and publicly available records to build rich data assets which they can leverage as part of their data services and solutions product offering.

340 Experian, 'Mosaic', http://www.experian.com.au/mosaic, accessed 9 April 2019.

341 Neumann, N. & Tucker, C., 2020, 'Buying Consumer Data? Tread Carefully', https://hbr.org/2020/05/buying-consumer-data-tread-carefully, accessed 9 June 2020.

342 The Next Web, 2019, 'Loyalty programs cost you your personal data – are the rewards worth it?', https://thenextweb.com/insights/2019/06/12/loyalty-programs-cost-you-your-personal-data-are-the-rewards-worth-it/, accessed 1 June 2020.

Acxiom also conduct propensity modelling and sell this data. For example, whether an individual has an 'online search propensity' for a certain ailment or prescription[343] can be sold to insurance companies which are looking to flag health related risks.

Datalogix

Datalogix are a data collection company that obtains and tracks offline and online data purchasing behaviour patterns alongside information from retailer loyalty programs. Datalogix says it has 'information on more than $1 trillion in consumer spending across 1400 leading brands'.[344]

They have partnered with Facebook to track whether Facebook users who see ads for certain products end up buying the products from local stores to better understand consumer behaviour and improve the various layers of information and communication touchpoints.

Data exchanges

A data exchange is similar to a data broker but operates in a slightly different way. Data exchanges allow companies to share data collected from their customers with other selected companies. This practice can provide loyalty programs with access to many data points, which they can use to build out member profiles. Contributors have full control of what gets exchanged, oversight of its use, and legal rights to protect against misuse. The platform ensures that the use of the data is reasonable and legal and provides a full audit trail for this to be monitored.

---

343 Beckett, L., 2013, 'Everything We Know About What Data Brokers Know about You', ProPublica, https://www.propublica.org/article/everything-we-know-about-what-data-brokers-know-about-you, accessed 1 June 2020.
344 Ibid.

Data Republic

Data Republic is a data exchange platform backed by Westpac's Reinventure, Qantas Loyalty, NAB Ventures, Qualgro and ANZ. According to their website, 'Data Republic has seen rapid adoption of their technology from major brands and service providers across Australia and the Asia Pacific, including banks, retailers, state governments and airlines. Data Republic's technology now underpins a fast-growing ecosystem and network of over 200 organisations who leverage the governance framework and technology as an emerging standard for secure data sharing, globally.'[345]

Database generators

A member database is highly valuable to any company, but they can be difficult to build. Some loyalty programs engage third-party database generators to grow their databases. This is achieved by partnering with other companies who offer online transactions.

For example, a member of a loyalty program may choose to purchase some tickets from the company which runs the program. At the end of the purchase journey, they are presented with offers from other companies. This may be a discount off a hotel stay, a flight, a pizza, a food delivery service, or any manner of products or services. They may also be invited to enter a competition.

The personal data which the member enters is collected by the database generator and provided to the sponsoring company to build their database. The member's personal data may be auto populated if the member is signed into their online account. The member will later begin to receive marketing communications from the company which funded the collection of the data.

The database generator uses powerful machine learning capabilities to deliver highly personalised messaging to target members as a way to boost their conversion rate.

---

345 Data Republic, 'About Us', https://www.datarepublic.com/company/about-us, accessed 16 April 2019.

Rokt

Rokt are a database generator operating around the globe.

Rokt state on their website they use, 'more than 2B user records during the Transaction Moment creating the ability to personalize the creative & user journey using data such as past purchases, event type and demographic.'[346] They also communicate that their algorithms 'consider 1B pieces of data every 40 milliseconds — getting smarter and more predictive with each user action—surfacing the most relevant message for each individual user.'

According to Rokt statistics, consumers making a purchase are two times more likely to engage with marketing offers (leveraging the priming bias), making their approach potentially powerful in building marketing databases.

Member data analysis and usage

Once member data sets are expanded and standardised, a detailed view of members becomes an important asset which can be used to drive revenue growth across multiple business functions. This section explores how member data is used by loyalty programs to achieve these objectives.

Marketing

Data enables the development of more sophisticated communications efforts, such as hyper-personalised digital marketing campaigns. This may include the use of machine learning/AI engines generating individualised messages, prices and product offers. It may also involve delivering messages via a variety of communications channels at specific times of the day which are more likely to generate a desired response from the member. According to Salesforce, 7 per cent of site visitors click on personalised product recommendations, however personalised recommendations account for 26 per cent of revenue.[347]

---

346 Rokt, https://rokt.com/, accessed 16 April 2019.

347 Young, H., 2017, 'Personalized product recommendations drive just 7% of Visits but 26% of Revenue', Salesforce, https://www.salesforce.com/blog/2017/11/personalized-product-recommendations-drive-just-7-visits-26-revenue.html, accessed

Airline industry commentator Mark Ross-Smith reported that airline programs know how much members are willing to pay (i.e. what they have historically paid), what they are not willing to pay (abandoned cart statistics), whether the member is committed to flying that day (based on friends/ colleagues already booked on the flight or whether a hotel is booked) and whether they are travelling for work or pleasure (path to purchase).[348] He theorised that the data is fed into direct booking channels in real time and may be used to customise pricing for the individual's situation.

Retargeting

With the increasing power of computers and the rise of AI, loyalty program data can be overlaid with predictive analytics to dynamically retarget and adjust offers based on individual behaviour patterns across multiple channels.

Retargeting promotions can be delivered via promotional websites, eDMs, apps and SMS to remind the member about a product they may have been considering, sometimes accompanied by an offer.

> **Adidas Creators Club**
>
> Adidas Creators Club[349] provides members with exclusive offers, early access to sales, inclusion in sports communities, free access to the Adidas Runtastic Premium app and birthday bonuses.
>
> Adidas utilise retargeting approaches to promote products which the member may have viewed to increase sales conversions. A member who browses a pair of shoes online may find the same shoes are advertised on a variety of different websites, such as the New York Times, increasing the likelihood they will return to the Adidas website and complete the transaction.
>
> Adidas also sends retargeting eDMs to members to encourage

13 May 2019.

348 Ross-Smith, M., 2015, 'How big data is changing the way you fly', https://www.linkedin.com/pulse/how-big-data-changing-way-you-fly-mark-ross-smith/, accessed 4 April 2019.

349 Adidas Creators Club, https://www.adidas.com.au/creatorsclub, accessed 23 June 2020

them to return to the site after they have detected browsing activity without a purchase. One eDM received by the authors was worded, 'THANKS FOR STOPPING BY. Not sure what size? We offer free returns for 30 days. Looking for the latest items? Check out our new arrivals here.'

Customer service

By knowing more about the member, and their history with the loyalty program and the parent company (e.g. that they are a premium tier member showing a higher than desired churn risk score), the company can tailor customer service support and responses to ensure an optimal outcome. This may also include using automated software programs which prompt the customer service agent to recommend a new product to the member. Data broker companies can provide this data to their clients so that even when an individual may be phoning a company for the first time, specific details about the individual (such as age, salary bracket and location) can be presented to the agent, helping them influence the outcome of the call.

Twilio

Twilio is a cloud communications platform used by companies such as ING, Deliveroo and Zendesk to deliver personalised customer experiences at scale.

By centralising the full member history from their data profile, transactions and conversations in real time, agents can deliver personalised member experiences.

The approach allows for rule-based call routing to ensure high profile customers reach specific call staff instantly.

The platform can also analyse sentiment and spot keywords which can be fed back up into the member's data profile and be used to improve subsequent member interaction.[350]

---

350 Twilio, 'Call Centre API's to Compose Modern Customer Experiences', https://www.twilio.com/learn/contact-center/customer-experience-technology, accessed 19 June 2020.

Segmentation

A standard segmentation approach involves dividing the member base into cohorts with similar characteristics, with the expectation they will be attracted to similar marketing campaigns, offers, products and services.

Examples include:

- **Psychographic**: based on the activities, interests, and opinions of customers.

- **Demographic**: based on age, gender, occupation, income, marital status, life stage, education, ethnicity, religion and more.

- **Geographic**: based on location.

- **Generational**: based on birth date. Assumes that people's values and attitudes are shaped by the key events that have occurred during their lives and that these attitudes translate into product and brand preferences.

- **Cultural**: based on cultural origin and their engagement with products, brands and channels as well as measures of recency, frequency and monetary value.

Segmentation modelling within loyalty programs is becoming increasingly sophisticated. In the past, a program may have utilised a single segmentation model (often based on demographic or transactional characteristics), however best-practice programs in the current era tend to generate multiple models, each of which are tailored to address specific opportunities or challenges.

For example, a program may be seeking to identify segments within its member base which display different propensities to take up credit card products. This segmentation model can be used to better understand the financial service needs among different member cohorts and influence more targeted advertising campaign approaches.

Lexer

Lexer, a customer data platform for retailers, provides sophisticated tools which enable companies to combine their data into an enriched single customer view, then apply machine learning and marketing models to create intelligent analysis and predict what customers will do next.

Lexer enables unique bespoke segments to be created in real time to address specific market opportunities or business challenges.

Member data can be enriched with third-party demographic, location and propensity data, allowing companies to segment by product interest, churn risk, buyer behaviour, campaign or channel preference.

Hyper-personalised marketing campaigns can be executed to any segment in minutes, with triggers supporting channel optimisation. For example, a member may open an eDM which triggers the send of a targeted ad via social media to boost conversion. A member may purchase a product featured in a campaign, and they are automatically removed from further campaign activity to save marketing budget.

Lexer also supports the personalisation of customer care and the in-store experience (topics discussed further in Chapter 11).

Reporting and analytics

Data provides the ability for loyalty program operators and parent companies to generate extensive insights into who members are, how they behave, how they respond to different marketing campaigns and offers, what their consumption patterns are over time, what life-stage they are in, what segments they belong to and more.

In many ways, loyalty program operators today are extremely fortunate compared to their peers in the past. The data analytics available to B.T. Babbitt, The Great Atlantic & Pacific Tea Co., The Grand Union Tea Company, S&H Green Stamps and The United Cigars Store Co. (detailed in Chapter 2) would have been rudimentary at best, limited to the names and addresses of redeeming members, their frequency of redemption and the types of rewards they generally claimed. There is no evidence to suggest how (or if) they used the data for analytics, however it can be assumed data played a role in influencing the evolution of the rewards range.

A loyalty program operator should be able to access data insights via a variety of means, such as standard reporting modules, an automated reporting dashboard, or the use of professional analysts and data scientists. Reporting modules should be flexible to meet the needs of different teams and business requirements. For example, being able to search by specified time periods and country/region/store/online across different campaigns, segments or tiers, and member behaviours.

Reporting dashboards should provide real-time updates, a single view of members across all channels, details of interactions with various online and offline business functions, and campaign results. Most importantly, they should evaluate changes in member behaviour, providing the program operator with real and actionable insights into how the program is driving revenue growth and building brand sentiment over time.

Reporting permissions are important to ensure the relevant persons are provided with the appropriate level of access to reports to be able to extract data insights, while protecting the data from unauthorised access by other parties.

Using data scientists and analysts for data mining can deliver an additional dimension to the quest for richer insights. They can bring technical expertise to validate the quality and accuracy of the data, then process and present relevant insights to support the evolution of the program. They may also play a role in building new reports into reporting modules, as well as evolving the information presented within dashboards.

Data is also important to measure and monitor the effectiveness of the loyalty program. The types of measures available are extensive, and include market research (qualitative and quantitative), social media engagement, marketing communications engagement, return on ad spend, churn rate and reasons, RFM (recency, frequency, monetary value) tracking, repeat purchase ratio, share of wallet, member lifetime value, cost per acquisition, status tier progression and call centre reporting. Financial models and formulas are detailed further in Chapter 14.

Refer to Appendix for a summary list of the types of reporting insights a loyalty program operator may wish to develop and utilise. The list provided is a guide only and will vary for different program designs, business structures and industries.

> **Best Western Rewards**
>
> Best Western International Inc owns the Best Western Hotels and Resorts brand which they licence to over 4,500 hotels in their global network across over 100 countries.
>
> With loyalty of paramount importance to the brand, Best Western Hotels adopted a strategy to leverage their member data to drive Best Western Rewards sign-ups and incrementality through the creation of relevant browsing experiences.
>
> They did this through tailored scenarios communicated to different customer groups:
>
> - Non logged-in members: those searching for a one-night or two-night stay received a pop-up communication with a relevant incentive to create an account and prolong their stay.
>
> - Logged-in members: those searching for a one-night stay received a pop-up communication with an incentive to prolong their stay.
>
> - Logged-in members searching for multiple night's stay: this was the desired member behaviour, so no additional incentive was provided.
>
> This personalised messaging approach had a significant effect on engagement with the most successful scenario (non-logged-in members searching for multiple night's stay) generating a 12 per cent increase in Best Western Rewards program sign-ups.[351]
>
> This strategy used member browsing data to deliver relevancy to the right members at the right time to stimulate desired behaviours, protect profit margins and generate additional member insights.

---

351 AB Tasty, 'How Best Western Hotels & Resorts Increased Loyalty Program Engagement', https://www.abtasty.com/resources/best-western-personalization/, accessed 1 July 2020.

Inventory management and product development

Data helps companies understand how customers are using their products and services, the reasons why, what they like and dislike, and any new features they might enjoy (and ideally pay more for). Data collected via loyalty programs plays an important role in inventory management, particularly for companies which have large product offerings (such as supermarkets and liquor retailers) or those which need to forecast sales levels up to twelve months out to optimise yields (such as airlines and hotels). Data also plays a critical role in the development of new products, as it allows for complex modelling to forecast the operational and profit impacts such innovations might deliver.

Lifecycle and life-stage journey

For members who engage with a loyalty program or company over a longer period of time, data will allow the loyalty program to determine the evolution of their lifecycle journey (how they change the way they interact with the company and its products over time) and life-stage journey (how their life situation changes over time), and the relevance of those changes to the company. These valuable insights can be utilised to maintain loyalty by leading the member along a consumption pathway by predicting which products will suit them at specific times and introducing those products with suitable messaging and offers.

Member lifecycle management is a critical underpinning of successful loyalty programs, and is covered in detail in Chapter 12.

Security and fraud monitoring

Security breaches and fraudulent activity are extensive in loyalty programs. Loyalty fraud is defined as where deception is used to intentionally secure unfair financial, personal or third-party gains from loyalty programs.

While security protocols provide the best opportunity to prevent fraud from happening, if (or when) it does happen, effective data monitoring processes will enable instances to be quickly identified, neutralised and prevented from occurring again.

To mitigate security and fraud risks, program operators want to quickly identify unusual earn and redemption activity, accounts created by bots, account take-over instances, and even database breaches.

Chapter 16 covers the potential risks and mitigation strategies associated with specific loyalty security and fraud instances.

Sharing and reselling insights to third parties

Major loyalty programs sell and share insights from their data, and data-powered marketing services, to generate additional revenue streams.

The monetisation of member personal data is covered In Chapter 14.

Member awareness and attitudes about personal data collection and usage

Research indicates members are becoming increasingly aware that loyalty programs are collecting personal information about them. They are also realising that their personal data has a tangible value, and they appear to be more willing to share their data with preferred brands and companies. Members expect that they will be rewarded for sharing or that the data will be used to personalise and enhance their experience engaging with that brand or company.

A 2017 global research report by Deloitte showed a marked increase in recent years in consumer willingness to share browsing history and social media activity data with 'companies whose products or services (they) purchase' although it was still a relatively low 15 per cent.[352]

A 2018 report by US firm Adlucent titled 'Data Wars' determined that 'seven out of ten consumers prefer content and advertising that is tailored to their personal interests and shopping habits', and most importantly, consumers are willing to provide 'a wide array of information ranging from name and email address to product preferences and updates on major life updates in order to get the personalized experiences they want'.[353] The challenge for loyalty programs is one of transparency. While consumers are increasingly willing to share personal data with preferred brands and programs, the Adlucent

---

352 Pingitore, G., Rao, V., Cavallaro, K., & Dwivedi, K., 2017, 'To share or not to share', Deloitte, https://www2.deloitte.com/insights/us/en/industry/retail-distribution/sharing-personal-information-consumer-privacy-concerns.html, accessed 16 April 2019.

353 McFarling, A., 2018, 'Data Wars: Information's Role in the New Era of Advertising', Adlucent, https://www.adlucent.com/blog/2018/data-wars-informations-role-in-the-new-era-of-advertising, accessed 17 April 2019.

report indicated that '96 per cent want brands to be more transparent about the collection and use of their personal data'.

A 2016 global report by loyalty agency Aimia indicated consumers are 'increasingly aware of the value of their personal data' and would put a price tag from $50 (Australia) to $70 (Germany) to $120 (South Korea) on their personal data if they could.[354] Snap My Eats, a case study featured earlier in this chapter, is an example of a transparent data exchange between members and a program for a cash-equivalent reward.

The Aimia report also found 71 per cent of global respondents believed their preferred brands are good at using their data to make online shopping experiences better, yet 77 per cent would like more control over what data companies hold on them. Transparency can also work to the loyalty program's advantage. For example, while 52 per cent said they would provide their mobile phone number without any context, the figure increased to 69 per cent when companies provided an explanation as to why they were asking for it.

Attitudes about sharing data differ across cultures. A 2018 Asia-Pacific survey by Mastercard reported 46 per cent of Japanese respondents would be willing to share personal information with their loyalty programs to receive more relevant experiences or benefits. This increased to 64 per cent for Australia, South Korea and Hong Kong, and up to 87 per cent for China, Indonesia and India.[355]

There is sharing and then there is taking. Research indicates members are not always aware of what type of information is being collected about them, and they seek more control and transparency over what data is collected and used. A report from the Consumer Policy Research Centre (CPRC) indicates consumers do not appear to read privacy policies which are designed to inform them of the ways in which their data is collected, used and shared.[356]

---

354 Cameron, N., 2016, 'Report: Aussie consumers value their online behavioural data at $50', CMO, https://www.cmo.com.au/article/611697/report-aussie-consumers-value-their-online-behavioural-data-50/, accessed 17 April 2019.

355 Mastercard, 2017, 'Achieving Advocacy and Influence in a Changing Loyalty Landscape', p22, https://newsroom.mastercard.com/asia-pacific/files/2018/01/Loyalty-Solutions-Whitepaper.-AP-Region-20171.pdf, accessed 16 April 2019.

356 Nguyen, P., & Solomon, L., 2017, 'Consumer data and the digital economy – Emerging issues in data collection, use and sharing', Consumer Policy Research

Key insights

- Loyalty programs can play a key role in the entire data value chain by facilitating the collection of member personal data, utilising loyalty platforms to analyse the data, and harnessing the insights generated to stimulate deeper member engagement by using sophisticated segmentation and lifecycle management models. This allows loyalty program operators to determine and subsequently influence when, why and how members engage with the program.

- Member personal data is collected directly by loyalty programs via the join process, digital interactions, transactions, surveys, apps, virtual home assistants, social media and household patterns.

- Data may also be collected indirectly via data brokers, data exchanges and database generators.

- Data is analysed and used to support marketing, retargeting, customer service, segmentation, reporting and analytics, inventory management, product development, lifecycle management, and security and fraud monitoring.

- Consumers are becoming increasingly aware that loyalty programs are collecting personal information about them, and that their data has a tangible value. They appear to be more willing to share their data with preferred brands and companies, but with the expectation they will be rewarded for sharing or that the data will be used to personalise and enhance their experience.

Suggested reading

- Van Rijmenam, M., 2013, 'A Short History Of Big Data, Datafloq, https://datafloq.com/read/big-data-history/239

- Cleary, Gillian, 2018, 'Mobile Privacy: What Do Your Apps Know

Centre, http://cprc.org.au/wp-content/uploads/Full_Data_Report_A4_FIN.pdf, accessed 17 April 2019.

About You?', Symantec Corporation, https://www.symantec.com/blogs/threat-intelligence/mobile-privacy-apps

- Molitorisz, Sacha, 2018, 'It's time for data brokers to emerge from the shadows', IT News, https://www.itnews.com.au/news/its-time-for-data-brokers-to-emerge-from-the-shadows-488450

- Ross-Smith, Mark, 2015, 'How big data is changing the way you fly', https://www.linkedin.com/pulse/how-big-data-changing-way-you-fly-mark-ross-smith/

- Nguyen, P., & Solomon, L., 2017, 'Consumer data and the digital economy – Emerging issues in data collection, use and sharing', Consumer Policy Research Centre, http://cprc.org.au/wp-content/uploads/Full_Data_Report_A4_FIN.pdf

CHAPTER 11

LOYALTY TECHNOLOGY AND EMERGING CAPABILITIES

'Artificial intelligence and machine learning are completely changing the way businesses deliver services and understand their potential customers. Though technology is no alternative to personalized human interactions in the hospitality business, in some circumstances tech simply does a better job.'

- Wajid Hussain, Advanced Hospitality Technologies, 2020[357]

Focus areas

This chapter will address the following questions:

- What role does technology play in the execution of best-practice loyalty programs?

- What are the types of technology solution providers available?

- What capabilities does a world-class loyalty platform incorporate?

- What are some of the emerging and major trends driven by technology within the loyalty industry?

LOYALTY TECHNOLOGY PLAYS an increasingly critical role in the execution

---

357 Wajid, H.,2020, 'Hotels are leveraging artificial intelligence to grow loyalty & revenue in 2020', Advanced Hospitality Industries, http://blog.advhtech.com/hotels-are-leveraging-artificial-intelligence-in-2020/ , accessed 19 July 2019.

of best-practice programs. In the opinion of the authors, the ultimate manifestation of loyalty technology application and operation is Digital EQ. Coined by Max Savransky,[358] the term refers to 'the ability to anticipate and recognise customer sentiment and deliver a digitally enabled response which optimises the customer experience in real time, serving to build a deeper emotional connection.'

This chapter reviews the core capabilities which leading loyalty platforms deliver, and explores technological innovations which support emerging and major loyalty trends, and the realisation of Digital EQ.

Loyalty technology platforms

Loyalty platforms have traditionally been expensive and lacking in flexibility, but more recently a range of high-quality, cost-effective platforms have entered the market, delivering companies the ability to better realise their innovative visions, while making the loyalty technology industry increasingly competitive.

Some of the best platforms available are less than 10 years old. They have been designed for easy Application Programming Interface (API) integration with other systems and provide highly complex campaign capabilities, app and digital wallet support, automated machine learning capabilities and extensive analytics functionality.

The purpose of the technology

A loyalty platform is ultimately a rules engine. Best-practice platforms can support complex rules supporting all manner of campaigns, earn promotions and tier progression. The loyalty program operator can feed in different transaction data (such as the date and time, product Stock Keeping Unit (SKU), cost and retailer), personal data (such as a member identifier, demographic data and status tier) and offers, and the platform can apply a range of rules in real time to deliver a variety of specified outcomes designed to generate member engagement. This may be bonus points, cashback, new status tiers, product discounts or many other rewards.

---

358 Savransky, M., 2020, 'The Power of Digital EQ', Loyalty & Reward Co, https://www.rewardco.com.au/the-power-of-digital-eq/ accessed 24 June 2020.

Platforms can support multi-step campaigns, whereby the member must complete a series of transactions and tasks to unlock a benefit, with each step tracked and recorded as the member progresses. Platforms also allow for advanced gamification campaigns and are useful for supporting automated member lifecycle marketing approaches.

Types of loyalty technology solution providers

Loyalty platform solution providers can be categorised into four main groups:

- **Full-service loyalty solutions**: provided by specialised loyalty agencies which deliver everything required to run the loyalty program as part of an outsourced approach. Services include delivery of a loyalty program website and/or app with the client's branding, the back-end platform holding member accounts and points balances, status tier and profile data, customer service support, analytics processing, supply of reward products, account management, consulting services for the future evolution of the loyalty program, full life-cycle marketing management (including trigger emails at key points of the member journey) and customer care support. With this type of solution, the client rarely has direct access to the platform itself, as it is generally limited to agency personnel.

- **Partial service loyalty solutions**: focused more on the technology rather than a full-service offering, but with the option to provide additional support if required. This solution usually allows the clients to have direct access to their platform, with the platform enabling the running of the loyalty program, rather than the service provider actually running it. The agency (usually a smaller agency) may also provide some marketing strategy formulation and execution, reward support co-ordination and customer care support, as required.

- **Off-the-shelf loyalty solutions**: come with an extensive array of features and functions that will deliver to most needs of a client looking to launch a loyalty program or replace the legacy platform of their existing loyalty program. They are designed to be user-friendly and configurable to minimise the amount of additional client support required post-launch. This type of platform is suitable for program operators seeking maximum control over their operations.

- **Niche loyalty solutions**: may provide a partial solution which solves a specific problem. Niche agencies specialise and excel in their area of expertise, with the ability to solve an issue effectively and efficiently, however additional technical solutions may be required to run the complete loyalty program. An example is a company providing a solution to support the collection of member transaction data across multiple disparate point of sale (POS) systems or from third-party retailers.

Best-practice loyalty platform capabilities

A loyalty platform's core capabilities are typically comprised of six areas. These are Integrations, Product, Marketing Execution, Financial Management, Security and Data Protection, and Account Management and Support. A loyalty program operator should consider all these areas and determine what is most important for them at time of program launch and for post-launch operations.

Post-launch considerations are important, as the program operator needs to ensure the platform will be able to scale to support their expansion plans without incurring significant additional cost.

1. Integrations:

- **Application programming interface (API's):** a set of programming code that enables data transmission between the loyalty platform and other systems. It also contains the terms of this data exchange.

- **Out of the box vendor integrations**: many loyalty platforms have existing integrations to major vendors (such as Salesforce, Twilio, etc).

- **Software development kit (SDK):** an installable package which can be integrated into a client's existing App to provide a gateway to all platform capabilities.

- **Social media monitor**: an automated monitoring tool which would typically be integrated with the major social media networks.

- **Reward partners**: integration with established reward supply partners to support automatic fulfilment (e.g. gift cards, movie vouchers) or order submission and tracking (e.g. consumer goods). This may extend to third-party partners where members can redeem points in real-time when transacting online or in-store.

2. Product:

- **Customer data platform (CDP)**: a unified customer database which combines multiple data sources into a single member view. This ideally will include zero/first party data and permissions.

- **Loyalty rules engine**: a configurable engine which underpins calculations for earning, redeeming, expiry, tiering, games, gamification, and anything else that requires rule sets and subsequent execution.

- **Offer management and promotion engine**: a configurable engine which provides the ability to set-up and deliver coupons, discounts, points bonuses and other offer types to members.

- **Analytics:** a reporting engine with pre-built loyalty metrics and customisable dashboards, which can be viewed within the platform or exported in several different file formats.

- **User interfaces:** platform access portals for different users within the business.

- **Multi market:** capability which supports global programs via a multi-language back-end and the ability to display and transact in multiple currencies.

- **Reward store**: a white label e-commerce store for members to use their points (or any other loyalty currency) to redeem for a range of reward options.

3. Marketing execution

- **Machine learning/AI:**

  - Machine learning involves creating algorithms that can recognise patterns in large, evolving data sets, and drawing conclusions from past experience by using that data.[359]

  - Artificial intelligence is the field of computer science that is associated with the concept of machines 'thinking like humans' to perform tasks such as learning, problem-solving, planning, reasoning and identifying patterns.[360]

  - Autonomous decisioning engines powered by machine learning/AI can process models such as affinity, propensity, churn risk, market and basket analysis, offer optimisation, Next Best Action and more. For marketing, the models can be designed to identify and send the right offer to the right customer at the right time, then learn from the member's response. Very few loyalty platforms provide full AI, with most operating machine learning modules which require manual intervention to train and evolve.

- **Communications:** campaign builder and messaging engine capability which supports multi-channel member engagement via in-app messaging, notifications, emails, SMS, direct mail, and other channels. It should also support multi-step campaigns.

- **Customer feedback loop:** survey and sentiment modules which can collect member feedback across various touch points based on pre-determined rules.

---

359 Burnett, S., 2018, 'Customer Loyalty Trend: Artificial Intelligence' Customer Insight Group, https://www.customerinsightgroup.com/loyaltyblog/loyalty-marketing/loyalty-trend-artificial-intelligence accessed 23 June 2020.
360 Ibid.

- **A/B testing:** ability to run marketing communication tests, where subject lines, designs, content and offers are compared for effectiveness and then fed back in.

- **Zero-party data capture:** ability to run campaigns to capture zero and first-party data and permissions (e.g. questionnaire, poll, quiz, social story).

- **Personalisation/segmentation:** capability to personalise campaigns at segmented and individual member level, leveraging any type of rewards currency available within the platform. This capability should work in tandem with the Offer Management & Promotion Engine.

- **Geolocation:** capability which captures user location data via a front-end app (once permission has been enabled) and then uses that data to enable marketing communications based on a wide range of criteria.

- **Referral:** capability to run automated friend-get-friend campaigns which reward both existing and new members, either immediately or after transactions have been completed.

- **Chatbots:** customer service support, with the option to support other system users, such as marketing.

4. Financial management

- **Points management:** capability to track and report points earn, burn and expiry activities across specified timeframes to manage points liabilities.

- **Billing and reporting:** capability to export transaction data into accounting systems to raise invoices or credit notes for third-party partners.

5. Security & data protection

- **Full compliance:** with GDPR and other regulatory requirements, fraud protection capabilities and proper adherence to best-practice data hosting (this could be an on-premises server, or AWS, Azure, etc).

- **Fraud monitoring:** automated fraud monitoring and reporting (ideally facilitated by machine learning/AI), including alerts for unusual activity and automatic freezing of suspicious accounts.

6. Account management and support

- **Helpdesk and technical support:** telephone and email support to address issues with different levels of criticality. This is primarily related to platform functions.

- **Program management:** primarily related to program operations functions and usually only available with the full-service or partial service loyalty platforms. They may engage external consultants to support managing functions such as campaign set-up, rewards store management, reporting and strategic evolution.

Technological innovation and emerging capabilities

Extensive innovation and the evolution of trends within the loyalty industry has led to the development of a wide range of complimentary technology solutions. These are used to enhance existing platforms or implement different types of engagement strategies altogether.

This section reviews loyalty trends and technology, with supportive examples of how they are being applied.

Utilising machine learning and AI within loyalty programs to deliver members more relevant experiences and communications is a major emerging trend.

Machine learning and AI

Advances in member personal data collection techniques, data science and computing are allowing specialised data agencies working on behalf of loyalty programs to develop, analyse and monetise datasets, generate insights, create decision support tools and embed automated decision engines into loyalty platforms.

These agencies employ teams of actuaries, statisticians, data scientists, product leaders, strategy consultants, software engineers, delivery managers, industry experts, designers, and futurists to capture, process and apply data on behalf of large loyalty programs seeking deeper member engagement, optimisation of marketing spend and a competitive edge.

Some of the services provided include in-depth analysis of brand and product performance, advertising effectiveness analysis, identifying high-priority shoppers and profiling their behaviour, developing unique member profiles, and delivering individualised marketing communications to millions of members.

Ways in which machine learning/AI is being employed to power loyalty programs are detailed below.

AI-powered marketing communications

While mass market offers (e.g. double points bonuses) can be highly effective in driving incremental visits and spend, they can also be costly and inefficient (e.g. the member may have already been intending to visit anyway, hence the additional promotional cost was unnecessary). An opportunity exists to optimise promotional activity to reduce overall program spend.

Machine learning/AI-powered marketing execution can automatically construct and send individualised communications to members across a variety of channels, then track responses and evolve future communications to optimise engagement potential. Their ability to serve up individualised communications to members across a variety of channels makes them highly effective, while helping to reduce marketing costs.

AI-powered marketing execution are primarily the domain of larger loyalty programs due to the cost and the enormous amount of data required to optimise the algorithms.

Jason Nathan, *dunnhumby*'s global managing director, directly referred to using member data to personalise communications and offers as a way for retailers to fight disruptive challengers like Aldi in the supermarket space. 'If you're up against somebody selling 2000 products at 10 per cent cheaper then clearly you have to do something different, and that something different is going to be able to stay in a personalised conversation with your customers.'[361]

A May 2019 Credit Suisse report[362] indicated that major supermarkets 'are almost uniquely positioned to leverage their growing digital capabilities to establish a competitive advantage in the promotional expenditure component of the food retail value chain. With material efficiency benefits feasible, it is likely that growing digitally-led efficiency will support market share gain and outperformance'. This includes the ability to offer discounts on products to members who are price sensitive, while charging full price to customers who regularly buy the product, with machine learning/AI tracking the campaign's success and adjusting accordingly.

The Nordy Club

Since 2015, Nordstrom[363] have been making conscious decisions to invest in digital. They began their phased approach to using AI by focusing first on identifying potential customer cohorts which shop with Nordstrom's discount brand (Nordstrom Rack) who may be willing to pay for full price Nordstrom items.[364] Converting the right customers from their existing member base was a way of improving product margins and decreasing customer acquisition costs.

Early in 2018, Nordstrom then invested in the BevyUp and

---

361 Hatch, P., 2019, 'Winning your loyalty: Australia's retail data war is heating up', Sydney Morning Herald, https://www.smh.com.au/business/companies/winning-your-loyalty-australia-s-retail-data-war-is-heating-up-20181221-p50npy.html, accessed 30 May 2019.

362 Credit Suisse, 2019, 'Asia Pacific/Australia Equity Research Food & Drug Retailing', accessed 30 May 2019.

363 Nordstrom, https://shop.nordstrom.com/, accessed 30 June 2020.

364 Townsend, T., 2018, 'How Nordstrom tapped into a century's worth of customer data', https://venturebeat.com/2018/08/21/how-nordstrom-tapped-into-a-centurys-worth-of-customer-data/#:~:text=Nordstrom%20is%20looking%20to%20continue,had%20bought%20BevyUp%20and%20MessageYes., accessed 30 June 2020.

MessageYes platforms to continue their momentum in the AI space by delivering style advice and personalised messages to members at strategic times from which they can purchase items.[365]

Nordstrom now leverage AI technology across both online and brick-and-mortar stores with a focus on personal shopping, style advice and local order collection services, with AI integrated across fulfilment, distribution, customer experience and loyalty.

Pixoneye

Pixoneye[366] SDK identifies numerous features within digital photos on a smartphone and condenses them into a single vector, representing the entire gallery. This can be matched to pre-programmed characteristics (e.g. water sports enthusiast, foodie, married with children). These insights are then presented on a dashboard which makes it easy for loyalty programs to tailor customer experiences to individual users.

Pixoneye's technology can predict when a member is going through a life-changing event – including the moments that matter most, such as marriage, moving home or having a baby. This enables companies to tailor their services directly to members in real-time.

AI-powered personalised digital experiences

Another area where AI platforms are being applied to hyper-personalise member experiences and communications is websites and apps.

AI platforms can identify individual members when they are engaging with a range of digital channels, access their profile information (encompassing

---

365 Ibid.

366 Peverelli, R., de Feniks, R., 2018, 'Pixoneye: analyses personal photo galleries using AI to help companies truly understand their mobile consumers & personalize their experience', https://www.digitalinsuranceagenda.com/245/pixoneye-analyses-personal-photo-galleries-using-ai-to-help-companies-truly-understand-their-mobile-consumers--personalize-their-experience/, accessed 30 June 2020.

hundreds of datasets) and automatically trigger a relevant promotion to stimulate a desired behaviour from the member.

The platforms use cookies, member logins, app tracking software and other methods to track browsing and shopping behaviour. AI is then harnessed to determine the right offer to provide to the member at the right time to maximise the chances of generating a specific outcome, which in most cases will be the purchase of a featured product, an increase in overall spend or the completion of check-out. The approach is designed to optimise advertising spend by ensuring budgets are invested in activities which have the maximum impact.

One advancement which is designed to support the manifestation of Digital EQ is AI which reads human facial expressions online to determine nuanced emotions and complex cognitive states. This allows digital technology to recognise member sentiment and respond with an appropriate digital experience.

Domino's and Tealium

Global player Tealium[367] provide AI capabilities to Domino's to grow online and app order spend and completion of transactions. The new capabilities have enabled the business to empower stakeholders on an international scale to make more timely data-driven decisions for user segmentation and marketing campaigns.

Spotify

Hundreds of millions of Spotify users receive new playlists tailored to their own tastes every single week, all generated by AI and machine learning. The brand uses a recommendation engine, a system which processes data to help subscribers find what they want and identify things they might be interested in based on preferences and previous behaviours.

Spotify's engine uses a combination of three models: collaborative

---

367 Tealium, https://tealium.com/products/standardize-data/, accessed 30 June 2020.

filtering (analysing and comparing an individual's behaviour to other people's taste), natural language processing (analysing text from the lyrics and the internet for key terms that describe a song or artist), and audio modelling (processing the raw audio of a song and matching it with songs of similar likeness). By combining this information, the engine can recommend new songs with a strong certainty of user interest.[368]

Features like Discover Weekly and the Daily Mix lend to the popularity of Spotify, as they provide more personalised experiences and unexpected delights. These engage the member and encourage repeat usage of the platform, leading to the formation of habitual behaviour.

Affectiva

Affectiva use 'computer vision, speech analytics, deep learning and a lot of data'[369] to analyse human states in context. Having analysed close to ten million faces and expressions, their AI-powered algorithm can detect human emotions, cognitive states, behaviours, activities and objects people use in real time.

Large scale analysis of emotional responses can be valuable to a loyalty program in providing predictive analytics, purchase intent recognition or friction point detection for each member, with the ability to adapt and tailor the member experience in real time based on their emotions.

AI-powered in-store personalisation

Some retail stores have begun to experiment with AI in ways which have the potential to change the traditional retail experience for good. AI is being applied directly to the in-store experience, whereby members can receive

---

368 Sen, I., 'How AI helps Spotify win in the music streaming world', https://outsideinsight.com/insights/how-ai-helps-spotify-win-in-the-music-streaming-world/, accessed 30 June 2020.

369 Affectiva, https://www.affectiva.com/, accessed 22 July 2020.

real-time recommendations, virtual assistants, and test products without physically trying them on. This level of hyper-personalisation in-store enriches the member experience and aids purchase decision stimulation.

Sephora

Customers of Sephora can walk into a store and find the perfect makeup shade by having their face scanned with Color IQ and Lip IQ systems.[370] The technology captures a customer's exact skin or lip tone and matches it with data from an existing 'shade library', producing a unique code and personalised recommendations. Once this code is added to a member's loyalty program account, recommendations are automatically applied as filters to online and mobile product searches and catalogue displays.

Uniqlo

Clothing store Uniqlo rolled out AI-powered kiosks to select stores that measure member facial reactions to a variety of colours and styles and provides recommendations based on the individual's reactions.

Kroger

Supermarket chain Kroger partnered with Microsoft to create a personalised shopping experience with smart shelves.[371] With the Kroger app open on their phone, members can walk down the aisle and sensors will highlight products the member might be interested in buying based on account information and previous shopping history. It also provides dynamic personalised pricing and will

370 Milnes, H., 2016, 'How Color IQ, Sephora's shade-matching skin care tool, boosts brand loyalty', Digiday, https://digiday.com/marketing/color-iq-sephoras-shade-matching-skin-care-tool-boosts-brand-loyalty/, accessed 30 June 2020.

371 Retail Insight, 2019, 'Kroger and Microsoft to launch new connected store concept', https://www.retail-insight-network.com/news/kroger-microsoft-connected-store/, accessed 30 June 2020.

show ads and point out items of interest, making the shopping experience efficient and convenient.

7-Eleven

7-Eleven is introducing facial recognition technology to its 11,000 stores in Thailand.[372] The technology will be used to identify loyalty members, analyse in-store traffic, monitor stock levels, recommend products and measure emotions while in the store.

Amazon Go

Amazon Go[373] is a chain of concept stores by the online retailer Amazon allowing members to conveniently purchase products without being checked by a cashier or using a self-checkout station. The 'Just Walk Out' system uses several technologies, including computer vision and deep learning algorithms to automate much of the steps associated with a traditional retail transaction. Several technology firms have emerged offering Amazon Go-like technologies to retailers; some of which are being trialled by major supermarket chains like Tesco in the UK and Giant Eagle in the US.

In-store personalisation can also be delivered via other technologies outside AI which also work to ensure the shopping experience for members is as hassle-free and convenient as possible. Members can choose to be identified, or self-identify, when they enter a store to be provided with a customised experience.

Additional technology utilised to identify members includes RFID, Wi-Fi tracking, beacons, facial recognition software and iPads.

372 Chan, T., 2018, '7-Eleven is bringing facial-recognition technology pioneered in China to its 11,000 stores in Thailand', Business Insider, https://www.businessinsider.com.au/7-eleven-facial-recognition-technology-introduced-in-thailand-2018-3?r=US&IR=T, accessed 30 June 2020.

373 Tillman, M., 2020, 'What is Amazon Go, where is it, and how does it work', https://www.pocket-lint.com/phones/news/amazon/139650-what-is-amazon-go-where-is-it-and-how-does-it-work, accessed 30 June 2020.

Musti Group Finland

Musti Group Finland[374] have invented a world first member recognition program for pets. 'Biscuit' is a smart collar with an RFID chip that recognises the pet, rather than the owner, when they walk into a pet store.

This gives staff access to 'personal dog data' including their name and birthday, favourite treat, and shopping history. A picture of the dog flashes up on a screen when they enter the store as a personalised welcome.

The program works to build an emotional connection with pet owners through pet owners deep emotional connection with their pets.

AI-powered virtual try-ons

Consumer brands are rolling out virtual try-on technology to allows members to try on clothes, shoes, cosmetics and more using the webcam on phones or laptops, or screens installed in stores.

The technology allows brands to load thousands (or even millions) of items into the platform for members to try. More advanced platforms can utilise member data to generate general recommendations, as well as suggesting items which complete their wider wardrobe.

Zeekit

Zeekit have developed the first dynamic virtual fitting room technology now adopted by large retail clothing brands including ASOS, Macy's, Modcloth, Net-a-Porter, Adidas and more.

Based on real-time image processing, Zeekit can map a member's image into thousands of segments with the equivalent points mapped against each piece of clothing to simulate how the garment and fabric will fit and fall.[375]

---

374 Musti Group, https://www.mustigroup.com/, accessed 30 June 2020.

375 Zeekit, https://zeekit.me/, accessed 22 July 2020.

Members are provided with ultra-convenience, whilst retail brands are provided with a large amount of additional data and upsell/cross-sell opportunities. This became particularly relevant with the Covid-19 pandemic when physically trying clothing on in-store was not possible, allowing retailers to not only stay alive, but to thrive.

Yael Vizel, the co-founder of Zeekit reported that 'shoppers who use the company's artificial intelligence to virtually try on clothing are five times more likely to purchase the item'. She also notes that member's 'are also more likely to keep what they buy with a reduction in return rates from 38 per cent to about 2 per cent'.[376]

Conversational AI

Conversational AI refers to the use of messaging and speech-based virtual assistants to automate communications and create personalised customer experiences at scale. These technologies are fuelled by the rise of messaging apps, voice assistant platforms and general advancements in AI, including deep learning and natural language understanding.

The most rudimentary form of conversational machine learning/AI currently in use is chatbots. Chatbots are primarily language text interfaces designed for a specific purpose. They typically follow linear-driven interaction based on predefined rules and are therefore restricted by the bot's limited understanding of conversation and inability to learn. Many online retailers and airlines have recognised the benefits of chatbots particularly in terms of improved efficiencies for customer support. However, since the rules are handwritten, developers must anticipate all scenarios of human interaction, and this presents some obvious problems.

True conversational AI is the next step where machines will be capable of understanding and responding to human language and behaviour in real-time, learn from these experiences, and then apply these learnings to future conversations. These intelligent assistants will not be limited by the functions anticipated by a programmer. This nascent technology will present new ways

---

376 Bhattarai, A., 2020, 'Virtual try-ons are replacing fitting rooms during the pandemic', https://www.washingtonpost.com/business/2020/07/09/virtual-try-ons-are-replacing-fitting-rooms-during-pandemic/, accessed 22 July 2020.

for brands to appear more lifelike, respond contextually and personally at scale, and shift the brand-customer dynamic from many-to-one to one-to-one.

KLM's BlueBot

KLM Royal Dutch Airlines implemented an AI-powered assistant, named BlueBot or BB, as a sustainable solution which supports the scale of its servicing team.[377] Available across all existing conversational platforms and virtual assistants, BB automates simple customer queries like finding a destination, booking a flight, and providing holiday preparation tips. BB helps make the customer journey as stress-free as possible and frees up time for human assistants to focus efforts where required.

Nestle's NINA

Nestlé India has built NINA (Nestlé India Nutrition Assistant), an AI-powered nutrition assistant.[378] Available via an online platform name AskNestlé, parents can track how their children are growing in relation to a paediatric database, get answers to daily nutrition questions and tips, and receive custom meal plans based on regional preferences and allergies. The system is designed to help parents and their children with real-time, personalised advice on nutrition which is relevant and accessible.

Rose, the Hotel Chatbot

The Cosmopolitan of Las Vegas is a luxury casino and resort which encourages hotel guests to interact with their virtual assistant during their stay. The hotel chatbot, known as Rose, is designed with a unique voice with over 1,000 conversation threads to offer

---

377 KLM, https://bb.klm.com/en, accessed 30 June 2020.

378 Deoras, S., 2019, ⊠Nestlé India Introduces NINA, A Virtual Nutrition Assistant In Association With Senseforth', Analytics India, https://analyticsindiamag.com/nestle-india-introduces-nina-a-virtual-nutrition-assistant-in-association-with-senseforth/, accessed 30 June 2020.

guests ways to book experiences such as restaurant reservations, spa treatments, events tickets, and other exciting adventures.

Rose can provide recommendations based on what the guest desires and provide insider information like secret menu items to drive guests to specific bars, clubs, and restaurants. For example, a guest can ask 'What should I have to drink?' and Rose may make a special drink recommendation which is not on the menu, both assisting and delighting the guest.[379]

AI-powered security and fraud monitoring

In addition to enhancing the member experience, machine learning/AI are being applied to protect programs and their members from security breaches and fraud. The advantage of an algorithm-based monitoring approach is speed, volume of account reviews, and the ability to learn and adapt to changing circumstances.

GetPlus Loyalty

GetPlus, a leading coalition loyalty program in Indonesia, utilise a fraud-management system powered by AI. With GetPlus OCR within the membership mobile app, members can scan their receipts from participating merchants to earn GetPlus reward points at their convenience.

According to Adrian Hoon (COO of Global Point Indonesia, the leading operator of the GetPlus program in Indonesia),[380] the AI system includes configurable, action-based scoring rules to evaluate the risk of loyalty fraud in real time. If a high-risk earn order is identified, it is suspended to be reviewed by human operators, or is automatically cancelled.

---

379 R/GA, https://www.rga.com/work/case-studies/rose-the-hotel-chatbot, accessed 30 June 2020.

380 Hoon, A., 'How AI can drive customer loyalty programs', The Jakarta Post, Feb 2020, https://www.thejakartapost.com/life/2020/02/20/how-ai-can-drive-customer-loyalty-programs.html accessed 24 June 2020

> The fraud-detection capability also provides reports to be actively monitored, and orders can be analysed by risk status. It can also make modifications to scoring algorithms as patterns of fraud change.

Machine learning/AI limitations and challenges

While the potential of machine learning/AI is significant, there are also some limitations and other challenges which need to be considered:

- **Data**: there is a direct relationship between the richness of data and the capability of a machine learning/AI application, meaning large volumes of clean data is critical. If the loyalty program systems are unable to provide this, the quality of the output will be compromised.[381]

- **Marketing stack**: the primary limitation of applying machine learning/AI to a marketing function lies in system constraints. These primarily come from the inputs into the model, the algorithms available to the model and/or the actions the model is capable of driving. Disparate, disconnected marketing systems can present a major obstacle. With a loss of the connection between data points, the machine learning/AI algorithms are only able to assess some behaviour in aggregate versus individual use cases. Delays in gathering data (e.g. batch process) will also limit the ability to act in real time or near real time.[382]

- **Responsiveness to rapid changes**: machine-learning/AI execution is not always operationally smooth and can be sensitive to changes in human behaviour. For instance, at the start of the Covid-19 pandemic, the top selling products on Amazon switched from phone cases, phone chargers and Lego to toilet paper, hand sanitiser and

---

381 Roetzer, P., '6 Limitations of Marketing Artificial Intelligence, According to Experts', Marketing Artificial Intelligence Institute, June 2017, https://www.marketingaiinstitute.com/blog/limitations-of-marketing-artificial-intelligence accessed 28 August 2020

382 Ibid.

face masks. According to an MIT Technical Review article, this caused issues for the AI algorithms powering marketing, inventory management, and more. 'Machine-learning models are designed to respond to changes. But most are also fragile; they perform badly when input data differs too much from the data they were trained on.'

The authors received reports from a number of loyalty programs operators which utilise AI for marketing who faced similar challenges at the start of the pandemic. Some stated they needed to turn their AI systems off for a period as they could not cope with the rapid change in member transaction behaviour, which had led the systems to generate illogical marketing campaign activity.

- **Ethical considerations**: some AI systems (particularly 'deep learning' platforms) work to solve problems and complete tasks, but data scientists are not really sure how it works. AI systems that are unexplainable should not be acceptable. Explainable AI needs to be part of the equation to ensure the AI system can be trusted. [383]

Deep learning relies heavily on training data, thus biased training data can lead to biased AI systems. Testing and monitoring are essential to identify and address any biases in the system.

---

383 Walch, K., 'Ethical Concerns of AI,' Forbes, Dec 2019, https://www.forbes.com/sites/cognitiveworld/2020/12/29/ethical-concerns-of-ai/#573ac23823a8 accessed 28 August 2020

Subscription loyalty memberships

Examples of companies which are using subscription loyalty programs include Lululemon, CVS and Loblaw,[384] as well as GameStop, Sephora and Restoration Hardware,[385] and more recently Pret a Manger[386] and Walmart.[387]

According to a 2015 survey by LoyaltyOne,[388] paid loyalty programs are particularly appealing to millennials. 76 per cent of millennials would consider joining a fee-based reward program from a favourite brand, compared to 61 per cent of Gen Xers and 48 per cent of Boomers. Acceptance of subscription products (Netflix, Naturebox, Spotify, etc.) is high among young shoppers.

62 per cent of respondents said they would consider joining a fee-based reward program if their favourite retailer offered one. This number was even higher among Millennials with 75 per cent of 18-24-year-olds and 77 per cent of 25-34-year-olds saying they would consider joining a fee-based reward program.

Subscription membership programs also have their challenges. It is critical for the model to be designed correctly to ensure the program will be profitable, as the company could make a loss if the program is too generous (the core

384 Pearson, B., 2019, 'Is 2019 The Year Of Paid Loyalty? Lululemon, CVS And Loblaw Are Game To Find Out', Forbes, https://www.forbes.com/sites/bryan-pearson/2019/01/04/is-2019-the-year-of-paid-loyalty-lululemon-cvs-and-loblaw-are-game-to-find-out/#7edb0d094276, accessed 12 May 2019.

385 Stephens, D., 2018, 'Why Paid Memberships Are the New Loyalty', Retail Prophet, https://www.retailprophet.com/why-paid-memberships-are-the-new-loyalty/, accessed 10 June 2019.

386 Sweney, M., 2020, 'Pret offers five coffees a day for £20 a month in move to boost sales', The Guardian, https://www.theguardian.com/business/2020/sep/04/pret-offers-monthly-subscription-to-boost-post-covid-pandemic-sales, accessed 9 September 2020.

387 Springer, J., 2020, 'Walmart Reveals Paid Loyalty Program', https://www-winsightgrocerybusiness-com.cdn.ampproject.org/c/s/www.winsightgrocerybusiness.com/amp/retailers/walmart-reveals-paid-loyalty-program, accessed 9 September 2020.

388 LoyaltyOne, 2015, 'Hard-to-please Millennials Most Open to Joining Fee-based Loyalty Programs', https://www.loyalty.com/home/insights/article-details/hard-to-please-millennials-most-open-to-joining-fee-based-loyalty-programs, accessed 29 January 2020.

reason the theatre subscription service MoviePass failed[389]). Members who pay will have higher expectations of their value and service experience, meaning an increased level of customer service support. For an annual fee membership program, additional administration will be required to remind the member to re-subscribe and chase them for payment.

My Panera

Panera Bread[390] launched a subscription service as a premium option for all members of the MyPanera loyalty program. The sub-scription provides unlimited hot coffee, iced coffee, or hot tea at all Panera Bread restaurants for a monthly fee of US$8.99. Members can redeem the benefit once up to every two hours, with no size restraints and unlimited refills while inside the café. The premium service adds value for loyal members, creates a lock-in effect, and drives more regular foot traffic and upsell opportunities in-store.

Loblaw and Eagle Eye

Loblaw, Canada's largest food and pharmacy retailer, utilised the Eagle Eye AIR digital marketing platform to facilitate the launch of a premium loyalty program, PC Insiders.[391]As part of the rollout, the platform enabled the integration of POS and eCommerce systems across Loblaw's massive network of stores, as well as facilitated the merger of two existing loyalty programs, with 8 million and 11 million members respectively.

PC Insiders offers an assortment of benefits for a US$99 annual fee to attract more customers to shop exclusively within the Loblaw

---

389 Statt, N., 2019, 'Why MoviePass Really Failed', https://www.theverge.com/2019/9/19/20872984/moviepass-shutdown-subscription-movies-helios-matheson-ted-farnsworth-explainer, accessed 30 June 2020.

390 Panera Bread, https://www.panerabread.com/en-us/mypanera/welcome.html, accessed 30 June 2020.

391 Eagle Eye, 'Eagle Eye works with Loblaw to unveil one of the largest digital loyalty programs in Canada', https://www.eagleeye.com/solutions/loblaw-launch-pc-optimum, accessed 30 June 2020.

network of grocery stores, pharmacies and travel agents. These benefits include points on every spend, free delivery or 'click and collect' services, discounts on branded products, US$99 annual travel credit, and a surprise box of curated products.

Card-linking and bank account-linking

Card-linked platforms have direct relationships with the major card payment providers (such as Visa, MasterCard and Amex) and allow retailers to set-up offers which can be linked to a consumer's credit card. When a consumer spends in-store or online with a participating merchant using their credit card, the offer (predominately cashback or points earn) is automatically triggered and applied without them having to also scan their membership card.

Bank account-linking platforms access authorised feeds of transactions from member accounts. This approach is more comprehensive than credit card linking because it provides all of the transaction data from an account, not just the transactions made with participating retailers. Thus, a member can access offers even if they do not pay with a specific credit card, while the program operator accesses significantly more member transaction data.

Some companies provide the option for participating merchants to access a portal to configure their own offers. The offers are sent to customers, who can click to activate them. This ties the offer to their card or bank account, ready to be unlocked when they transact with the merchant.

Bits of Stock

Bits of Stock[392] is a brand loyalty and investment app which allows members to receive a cashback reward in the form of fractional shares of stock.

Members can shop with participating brands and earn a cashback amount. They can then select which companies to invest the cashback in, and receive a small amount of shares in the company they choose.

This vested interest may also increase the propensity for the

392 Bits of Stock, https://www.bitsofstock.com/nl, accessed 30 June 2020.

member to contribute to the brand through repeat purchases, potentially because they might feel a stronger bond with the brand in which they own a stake.

Digital wallets, payments and convergence

Loyalty programs can introduce payments and digital wallet capabilities via app solutions which allow members to hold everything in a single place (convergence). This feature allows members to use their loyalty account as an all-in-one wallet, which can support any established currency such as fiat currency, loyalty currencies and even a range of cryptocurrencies. The member can connect a bank account or a credit card to facilitate instant payments. The payments capability lets the member pay via their smartphone app, after selecting the funding source.

For example, payment apps in the Quick Service Restaurants (QSR) industry allow members to register a credit card in the app. The member then orders via the menu in the app, with the payment automatically transacted. This process allows personalisation of experience by delivering offers relevant to member consumption history and time of day.

A range of apps allow consumers to store all their loyalty cards digitally, removing the need to carry plastic versions in their wallet. This allows quick access to any membership card that the member requires when transacting with a loyalty program. Some apps have API connections to certain loyalty programs, allowing them to access their points balances within the same app. As they hold the membership card for millions of members of different loyalty programs, the app companies may provide marketing services to the loyalty programs by sending offers directly through the app to members.

Stocard

Stocard[393] allows users to store all their reward cards in one app on their smartphone and collect points and rewards without having to carry around plastic loyalty cards. Their 50m users across 11 countries access the app on average every eight days, with over 500m plastic cards digitised. Users simply need to add one of their

---

393 Stocard, https://stocardapp.com/en/au, accessed 30 June 2020.

loyalty cards into Stocard by scanning the barcode or entering the member number manually.

Users can access discount offers from participating partners, who pay advertising fees to Stocard to promote their brands to users.

In 2020, Stocard introduced mobile payments, with UK-based Stocard users able to pay via a virtual Mastercard issued in the app.

According to an EU-Startups article,[394] 'in the long run, Stocard wants to offer more financial products such as Point Of Sale lending (buy now, pay later), cashback, savings, allowing consumers to access them where it's easiest and most convenient – all within their digital wallet. The company will offer these services at much better terms than banks by leveraging their existing relationship with the biggest and leading retailers across Europe.'

While China embraced app convergence many years ago (via Alipay and WeChat), the rest of the world is now slowly catching up. Björn Goß, founder and CEO of Stocard, sees a future involving the consolidation of shopping, payments and financial services in the digital wallet, where 'our wallets are moving to our mobile phones, the digital wallet is becoming the central hub in our lives for anything around money, shopping, and banking.'

Receipt scanning apps

Receipt scanning capabilities allow a member of a loyalty program to take a photo of the entire receipt via their smartphone. In the back end, the information is broken down and translated into a digital record, all of which is stored against a member profile, thus providing insightful product purchase information. The loyalty program not only verifies that the member purchased their

---

394 Tucker, C., 2020, 'German-based Stocard launches mobile wallet in the UK and a mobile payment feature, reaching 50 million users', EU-Startups, https://www.eu-startups.com/2020/06/german-based-stocard-launches-mobile-wallet-in-the-uk-and-a-mobile-payment-feature-reaching-50-million-users/#:~:text=Today%20German%20fintech%20startup%20Stocard,reaches%2050%20million%20users%20globally. accessed 24 June 2020.

product, but also captures details of all the products the member bought in the same transaction.

Loyalty programs can use this to personalise communications and offers to a product level, rather than just a transaction level. The member can be provided with rewards for their entire spend, or for buying specific products.

> **Kellogg's Family Rewards**
>
> Kellogg's Family Rewards[395] was one of the first FMCG companies to adopt receipt scanning for point collection. Members earn points by scanning receipts for eligible products and redeem on a range of rewards including branded merchandise, discount coupons, entry into sweepstakes, donations and gift cards.
>
> Kellogg's then pivoted to allow members to automatically earn points by connecting retailer loyalty cards with their membership. However, as of July 2020 Kellogg's have returned to the original receipt scanning only model. This is potentially a result of the inability to capture additional data which allows Kellogg's to more deeply understand their members' purchasing behaviours outside of the Kellogg's brands they buy.

Third-party aggregators

With member benefits programs increasing in prevalence and popularity (where loyalty programs provide third-party offers to their members such as discount movie tickets, gift cards, accommodation, experiences and more), an industry has developed to provide support. Third-party aggregators have evolved to provide both a white-label transaction platform and the relationships with the third-party partners, such as gift card providers, cinemas, travel companies and experience companies.

This can save a program operator years of work as the establishment of many relationships can be time-consuming and expensive. Aggregators

---

395 Kelloggs, Family Rewards, https://www.kelloggsfamilyrewards.com/en_US/how-v2.html, accessed 30 June 2020.

typically charge a per member annual fee or a flat rate annual fee for a certain number of members.

> **The Ambassador Card**
>
> The Ambassador Card[396] is a large, third-party aggregator providing a white-label platform that includes over 3,500 offers in one solution. The Ambassador Card network gives brands an effortless way to provide their loyal customers and member base with instant discounts and exclusive offers on a wide range of goods and services from restaurants, hotels and cinemas to tourist attractions, accommodation, and health and wellbeing resources.
>
> As a white-label solution, The Ambassador Card provides a high degree of scalability and customisation, which allows loyalty program operators to tailor offers and communications to their audience and objectives.
>
> New offers, partnerships and platform features are continuously developed by The Ambassador Card, which evolves the platform and thus extends the overall value given to loyalty program operators and their members.

Next best action platforms

By creating rich member profiles, loyalty programs provide a foundation for the installation of a Next Best Action (NBA) platform. These are primarily used in call centres and prompt the call centre agent or sales agent to recommend a specific product to the member at the end of the call.

For example, a member may call their bank to address an issue with their account, and at the end of the call the NBA system will prompt the call centre agent to recommend that the member consider applying for a credit card which enables them to earn loyalty points. The recommendation provided by the NBA platform is based on all the data held against the member's profile, including their propensity for loyalty program engagement, their credit

---

396 The Ambassador Card, https://www.ambassadorcard.com.au/, accessed 30 June 2020.

card usage history and current cards, their credit score, their preferred loyalty points (bank or airline) and many other datasets.

According to Deloitte,[397] 'NBA is focused on using sophisticated rules, analytics and algorithms to better predict customer needs and in turn, present more relevant actions and offers leading to improved wallet share and loyalty'. The NBA approach enables organisations to shift from a product-centric view to a customer-centric focus with product offerings tailored to the individual.

Financial Times

The Financial Times (FT) adopted an NBA model[398] to make communication with members more efficient by using the model to prioritise and potentially limit product promotions based on each reader's needs.

Their research team investigated correlations between reader engagement and specific member actions with FT products (e.g. Newsletters, Gift links, FT App, MyFT Feedpage), identifying reader habits that are more frequent with engaged users. These member actions and habits were given values based on the expected impact and probability of engagement to ultimately determine a reader personalised Next Best Action. The implemented model increased reader engagement by suggesting actions that an individual was more likely to take based on existing habits and engagement.

Geolocation tracking

Geolocation systems capture user location data (once permission has been enabled) and then use that data to enable targeted marketing communications based on a range of criteria. Tracking the location of a member adds a valuable

---

397 White, D., 2017, 'Customer loyalty: A relationship, not just a scheme', The Deloitte Consumer Review, https://www2.deloitte.com/au/en/pages/consumer-business/articles/consumer-review.html, accessed 15 June 2020.

398 Kastrinakis, G., 'How we calculate the Next Best Action for FT readers', https://medium.com/ft-product-technology/how-we-calculate-the-next-best-action-for-ft-readers-30e059d94aba, accessed 30 June 2020.

layer of data to the member's profile which helps to provide a better understanding into their lifestyle, habits, interests and motivations.

Tracking a member's location can be done through several channels, with apps and Wi-Fi being the most prevalent channels. This can be done in several ways:

- **Geofencing**: the program operator can set a virtual boundary around a location, together with a specific offer, so that if a member comes within the boundary, the offer is triggered. For example, an offer could be strategically triggered when a member is within 500m of a retail location to entice them to visit, or near a competitor's location to entice them to switch.

- **Geotargeting**: the program operator can segment members based on the location data stored within their profile and target them with a specific offer aimed at driving a desired behaviour. Geotargeting does not need to be based on the real-time location of a member, it can also be based on historical location. For example, the retailer may wish to target members who usually travel within a 1km radius of a store between 12 noon-2pm with a lunch offer.

- **Wi-Fi tracking**: Wi-Fi platforms can be used to capture personal details, send targeted and real-time offers and promotions to an individual when they are at a specific location (via geolocation tracking), and track the movement of members and non-members around stores. A retailer's existing Wi-Fi network could be effectively leveraged to drive incremental sales by tracking a member's connection time and sending a curated offer to stimulate an additional purchase if they have been in-store for a specified period of time.

- **Beacons**: working in a comparable way to Wi-Fi tracking platforms, beacons allow for more localised engagement. A beacon is essentially a small Bluetooth radio transmitter. A Bluetooth-equipped device like a smartphone can 'see' a beacon once it is in range. The key capability of this type of platform is to send coupons and offers to consumers via an app. The beacon sends out its ID number about ten times every second (sometimes more, sometimes less, depending on its settings). A nearby Bluetooth-enabled device picks up that signal. When a dedicated app recognises it, it links it to an action or piece of content stored in the cloud and displays it to the consumer. Platforms can 'teach' the app how to react to a beacon signal.

LANDMARKS ID

One company operating in the geolocation tracking space is LANDMARKS ID.[399] They provide a platform which collects location and mobile device data, delivering rich member datasets. Insertion of the LANDMARKS ID SDK into an app allows tracking of member movements to specific locations (e.g. supermarkets, restaurants, public landmarks, attractions) as well as recording what other apps are on their smartphone.

Westfield Group

Major shopping centre group Westfield[400] uses shopping centre-wide free Wi-Fi to run a customer engagement program. It captures a range of member data which they use for marketing purposes, and to find out which webpages are the most popular and where different shopper segments spend most of their time. Customers can access competitions, news, events and offers for mall retailers and get directions to any store.

Westfield also use the customer data gathered to pinpoint the types of customers within their shopping centres at any point in time. They then adjust the advertisements displayed on their digital billboards within the mall to appeal to those customers to stimulate increased buying behaviour. For example, advertisements targeted towards mothers with young children are shown during the middle of the day.

---

399 LANDMARKS ID, https://www.landmarksid.com/, accessed 30 June 2020.

400 Westfield Group, https://www.westfield.com/, accessed 30 June 2020.

Stock keeping unit (SKU) capture platforms

New hardware solutions allow loyalty program operators to capture SKU data (i.e. a line by line summary of what items the member has purchased). Traditionally, this capability has been available primarily to supermarket programs and other retail programs which capture all the transaction data of individual members. Coalition loyalty programs, such as frequent flyer programs and bank programs, do not normally have access to this data as the supermarkets and retailers do not share it with them.

SKU data allows the loyalty program to not only understand where a member is spending and how much they are spending, but also what they are spending on. They can use this information to build a more comprehensive profile of the member, as well as promote offers tied to the products they like, to stimulate increased visits and spend. The loyalty program can also provide data services to third-parties suppliers who are interested to understand the profile of their customers.

> **PiCo**
>
> Hardware and software provider, PiCo,[401] has created a black-box solution which plugs into any Point of Sale (POS) system to capture the SKU data. The data is sent to the cloud, where it can be fed into the loyalty program's platform for processing. The solution can also input personalised member discounts directly into the POS, and support earn and redemption activity, all without any direct POS integration.

Affiliate marketing platforms

As detailed in Chapter 8, advertisers can reward promoters (or 'affiliates') with a set amount of commission for each customer that they refer to their online store (and increasingly, physical stores). This may be for a visit, but more commonly it is for a transaction.

Affiliate marketing platforms have evolved to act as middlemen to track transactions and attribute the correct affiliate to the sale. They track member

---

401 PiCo, http://picolabs.co/, accessed 30 June 2020.

progress using cookies or APIs and organise the transfer of the affiliate marketing revenue from the third-party retailer to the loyalty program.

> **Partnerize**
>
> Partnerize[402] work with over 300 of the world's leading brands to track online sales and pay commissions to affiliate marketers. The company has developed their Partner Management Platform (PMP), a SaaS-based solution which streamlines the process of managing affiliate partnerships.
>
> Brand partnerships are complex and fragmented across different networks and channel partners (e.g. loyalty programs, cashback programs, bloggers, influencers, resellers, and brand alliances). The traditional model of building affiliate partnerships would require a loyalty program operator to establish and manage ongoing relationships with brands on an individual basis, which is costly and onerous. Partnerize solves this issue by acting as the intermediary, allowing a loyalty program operator to create, build and manage brand relationships, affiliate revenue, and integrate partnership insights via a single platform.

Blockchain

A blockchain is a continuously growing list of records, called 'blocks', which are cryptographically secured and linked into a 'chain'. Blockchains are inherently resistant to modification of the data because the data in all the blocks (held by millions of computers around the world) must match for a record to be valid.

Blocks are a ledger which are not controlled by a central entity. The 'millions of computers around the world' are run by Miners. Miners use special software to solve math problems and are rewarded with cryptocurrency bonuses. This creates an incentive for more people to mine, increasing the network size and expanding the decentralisation and security of the blockchain platform.

---

402 Partnerize, https://partnerize.com/, accessed 6th October 2020.

Because blockchain is so secure, it allows for the creation of a trustworthy digital currency, or cryptocurrency, without the need for a centralised authority (such as a bank or loyalty program) to maintain a ledger. Prior to blockchain, a decentralised digital currency could not be trusted because there was no way for the holder to ascertain whether it had already been spent or not. Blockchain solves this problem because a transaction creates a decentralised, immutable record stored on the blockchain for everyone to see, making it easy to verify who the actual owner of the cryptocurrency is.

Blockchain can be applied to loyalty programs in two main ways:

- **By the development of cryptocurrency rewards**: a blockchain loyalty program rewards members for their spend with a cryptocurrency (or cryptotoken) instead of traditional points and miles. The cryptocurrency can be actively traded on a digital exchange, similar to a Forex exchange, meaning the value can fluctuate. Thus, rather than holding a balance of points and miles where the value remains static, the member holds a new type of digital currency with a value which constantly adjusts based on speculative investor behaviour and the market forces of supply and demand. The loyalty currency itself becomes a game; one of acquiring, holding and trading. The potential exists to drive much deeper member engagement with a cryptocurrency than with points and miles as members can become fascinated with the idea of earning a currency which is 'alive'. Variations of this model exist, where the cryptotoken value remains static but the program allows members to easily transfer cryptotokens between different programs to unlock value.

Lolli

Lolli is an affiliate loyalty program which rewards members with Bitcoin when they shop at over 500 participating online retailers.[403]

Members can click through to the retailer's website via the Lolli website or utilise the Lolli browser extension when visiting retailer sites.

---

403 Lolli, https://www.lolli.com/about, accessed 23rd June 2020

Lolli use the affiliate marketing revenue paid by the advertisers to purchase Bitcoin for members, which they hold in a Lolli wallet on their behalf.

Members can transfer their Bitcoin from their Lolli wallet to their own Crypto wallet once they have accumulated US$15 worth.

Participating retailers include 1-800-Flowers, Best Buy, Bloomingdale's, CVS, Hilton, Macy's, Marriott, Office Depot and OfficeMax, Old Navy, Topman, and Walmart.

- **Via enterprise blockchain loyalty solutions**: a blockchain platform can be integrated with a loyalty platform and retail partner platforms to facilitate secure, real-time, auto-reconciled transactions. This approach provides specific advantages for major loyalty programs which have large, expensive legacy systems. While the legacy systems can process enormous volumes of transactions with high stability, they are often inflexible, limiting the ability of the loyalty program operators to innovate. Back-end blockchain platforms connect to the system and allow campaign rules to be exported, meaning the operator can more easily execute complex campaigns without having to develop or replace their legacy platform. They also allow for easier onboarding of partners where members can earn or redeem points and miles, and more efficient processing of transactions, reducing administrative overheads. The approach focuses specifically on the application of blockchain solutions, with cryptocurrencies only used if the existing loyalty currency requires tokenisation to improve transactional processing efficiencies.

Singapore Airlines and KrisPay

Singapore Airlines uses KrisPay,[404] a digital blockchain wallet that allows members of KrisFlyer to convert their miles and partner reward points into a digital currency for everyday spending in

---

404 Singapore Airlines, https://www.singaporeair.com/en_UK/sg/ppsclub-krisflyer/use-miles/krispay/, accessed 30 June 2020.

Singapore. Members can use their KrisPay miles to pay for items at the airline's partner merchants, including gas stations, retailers, and food and beverage outlets. The KrisPay app also provides members with personalised offers based on member interests and location services. For Singapore airlines, the benefits include reducing inventory by giving members new ways to spend their miles, a decentralised network improving system resiliency, and removing third-party involvement in processing transactions.

Emirates and Loyyal

Emirates utilises the enterprise blockchain platform Loyyal[405] for their Emirates Skywards reward program. Loyyal's platform is designed to extend and enhance existing loyalty legacy technology, rather than to replace. The backend blockchain loyalty solution integrates with legacy loyalty systems to deliver faster onboarding of new earn and redemption partners, streamlined reconciliation and settlement processes and simplified data sharing among partners. Emirates Skywards use these capabilities to achieve operational cost-savings, reduce their financial liability and improve customer experiences for their 25 million global members.

*

As can be seen, the technology innovation in the loyalty industry is extensive and provides loyalty program operators with a wide range of options to deliver any manner of program designs and member engagement approaches.

Key insights

- Loyalty technology plays an increasingly critical role in the execution of best-practice programs, both by providing the core capabilities required to run the program, and by providing

---

405 Loyyal, 2019, 'Loyyal Announces Endorsement From Emirates Skywards', https://loyyal.com/loyyal-announces-endorsement-from-emirates-skywards/, accessed 30 June 2020.

technological innovations to support emerging and major loyalty trends.

- Types of loyalty solution providers can range from full-service providers, partial service providers, off-the-shelf solutions or niche solutions, each with their own benefits and challenges.

- A loyalty platform is ultimately a rules engine. Best-practice platforms can support complex rules underpinning all manner of campaigns, earn/burn promotions and member movements between tiers. Platform capabilities are typically comprised of six overarching areas; integrations, product functionality, marketing execution, financial management, security and data protection, and account management and support.

- Extensive innovation and the evolution of trends within the loyalty industry has led to the development of a wide range of complimentary technology solutions. These are used to enhance existing platforms or implement different types of engagement strategies.

- Emerging and major trends within the loyalty industry include machine learning and AI, in-store personalisation, subscription memberships, card and bank account linking, digital wallets and payments, receipt scanning, third-party aggregators, next best action platforms, geolocation tracking, SKU capture platforms, affiliate marketing and blockchain.

Suggested reading

- Credit Suisse, 2019, 'Asia Pacific/Australia Equity Research Food & Drug Retailing'.

- Heaven, W. D., 'Our weird behavior during the pandemic is messing with AI models', MIT Technology Review, May 2020, https://www.technologyreview.com/2020/05/11/1001563/covid-pandemic-broken-ai-machine-learning-amazon-retail-fraud-humans-in-the-loop/

- Hoon, A., 'How AI can drive customer loyalty programs', The

Jakarta Post, Feb 2020, https://www.thejakartapost.com/life/2020/02/20/how-ai-can-drive-customer-loyalty-programs.html

- Pearson, Bryan, 2019, Is 2019 The Year Of Paid Loyalty? Lululemon, CVS And Loblaw Are Game To Find Out, Forbes, https://www.forbes.com/sites/bryanpearson/2019/01/04/is-2019-the-year-of-paid-loyalty-lululemon-cvs-and-loblaw-are-game-to-find-out/#7edb0d094276

- White, D.,2017, 'Customer loyalty: A relationship, not just a scheme', The Deloitte Consumer Review, https://www2.deloitte.com/au/en/pages/consumer-business/articles/consumer-review.html

CHAPTER 12

MEMBER LIFECYCLE MANAGEMENT

'Yowza… so I said back to that – ever so eloquently – 'the seeds of churn are planted early, my friend'… and then I went on to explain that churn is not an end-of-lifecycle issue, it's a LIFECYCLE issue; meaning it can be caused during – and happen at – anytime in their customer lifecycle.'

- Lincoln Murphy, 2013[406]

Focus areas

This chapter will address the following questions:

- What is member lifecycle management?
- What are the elements of a basic member lifecycle management model?
- What approaches are taken for more complex lifecycle management models?

A SIGNIFICANT ADVANTAGE loyalty programs provide to companies is the ability to track the lifecycle engagement of an individual member. If a repeat customer transacts with a company but does not belong to their loyalty program, it is challenging for the company to determine that multiple

---

406 Murphy, L., 2013, 'The Seeds of Churn are Planted Early', Sixteen Ventures, https://sixteenventures.com/seeds-of-churn, accessed 18 February 2020.

transactions were made by a single individual. If the same customer is a loyalty program member, the company can efficiently track their engagement, build a comprehensive member profile, and use that profile to develop a personalised management strategy. This increases the likelihood they will feel recognised, rewarded, valued and appreciated, and continue to transact with the company.

More relevant customer experiences are increasingly being sought after by consumers.[407] Recognising where a member is within their lifecycle, and providing them with relevant communications and offers, can stimulate increased engagement to generate significant business growth, profitability and competitive differentiation.

Lifecycle models tend to be transaction based. They do not consider any psychographic insights, meaning they can indicate what the member is doing but cannot answer why.

More complex models are also used by loyalty programs, which are reviewed later in this chapter.

Basic member lifecycle management model

A basic member lifecycle management approach focuses on six key areas, as demonstrated in Figure 15. The presented member lifecycle management model is relatively simple, however the experience of the authors suggests many companies fail to execute even at this level. It involves using analytics to segment the member base, allowing the program operator to manage each segment in a way which attempts to transition them to a more ideal lifecycle segment. For example, a member in the Retention phase may be targeted with specific offers to reduce the likelihood they will churn, and by doing so transition them back to the Growth phase.

---

407 Deloitte, 2017, 'Customer loyalty: A relationship, not just a scheme', The Deloitte Consumer review, p9, https://www2.deloitte.com/au/en/pages/consumer-business/articles/consumer-review.html, accessed 3 January 2020.

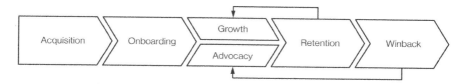

Figure 15: a basic member lifecycle management model.

Most models broadly follow a similar framework to the basic member lifecycle management model, the phases of which are outlined below.

Acquisition

Acquiring new loyalty program members follows a similar conversion funnel pathway to product and service sales.

Best-practice loyalty programs are simple to join. With a near-saturation amount of loyalty programs provided within many industries, this is where member acquisition strategies should focus. This is because any perceived barrier-to-entry is likely to have a negative impact on member base growth.

Common ways in which members can join loyalty programs include:

- **In-store registration:** in many cases the member is provided with a plastic membership card, although digital cards which can be stored on mobile phones are becoming more prevalent. The member may be asked to fill in a paper form, with the details entered into a database at a later date, or a staff member may enter the details directly into a database as part of the check-out process. Alternatively, the member may be provided with a registration pack and directed to complete their registration online.

- **Online registration:** the new member accesses a web page to register for the loyalty program. This may be as a separate action or as part of an online shopping journey. The loyalty program may send the member a join pack in the mail containing a membership card and educational/promotional material, or they may be sent a link to a digital membership card.

- **App download:** the new member downloads an app and completes the registration process within the app. This will likely include them being asked to provide approval to receive notifications and track their location. They may also be asked to link a credit/debit card or bank account to their profile.

KPMG's The Truth About Loyalty Report (2019)[408] identified that 69 per cent of Millennials agree that most programs are too difficult to join and/or earn rewards. This indicates loyalty program operators need to try harder to simplify the registration process, which may include providing multiple channel options giving members flexibility around how they wish to join.

Some loyalty programs provide only a single option for members to join, while others will present prospective members with a range of different channels and options in an effort to increase the program's effectiveness in acquiring new members.

Two-step join processes can be challenging, such as programs which provide a membership card in-store and require the member to complete their registration online. Industry insight suggests completion rates can be low for many of these programs (due to the member forgetting, being apathetic or losing their card), and the company has no opportunity to contact them to provide a reminder. A better approach involves the member submitting their email address or mobile number in-store to commence the registration process. They can then be reminded via email or text message to complete the registration process online if they do not.

Increasingly, companies are structuring loyalty programs around smartphones, with the member required to download an app to join the program. This has its advantages; global mobile phone usage increased 35 per cent on average from 2017 to 2019,[409] while apps provide the ability to deliver a rich and convenient member experience. It also has its challenges; the average consumer in the US, South Korea, Japan and Australia has over 100 apps on their

408 KPMG, 2019, 'The Truth About Loyalty Report', https://assets.kpmg/content/dam/kpmg/xx/pdf/2019/11/customer-loyalty-report.pdf, accessed 10 June 2019.

409 App Annie, 'The state of mobile 2020', https://www.appannie.com/en/go/state-of-mobile-2020/, accessed 10 June 2020.

smartphone,[410] making it increasingly difficult to convince new members to download yet another app as an essential step to joining their program.

As detailed in Chapter 10, member data is also captured during the member acquisition process. Best-practice loyalty programs initially focus on capturing essential data, knowing the establishment of the member account is the first step on a pathway to collecting additional data which can be used to tailor the member's experience and stimulate early engagement with the program.

> **Vans Family**
>
> Customers of Vans, the 1966 skateboarding company which evolved into the world's largest youth culture brand, can join the Vans Family loyalty program simply by providing their email address in-store when they transact. New members are then sent an email requesting that they complete the registration process online at www.vans.com.[411]
>
> Once the member has provided their email address in-store, they are considered a Vans Family member and they can start earning points for product purchases at Vans stores and online at www.vans.com.
>
> For complete access to all available benefits, the member must complete their registration, providing an incentive for them to finish the process.

Onboarding

The 'Halo Effect' which occurs when positive first impressions positively influence future judgments or ratings of unrelated factors.

Asch (1946)[412] conducted an experiment which identified that first

---

410 Ibid.

411 Vans Family, Terms and Conditions, https://www.vans.com/family/terms-conditions.html, access 20 June 2020.

412 Asch, S. E., 1946, 'Forming impressions of personality', The Journal of Abnormal and Social Psychology, Vol 41, Iss 3, pp258–290.

impressions are more heavily weighted in forming an overall impression of a person than subsequent impressions. Subjects were read lists of adjectives about an individual. Half the subjects heard a list where the adjectives went from positive to negative, while the other half heard a list where the adjectives went from negative to positive. Asch determined that the order in which the adjectives were read influenced how the subject rated the individual, and that adjectives presented first had more influence on the rating than adjectives presented later. When positive traits were presented first, the participants rated the person more favourably and visa-versa. In other words, first impressions count.

Companies and loyalty program operators can harness the halo effect by developing excellent quality join and onboarding processes.

According to Murphy, 'The seeds of churn are planted early.' [413] This further stresses that the early days of a relationship with a new member are critical for educating them about the program and convincing them that they will be able to access value ongoing, thereby reducing the likelihood they will disengage immediately or over the longer term. Onboarding is one of the most critical strategies for increasing the lifetime value of members.

Best-practice program operators utilise sophisticated onboarding processes to educate and excite members about the program, encourage them to self-discover, start them on the pathway towards claiming their first reward, stimulate them to make a follow-up transaction earlier in the purchase cycle, and motivate them to share their positive experiences with family and friends.

Leading a new member towards their first reward is critical for long-term engagement. For example, if a new member successfully registers, earns points for transacting, then redeems those points for a reward, they have worked through the earn and redeem cycle once, and are hence likely to understand how it works. Consequently, there will be an increased likelihood of further engagement with the program.

Onboarding approaches can incorporate a range of strategies to ensure they are sufficiently optimised and continue to evolve with changing consumer needs:

---

413 Murphy, L., 2013, 'The Seeds of Churn are Planted Early', Sixteen Ventures, https://sixteenventures.com/seeds-of-churn, accessed 18 February 2020.

- **Optimised messaging**: the onboarding process is critical to ensure the new member feels adequately educated about the program and suitably rewarded for their early engagement. Best-practice program operators run focus groups and user testing with members to seek feedback on communication styles, thereby ensuring messaging is clear and understandable.

- **A/B testing**: optimisation of the onboarding process can be supported by A/B testing across communications frequency (how many communications), channels (eDM, DM, SMS, app, website and outbound call combinations), design, content, urgency (standard vs FOMO), and value (education vs offer).

- **Interactive walk-throughs**: for digital products, walk-throughs lead members through the product, introduce them to different elements, provide usage tips and help them establish their account to access value more quickly.

- **Preference centre:** establishing an approach to preference setting involves asking members to specify their product, communications, or interest-based preferences, encouraging them to share additional data. This enables program operators to tailor elements of the program with member desires to ensure they are provided with information genuinely relevant to them in a way that is palatable from the outset of their engagement. Preference centres have been shown to increase member engagement rates and reduce churn rates.

- **Dynamic communications**: a refined onboarding communications process will seamlessly transition the customer from Acquisition to Growth by acknowledging how they interact with each communication and adjusting accordingly using trigger and behavioural-based rules.

- **Progress trackers**: the early introduction of progress trackers can help communicate to the member that they are on the pathway to unlocking a reward, inspiring them to discover ways in which they can continue their progression.

- **Celebrations**: acknowledging that members have completed a key step can reinforce the behaviour and influence their motivation to continue engaging. This may be a pop-up, some bonus points, a badge or other low-cost reward.

Growth

The primary ambition of a loyalty program is to generate deeper member engagement with the brand, leading to a greater share of wallet spend. The opportunities to stimulate incremental spend by members via well-designed loyalty programs are numerous.

Engaged members desire to earn more points, so many programs promote bonus points offers to stimulate member spend.

Within member benefits programs, members are motivated by discounts and value-adds. Therefore, the focus to grow engagement often revolves around highlighting the savings which members can access from third-party partners.

Status tier programs entice members to engage more to progress to higher tiers, and then encourage them to maintain their high engagement to continue to enjoy the benefits which come with their privileged status.

Best-practice loyalty programs deliver personalised communications to ensure members primarily receive offers which are relevant to them. They aim for a major proportion of their member base to be within the Growth segment to maximise program and company profitability.

---

414 Groove, https://www.groovehq.com/, accessed 27 January 2020.

Tesco Clubcard

While supermarket programs offer very low return on spend levels (generally 0.5 per cent of spend is returned in points), they successfully drive growth by running consistent bonus points campaigns (e.g. double and triple bonus points or fixed amount bonus points). This makes the customer feel they are being continuously well rewarded, despite the return only being increased to 1-1.5 per cent.

To capitalise on growth opportunities, Tesco[415] have leveraged the power of Machine Learning and AI technology to target their campaigns in an efficient and effective way, positively influencing purchase intervals and spend. The technology is used to automatically construct and send individualised communications with product promotions and specials to each member. They track member responses and evolve future communications to optimise engagement potential in an effort to continually keep members within the growth phase.

Opening up an increased number of compelling bonus points opportunities for members has also resulted in several news articles about Tesco being published which provide tips to readers on how they can boost their points balances, turning bloggers into program advocates and supporting program growth.

Advocacy

Best-practice loyalty programs harness member advocacy to grow their program's brand awareness and perception, and to boost member acquisition and engagement.

According to Neilsen's Global Trust in Advertising survey (2015),[416] 83 per cent of respondents reported that they completely or somewhat trust the

---

415 King, K., 2019, 'Using Artificial Intelligence in Marketing: How to Harness AI and Maintain the Competitive Edge', Kogan Page Ltd.

416 Neilsen, 2015, 'Global Trust in Advertising', https://www.nielsen.com/au/en/insights/report/2015/global-trust-in-advertising-2015/, accessed 13 March 2020.

recommendations of friends and family, while 66 per cent said they trust consumer opinions posted online. Noteworthy to loyalty program operators, 70 per cent of global respondents said they completely or somewhat trust branded websites, while 56 per cent trust emails they signed up for.

A 2010 McKinsey study identified that word of mouth is the primary factor behind 20 to 50 per cent of all purchasing decisions. They defined word of mouth as either experiential (resulting from a consumer's direct experience with a product or service), consequential (when consumers directly exposed to traditional marketing campaigns pass on messages about them) or intentional (when marketers use celebrity endorsements to generate consumer discussion). Loyalty programs can play a key role in all three areas, but particularly in experiential and consequential, by ensuring the product and service experience is exceptional and the marketing messaging is relevant and tailored.

Program operators can utilise a range of activities to stimulate advocacy:

- **Referral programs**: as detailed in Chapter 8, referral programs can be effective in incentivising and harnessing the member base to recruit new members.

- **Social media sharing**: programs can reward members with points, status credits or competition entries for following them, and sharing content on social media.

- **Recognition**: status tiers can harness social identity theory (as discussed in Chapter 5) by influencing the member to adopt their status within the program as part of their own self, motivating them to share their experience.

- **Reviews**: programs can invite satisfied and delighted members to write reviews which can be shared publicly.

- **Recommendations**: programs may reward existing clients who provide recommendations which result in new business opportunities. This is especially true of B2B programs.

Dropbox

The Dropbox referral program resulted in exponential success with 3,900 per cent growth in a 15-month period.[417]

Since the Dropbox product offers storage space in the cloud, the referral program provides more storage space for referees. This perfectly structured reward means that referees are getting further benefits from the product enhancing their positive attitudes towards it.

Instead of 'Invite your friends', Dropbox framed the referral program as 'get more space' so referees are motivated to get something extra, taking advantage of the framing bias.

The invitation process is simple with the flexibility to invite contacts via Gmail, Facebook or copying a link, with referral statuses and rewards tracked and displayed to the member within their profile so they can see how much additional space they have earned (gamification).

Retention

Irrespective of how successful a loyalty program is, a percentage of the member base will at some stage show signs of disengagement. Best-practice loyalty programs monitor member engagement and detect members who are showing such signs. This may be via an identified lapse in transactions, a big 'cash-out' redemption event, a sudden increase in customer service enquiries, a reduction in account access or even tracking showing engagement with competitors. These signs can often be a precursor to the member ceasing any involvement with the loyalty program altogether, enabling loyalty program operators to respond early with retention campaign activity.

A best-practice retention process involves two steps; firstly, developing a churn-risk score and secondly, developing automated retention campaigns triggered by high scores which indicate a risk that the member may churn.

---

417 Mengoulis, A., 2019, 'Dropbox grew 3900% with a simple referral program. Here's how!', Inside Viral Loops, https://viral-loops.com/blog/dropbox-grew-3900-simple-referral-program/, accessed 22 May 2020.

Churn-risk score formulation is a machine learning/AI method which utilises data to indicate the likelihood that a member will churn within a predefined amount of time. A study by Kahn et al (2015)[418] used several terabytes of data from a large mobile phone network to build a model which they reported could predict whether a subscriber will churn with 89.4 per cent accuracy.

Developing a churn-risk score allows program operators to tailor communications to specific segments, measure member health and make strategic decisions to nudge member engagement. A churn-risk score can be automatically generated via a loyalty platform utilising a range of engagement metrics (e.g. frequency of engagement, recency of engagement, transaction patterns, changes in order type, seasonality or changes in points balance). If the churn-risk score increases past a certain threshold, automated trigger campaigns can target the member with an exclusive, tailored offer to arrest and reverse the decline.

As an example, a member may reduce their visit pattern over a three-month period, reduce their app usage and stop opening eDMs. These would all be obvious signs the member is reducing their engagement, but they may not be obvious to a busy marketing team managing millions of customers. A churn-risk score algorithm would calculate and identify the increase in the member's score, trigger an alert (the member now appears on a list as a potential churn risk) and automatically send the member a retention offer which is more valuable, and ideally more effective, than regular offers.

To offset the loss of a valuable member, the loyalty program operator will attempt to understand why the member is disengaging (e.g. ineffective campaigns, a service issue, strong competition) and rectify this if possible. Loyalty program operators may also try to tease out potential irritants which may trigger a disengagement event, implement analytics to track and identify affected members and develop solid strategies to address the irritants. Examples of irritants include missing points, delayed flights, a poor service experience, a lack of available rewards or other issues where the member experience falls short of their expectations.

---

418 Khan, M. R., Manoj, J., Singh, A. & Blumenstock, J. E., 2015, 'Behavioral Modeling for Churn Prediction: Early Indicators and Accurate Predictors of Custom Defection and Loyalty', IEEE International Congress on Big Data, pp 677-680.

In that sense, a loyalty program team can expand their role into being advocates for a better customer experience across all areas of the business.

> ### Qitaf
>
> Saudi Telecom Qitaf rebuilt their loyalty program with the aim to deliver highly personalised and relevant engagement experiences in real-time. Members can earn points when paying bills and buying products from Qitaf, but also earn across 170+ brand partners and 3,700 retail locations across Saudi Arabia. Earn transactions are processed instantly and customers receive notifications while shopping, detailing opportunities to earn more points.
>
> In this tiered program, the primary goal is to reduce churn while upselling more products and services. Without revealing the exact data, the 2020 Loyalty Magazine Awards recognised that lower-tier members of the Qitaf program showed a material reduction in churn, while the higher tier members could access so many benefits that churn was almost at zero. Customer lifetime value subsequently increased dramatically.[419]

Winback

Despite best efforts, a percentage of members will cease to engage with the program altogether.

One major reason is they do not perceive they are accessing meaningful value. Another is they may not have attitudinal commitment to the brand. They may find interacting with the loyalty program to be too complicated and onerous. Or they may have changed their career path (e.g. different role) or life path (e.g. retirement) and no longer need to consume the product or service offered.

For example, frequent flyer programs often see complete disengagement from previously frequent travellers who no longer need to fly regularly, if at all. The airline can invest in incentivising the member to re-stimulate their

---

419 Ehredt, C., 'Innovators Break The Mould, At The 2020 Loyalty Magazine Awards', Currency Alliance, https://www.linkedin.com/pulse/innovators-break-mould-2020-loyalty-magazine-awards-charles-ehredt/, accessed 18 June 2020.

engagement, but it may not be successful if the member no longer has a demand for their product or services. Knowing why members have disengaged can help companies optimise usage of their retention and winback budget.

Inevitably, a program will end up with a percentage of their member base who are completely inactive. Major coalition loyalty programs can have 30 to 60 per cent of their member base inactive. Even so, the opportunity still exists for the program to attempt to win a proportion of these members back using a variety of best-practice campaign approaches.

Kumar et al (2015)[420] ran a study which identified that the stronger the first-lifetime relationship with the firm, the more likely a customer was to accept a winback offer. One specific identifier was if the member had referred the company to family and friends in the past, they were more likely to accept the offer. A service recovery experience which occurred when they were a customer was also positively associated with the likelihood of successful winback.

This research not only emphasises the key role loyalty programs can play when the member is a customer, but the value the program has provided even after the customer has churned.

One advantage a company has in trying to win back members is their data profile, as they can tailor communications and offers in a way that is not possible with non-members or potential new members.

The winback process generally starts with experimentation. Loyalty program operators may try a variety of different campaign approaches to determine which is most effective, with a strategy to stimulate a simple engagement from the member, then build on the successful response. Winback campaigns can be structured to run centrally and/or automatically from the loyalty platform. This may be a generic campaign to all target members on a monthly basis, or a tailored, targeted campaign run automatically utilising the dataset held against individual members.

---

420 Kumar, V., Bhagwat, Y. & Zhang, X., 2015, 'Regaining "Lost" Customers: The Predictive Power of First-Lifetime Behavior, the Reason for Defection, and the Nature of the Win-Back Offer', Journal of Marketing, Vol 79.

Audible

Audible[421] have a best-practice automated winback approach which consists of the following sequence (as observed by the authors):

- Three hours after unsubscribe: a list of personalised recommendations for audiobooks similar to those most recently enjoyed by the member (a subtle prompt to remind the member why they became a member in the first place).

- 60 days after unsubscribe: a 'get $8 off for 4 months' offer followed by a list of personalised recommendations (an incentive to nudge membership renewal with an offer that helps re-establish habitual membership rollover).

- 65 days after unsubscribe: a reminder to take advantage of the 'get $8 off for 4 months' offer, highlighting that the member will save 45 per cent off the normal price (a reinforcer).

- 90 days after unsubscribe: a new offer of 'come back for $2' together with a list of new benefits now available to the member since they last left (a more direct sell and more valuable offer with higher levels of instant gratification).

- 93 days after unsubscribe: a reminder to 'come back for $2' plus a 'free editors pick audiobook', together with a list of new benefits for being a member and personalised recommendations (a bonus benefit and harder sell).

- 102 days after unsubscribe: a 'hurry last days to come back for $2 plus a free editors pick audiobook' push, together with other popular book recommendations and personalised recommendations (creates urgency and generates FOMO).

- 104 days after unsubscribe: 'last chance to come back for $2 plus a free editors pick audiobook' push, together with other popular book recommendations and personalised recommendations (triggers loss aversion bias and FOMO).

- 106 days after unsubscribe: 'come back and get $8 off for the first

---

421 Audible, https://www.audible.com, accessed 30 June 2020.

> three months (the start of a new winback series with a different offer' based on member reactions to previous offers).
>
> It is likely the sequence will continue to be adjusted and refined over time to further optimise the retention/winback approach.

More complex member lifecycle management models

A more complex lifecycle management model typically involves developing granular member segments, which allows for better insight and communication approaches. For example:

- Members are segmented into Onboarding or Onboarded status.

- The Onboarding segment are categorised based on transactions made within a specified timeframe. This includes Retention (if they have only made a single transaction) or Winback (if they have not made any transactions), for which different engagement strategies can be triggered. If they make multiple transactions, they are reclassified as Onboarded.

- The Onboarded segment are categorised into tiers (e.g. Silver, Gold, Platinum) based on the total amount spent within a specified period. These tiers are generally covert, meaning the customer is unaware they have been segmented into a particular tier.

- The Onboarded tiers are further categorised based on the trajectory of total spend made within a specified timeframe. This includes Retention and Winback, as well as Growth (for increasing spend), Stable (for maintaining spend) and Reduced (for declining spend).

Other variations of complex models have also been developed. For example, Hu et al (2018)[422] proposed a two-part framework involving the development of a downward trend prediction process and the establishment of a methodology to identify the reasons why members may be in a downward trend. Their model identified at risk customers when they started to show a downward trend in engagement, often in an earlier stage of the customer

---

422 Hu, K., Li, Z.,Liu, Y., Cheng, L., Yang, Q. & Li, Y., 2018, 'A Framework in CRM Customer Lifecycle: Identify Downward Trend and Potential Issues Detection'.

lifecycle than the Retention phase. Their methodology utilised bad shopping experiences as inputs, which they then validate via A/B market testing. Their initial research demonstrated an 88.5 per cent incremental lift in spend.

Sawhney[423] developed an innovative lifecycle management approach titled CxDNA (customer experience DNA). The design involves two interwoven strands; Customer Action (the customer journey) and Organisational Action (the customer funnel management journey):

- **Customer Action**: focuses on optimising the Discover, Learn, Evaluate, Buy, Engage and Advocate stages of the member lifecycle.

- **Organisational Action**: focuses on Reach, Acquire, Convert, Develop, Retain and Bond stages.

By qualitatively and quantitatively detailing what each stage of the Customer Action strand looks like from a customer perspective, companies can clarify what information and content will be most useful for customers at each stage. Applying those insights across the Organisational Action strand will enable the organisation to identify the actions and processes needed to nurture customers across the lifecycle, ensuring the customer is at the centre of all actions taken.

The ultimate application of complex member lifecycle management involves machine learning/AI. As detailed in Chapter 11, such platforms can categorise members into a myriad of segments based on extensive transactional, demographic and psychographic information. Onboarding communications can be fully dynamic across multiple channels, automatically adjusting based on how the member responds. Growth communications can be tailored specifically to the individual with the aim of delivering the right message to the right member at the right time, while reducing overall marketing spend. Retention and Winback communications can be triggered at the optimal time with the right offer to maximise impact at minimal cost.

If set-up and executed optimally, Machine learning/AI allows each individual member to be supported by their own tailored, multi-faceted lifecycle

---

423 Sawhney, M. S., 2019, 'It's Time to Radically Rethink the Customer Experience. Here's How to Get Started.', Kellogg Insight, Kellogg School Of Management at Northwestern University.

management strategy. This is a core technology foundation for the delivery of Digital EQ, with the growth of member attitudinal commitment a valuable and desirable outcome.

Key insights

- A member lifecycle management model involves using analytics to segment a member database into lifecycle stages, allowing the program operator to manage members in a way which makes them feel recognised, rewarded, valued and appreciated, increasing the likelihood they will continue transacting with the company.

- A basic member lifecycle management model includes acquisition, onboarding, growth, advocacy, retention and winback stages, with each stage requiring different communications strategies.

- More complex lifecycle management models may involve developing granular member segments or trend prediction methodology which allows for better insight and more effective communications.

- The ultimate application of complex member lifecycle management involves machine learning/AI, which categorises members into a myriad of segments based on extensive transactional, demographic and psychographic information. This approach allows each individual member to be supported by their own tailored, multi-faceted lifecycle management strategy.

Suggested reading

- Murphy, Lincoln, 2013, 'The Seeds of Churn are Planted Early', Sixteen Ventures, https://sixteenventures.com/seeds-of-churn

- Mengoulis, A., 2019, 'Dropbox grew 3900% with a simple referral program. Here's how!', Inside Viral Loops, https://viral-loops.com/blog/dropbox-grew-3900-simple-referral-program/

- Kumar, V. & Bhagwat, Yashoda & Zhang, Xi., 2015, 'Regaining 'Lost' Customers: The Predictive Power of First-Lifetime Behavior, the Reason for Defection, and the Nature of the Win-Back Offer', Journal of Marketing, Vol 79.

- Hu, Kun & Li, Zhe & Liu, Ying & Cheng, Luyin & Yang, Qi & Li, Yan, 2018, 'A Framework in CRM Customer Lifecycle: Identify Downward Trend and Potential Issues Detection'.

- Mohanbir S. Sawhney, 2019, 'It's Time to Radically Rethink the Customer Experience. Here's How to Get Started', Kellogg Insight, Kellogg School Of Management at Northwestern University.

CHAPTER 13

GAMES AND GAMIFICATION

'In every job that must be done, there is an element of fun. You find the fun and snap! The job's a game.'

- Mary Poppins

Focus areas

This chapter will address the following questions:

- What is the difference between games and gamification?

- How are games used in loyalty programs to drive deeper member engagement?

- How is gamification used in loyalty programs to motivate specific member behaviours?

GAMES ARE DEFINED as 'an activity that one engages in for amusement or fun', and 'a complete episode or period of play, ending in a final result'.[424]

Gamification is the use of elements of gameplay in non-game contexts to stimulate specific behaviours.

These distinctions are important. Games and gamification are different approaches which deliver different outcomes within loyalty programs.

In modern loyalty programs, both games and gamification are being used

---

424 Oxford dictionary.

to drive deeper member engagement. Applied intelligently, gamification and games can support the stimulation of a wide range of desirable member behaviours, including sharing of personal data (to support analytical modelling and hyper-personalised communications), advocacy and referrals (to grow the member base and promote tactical offers), and incremental visits and spend.

Approaches are becoming increasingly sophisticated and more prevalent. Momentum is building in both areas as companies are inspired by the efforts of their competitors and other loyalty program operators, while technological advances (smartphone market penetration and better software platforms) has allowed gaming and gamification to become more low cost and mainstream.

While much has been written about the potential of gamification within loyalty programs, it is games which are booming, rapidly developing into one of the loyalty industry's mega-trends.

Games

According to the Entertainment Software Association (ESA), in 2019, '164 million adults in the United States play video games and three-quarters of all Americans have at least one gamer in their household.'[425] The ESA also identified that smartphones are the most common device for playing games (60 per cent) compared to personal computers (52 per cent) and dedicated game consoles (49 per cent). There is only minimal gender imbalance, with 46 per cent of gamers being female.

Assuming similar statistics in other modern or modernising countries, this represents a sizeable population of consumers who are likely to be open to engaging with quality games provided through a loyalty program.

Games can be both entertainment in themselves and a pathway towards a reward, making them a useful tool. Members can be invited to play a physical or digital game, enjoy the experience and unlock a prize, reinforcing the positive experience.

Lazzaro (2004)[426] conducted a comprehensive study of the role of emo-

---

425 Entertainment Software Industry, 2019, '2019 Essential Facts about the Computer and Video Game Industry', https://www.theesa.com/wp-content/uploads/2019/05/ESA_Essential_facts_2019_final.pdf, accessed 15 June 2020.
426 Lazzaro, N., 2004, 'Why we Play Games: Four Keys to More Emotion without

tions in video games. She identified four key emotion-based reasons why people play games:

1. **Hard fun**: players like the opportunities for challenge, strategy, and problem solving.
2. **Easy fun**: players enjoy intrigue and curiosity. Players become immersed in games when it absorbs their complete attention, or when it takes them on an exciting adventure.
3. **Altered states**: players treasure the enjoyment from their internal experiences in reaction to the visceral, behaviour, cognitive, and social properties.
4. **The people factor**: players use games as mechanisms for social experiences.

Lazzaro reported being surprised by the 'dramatic contrast in emotional displays between one vs. several people playing together. Players in groups emote more frequently and with more intensity than those who play on their own. Group play adds new behaviours, rituals, and emotions that make games more exciting.' This insight should be of particular interest to loyalty program operators that are contemplating games, as campaigns which stimulate group and social discussion may tap into this greater intensity to the benefit of the operator.

Brands can enjoy some valuable benefits from providing members with access to compelling games:

- **Acquisition:** if a consumer is required to join the program to play the game, they are provided with an additional motivation to join. If an existing member needs to download an app to play, they are provided with an incentive to complete that action.

- **Brand exposure**: members playing a game will focus their attention for an extended period of time on a field or game board which will likely contain overt branding, as well as subtle brand associations. This can tap into a psychological bias known as the mere-exposure

---

Story', Game Dev Conf, http://twvideo01.ubm-us.net/o1/vault/gdc04/slides/why_ we_play_games.pdf, accessed 2 June 2020.

effect. Zajonc (1968)[427] found that mere repeated exposure of individuals to a stimulus object enhances their attitude toward it. His study focused on exposure to images such as foreign words, Chinese characters and faces of strangers. Later research has replicated the effect across paintings, colours, flavours, geometric shapes and people.[428] Baker (1999) [429] found the effect also works for brands, and recommended that advertisers should place a higher priority on maximising the prominence of the brand name and package in advertisements to capitalise on the effect.

Games provide an engaging medium for intense, repeated exposure. Examples of luxury brands which have embraced games as promotional channels include Louis Vuitton, Guerlain, Dior, Hermes, Burberry, Gucci and Chanel.[430]

Dior

Discounting is never a strategy used by Dior to generate engagement with their luxury fashion lines. Instead, to drive hype around a new store opening in Shanghai, they created a playful, competitive, interactive game on their WeChat account.

Dior invited users to collect six Dior branded in-game tokens via an interactive treasure hunt, allowing them to launch a virtual hot air balloon into the sky upon successful completion. Launching a balloon gave shoppers the opportunity to win tickets to the store's grand opening.

427 Zajonc, R. B., 1968, 'Attitudinal effects of mere exposure', Journal of Personality and Social Psychology, Vol 9, Iss 2 Pt.2, pp1-27.

428 Moreland, R. L. & Beach, S. R., 1992, 'Exposure effects in the classroom: The development of affinity among students', Journal of Experimental Social Psychology, Vol 28, Iss 3, pp255–276.

429 Baker, W. E., 1999, 'When Can Affective Conditioning and Mere Exposure Directly Influence Brand Choice?', Journal of Advertising, Vol 28, Iss 4, pp31-46.

430 Page, R., 2020, 'Game on: 7 brands getting into gaming', CMO, https://www.cmo.com.au/article/670396/game-7-brands-getting-into-gaming/, accessed 4 April 2020.

Dior gave repeated exposure to their logo within the game, while effectively using it to meld online and offline engagement experiences.

- **Education**: according to Tulleken,[431] games provide a unique opportunity for brands to represent their values and involve their customers in their mission. He cites the examples of Chipotle (who used a game called Scarecrow to allow customers to save produce and animals from industrial food corporations) and Burger King (who created their Sneak King game to incorporate their promise to 'feed your hunger' by having players feed hungry people). Loyalty programs can further utilise this approach by better educating members on how to extract more value from the program.

Porsche

Porsche consolidated their brand values and commitment for fast cars with the launch of their racing game *Need For Speed: Porsche Unleashed*. The game let users race with different Porsche sports car models, bringing to life the history of the Porsche designs and how they have been refined and evolved over time with each model. With speed and style always at the core, the game is a classic portrait of the brand and its values, with the game itself now a collector's item.

Boost Juice Vibe Club

Boost Juice launched two games in two years for their Vibe Club loyalty program members to play within their app. The games educate members on the healthy fruit contained within Boost drinks and incorporate elements of their brand story and founder. It also allowed members to win prizes.

Boost Juice said in a statement that their first 'Free the Fruit' app

431 Tulleken, H., 2019, '5 ways games increase brand awareness', Plinq, https://www.plinq.co/blog/5-ways-games-increase-brand-awareness, accessed 4 April 2020.

saw over 329,889 downloads and 225,970 prizes given away, while reaching number one on the Apple App Store and remaining in this position for four weeks.[432] During this time, Vibe Club members spent close to 56 million minutes of gameplay at an average 173 minutes per user. This level of app engagement (which rewarded members with digital discount vouchers), drove high traffic into their bricks and mortar stores and resulted in significant sales uplifts.

The game was quickly followed by a second game 'Find the Fruit', capitalising on the success of Free the Fruit.

- **Advocacy**: games are effective in generating word of mouth promotion. In 2009, The NDP Group revealed that 41 per cent of all gamers report that they rely on word of mouth to obtain information on video games.[433]

  Further research from Poretski et al (2019)[434] found that word of mouth increases game consumption, particularly for online games. Loyalty program operators that develop games with a 'talkability' factor can benefit from generating a buzz amongst social groups.

KFC China

KFC China identified that the country's 564 million gamers were a core target market which was key to achieving their goals of connecting with the youth population. They strategically partnered with the most popular Esports gaming franchise in China, League Of

---

432 McGilloway, C., 2018, cited in 'Boost Juice launches new "Find the Fruit" game app', Inside FMCG Magazine, https://insidefmcg.com.au/2018/04/19/boost-juice-launches-new-find-the-fruit-game-app/, accessed 16th May 2019

433 The NPD Group, 2009, 'Gaming Device Profiles'.

434 Poretski, L., Zalmanson, L. & Arazy, O., 2019, 'The Effects of Co-Creation and Word-of- Mouth on Content Consumption - Findings from the Video Game Industry', Fortieth International Conference on Information Systems Munich 2019, https://aisel.aisnet.org/cgi/viewcontent.cgi?article=1639&context=icis2019, accessed 15 June 2020.

Legends, to create an AI commentator (which they called Colonel KI) that predicted outcomes of League of Legends tournaments in real time. Fans could log into the KFC app to track predictions throughout the match. During the most exciting moments in the match, the Colonel would virtually distribute QR coupons to fans inviting them to order KFC online and enjoy fried chicken during the game.

Results generated impressive metrics in both social buzz and sales. There were 203 million viewers on League of Legends live streams, 35 million topic views on Weibo, 1.9 million on screen comments, 100 per cent of coupons accepted and 25 per cent of coupons redeemed (2,500 per cent above the benchmark).[435]

To increase talkability further, KFC also themed some of their restaurants with League of Legends branding, and saw a 35 per cent uplift in sales in themed stores.[436]

- **Social sharing**: gamers are increasingly sharing their experiences and successes on social media. According to Minguez,[437] this commenced with interactive browser-based Facebook games like Zynga Poker, Mafia Wars and FarmVille, where it was observed that 'players not only loved to play against one another, but also liked the bragging rights that came with getting high scores or passing a particularly tough level'. Loyalty programs which develop more comprehensive, challenging games have the opportunity to tap into social sharing, and even harness it by making it easy to share (via strategically positioned buttons) and rewarding the behaviour (by providing incremental rewards).

435 The Esports Ads, Colonel KI campaign, https://theesportsads.com/campaigns/colonelki, accessed 27 May 2020.

436 Thomas, P., 2019, Digital Driving Growth in KFC China, Global Convenience Store Focus, https://www.globalconveniencestorefocus.co.uk/features/digital-driving-growth-in-kfc-china/, accessed 14 January 2020.

437 Minguez, K., 2014, 'The Merging of Social Media and Gaming', Social Media Today, https://www.socialmediatoday.com/content/merging-social-media-and-gaming, accessed 14 January 2020.

Candy Crush

Candy Crush was designed to be played and completed for free (70 per cent of users on the last level have never paid to play) but with limitations, including limits on the amount of lives and moves players can access for free each day. Players can get more lives by either buying them or asking their friends on Facebook to accept their request for free lives. Using Facebook as a platform to expand the program throughout social friend networks was the primary source of new Candy Crush players through their growth phase.

The ability to compete against friends was another social element which motivated users to want to progress faster, compelling them to pay for more lives to win against their friends. Players also like to show off their scores to people they know, feeling a sense of pride in their level of achievement.

Tapping into social sharing helped the Candy Crush series bring in more than US$1.5 billion in revenue from micro-transactions in 2018 across iOS and Android.[438] For loyalty program designers, it demonstrated what is possible when a hot game goes viral.

- **Habit formation**: games can be used to generate more sustained and habitual behaviour. A program operator may apply simple, low skill and randomness elements to turn their delivery of offers into a game. This provides the opportunity for a member to reveal a new offer every day by playing, exposing them to the brand on a frequent basis and entering their consideration set frequently and consistently.

---

438 Makuch, E., 2019, Gamespot, 'Here's How Much Money Candy Crush Makes Compared To Fortnite And Pokemon Go On Mobile', https://www.gamespot.com/articles/heres-how-much-money-candy-crush-makes-compared-to/1100-6464305/, accessed 28 May 2020.

Maccas Mini Games

'Maccas Mini Games', a 2020 promotion provided by McDonald's, gave players one opportunity per day to unlock a prize by playing an in-app game. Players could choose to dunk a chicken nugget, play mini-golf or run through a maze, where everyone won a prize.

On successful completion of the game, an offer was presented to the player which expired within 16 hours, generating engagement urgency.

The player could revisit the app and play again the next day, helping to develop habitual behaviours.

- **Endowment effect**: as detailed in Chapter 6, Thaler, (1980)[439] identified that consumers place a greater value on things once they have established ownership. The endowment effect can be harnessed by loyalty programs when distributing offers as prizes. While not proven, it can be hypothesised that a member who earns an offer after successfully completing a challenging game is likely to value the offer more than a member who has just been provided with it. As a result, they are potentially more likely to use the offer.

With all these benefits, it is important to acknowledge that developing a compelling, engaging, likeable and shareable game within a reasonable budget can be challenging. Phan et al (2016)[440] developed a Game User Experience Satisfaction Scale (GUESS) to comprehensively measure video game satisfaction based on nine key factors; usability/playability, narratives, play engrossment, enjoyment, creative freedom, audio aesthetics, personal gratification, social connectivity and visual aesthetics. Developing a game which measures highly across most or all factors would be challenging, although it should be recognised that games developed for short-term loyalty program

---

439 Thaler, R., 1980, 'Toward a Positive Theory of Consumer Choice,' Journal of Economic Behavior and Organization, Vol 1, pp39-60.

440 Phan, M., Keebler, J. & Chaparro, B., 2016, 'The Development and Validation of the Game User Experience Satisfaction Scale (GUESS)', Human Factors: The Journal of the Human Factors and Ergonomics Society, Vol 58, Iss 8.

promotional campaigns are likely not going to be judged in the same light as a major label release.

To support loyalty programs interested in experimenting with games, platform providers have evolved offering white-label game solutions specialising in rapid, low-cost development, deployment and analytics.

Gamification

Gamification can play a key role in loyalty programs by making mundane actions fun, as well as motivating members to engage in desirable behaviours. Gamification incorporates a range of useful tools to facilitate engagement; points, badges, levels, leaderboards, progress trackers and challenges. It can be argued that many loyalty programs are gamification programs. Members are motivated to complete specific tasks in non-game contexts to accumulate points, earn badges and move up levels (status tiers), climb leaderboards and complete challenges (e.g. shop at new coalition partners to earn bonus points).

The term gamification was first coined by games designer Nick Pelling. He launched a company in 2003 which focused on 'applying game-like accelerated user interface design to make electronic transactions both enjoyable and fast.'[441] Pelling claims his vision was a decade too early for its time, and the company was closed in 2006. To his credit, gamification has blossomed, with Pelling identifying Apple as the company which has run furthest with it by embracing 'the underlying idea of gamification – making hard things easy, expressive, near-effortless to use.'

During that same period, others in the gaming industry were also contemplating the expansion of game thinking into non-game areas, such as technology use and work environments. Much of the conceptual focus was on fun and enjoyment. Brandtzaeg et al (2004)[442] explored a theoretical model for understanding the components and nature of enjoyment, and how designers could use their model to predict and evaluate enjoyment. McCarthy and

---

441 Pelling, N., 2011, 'The (short) prehistory of "gamification"', https://nanodome. wordpress.com/2011/08/09/the-short-prehistory-of-gamification/, accessed 22 May 2020.

442 Brandtzæg, P. B., Følstad, A. & Heim, J., 2004, 'Enjoyment: Lessons from Karasek', Funology; From Usability to Enjoyment, Springer.

Wright (2004)[443] wrote of feeling attached to technology brands which had provided them with a sense of 'enchantment' when using their products. Anderson et al (2004)[444] proposed using tools for market research that were both provocative and aesthetically pleasant to involve people in engaging experiences as a way to access their intimate sphere and collect revealing data. Overbeeke et al (2004)[445] argued that technology could be made more engaging by appealing more to the senses to make the interaction more tangible.

In 2008, Currier[446] argued that 'there is no more consistent way to predictably induce desired behaviour in humans than engaging them in a context that uses game mechanics such as leader boards, levelling, currencies, stored value, privileges, super-powers, status indicators, random reward schedules, etc.' He provided examples of Tencent in China, where members could be sold virtual medicine for their virtual pets if they became sick, and MyCokeRewards, where members could engage with a virtual currency, leaderboards, quests and each other.

The Loyalty360 Expo in Hollywood, Florida in 2009 featured a presentation on gamification by Barry Kirk and Tim Crank of Maritz.[447] 'Games tap into competition, status, flow, play, reward, achievement and mastery—primal psychological needs', Kirk was quoted as saying. He provided a long list of game mechanics, including points, tiers, collecting (e.g. badges), leaderboards, exchanges (sharing gifts on social media), customisation (encouraging members to invest in creating their profile, as it develops exit barriers), feedback (progress tracking), randomness (elements where the member does not know when an event will occur), spectators and bosses (those who climb to

443 McCarthy, J. C. & Wright, P. C., 2004, 'The enchantments of technology', Funology; From Usability to Enjoyment, Springer.

444 Anderson, K., Jacobs, M. & Polazzi, L., 2004, 'Playing Games in the Emotional Space', Funology; From Usability to Enjoyment, Springer.

445 Overbeeke, K., Djajadiningrat, T., Hummels, C., Wensveen, S. & Pens, J., 2004, 'Let's make things engaging', Funology; From Usability to Enjoyment, Springer.

446 Currier, J., 2008, 'Gamification: Game Mechanics is the New Marketing', Oogalabs, https://blog.oogalabs.com/2008/11/05/gamification-game-mechanics-is-the-new-marketing/, accessed 19 April 2020.

447 Loyalty Management Magazine, 2009, Loyalty 360, Vol 3, Iss 1.

the highest tiers). Of interest is that more modern gamification theory tends to focus on a more refined list (points, badges tiers, leaderboards and challenges), indicating that along the way the full scope of gamification appears to have been watered down.

Earlier that year, Foursquare (acknowledged as one of the first mass-market applications of gamification) had been unofficially launched at the SXSW conference in Austin.[448] Creators Dennis Crowley and Naveen Selvadurai spent the conference walking around showing attendees the app, and in the space of a few days grew the member base from one hundred to over four thousand. The iPhone app let members explore cities, check-in at restaurants and bars (to let friends know where they were), read and write reviews, and access special offers. Gamification elements included the ability to earn points and badges, achieve status levels and become 'mayor' of a particular venue (for checking in multiple times in a set period). Inspired by Dodgeball (a texting app launched in 2000, which allowed users to check-in, and view crushes, friends, friends of friends and interesting venues nearby), Foursquare demonstrated to a much wider, global audience the potential of gamification in the new age of smartphones and increasingly sophisticated internet applications.

Deterding et al (2011)[449] reported that Foursquare helped gamification gain rapid traction in interaction design and digital marketing, with numerous applications developed across productivity, finance, health, education, sustainability, news and entertainment media, and software service layers just two years later.

A 2019 whitepaper from Bunchball[450] expanded on the concept of game mechanics by also focusing on 'game dynamics' or desires. They argued that

---

448 McKracken, H., 2009, 'Foursquare's first decade, from viral hit to real business and beyond', Fast Company, https://www.fastcompany.com/90318329/foursquares-first-decade-from-viral-hit-to-real-business-and-beyond, accessed 14 April 2020.

449 Deterding, S., Dixon, D., Nacke, L. E., O'Hara, K. & Sicart, M., 2011, 'Gamification: Using game design elements in non-gaming contexts', Paper presented at the 2011 Annual Conference Extended Abstracts on Human Factors in Computing Systems (CHI EA'11), Vancouver, BC, Canada.

450 Bunchball Whitepaper, 2019, 'Gamification 101: An Introduction to the Use of Game Dynamics to Influence Behavior', https://www.bunchball.com/gamification101, accessed 5 May 2020.

through the application of game mechanics, companies could create an experience that drives behaviour by satisfying one or more desires. These included status, reward, competitive nature, altruism, self-expression and achievement. Bunchball maintained that these desires are universal, crossing generations, demographics, cultures, and genders.

> **Waze**
>
> Waze is a peer community of users who aim to 'outsmart traffic together'. They use their pool of crowdsourced information to allow Waze to adapt to traffic patterns, avoid traffic jams, avoid police, regulate roads, and generally get around faster and more efficiently.
>
> Waze achieved the critical scale of users necessary to make their user generated sharing economy succeed by employing gamification tactics to reward user participation. Wazers (drivers) can earn points and achieve a higher ranking (5 levels) for anything which will improve the map data and make the roads safer for other drivers. These rewardable actions include reporting incidents, reporting hazards (e.g. roadkill), mapping new roads, updating house numbers or marking police sightings on the map.
>
> Wazers can see other Wazers on the road (as well as their ranking) and can send notifications thanking other Wazers for sharing useful traffic information which helps increase their ranking further. Having the rank visual and being appreciated by peers are both powerful motivators from a consumer psychology perspective, reinforcing the idea that users feel accepted, important and useful to the group (social identity and social proof biases).

A model which is widely applied to gamification theory is the 'Fogg Behavior Model', developed by Stanford professor B.J. Fogg.[451] The model

---

451 http://www.behaviormodel.org/. Reproduced with permission Professor B.J. Fogg.

proposed that three elements (Motivation, Ability and a Prompt) must converge at the same moment for a behaviour to occur.

To illustrate, if a loyalty program operator aims for members to increase spend at a particular coalition partner, the model provides guidance on how to stimulate the base. Specifically:

- **Motivation**: the key motivation of the community is their desire to earn more points and status credits.

- **Ability**: most members of the community will have the ability to access the partner via a retail store or online.

- **Prompt**: the program operator can prompt the behaviour with bonus points and status credits for spending with the partner and promoting their purchase on social media.

The 'Fogg Behaviour Model' further elaborates on Prompt types, which can differ in effectiveness dependent on the level of motivation and ability of the member:

- **High motivation-low ability**: a Facilitator Prompt is required, where the member is provided with a higher level of support to commence and complete the behaviour. For example, a short training video on how to progress status tiers.

- **High motivation-high ability**: a Signal Prompt is required, where the member simply requires a cue to commence the behaviour. For example, a text message that the campaign has commenced.

- **Low motivation-high ability**: a Spark Prompt is required, where the member requires additional motivation to commence the behaviour. For example, double status credits for purchases made in a defined period.

Taylor Swift

Taylor Swift launched a 'Taylor's Biggest Fan'[452] program in 2017, pitching to her fans that she was committed to getting tickets into the hands of her most committed fans (not scalpers or bots) through the exclusive program. Using the 'verified fan' system introduced by Ticketmaster, fans could watch and repost her latest music video, buy her new album or buy Taylor Swift merchandise to increase their chances of accessing tickets. Those fans with the highest motivation (with some fans reportedly buying the same album multiple times from different stores to boost their chances) were rewarded with ticket access.

The program received significant criticism due to all fans not having the same financial means to prove they were Taylor's biggest fan, earning the program a derogatory name of 'Taylor's Richest Fan'. Although the intention was to reward motivation, the campaign design was weighted towards those with high financial ability to purchase more products.

Gamification has since extended into many areas, not just limited to loyalty programs. But does gamification work? A literature review of 25 empirical studies by Hamari et al (2014)[453] where the principal research question was 'Does gamification work?' found that the majority of the programs produced positive effects and benefits. It is important to note that most of the programs studied were for education and learning or for intra-organisational systems. Hamari et al were surprised that none of the studies were conducted on marketing gamification, despite the wide range of applications already in market

452 Hann, M., 2017, 'Bad blood! Is Taylor Swift's 'verified fan' system a way to reward followers – or rip them off?', The Guardian, https://www.theguardian.com/music/2017/aug/31/bad-blood-is-taylor-swifts-verified-fan-system-a-way-to-reward-followers-or-rip-them-off, accessed 20 July 2020.

453 Hamari, J., Koivisto, J. & Sarsa, H., 2014, 'Does Gamification Work? – A Literature Review of Empirical Studies on Gamification', In proceedings of the 47th Hawaii International Conference on System Sciences, Hawaii, USA, January 6-9, 2014.

by that time, and that no studies focused on the relationship between gamification and purchase behaviour.

Sailer et al (2017)[454] reported support for gamification in a study where they deliberately varied different configurations of game design elements, and analysed them in regard to their effect on the fulfilment of basic psychological needs. They found that badges, leaderboards and performance graphs positively affected competence need satisfaction, as well as perceived task meaningfulness, while avatars, meaningful stories and teammates affected experiences of social relatedness. Their conclusion was that specific game design elements have specific psychological effects.

This insight is important for loyalty program designers seeking to apply gamification, indicating they should have clarity on the types of psychological and emotional reactions they are attempting to arouse to guide their use of the appropriate game elements.

Hwang and Choi (2019)[455] conducted a study of U.S. consumers responding to gamification elements within app-based loyalty programs. The results confirmed that gamified loyalty programs increased consumer loyalty towards the program, which in turn enhanced consumers' participation intention and app download intention. The findings also suggested that gamified loyalty programs can help companies differentiate their program from other conventional programs, acting to improve overall member loyalty.

Google Local Guides

Google's Local Guides[456] program was designed to generate business related content for Search and Google Maps. Local Guides members all around the world earn points for different activities, including writing a review (10 points), providing a rating (1 point),

---

454 Sailer, M., Hense, J., Mayr, S. & Mandl, H., 2017, 'How gamification motivates: An experimental study of the effects of specific game design elements on psychological need satisfaction', Computers in Human Behavior. Vol 69, pp371-380.

455 Hwang, J. & Choi, L., 2020. 'Having fun while receiving rewards?: Exploration of gamification in loyalty programs for consumer loyalty', Journal of Business Research. Vol 106, pp365-376.

456 Google, Local Guides, https://maps.google.com/localguides, accessed 29 June 2020.

submitting a photo (5 points), answering a question (1 point), editing incorrect details (5 points) and adding a new place (15 points).

Points can be accumulated to unlock ten levels and seven badges, which provide different benefits such as exclusive contests, early access to new Google products and features, Google Drive storage upgrades, the option to be featured in Local Guides online channels and special perks from partners.

Any reviews posted by the member display their profile, which includes their level and their badge. Higher level tiers also have an opportunity to win a trip to the annual Local Guides summit, a conference where Google hosts a select group of Local Guides from around the world.

An interesting element of the program is Google Communities. Local Guides allows reviewers to host meet ups, where they can invite other local reviewers to get together and explore the neighbourhood, then post their experience onto Google Maps. Examples include San Francisco (the group mapped an interesting walking path through the city and photographed the whole thing), London (the group mapped out a route of the cafes with the best coffee) and New York (the group mapped out the city's finest ramen joints).

TripAdvisor (B2B gamification)

TripAdvisor[457] gives each business (e.g. hotels, restaurants, tour companies) a ranking within their specific category and overtly display this ranking to users. For example, if a user searches for restaurants within their city, the list is showcased to them in the order of the restaurant rank together with a label on each restaurant displaying the rank (i.e. #13 of 181 restaurants in Zurich). This is aimed at motivating businesses to rally their customers to

---

457 Tripadvisor, 'Tripadvisor Popularity Ranking: Key Factors and How to Improve', https://www.tripadvisor.com/TripAdvisorInsights/w722#:~:text=Your%20 Tripadvisor%20Popularity%20Ranking%20is,when%20they%20search%20 your%20area., accessed 30 June 2020.

provide positive reviews, with the reward to the business being an improved ranking, exposure to new customers and likelihood of driving additional business.

This strategy also forces businesses to think about the elements which contribute to a positive review (food + service + value) and improve certain aspects of the customer experience to ensure they work towards progressing and/or maintaining their valuable ranking.

TripAdvisor uses a ranking/leaderboard system to stimulate businesses to leverage their customer bases to drive acquisition and engagement on the TripAdvisor platform.

Key insights

- Games and gamification are different approaches which deliver different outcomes within loyalty programs.

- Games are defined as 'an activity that one engages in for amusement or fun', and 'a complete episode or period of play, ending in a final result'.

- Gamification is the use of elements of gameplay in non-game contexts to stimulate specific behaviours.

- Games can be used to acquire new members, expose consumers to the brand for extended periods, be used to promote company values and mission, generate word of mouth promotion, stimulate social media sharing, generate habitual behaviours and make members value offers more highly than if they are simply conferred.

- It can be argued that loyalty programs are gamification programs. Gamification incorporates a range of useful tools to facilitate engagement within loyalty programs; points, tiers, collecting, leaderboards, progress trackers, exchanges, customisation, feedback, randomness, spectators and bosses.

Suggested reading

- Lazzaro, Nicole., 2004, 'Why we Play Games: Four Keys to More Emotion without Story', Game Dev Conf, http://twvideo01.ubm-us.net/o1/vault/gdc04/slides/why_we_play_games.pdf

- William E. Baker, 1999, 'When Can Affective Conditioning and Mere Exposure Directly Influence Brand Choice?', Journal of Advertising, Vol 28, Iss 4, pp31-46.

- Pelling, N., 2011, 'The (short) prehistory of 'gamification'', https://nanodome.wordpress.com/2011/08/09/the-short-prehistory-of-gamification/

- McKracken, H., 2009, 'Foursquare's first decade, from viral hit to real business and beyond', Fast Company, https://www.fastcompany.com/90318329/foursquares-first-decade-from-viral-hit-to-real-business-and-beyond

- Sailer, Michael & Hense, Jan & Mayr, Sarah & Mandl, Heinz., 2017, 'How gamification motivates: An experimental study of the effects of specific game design elements on psychological need satisfaction', Computers in Human Behavior, Vol 69, pp371-380.

CHAPTER 14

MONETISATION AND COMMERCIAL MODELLING

This chapter was co-written by Stuart Dinnis,
global expert in Loyalty Finance.

'… brand managers may overestimate the importance of targeting heavy users (or frequent users) and may underestimate the effectiveness of inexpensive reward programs. In reality, low and moderate reward programs that target light users may generate higher incremental sales and may tend to be more profitable than is generally expected.'

- Brian Wansink, 2003[458]

Focus areas

This chapter will address the following questions:

- What does monetisation of a loyalty program involve?

- How can companies monetise loyalty programs?

- How can member personal data be monetised?

- What are the different approaches which can be taken to measure the cost-effectiveness and return on investment for loyalty programs?

---

458 Wansink, B., 2003, 'Developing a cost-effective brand loyalty program', Journal of Advertising Research, Vol 43, Iss 3, pp301-309.

Monetisation

Many loyalty programs are a direct cost to the company, representing a form of marketing spend. This is viewed as a strategic investment intended to boost customer engagement, leading to profit growth, reduced churn and other benefits, delivering an overall positive financial and brand health outcome.

Some loyalty programs generate direct incremental revenue. This may be enough solely to offset some of the operational costs, or it may be of such magnitude that the program operates profitably. Many loyalty programs can be structured to be profitable, taking into consideration value to both the customers and the program partners.

There are a range of ways loyalty programs can generate income for the program operator. These include:

1. Third-party partners paying for members to earn points.
2. Earning revenue for selling membership subscriptions.
3. Earning commission when selling discount products to members.
4. Earning merchant funded revenue via member transactions.
5. Selling and supplying program-branded products and services.

Some bigger programs have also evolved business units that are responsible for using member personal data to generate incremental revenue for the loyalty program or parent company. As referenced in Chapter 10, there are data brokers that collect data from publicly available digital sources (such as social media and apps) which they sell to loyalty programs, and database generators, which specialise in building marketing databases on behalf of loyalty programs.

The ways revenue is generated using member personal data include:

6. Consumer insight reports created by loyalty programs to sell to third parties.
7. Marketing services provided by loyalty programs.
8. Data brokers and data exchanges selling data and services to loyalty programs.
9. Database generators creating new databases to sell to loyalty programs.

Each of these nine monetisation approaches will be explored in turn.

Third-party partners paying for members to earn points

Globally, a small number of coalition loyalty programs are highly profitable, with their annual billings in the billions and profits in the hundreds of millions, or even billions. According to IdeaWorksCompany,[459] in 2017, American Airlines generated US$3.1 billion from AAdvantage program points sales, while Delta SkyMiles generated US$3 billion, and United MileagePlus generated US$2.3 billion.

The United MileagePlus June 2020 Investor Presentation[460] stated the program had over 100 million members, US$5.3 billion in cash flow from miles sales in 2019 (12 per cent of total United revenue) and US$1.8 billion EBITDA (26 per cent of total United adjusted EBITDAR). Of interest, due to the massive impact of Covid-19 on the airline industry globally, United obtained a US$6.8 billion financing commitment through a financing structure secured by MileagePlus, indicating the critical importance of the loyalty program to the airline.

Coalition loyalty programs generate *billings* when a partner company pays for a member to earn points. For example, if an Emirates Skywards member hires a car from Sixt, they will earn 2,000 miles. Emirates will invoice Sixt for the cost of those miles. Sixt will view the cost as a marketing expense, because by offering Skywards miles, Sixt is more likely to attract Skywards members, plus Emirates may promote them to their member base, helping to boost sales.

Coalition loyalty programs generate revenue when the member earns points, redeems points, when points expire, and when interest is paid on deferred billings.[461]

To illustrate the coalition loyalty program monetisation model, consider this hypothetical example.

---

459 Silk, R., 2019, 'Airlines' credit cards in "arms race" to profits,' Travel Weekly, https://www.travelweekly.com/Travel-News/Airline-News/Airlines-credit-cards-in-arms-race-to-profits, accessed 26th May 2020.

460 United Airlines, 2020, 'MileagePlus Investor Presentation 15 June 2020', https://ir.united.com/static-files/1c0f0c79-23ca-4fd2-80c1-cf975348bab9, accessed 23 June 2020.

461 Catchit Loyalty, 2016, "How Frequent Flyer Programs Make Money", YouTube, https://www.youtube.com/watch?v=-i50YVaD-tk, accessed 13th May 2019.

1. A member of a coalition loyalty program spends $10,000 with participating retailers (this may be a single transaction or multiple transactions). They swipe their membership card and earn 10,000 points at the rate of 1.0 point per dollar spent. The coalition loyalty program invoices the retailer/s for the cost of the points at a rate of 1.5 cents per point, costing the retailer/s $150.

2. The $150 billings earned is transferred to a holding account. International accounting standards dictate the program operator must hold sufficient billings to cover the cost of the future points liability (referred to as 'Fair Value'). In other words, the program operator must retain enough cash to cover the cost of the reward when the member decides to redeem the points.

    For our example, the Fair Value is 1.0 cent per point, so the extra 0.5 cent can be recognised immediately as revenue (IFRS13 refers to this as marketing revenue, while under US-GAAP this is done through a bifurcation clause in the partner contract). The 1.0 cent per point is transferred to the Balance Sheet and added to a Deferred Liability account. It is held there until either the points are redeemed or they expire.

3. When the member redeems the points, the coalition loyalty program may assign a lower value than the 1.0 cent held as Fair Value for the points. In this example, the member will redeem their points for a gift card, where the value per point is just 0.6 cent. Thus, the program operator will earn an additional 1.0c − 0.6c = 0.4c per point. The program recognises both the 1.0 cent as redemption revenue (removing it from the Deferred Liability account on the Balance Sheet) and the 0.6 cent as a redemption expense, thus reflecting the marginal profit of 0.4 cents in the Profit and Loss.

4. If the member does not have any further account activity or does not redeem the points within a specified time period, the points may eventually expire. In this instance, the program operator will earn the full 1.0c per point as revenue.

The below diagram reflects the timing of recognising various parts of the point value through its lifecycle:

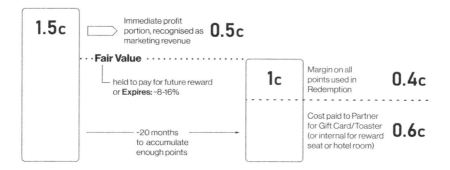

Figure 16: a monetisation model for a points-based coalition program, demonstrating the point value through its lifecycle. Designed by Stuart Dinnis.

A large coalition loyalty program can sell hundreds of billions of points each year, making those fraction of a cent profits quickly add up.

The below table illustrates the calculations for the example:

Action	Earn/ Redeem/ Expire	Net Points Balance	Billings/ Cost Paid	Revenue
Member spends $10,000	Earn 10,000 points	10,000	1.5c x 10,000 points = $150	0.5c x 10,000 points = $50
Deferred revenue earns interest				$100 x 3% p.a. = $3.00
Member redeems for a $50 gift card	Redeem 8,000 points	10,000 – 8,000 = 2,000	Paid - $48	8,000 x (1.0c- 0.6c) = $32
Remaining points expire	Expire 2,000 points	2,000 – 2,000 = 0		2,000 x 1.0c = $20
Total			**Net $102**	**$50 + $3 + $32 + $20 = $105.00**

Table 1: Basic gross margin calculation for a coalition loyalty program earn and redemption transaction

Thus, for a transaction of $10,000, the loyalty program operator collects billings of $150. Of that amount, $105 revenue is earned with $48 paid in cost to provide a reward.

Coalition loyalty program operators may price discriminate by offering volume discounts to third-party partners. Smaller retailers buying fewer points each year can expect to pay more per point than larger retailers buying more points. Some retailers may agree to provide multiple points for each dollar spent by the member, so they end up investing a larger percentage of the member's spend on points.

Loyalty program operators may also negotiate with the third-party partner to commit to rewarding their customers with a minimum amount of points each year to ensure they are fully committed to promoting the partnership within their marketing channels. In return, loyalty program operators may agree to specified marketing promotion of the partner to their member base to help them grow their business. Loyalty program operators may also negotiate for the partner to commit to running a number of bonus points campaigns each year. In some instances, the cost of the bonus points to the third-party partner may be higher than standard points in order to cover the campaign marketing costs of the loyalty program, while acting as an incentive for the program to run the campaign.

As detailed in the example, if the member does not redeem or transfer the points, they may expire (which is known as 'breakage' in the loyalty industry). This may be because the member has had no account activity for a specified period, meaning they have not earned or redeemed at least one point in the required time frame. For example, miles in the Air France/KLM Flying Blue program expire if members have no qualifying flight or credit card activity on their account within a 24 month period.[462] Alternatively, points may expire because a specified period of time has passed from when the points were earned. For example, Singapore Airlines Krisflyer miles expire after three years at the end of the equivalent month in which they were earned.[463]

The expiry of points is a key factor in the financial management of a coalition loyalty program's profitability, with both push and pull factors. Higher levels of expiry directly translate into higher immediate revenue.[464] However, it also represents members disengaging from the program, hence can have a negative impact on the future profitability potential of the program. Due to this, some coalition loyalty programs engage actuaries to help manage their

---

462 Air France, 'Air France FAQ's',https://www.airfrance.us/US/en/common/faq/flying-blue/how-long-do-your-miles-stay-valid.htm, accessed 25 May 2020

463 Singapore Airlines Krisflyer terms and conditions https://www.singaporeair.com/registerKFUser.form?showTnC=y#:~:text=A%20member's%20KrisFlyer%20miles%20will,in%20which%20they%20were%20earned. Accessed 26 August 2020

464 Feldman, D., 2017, 'LOYALTY MYTHS: IS BREAKAGE GOOD?', Medium, https://medium.com/@dfcatch/loyalty-myths-is-breakage-good-873950da26dc, accessed 16 May 2019.

expiry strategies, with the aim of maintaining it within a specified percentage range.

> **Qantas Frequent Flyer**
>
> A Qantas Frequent Flyer presentation to the Actuaries Institute in 2012 stated that within the loyalty program, 'modelling future points expiry (breakage) helps inform the setting of assumptions by management,' and that 'breakage is modelled with a multi-state transition model based on the level of customer activity.'[465]

This issue of points expiry has also attracted the attention of regulators, with some countries acting to outlaw the practice in the interests of consumer protection.

> **Ontario Government**
>
> In 2018, the Government of Ontario, Canada, legislated a ban on loyalty and reward points expiry as part of a series of consumer-side protections, allowing consumers to request that businesses reimburse them for improperly expired points.[466]
>
> These consumer protection laws do not come into play if the loyalty program operator decides to close a member's account due to reasonable grounds of inactivity or fraud.

Some loyalty program operators aim to maximise the profit they make on each point which is sold and redeemed. They may do this by adjusting the price and value of points. Depending on what reward a member redeems their points on, the value they receive for their points can vary. For example, points

465 Chandler and Tubman, 2012, 'The Analytics of Loyalty – Qantas Frequent Flyer', Actuaries Institute, https://www.actuaries.asn.au/Library/Events/FSF/2012/AnalyticsOfLoyalty3BChandlerTubman.pdf,accessed 15 May 2019.

466 Chharbra, S., 2018, 'Ontario's reward points expiry ban is now in effect,' https://mobilesyrup.com/2018/01/01/ontarios-reward-points-expiry-ban-now-effect/, Mobile Syrup, accessed 27 May 2020

redeemed on a flight may deliver a value of 1 cent per point but if redeemed on a gift card (as per our example) they may deliver a value of 0.6 cents per point, while a toaster may give just 0.25 cents value per point.

This approach utilises efficient rewards to maximise the value accessed by members for flights, ensuring the majority of points revenue remains within the airline. The approach also takes advantage of wholesale margins on third-party products to boost revenue earned on redemptions. To further boost revenues, some airline programs have been observed to apply surcharges on reward flights which are not applied on flights paid for with cash.[467]

Other loyalty program operators take a more balanced approach; attempting to maintain as much of a value return as possible for members, with the outcome being lower program profits but (ideally) higher member engagement.

As illustrated, the coalition loyalty program operator also earns interest on deferred billings. When the points are sold to third-party partners, the loyalty program operator must defer enough to cover the cost of the future reward (or liability)[468]. A deferred holding of several billion dollars is not unusual for a large loyalty coalition program.

*

Interest and breakage are not always related to points earn and expiry.

With the rise of payment apps, members of some loyalty programs are required to pre-load credit into their accounts to draw-down on when placing orders. Interest is earned on the holdings (or they can be used as working capital).

In addition, under some accounting standards if the credit is not used, it can be accounted for as breakage, allowing the company to draw-down on the deferred holding.

---

467 Moffitt, M., 2018, 'Lock in your Velocity redemptions before the end of the year to avoid new charges', Point Hacks, https://www.pointhacks.com.au/reduce-surcharges-frequent-flyer-programs-guide/, accessed 13 May 2019.

468 Australian Accounting Standards Board, 'Customer Loyalty Programmes, Compiled Interpretation, Interpretation 13', https://www.aasb.gov.au/admin/file/content105/c9/INT13_08-07_COMPjun10_01-11.pdf, accessed 26 November 2010.

Starbucks Rewards

Members of Starbucks Rewards who wish to place an order via the app are required to pre-load credit.

According to The Motley Fool,[469] 'Starbucks is essentially gaining access to an interest-free line of credit, one that equates to roughly 4 per cent of the company's total liabilities.'

A sizeable portion of the credit ends up going unused. The value stored has no expiration date, so Starbucks uses historical data to determine the amount of anticipated breakage. The Motley Fool reported that in FY19, Starbucks generated US$141 million breakage revenue.

Earning revenue for selling membership subscriptions

As detailed in Chapter 11, some loyalty programs charge a one-off or annual subscription fee for members to join the program. This is a source of revenue, which if structured correctly can make the program quite profitable.

This type of program approach can be particularly profitable if the rewards provided are efficient, as the cost to the company is negligible, allowing them to bank much of the membership fee.

Nike Adventure Club

Nike Adventure Club[470] is a subscription plan for children's sneakers aimed at encouraging healthy active lifestyles and ensuring growing children always have properly fitting sneakers without needing to be dragged to the shops.

Members choose an Adventure Club plan (4, 6 or 12 pairs per year), pick from a selection of sneaker styles and receive their delivery kit at the chosen intervals. The delivery kit includes a new pair of

469 Patel, N., 2020, 'How Starbucks Quietly Benefits From Its Most Passionate Customers', The Motley Fool, https://www.fool.com/investing/2020/06/17/how-starbucks-quietly-benefits-from-its-most-passi.aspx, accessed 24 June 2020

470 Nike, 'Nike Adventure Club', https://news.nike.com/news/nike-adventure-club, accessed 30 June 2020.

sneakers, plus other activities such as books, adventure guides and outdoor games. These are designed to inspire adventure and bonding between parents and children, whilst directly generating consistent revenue and brand stickiness for Nike.

Earning commission when selling discount products to members

As detailed in Chapter 8, a popular alternative to points and status tier programs is the member benefits program design, where members can gain access to a range of discount products and services provided by third-party suppliers, such as gift cards, movie tickets, accommodation, experiences, restaurants, travel and more.

Loyalty program operators tend to follow one of two approaches for the member benefits model. They may provide members with the full discount that has been negotiated with the third-party supplier, or they may retain part of the discount and pass on the remainder to the member.

The second approach allows for monetisation of the program. For example, if a program has negotiated access to discount movie tickets, the operator may choose to add a 50 cent surcharge on top, such that each time a movie ticket is sold, the loyalty program operator earns a small profit.

While big coalition loyalty programs can earn hundreds of millions of dollars profit each year, member benefits programs are not nearly as lucrative, primarily because the margin they earn on each transaction is much less, the size of their member bases are generally smaller and the amount of transaction activity is lower. Programs operating in this way will commonly view this approach as a method to offset their operational costs.

Earning merchant funded revenue via member transactions

As detailed in Chapter 8, loyalty programs can establish merchant funded programs where a third-party partner (or merchant) covers the cost of the benefits provided to the member. This is generally as a result of the loyalty program promoting the third-party partner to the member, leading to the member transacting with the partner. Different approaches to merchant funded programs include affiliate, card-linked and gift card-linked.

This model is becoming more prevalent, either within major coalition loyalty programs or standalone, such as cashback loyalty programs. The loyalty program operator can monetise the model by retaining some of the commission paid to them by the merchant partner website and take this as profit or use it to further fund the program. For the merchant, the incentive is the potential to gain access to highly engaged customers.

For example, if a member clicks through from their loyalty website to a partner website and spends $100, the loyalty program may earn commission of $8. They may choose to reward the member with $5 of points or cashback and retain the remaining $3 as incremental margin. The commission now becomes an added benefit to the members and a profit centre for the loyalty program operator.

> ### ClickBank
>
> ClickBank[471] is a leading global retailer and affiliate marketplace serving digital and physical goods and services with distribution in over 200 countries. Loyalty program operators can join as ClickBank affiliates to access a marketplace of over 4,000 products and receive commission when their members transact.

Selling and supplying program-branded products and services

Major loyalty programs generate additional revenue by developing branded products and services to market to their members. This may include credit cards, insurance, personal loans, travel services, food and wine clubs, and even golf clubs.

The approach delivers several benefits; additional revenue from the products or services sold, additional points earn for the member (which generates additional revenue for the loyalty program when the points are redeemed), and deeper engagement from the member who is actively choosing to consume program-branded and affiliated products.

---

471 ClickBank, https://www.clickbank.com/, accessed 30 June 2020.

Tesco Clubcard

Tesco[472] has diversified into many different areas over the years, including Tesco Bank credit cards and insurance, Tesco Mobile, Tesco Express/Esso petrol stations and the variety of Tesco and non-branded shopping and convenience stores.

Branded financial services products, such as Tesco Bank credit cards, provide members the opportunity to earn Clubcard points on every day spends and even more when they shop within the Tesco ecosystem.

For other financial services, such as home, pet or car insurance, Clubcard holders are entitled to policy discounts and new policy bonus points.

The launch of the subscription-based Tesco Clubcard Plus brought additional value to members across all Tesco brands and encourages them to remain within the brand.

Consumer insight reports created by loyalty programs to sell to third parties

One of the more common ways loyalty program data is monetised is via the creation of bespoke reports. These are sold to third-party companies seeking additional consumer insights which they are normally unable to generate themselves.

One approach is 'database matching'. This is where the third-party company provides a list containing basic customer identifiers (such as email address or mobile phone number) of their entire database to the loyalty program (or an independent broker). The data is then matched against the loyalty program's database to determine the third-party company's customers who are also members of the loyalty program.

The loyalty program is then able to create a detailed insights report about the third-party company's customers using the data it possesses about them. In most instances, the report is de-personalised or de-identified, meaning it does

---

472 Tesco, Clubcard, https://www.tesco.com.my/Clubcard/About-Clubcard/, accessed 30 June 2020

not contain any specific details about individual members. Instead, it provides more segmentation style data summaries, such as demographic, behavioural, psychographic, and other cohort clusters.

Other loyalty programs create analytical insight reports (in print or via secure online channels) to sell to their product or service supplier base.[473] Because some loyalty programs build up complex data profiles about their member base, including the products they buy (and do not buy), they are well positioned to sell reports to companies that supply products or services to them. The loyalty programs can provide extensive insights into what customers who buy their products look like and even compare them to customers who buy competitor products.

This is valuable information for a wholesale product supplier that does not have any direct consumer interaction as part of the sales process. Though the reports are also de-identified at an individual level, they can help companies gain a deep understanding of what their typical customers look like and even how they think, allowing them to tailor branding, marketing campaigns and new product development. Accessing a profile of their competitor's customers can help them grow their customer base by developing campaigns and product lines designed to persuade the customer to switch.

According to one report, less than 2 per cent of supermarket suppliers subscribe to such reports, although it notes, 'the users are likely to be the bigger suppliers in the market'.[474] This type of report may provide larger, wealthier companies with a competitive advantage by arming them with data insights which smaller companies may not be able to afford.

473 AFN Staff Writers, 'Woolworths gives suppliers unprecedented access to consumer data',Australian Food News, http://www.ausfoodnews.com.au/2017/01/09/woolworths-gives-suppliers-unprecedented-access-to-consumer-data.html, 9 January 2017, accessed 18th April 2019.

474 Thompson, J., 'Woolworths stirs a data debate with suppliers'Australian Association Of Convenience Stores, https://www.aacs.org.au/media/woolworths-stirs-a-data-debate-with-suppliers/, 17 July 2018, accessed 18 April 2019.

Amazon

Amazon is notoriously conservative with the kind of customer data it passes on to brands. However, there are some options for brands to access rich e-commerce data depending on how brands choose to sell their products via the major online retailer.[475]

- Vendor Central: vendors who sell wholesale to Amazon are provided with basic analytics such as search relevance and product competition comparisons, with the option to pay an additional fee to access 'basket analysis', which tells brands what people bought after looking at their products. The downside is retailers receive little customer information, as Amazon owns the customer relationship, not the retailer.

- Seller Central: the alternative is for brands to utilise the third-party selling method, which offers them greater control and more data on who is buying their products, as well as conversion metrics.

Walmart

Nielsen became Walmart's preferred sole provider of POS data, enabling the two to collaborate data and grow with a consistent view of the marketplace. As a result, Nielsen has a total consumer view of 90 per cent of fast-moving consumer goods (FMCG) online sales within the U.S. market, providing clients with a significant understanding of the channel.[476] The partnership helped Walmart and its partners streamline the way data is used across the supplier ecosystem by connecting fragmented customer behaviour across channel segments, enabling faster and better-informed decisions.

---

475 Pathak, S., 2017, 'Retailers chafe at Amazon's tight hold on data', Digiday, https://digiday.com/marketing/retailers-chafe-amazons-tight-hold-data/, accessed 28 May 2020.

476 Grill-Goodman, J., 2017, 'Nielsen, Walmart and Jet.com Team Up on Data Sharing', Retail Info Systems, https://risnews.com/nielsen-walmart-and-jetcom-team-data-sharing, accessed 29 May 2020.

Marketing services provided by loyalty programs

Some loyalty programs provide the opportunity for product suppliers to promote to segments of their member base, which may include the customers of their competitors. A brand aiming to build their customer base may pay the program operator to send a discount coupon or bonus points offers to competitor customers with the aim of encouraging them to try their brand, with the ultimate ambition of winning them over.

Sainsbury's

Some supermarket giants around the globe, such as Sainsbury's, offer brands access to selected insights, for a price. These data-sharing services provide suppliers with a multitude of data sets from product to category performance, and sometimes even competitor data.

Brands can approach Sainsbury's and request for access to customers purchasing competing products with the intent to market to these customers in an attempt to win them over with a valuable and competitive offer.[477] This saves an enormous cost for some brands as they avoid the need to invest in their own research efforts.

Other loyalty programs have established separate digital marketing agencies to generate incremental revenue from their large and highly engaged marketing databases. The agencies use their extensive data insights to implement hyper-targeted digital marketing campaigns (such as banner advertising) on behalf of third-party clients.

---

477 Ferguson, D., 2013, 'How supermarkets get your data – and what they do with it', The Guardian,<https://www.theguardian.com/money/2013/jun/08/supermarkets-get-your-data>, accessed 27 May 2020

Red Planet

Red Planet[478] is a data marketing business set up by Qantas Airways which offers other businesses access to the rich database of the Qantas Frequent Flyer program. The move was part of the airline's push to diversify its offering and provide the opportunity for others to tap into the brand's rich data and optimise who to target, with what messaging, and which media channels to use.

Other Red Planet services include:

- Database matching of website visitors to better tailor site experiences.
- Survey panel research across large numbers of loyalty program members.
- Call centre plugins to provide member profile data in real-time when a member makes contact.

Data brokers and data exchanges selling data and services to loyalty programs

As detailed in Chapter 10, data brokers collect extensive personal data about billions of individuals from all around the world, which they may package up and sell to loyalty programs to help build out and standardise their member profiles. Loyalty programs may also join data exchanges to share data with other companies.

According to Mott, in 2014, the global data broker industry was estimated to comprise thousands of companies of various sizes generating some US$200 billion in annual revenue.[479] Data brokers generally sell data in lists generated using specific criteria.

---

478 Red Planet, https://www.redplanetgroup.com.au/, accessed 30 June 2020.

479 Mott, N., 'The FTC condemns the data brokerage industry's collection practices.' Pando Daily, May 2014. https://pando.com/2014/05/27/the-ftc-condemns-the-data-brokerageindustrys-collection-practices/, accessed 26 May 2020

InfoUSA

InfoUSA[480] deliver a full range of U.S. business and consumer contact databases for targeted marketing, direct marketing, and ongoing sales leads. The service allows clients to create custom lists based on factors including geographic, demographics, housing and finance, and other personal identifiers and interests, which will determine the number of contacts and price. For example, one could create a list targeting people aged 35-44 with children under the age of 13, and a mortgage in the metro area of Philadelphia, Pennsylvania - creating a list of over 100,000 potential leads.

Impact Lists

Impact Lists[481] supplies a range of business and consumer data lists to direct marketers and clients. Business lists enable clients to target specific B2B target audiences such as those in banking, real estate professionals or the FMCG industry; and consumer lists help clients reach a diverse range of consumer target audiences such as a list of people who are frequent global travellers or those who specifically own real estate properties with solar.

These lists range in size from thousands to millions of contacts and can be bought for as little as approximately US$150 per 1000 contacts for standard data, including age, gender, location, job title and interests.

Database generators creating new databases to sell to loyalty programs

As detailed in Chapter 10, database generators specialise in partnering with other companies to collect marketing databases to on-sell to loyalty programs. The monetisation of the data occurs in two ways; firstly, the company which the member transacted with receives a payment from the database generator

---

480 infoUSA, 2020, 'Data and Marketing Solutions for Your Business', infoUSA, https://www.infousa.com/, accessed 29 May 2020.

481 Impact Lists, 2012, 'About', Impact List, http://www.impactlists.com.au/About. aspx, accessed 29 May 2020.

for the data, and secondly, the database generator receives a payment from the sponsoring loyalty program for providing them with their new marketing database.

> **Velocity Frequent Flyer and Rokt**
>
> Velocity partnered with Rokt to launch an acquisition campaign using Acquire Prime, their premium ad placement sign-up module.[482] The platform serves native ads into the user transaction journey of major e-commerce websites when ideal customers are at their most receptive – immediately after they have made an online purchase.
>
> In this example, customers were invited to join the Velocity Frequent Flyer program as they transacted which was paired with a sweepstakes entry and another relevant offer from a different retailer based on data gathered at the point of purchase.

Measuring loyalty program cost-effectiveness and return on investment

Depending on the design framework, there are a variety of ways program operators can measure the cost-effectiveness and return on investment of a loyalty program.

Wansink's cost-effectiveness model

Wansink (2003)[483] developed a mathematical model to determine the cost-effectiveness of loyalty programs, with a focus on guiding program operators to spend less and gain more by optimising the rewards (and cost of rewards) provided. His model was as follows:

---

482 Rokt, 2017, 'Velocity Frequent Flyer surpasses 8 million members', Rokt, https://rokt.com/wp-content/uploads/2017/10/20170921-Velocity-Frequent-Flyer-Case-Study-UK-AT-Final-.pdf, accessed 30 May 2020.

483 Wansink, B. (2003). Developing a cost-effective brand loyalty program. Journal of Advertising Research, 43(3), 301-309.

> **Gain/Loss = (Ua*P) – D – (Uw *P) – A**
>
> Ua = Unit sales after program implementation
>
> P = Price per unit
>
> D = Dollar amount of coupons or other incentives used
>
> Uw = Unit sales before program
>
> A = Administrative costs of program

To illustrate, if a cinema is selling movie tickets and runs a double points campaign to boost sales, their model may look as follows:

Ua = Unit sales after program implementation = 220,000

P = Price per unit = $15

D = Dollar amount of coupons or other incentives used = $165,000

Uw = Unit sales before program = 200,000

A = Administrative costs of program = $80,000

Gain = (Ua*P) – D – (Uw *P) – A = (220,000*$15) - $165,000 - (200,000*15) - $80,000 = $55,000

Thus, providing members with bonus points (which cost an incremental 5 per cent of revenue) to generate a 10 per cent increase in ticket sales delivers a net gain of $55,000.

This approach assumes all members are targeted with the same double points offer. However, Wansink argued (and demonstrated) that marketers can motivate some members to participate in the campaign with lesser benefits, as only a marginal push would be necessary to change their behaviour. An extension of this is identifying members who are likely to transact even without the campaign stimulus.

Using our example, some segments may respond equally well with a 1.5x points bonus, while other regular members may be excluded from the campaign because their transaction history suggests they are highly likely to attend the cinema during the campaign period anyway. Under this model, the cost of the campaign of $165,000 can be reduced to $95,000.

Gain = (Ua*P) – D – (Uw *P) – A = (220,000*$15) - $95,000 - (200,000*15) - $80,000 = $125,000

As can be seen, utilising a data-enabled segmentation approach more than doubles the profitability of the campaign. This is a basic example of the approach large retailers are attempting to apply using machine learning/AI models to optimise their marketing spend, where small percentage gains across enormous budgets and member bases can deliver substantial financial results.

Lifecycle management model

Wansink's model is particularly relevant for retail programs which are selling products or services and are utilising a loyalty program to boost sales.

When considering a program applied across a company which generates consistent, periodic purchases (e.g. telecommunications, insurance or utilities) some limitations are exposed. Specifically, Wansink's model does not account for incremental revenue generated from new customer acquisition and existing customer retention.

The lifecycle management model, developed by the authors, attempts to address these shortcomings. While revenue has been used, some companies may prefer to use gross margin:

Gain/Loss = (Mn*Ra) + (Mm*Ri) + (Mr*Ra) – D – A

Ra = Average revenue per customer

Mn = New customers acquired as a result of the program

Ri = Average increase in revenue by existing customer participating in the program

Mm = Number of existing customers participating in the program (members)

Mr = Number of existing customers forecast to churn who stay because of the program

D = Dollar amount of incentives used

A = Administrative costs of program

To illustrate, if a telecommunications company introduces an attractive member benefits program, the model may look as follows:

Ra = Average revenue per customer = $660 per annum

Mn = New customers acquired as a result of the program = 30,000

Ri = Average increase in revenue by existing customer participating in the program = $10 per annum

Mm = Number of existing customers participating in the program (members) = 1,500,000

Mr = Number of existing customers forecast to churn who stay because of the program = 80,000

D = Dollar amount of incentives used = $25,000,000

A = Administrative costs of program = $4,000,000

Gain = (30,000*$660) + (1,500,000*$10) + (80,000*$660) – $25,000,000 – $4,000,000 = $58,600,000

While the revenues from new customer acquisition and the incremental increase in spend by existing members are material, the biggest opportunity is to increase existing customer retention. The model demonstrates that companies which are not investing heavily in retaining their most valuable customers are missing a valuable opportunity.

Recency frequency monetary value (RFM) model

An alternative model which is suitable for tier-based programs is the RFM model. This involves dividing members into different segments based on their amount of spend (average per transaction) and how often they transact. Strategies can then be applied to stimulate higher per transaction spend or more frequent transactions in order to either shift them to higher, more valuable tiers (if they are in lower tiers) or maintain their frequency and monetary value behaviour (if they are in the highest tiers).

The RFM model developed by the authors, can be used to calculate the return on investment. While revenue has been used, some companies may prefer to use gross margin:

$$\begin{aligned}
\text{Gain/Loss} = &((\text{Ma1*Ra}) + (\text{Mb1*Rb}) + (\text{Mn1*Rn})) - \\
&((\text{Mab*Ra}) + (\text{Mbb*Rb}) + (\text{Mnb*Rn})) - D - A
\end{aligned}$$

Mab = Members in Tier A at start of program (baseline)

Mbb = Members in Tier B at start of program (baseline)

Mnb = Members in Tier n at start of program (baseline)

Ra = Average revenue Tier A

Rb = Average revenue Tier B

Rn = Average revenue Tier n

Ma1 = Members in Tier A at end of period post-program launch

Mb1 = Members in Tier B at end of period post-program launch

Mn1 = Members in Tier n at end of period post-program launch

D = Dollar amount of incentives used

A = Administrative costs of program

To illustrate, if a B2B company implements a tier-based program, the model may look as follows. Unlimited additional tiers can be added as required:

Mab = Members in Tier A at start of program (baseline) = 50,000

Mbb = Members in Tier B at start of program (baseline) = 20,000

Mnb = Members in Tier n at start of program (baseline) = 5,000

Ra = Average revenue Tier A = $5,000

Rb = Average revenue Tier B = $10,000

Rn = Average revenue Tier n = $20,000

Ma1 = Members in Tier A at end of period post-program launch = 47,000

Mb1 = Members in Tier B at end of period post-program launch = 22,500

Mn1 = Members in Tier n at end of period post-program launch = 5,500

D = Dollar amount of incentives used = $7,500,000

A = Administrative costs of program = $1,500,000

Gain = ((47,000*$5,000) + (22,500*$10,000) + (5,500*$20,000)) − ((50,000*$5,000) + (20,000*$10,000) + (5,000*$20,000)) − $7,500,000 − $1,500,000 = $11,000,000

The advantage of this type of model is that the segmentation by value allows the program operator to be very targeted in how the benefits and incentives are applied, helping with budget management. It also supports a test and learn methodology to determine the most effective methods to stimulate the increases in per transaction spend and/or frequency of spend required to move members up the value chain.

Coalition program model

Coalition loyalty programs generate billings from third-party partners providing points to their customers, and revenue from points earn, redemptions, interest and breakage. While Wansink's model is relevant for third-party partners offering points to members, a different model, developed by the authors, is required to enable the calculation of gain/loss for the program itself:

Billings = (Tp * BPP)

BPP, or Billings Per Point, acknowledges that different coalition partners may pay different amounts for points, primarily based on volume. For example, a bank may pay 1.2c per point, while a smaller retailer may pay 2c per point. BPP is calculated by dividing the total of billings by the total number of points conferred on members as a result of third-party partner transactions.

> **Gain/Loss = ((BPP – CPP) * Pe) + ((CPPf – CPPa) * Pr) +**
> **(B * BPP) + I – A**
>
> Pe = Total points earned
>
> Pr = Total points redeemed
>
> BPP = Billings per point (weighted average value of total points earned)
>
> CPPf = Cost per point forecast
>
> CPPa = Cost per point actual
>
> I = Interest
>
> B = Breakage (total points expired)
>
> A = Administrative costs of program

The Gain/Loss calculation is more complex. To illustrate, using a full year of program activity for a large, hypothetical coalition program:

Pe = Total points earned = 120,000,000,000

Pr = Total points redeemed = 70,000,000,000

BPP = Billings per point = 1c per point

CPPf = Cost per point forecast = 0.75c per point

CPPa = Cost per point actual = 0.7c per point

I = Interest = $30,000,000

B = Breakage (total points expired) = 5% of total points earned = 6,000,000,000

A = Administrative costs of program = $65,000,000

Gain = (1c – 0.75c) * 120bn + ((0.75c – 0.7c) * 70bn) + (6bn * 1c) + $30m – $65m = $330m

Of interest is the boost in Gain if the program is successful in either increasing their BPP or reducing their CPPf or CPPa. All else remaining equal, increasing the BPP to 1.1c will increase the gain to $486 million, while reducing the CPPf to 0.7c will increase the gain to $420 million.

Understanding the potential of these minor adjustments, some major coalition programs invest time and resources in increasing BPP or reducing redemption costs, with marginal adjustments generating substantial profit boosts. The challenge with this approach is the negative member sentiment it can create due to the erosion of value, leading to disengagement and potential brand damage.

> ### Delta SkyMiles
>
> Most loyalty programs will announce devaluations or changes far in advance, but not all operators are so open. On multiple occurrences, Delta Airlines has raised the costs of award tickets on partner airlines with no notice to its members.[484] In 2017, if you travelled exclusively on partner airlines, award costs increased, while if you travelled exclusively on Delta, or a combination of Delta and partner airlines, award costs remained the same. The lack of announcement creates negative sentiment as members are left in the dark questioning whether the change is a mistake or intentional.

Member lifetime value (MLV)

Many companies calculate and utilise Customer Lifetime Value (CLV) which is defined as the total worth to a company of a customer over the complete period of their relationship. A simple CLV calculation would be:

CLV = R*T – C

R = Annual revenue generated from customer

T = Tenure of customer in years

C = Costs of acquiring, serving and retaining the customer

A company operating a points-based program which directly generates revenue (such as a large coalition program) requires a more complex calculation, as the member generates revenue directly (via purchasing the company's

---

484 Lucky, B., 2017, 'Delta's Latest SkyMiles Devaluation Gets Even Worse', One Mile At A Time, <https://onemileatatime.com/delta-partner-award-price-increase/>, accessed 29th May 2020

products and services) as well as indirectly (via points earn and redemption, interest and breakage).

A more appropriate formula, developed by the authors, is Member Lifetime Value (MLV):

$$MLV = ((R - Cg)*T) + (((BPP - CPPf) *Pe)) + ((CPPf - CPPa) * Pr)) + (B * BPP) + Ia - Cp) * T))$$

R = Annual revenue generated from customer

Cg = Annual general costs of acquiring, serving and retaining the customer

T = Tenure of customer in years

Pe = Total points earned per annum

Pr = Total points redeemed per annum

BPP = Billings per point

CPPf = Cost per point forecast

CPPa = Cost per point actual

Ia = Annual interest earned on individual's points revenue deferred

B = Breakage (total points expired)

Cp = Program costs of acquiring, serving and retaining the customer

To illustrate, if a large, hypothetical coalition program is calculating the MLV for a single member:

R = Annual revenue generated from customer = $5,270

Cg = Annual general costs of acquiring, serving and retaining the customer = $1,472

T = Tenure of customer in years = 11 years

Pe = Total points earned per annum = 70,894

Pr = Total points redeemed per annum = 61,849

BPP = Billings per point = 1.4c

CPPf = Cost per point forecast = 0.75c per point

CPPa = Cost per point actual = 0.65c per point

Ia = Annual interest earned on individual's points revenue deferred = $27

B = Breakage (total points expired) = 0

Cp = Program costs of acquiring, serving and retaining the customer = $53

MLV = (($5,260 − $1,472)*11) + (((1.4c − 0.75) *70,894) + ((0.75c − 0.65c) * 61,849) + (0 * 1.4c) + $27 − $53) * 11)) = $47,137

Key Insights

- Some loyalty programs directly generate incremental revenue, which may only be enough to offset some of the operational costs, or it may be of such magnitude that the program operates profitably.

- There are a range of ways loyalty programs can generate revenue for the program operator, which includes partners paying for members to earn coalition program points, earning revenue for selling membership subscriptions, earning commission when selling discount products to members, earning merchant funded revenue via member transactions, or selling and supplying program-branded products and services.

- Member personal data can be monetised by selling consumer insight reports created using loyalty program data, providing digital marketing services using a loyalty program member database, data brokers and data exchanges selling data and services to loyalty programs, and database generators creating new databases to sell to loyalty programs.

- Depending on the program design framework, there are a variety of ways program operators can measure the cost-effectiveness and return on investment of a loyalty program to ascertain whether it is profitable, or needs to be adjusted or redesigned to return it to profitability.

Suggested reading

- Feldman, David, 2017, 'LOYALTY MYTHS: IS BREAKAGE GOOD?', https://medium.com/@dfcatch/loyalty-myths-is-breakage-good-873950da26dc

- Grill-Goodman, J. 2017, 'Nielsen, Walmart and Jet.com Team Up on Data Sharing', Retail Info Systems, https://risnews.com/nielsen-walmart-and-jetcom-team-data-sharing

- Wansink, B., 2003, 'Developing a cost-effective brand loyalty program', Journal of Advertising Research, Vol 43, Iss 3, pp301-309.

CHAPTER 15

LEGAL

This chapter was co-written by Lincoln Hunter,
Principal and Founder, Loyalty Legal.

*'Any abuse of the Program or failure to follow the Rules, United's
Contract of Carriage, United's fare rules, Partner rules, terms and
conditions or any abuse of any Partner offers or programs, any violation
of law, rule, or regulation, any conduct detrimental to the interests
of United, any fraudulent activity or attempted fraudulent activity,
any dissemination of information designed to defraud United, or
any misrepresentation of any information furnished to United or
its affiliates by any Member, anyone else acting on the Member's
behalf, or any third-party (collectively, "Prohibited Conduct"), may
result in United exercising any one or more of the following remedies
("United's Remedies"), with or without notice to the Member…* [485]*

*- An example of programs regulating members: United Airlines,
Rules for the MileagePlus Program, www.united.com, 2020*

Focus areas

This chapter will briefly address the following questions:

- What are the main regulatory regimes that may apply to
operating a loyalty program? (Noting the context outlined below

and that each jurisdiction has different laws and may address issues differently).

- What are some of the key legal considerations a loyalty program operator should address in the program agreement for members?

- What are some of the key legal considerations a loyalty program operator should address in a coalition merchant participation agreement?

Note on context

Writing a chapter on regulatory considerations for loyalty programs with a global context is challenging because laws and regulations are jurisdiction specific. Which means that any item included in this chapter may or may not apply to loyalty programs in a particular jurisdiction, and the chapter of necessity contains generalities and not specifics.

It also means that:

- The chapter gives a brief snapshot only of some of the key sorts of regulatory regimes and legal issues that loyalty programs typically face, without specifically referring to particular laws or jurisdictions;

- The reader cannot rely on the content of this chapter as relevant or applicable to any particular loyalty program or jurisdiction;

- This chapter is not legal advice, and appropriate legal professionals should be consulted for specific advice relevant to the jurisdiction/s in which the program is operating;

- The information provided in this chapter is general only, may not apply to all jurisdictions and there will certainly be other regulatory and legal issues that program operators will need to consider, address and comply with in designing and operating their loyalty program, wherever it is located or offered; and

- How (and if) the principles outlined in this chapter apply to any particular loyalty program or jurisdiction will depend on the specific applicable laws.

Note also that the writer has not conducted a comprehensive survey of all regulatory regimes throughout the world. Instead, the general propositions set out in this chapter are based on general principles applied in Australia (the writer's home country) and the writer's basic understanding and expectations of other similar jurisdictions.

For the purposes of this chapter, a jurisdiction is defined as 'the territory over which legal authority is exercised'. This may be a single state, a single country or multiple countries. In the context of loyalty programs, this could refer to any territory in which the program operates or is available to members. Hence, a loyalty program may need to adhere to the laws of a single jurisdiction or multiple jurisdictions.

Regulatory Regimes

Generally, loyalty program operators can expect that most advanced jurisdictions will seek to protect consumers from adverse or unfair trading practices by businesses (and by doing so also seek to address the imbalance of power when large businesses trade with individuals, as is often the case with loyalty programs), by way of a variety of laws and regulations which are often typically grouped into the following bundles:

- Consumer protection
- Privacy and data protection
- Competition laws
- Financial products and financial services regulation

Some of the key elements of each of these that are often applied by law makers are set out in this chapter, noting the context above and that there can be significant variations in how these are construed and applied across different jurisdictions (and that some of these elements may not apply at all in a given jurisdiction). In addition, certain jurisdictions may have other regimes in addition to these, which also need to be considered.

Consumer protection

Typical elements of consumer protection regulation include some form of prohibition of certain activities, such as misleading or deceptive conduct, unfair trading practices (such as making false or misleading representations in advertising) and unconscionable conduct, rules for addressing unfair terms in consumer contracts, and statutory implied product and service warranties.

Misleading or deceptive conduct

Generally, a prohibition of misleading or deceptive conduct (which may also extend to a prohibition of conduct that is likely to mislead or deceive) is usually an extremely broad provision that applies across most areas of doing business, and typically it does not matter if there is an intention to mislead or not.

This sort of regulation could address many wide and varied business practices, such as misleading headlines in advertising (and the extent to which small print can be used to clarify headline meanings), offers of 'free' items to customers, the use of puffery or hyperbole in advertising and comparative advertising. It could also apply to statements about how member data is collected, used or shared.

In a loyalty program context, the most obvious area (though by no means the only area) that this sort of a regulation may apply is in the advertising and marketing of offers and benefits to program members. Loyalty program operators should ensure that every area of their business (including their advertising and marketing to members, and that of participants who advertise through the program) complies with regulations applicable in the jurisdictions in which they operate.

Unfair trading practices

In the context of consumer protection, law makers may seek to prohibit or regulate certain adverse or unfair trading practices, such as businesses making false or misleading representations about goods or services. If so, it will often not matter if there is an intention to mislead or not, as the test is typically an objective one (such as, are the representations incorrect or likely to mislead).

In practice, depending on the relevant activity, there can be overlap between misleading or deceptive conduct prohibitions and prohibitions on false or misleading representations, as well as other principles of consumer protection. As a result, more than one regulation could apply to a particular statement or representation.

Other unfair trading practices regulations of relevance to loyalty programs may include rules around offering rebates, gifts, prizes or other 'free' items in connection with the supply of goods or services, making 'premium' claims in relation to goods or services (e.g. descriptions that infer that a product has a particular premium quality over generic substitutes, such as nutritional claims, environmental or organic claims and country or place of origin claims), and 'bait and switch' advertising.

Although compliance with these regulations will typically apply to most businesses in the relevant jurisdiction, given the nature of loyalty programs, program operators will need a full understanding of these sorts of regimes specific to their jurisdiction/s (if applicable) and how they apply to program operations, as well as members, merchant participants and other stakeholders.

Unconscionable conduct

At the more extreme level, law makers may also legislate that businesses must not engage in unconscionable conduct in connection with the supply or acquisition of goods or services (or similar).

Generally, to be considered unconscionable, conduct will need to be more than simply unfair – it will usually need to be against good conscience as judged against the norms of society (or some other prescribed test in the applicable jurisdiction) and may also need to be harsh and/or oppressive.

For the most part, loyalty programs should have little trouble in complying with these sorts of requirements (given that they usually apply to reasonably extreme activities) – but, for example, a sudden large devaluation of points redemption values or introducing a short points expiry period where one did not previously apply (in each case without reasonable notice or compensation) could arguably give rise to unconscionable conduct allegations.

Unfair contract terms (in consumer contracts)

In the context of consumer protection, law makers may also seek to prohibit or regulate unfair contract terms in certain consumer contracts. In connection with these sorts of regulations, a contract term determined to be unfair could be voided or prohibited, or some other remedy applied.

It is likely that each jurisdiction that imposes these sorts of regulations will apply its own definition of what is unfair and what contracts are covered by the regulations. Typically though, they are aimed at contracts where consumers do not get the opportunity to negotiate the terms (or accept or reject particular terms), such as a standard form contract that has been prepared by a trading business and presented to a consumer on a 'take it or leave it' basis. Similarly, an unfair term might include a clause that causes a significant imbalance in the parties' rights and obligations and would cause significant detriment to the consumer if it were applied (and where there is no reasonable business need for the clause).

In most circumstances, one would expect that loyalty program consumer-facing terms and conditions may be subject to these sorts of regulations (if applicable) given the nature of loyalty program contracts with members. If so, the loyalty program operator will need to ensure that the program and the program terms and conditions will not be impacted by the applicable unfair contract terms regime (to ensure the terms are enforceable and to avoid the remedy imposed by law or claims by members). This may also extend to the privacy policies of the program (depending on how they are presented to members), particularly if they are part of the standard form member contract or comprise a separate one.

In some jurisdictions, unfair contract terms regulation may extend beyond consumer contracts to small business or other contracts. Loyalty program operators may also need to consider any such laws.

Statutory product and service warranties

Some jurisdictions may also have laws which apply a basic set of product and service warranties (or guarantees) to certain goods and services acquired by consumers (or other purchasers).

If so, these statutory warranties are typically designed to give consumers a basic, guaranteed level of protection for the goods and services they buy (e.g. that the goods are of an acceptable quality and match the advertised description etc). While businesses may also offer extra product warranties (e.g. voluntary or extended warranties) in relation to their goods or services, the statutory warranties will typically apply regardless of any other warranties offered by a seller or manufacturer of goods or services. And typically, the statutory warranties cannot be contracted out of, or avoided, by using a 'drop ship' model.

If the statutory warranties are not complied with, consumers can typically take action to obtain a remedy from the supplier or, in some cases, the manufacturer or importer. The remedies are generally a repair, replacement, refund or having a service performed again (but may also include compensation in certain circumstances).

Statutory warranties such as this are likely to be relevant to loyalty programs primarily in connection with the supply of rewards. If applicable, loyalty program operators should address this risk in relation to the supply of rewards and also in their arrangements with the original product/service supplier/manufacturer.

Loyalty program operators should also be careful not to mislead members about their rights under relevant statutory warranties (e.g. referring members to the original supplier for defective goods and indicating that the program is not liable for defects, etc) as that could itself breach other consumer protection regulations.

Other rules may also apply to extra product warranties (e.g. voluntary or extended warranties) provided by a supplier or manufacturer.

Privacy and Data protection

These days, the collection, use and disclosure of personal data, and the sending of electronic marketing messages, are regulated in most advanced economies. Note that 'personal data' is also referred to as 'personal information' or 'personally identifiable information' (or similar) depending on the jurisdiction and each jurisdiction often applies a slightly different definition of the same concept. So, in this chapter 'personal data' is used to refer to the relevant personal data/information that is the subject of relevant privacy laws in the relevant jurisdiction.

At their core, loyalty programs are essentially a marketing, promotional and data capture tool for businesses, with data captured directly by the program via multiple member touchpoints, as well as indirectly, as detailed in Chapter 10. As such, privacy and data protection laws are particularly relevant and it is expected that compliance with privacy, data protection, member consent and marketing related regulations will be part of the 'DNA' and the corporate culture of program operations in order to safeguard the significant data assets of the loyalty program.

Privacy regulations and loyalty programs

As a first step, loyalty programs will need to ensure that the program terms and conditions and the program privacy policy reflect applicable regulations, and all required consents are obtained from members, in the applicable jurisdiction. Further, the internal policies and procedures applied by the loyalty program (e.g. marketing preferences and member profile records) will need to comply with and enact these requirements.

While there is significant variation between various jurisdictions in the content and approach adopted by privacy laws and regulations, it is also expected that at a minimum loyalty programs (who are regulated under the applicable regulations) will typically need to comply with the following sorts of requirements when handling personal data (these requirements are loosely based on Australian laws but requirements in other jurisdictions may be more onerous than these and additional requirements may also need to be complied with in more prescriptive jurisdictions such as the EU, if those laws apply):

- To maintain and make available a privacy policy about the program's management of member personal data, including how personal data is collected, held and disclosed.

- To collect personal data only where reasonably necessary for one or more of the program's legitimate functions or activities, and directly from the member to whom it relates (unless impracticable or consent or an exception applies).

- To notify a member, at or before the time of collection, of the particulars of collection and provide the member with access to the program's privacy policy.

- Not to use or disclose member personal data for a purpose other than that for which it was collected, unless the member consents, the member would reasonably expect their personal data to be used for the other purpose, or an exception applies.

- Not to use personal data for direct marketing purposes unless the member reasonably expects it, or consents to it, and prescribed 'opt out' processes are in place but have not been actioned.

- Before personal data is disclosed to an overseas recipient, to comply with certain prescribed requirements and/or assume liability for the overseas recipient's handling of the personal data.

- To take reasonable steps to ensure the personal data that the program collects, uses or discloses is accurate, up to date and complete.

- To take reasonable steps to protect the personal data that the program holds from misuse, interference and loss, and from unauthorised access, modification or disclosure.

- To take reasonable steps to destroy or de-identify personal data that the program no longer needs, unless otherwise required to retain it by law.

- To provide a member, upon request, with access to their personal data and other relevant data unless a prescribed exception applies.

Data breaches

Generally, privacy regulations will also require program operators (who are regulated entities) to notify members (and the regulator) about certain 'data breaches'. A relevant data breach for a loyalty program (that is a regulated entity) would typically include an event where there is unauthorised access to, or unauthorised disclosure of, or a loss of, personal data that a program holds which is likely to result in serious harm to one or more members, and the program operator has not been able to prevent the likely risk of serious harm with remedial action. This definition is likely to be different in each jurisdiction so program operators will need to refer to their privacy advisers.

Risk and mitigations strategies associated with data breaches are covered in Chapter 16.

Direct marketing or Spam regulation

Many jurisdictions have implemented restrictions on direct marketing or electronic spam which apply to any commercial/marketing electronic messages that an organisation sends or causes to be sent. If so, in the case of commercial electronic messages sent by a loyalty program, the program will generally be required to comply with a variety of requirements which typically include the following:

- **Consent**: the message must be sent with the member's consent.

- **Identification**: the message must contain accurate information about the loyalty program that authorised the sending of the message.

- **Unsubscribe**: the message must contain a functional 'unsubscribe' facility to allow the member to opt out of future marketing.

Foreign regulations

Whatever jurisdiction a loyalty program operates from, in addition to complying with local regulations in that jurisdiction, the operator may also need to comply with personal data and data protection regulations in foreign jurisdictions. This can depend on factors such as where else they are located and/or operate, where the program is offered, where their data processing activities take place, where their members or data subjects reside, and the applicable laws.

For example, the EU General Data Protection Regulation (the GDPR)[486] which commenced on 25 May 2018, is the primary source of personal data regulation in the EU. Businesses are generally required to comply with this regime if they have an establishment in the EU (regardless of whether they process personal data in the EU). They are also required to comply if they do not have an establishment in the EU, but offer goods and services in the EU, or monitor the behaviour of individuals in the EU.

Competition laws

Although ordinarily the conduct of a loyalty program should not give rise to any particular concerns regarding anti-competitive conduct per se (other than in relation to the regulations outlined earlier in this chapter), there are circumstances under which a particular jurisdiction's competition law regulations may need to be considered in relation to loyalty programs, particularly for large

---

486 GDPR https://gdpr-info.eu/ accessed 20 July 2020

coalition programs. This may include where coalition programs operate in concentrated markets, where competing loyalty programs wish to coordinate activities (e.g. under a points transfer agreement) or where independent operators wish to, or are required to, collectively bargain with a loyalty program.

Restrictive trade practices/Anti-competitive conduct

Most advanced economies will have a variety of regulations in place aimed at prohibiting or regulating anti-competitive conduct by businesses. The key elements of such regulations may prohibit activities such as:

- Anti-competitive agreements or contracts and practices which substantially lessen competition in a market.
- General cartel conduct or collusion (including price fixing and collective boycotts).
- Exclusive dealing (when it substantially lessens competition in a relevant market).
- Resale price maintenance.
- Misuse of market power.

Depending on local laws, this conduct may only be unlawful if it results in the substantial lessening of competition in a relevant market and sometimes the conduct can be exempted by a regulator if a relevant public benefit can be established.

Specific to loyalty programs, Chapter 3 provided the example of SAS in Norway, where the operation of their frequent flyer program was deemed sufficiently anti-competitive for the program to be curtailed, demonstrating the power of competition regulators in some jurisdictions.

Exclusive dealing - Third line forcing

In Australia, a form of exclusive dealing known as 'third line forcing' occurs when the supply of goods or services is made on the condition that the purchaser buys goods or services from a particular third-party, or supply is refused because the purchaser will not agree to do so or has not acquired certain goods/services from a third-party. This activity (in Australia) is generally prohibited if the activity has or is likely to have a substantial lessening of competition in a relevant market. Variations of this law may apply in other jurisdictions.

In any jurisdiction that applies these sorts of regulations, loyalty program operators and merchant participants should consider these third line forcing laws (typically in relation to program benefits offered to customers of merchant participants) to ensure they either do not apply (and no third line force arises) or that no substantial lessening of competition arises in the relevant markets.

Exclusive dealing - Exclusivity

Another form of exclusive dealing conduct could potentially arise (depending on local laws) where the supply of goods or services, or the supply of goods or services at a discount, is conditional upon the buyer not acquiring, or limiting the acquisition of, goods or services from a competitor of the supplier. Again, depending on local laws this conduct may only be unlawful if it results in substantial lessening of competition in a relevant market.

Typically, coalition loyalty programs will require 'exclusivity' from any third-party merchant participant in the program, and merchant participants will require category exclusivity, as part of the negotiations for the participation agreement.

Loyalty program operators should consider any applicable exclusive dealing laws (if any) to ensure they either do not apply or that no substantial lessening of competition arises in their relevant market.

Financial products and financial services regulation

Similar to the consumer protection regulations outlined above, generally advanced economies will seek to regulate offering, marketing, dealing in and issuing financial products and financial services to protect consumers from adverse or unfair trading practices by businesses (and by doing so also seek to address the imbalance of information and knowledge that applies to financial products and financial services such as securities).

If so, some of the key financial products/services and related regulatory issues that may arise in relation to a loyalty program are summarised below. Again, not all of these may apply in all jurisdictions (and where they do apply they may be implemented and construed quite differently) and there may be other issues specific to certain jurisdictions.

Financial products regulation and the program

As a general definition, a financial product is often referred to as a facility through which, or through the acquisition of which, a person makes a financial investment, manages a financial risk, or makes non-cash payments. A non-cash payment facility allows payments to be made otherwise than by physical delivery of fiat currency (in the form of notes and coins).

It could be argued that currency-based loyalty programs may be considered a non-cash payment facility, and could therefore be considered a financial product in certain jurisdictions. If so, the loyalty program provider may require a financial services licence in the jurisdiction in which the program operates (if such laws apply in that jurisdiction).

It is possible that where this sort of regulation applies, the law makers or the regulator will create an exemption which allows loyalty programs to operate without the need for a financial services licence, on certain prescribed conditions (as is the case in Australia).

Financial services regulation and operating a program

Even if the loyalty program is not considered a non-cash payment facility or financial product under local legislation, financial services regulations may still be relevant.

Typically, these days large coalition loyalty programs have banking and financial services earn participants. In this situation, a variety of related financial services regulations may apply, depending on the exact nature of the services that are being provided by or through the loyalty program (and naturally the applicable regulations in the jurisdiction).

A loyalty program operator may be deemed to be providing a financial service where it provides advice regarding a financial product or deals in a financial product, which may require the program operator to hold a financial services licence. This may include providing advice regarding financial products (such as banking products, mortgages and general insurance) issued by third-party participants to the program members. Other restrictions may also apply. The loyalty program operator will need to consult its financial services advisors in relation to these sorts of regulations to ensure compliance.

Key legal considerations for loyalty program agreements and documentation

Generally, the types of agreements and documents that a loyalty program operator should provide to members include program terms and conditions (the contract with the member), privacy policies, cookie policies, data collection statements and website terms of use (as well as all other marketing and service communications etc).

The operator may also need merchant participant participation agreements, as well as third-party supplier agreements (e.g. for platform, data services, analytics, marketing agencies, call centres and reward suppliers, etc).

The loyalty program operator will need appropriate legal advice (in all applicable jurisdictions) on all of these documents. This section focusses on some key items only for the contract with the members and a basic merchant participant participation agreement.

A valid contract with members

A critical, but often overlooked aspect, of running a loyalty program is the importance of ensuring that a valid contract is in place with members. This requires ensuring that all of the elements of a contract are present and that the mechanics of offer and acceptance are adequate to confirm those elements on the applicable terms. However it is done, the loyalty program operator needs to ensure that under the laws applicable to the jurisdiction in which it operates, a valid and binding contract is entered into by the member and the program, so the terms of the program (and data consents, etc) can be enforced.

Among many other terms and conditions, loyalty programs typically need to ensure that the following key program terms are set out clearly and accepted by the member:

- When points will expire and how members will be made aware of this. The expiry of points is usually an important issue for consumers and regulators, as well as for loyalty program operators who require the flexibility to expire points in order to manage liabilities. Accordingly, this is a contentious issue on which it is likely loyalty program operators will need legal advice in applicable jurisdictions. In a small number of jurisdictions, points expiry rules have been the subject of specific regulation. As discussed in Chapter 14, in 2016/17, Ontario and Quebec, Canada, prohibited the expiry of rewards points due to the passage of time.

- The conditions on which discount and value-add offers from third-party merchant participants can be accessed.

- The precise terms on which the member agrees that his/her personal data can be collected, used and disclosed by the program.

- Marketing communication permissions.

- The ability of the loyalty program operator to change the value proposition and terms unilaterally – again, this is usually an important issue for consumers and regulators and it is also critical to ensure that the program operator can change the terms to reflect market practice and to ensure the operator's liability is manageable, under an agreement that usually has an open ended term.

- Earn rates and redemption rates for loyalty currency transactions.

- Circumstances in which the program may be terminated, and the member can terminate his/her membership, or it can be terminated by the program operator.

- Other benefits and restrictions, as applicable.

- What happens at the end? The account termination process and any terms which apply post termination.

Many of these terms may be affected by the regulatory issues outlined above, as well as the need to make the program attractive and rewarding for the members.

Participation agreements – merchant participants

The terms on which third-party merchant participants participate in a coalition program or member benefits program are typically set out in a 'program participation agreement'. These agreements and their terms are critical, as they often generate third-party revenue earned by the program and provide for offers to be made available to members. They also give rise to important costs and administration issues.

Many of the terms included in such an agreement may be affected by the regulatory issues outlined above, as well as the commercial objectives of the parties, and the need to make the program attractive and rewarding for the members.

Some of the key issues include:

- **Commercial terms and offers**: this may cover themes including points or discount offers to members, services to be provided by each party, fees to be paid by the merchant participant, the details of, and payments applicable to, any redemption opportunity, payment terms, liability, etc.

- **Data and data use rights**: the data received by the loyalty program from merchant participants and the loyalty program's ability to use that data, is one of the primary drivers of value for the loyalty program. Accordingly, the provisions for data exchanges and each party's data use rights are therefore critical.

- **Exclusivity**: an undertaking that the merchant participant participates exclusively in the relevant loyalty program is often critical for the loyalty program to manage risk and differentiate itself from other offerings in a market. Equally, and arguably more so, merchant participants often require category exclusivity within the program for similar reasons, and to avoid exposing customers to competitor offers. The bifurcated nature of the customer relationship, together with the regulatory requirements and the genuine interest each party has in relation to their customer relationships, ensures that this issue is often the most hotly contested during negotiation of participation agreements. Legal advice should be obtained in each applicable jurisdiction on this issue and the commercial consequences.

- **What happens at the end?**: it is important to include arrangements that should apply at and after the end of participation. This is important because at the end of a lengthy participation arrangement each party can often hold details of the members/customers of the other party, which can then be exposed to offers from that other party's competitors after the participation agreement ends.

Other comments / issues

Although the following issues are not dealt with in detail in this chapter, note:

- A loyalty program operator (especially when designing a loyalty program) should ensure that it obtains thorough and detailed tax advice in relation to potential treatment for tax purposes of loyalty currency issued as part of the program (in respect of members, merchant participants and the loyalty program operator) and in all applicable jurisdictions. This advice may impact directly on the value of the program to those stakeholders and may need to be reflected in the member terms.

- There will be many other laws and regulatory issues (and industry codes and guidelines, etc) to be considered in addition to those mentioned in the chapter. Early legal advice should be obtained on all potential issues.

Key insights

- Appropriate legal professionals should be consulted for specific loyalty program legal guidance relevant to the jurisdiction/s in which the program is operating.

- The main regulatory regimes that a loyalty program operator will typically need to comply with when designing and operating a loyalty program include consumer protection regulations, privacy and data protection laws, competition laws, and financial products and financial services regulations. Not all of these regimes and the typical elements of them outlined in this chapter will apply in all jurisdictions, and certain jurisdictions may apply other regimes in addition to these.

- The following good practice principles should help loyalty programs comply with the key day to day regulatory requirements outlined in this chapter:

    ○ Present terms, conditions and privacy policies in a way that members can readily understand.

- Avoid making unilateral changes to terms and conditions in a way that may be unfair to members.

- Collect, use and disclose member data in ways that comply with applicable laws and also align with members' preferences. This could include providing members with full transparency regarding and control over the sharing of their data (especially with unknown third parties), and the ability to opt out of targeted advertising.

- Generally, the types of agreements and documents that a loyalty program operator should provide to members include program terms and conditions, privacy policies, cookie policies, data collection statements and website terms of use.

- The loyalty program operator needs to ensure that under the laws applicable in the jurisdiction(s) in which it operates, a valid and binding contract is entered into by the member and the program, so the terms of the program can be enforced.

- Program participation agreements for third-party merchant participants in coalition programs and member benefits programs are critical, as they often generate third-party revenue for the program and provide for some of the offers made available to members.

CHAPTER 16

SECURITY AND FRAUD RISKS, AND MITIGATIONS

This chapter was co-written by Michael Smith,
Co-Founder, Loyalty Security Association.

'IN NOVEMBER 2018, hotel giant Marriott disclosed that it had suffered one of the largest breaches in history. That hack compromised the information of 500 million people who had made a reservation at a Starwood hotel. On Tuesday, Marriott announced that it had once again been hit, with up to 5.2 million guests at risk. Which is a kind of progress, in a way?'

- Brian Barrett, Wired, 2020[487]

Focus areas

This chapter will address the following questions:

- What is loyalty fraud?
- What are the different types of security and fraud issues which can affect loyalty programs?
- How can security and fraud risks to loyalty programs be mitigated?

SECURITY BREACHES AND fraudulent activity are extensive in loyalty programs. With an estimated US$320 billion[488] of value sitting in points accounts around the globe, and many loyalty program operators not taking necessary steps to properly address security risks, account hacks and fraud continue to be perpetrated.

Loyalty fraud is defined as where deception is used to intentionally secure unfair financial, personal or third-party gains from loyalty programs.

Balancing easy join, earn, and redemption with proper security and fraud prevention processes is challenging, however understanding potential risks helps to identify issues early so they can be addressed quickly.

One of the main risk exposures for many loyalty programs is a lack of Know Your Customer (KYC) protocols. Unlike financial institutions, where KYC is usually a legal requirement, usually anyone can join a loyalty program by entering unverified credentials. This makes instances of fraud more possible as potential fraudsters can enter any details they wish.

Best-practice program operators utilise anti-fraud companies to check everything from the age of an email address to its validity as part of an automated background check. They also execute two-factor authentication (2FA) on the email address and/or mobile number as part of the registration process.

2FA requires members to provide an additional piece of information as part of the authentication process. This may be something they know (e.g. a PIN or a secret question), something they have (e.g. a unique code sent to their mobile, or a security token) or something they are (e.g. a fingerprint or voice scan). This makes it difficult for fraudsters to access accounts, and if they do, to complete transactions.

Building loyalty fraud into the overall business model as a line item in the P&L can help; both in terms of the old adage of 'what gets measured, gets

---

488 Statistic is taken from this article: https://medium.com/@simoncheong/gatcoin-is-blockchains-answer-to-loyalty-programs-d0193c2f4cef. Exact calculation of the value of unredeemed miles/points is hard to get at as many programs do not publish publicly available information. Consultant estimates give a figure in excess of US$220 billion. Other market research estimates of the size of the 'global market for loyalty programs' (which is not defined in terms of outstanding value of points) are also north of US$200 billion (from this article: https://www.prnewswire.com/news-releases/loyalty-programs-market-to-reach-201-billion-by-2022-according-to-beroe-inc300794907.html). It is safe to say that the amount is an enormous number.

done' but also because it forces the business to work out how to gather the data from the loyalty platform to calculate the amount of potential exposure.

This chapter focuses on loyalty-specific security and fraud issues, and suggests mitigation approaches for each.

Mass data breaches and account take-overs

<u>Risk</u>

Loyalty programs are attractive targets for database hacks, with enormous amounts of valuable member personal data held within systems which may lack appropriate security protections. Once accessed, hackers can extract authentication credentials and financial information.

Authentication credentials can be used for further hacks of other databases using 'credentials stuffing' attacks. This is where the hacked username and password is used to access the member's account on other sites. The approach preys on the tendency for consumers to use the same credentials across multiple websites.

Hackers may use phishing malware and other techniques (e.g. brute force, using common passwords) to capture member password details.

Financial information, such as credit card details, can be accessed and potentially used to conduct fraudulent payments.

Hackers may also sell member data on the internet rather than using it themselves. In recent years, there has been an increase in personal data for sale on the dark web. An article by Quartz[489] indicated a stolen identity can sell for an average of US$20, with a range from less than US$1 to about US$450.

Hackers may even lock out the owner of the database and demand a ransom for control to be provided back to them.

---

489 Collins, K., 2015, 'Here's what your stolen identity goes for on the internet's black market', Quartz, https://qz.com/460482/heres-what-your-stolen-identity-goes-for-on-the-internets-black-market/, accessed 9 June 2020.

Mitigation

Member data should be encrypted 'in motion' (active data traveling between devices, either through private networks or over a public or untrusted network) and 'at rest' (inactive data stored physically in any digital format in persistent storage). While many companies apply encryption in motion, fewer apply encryption at rest. Both are important, because if a hacker manages to intercept data during transit or access the database directly, the encrypted data cannot be used, ensuring the member is adequately protected.

Companies should conduct regular monitoring of online marketplaces that are buying/selling points. In addition, they should check all sections of the web (especially the dark web) to identify if their program data is for sale. Companies such as Amazon have started actively scanning member email addresses for known data breaches on other platforms and then recommending to their customers to change their passwords to prevent credentials stuffing attacks.

An account take-over can sometimes be identified by monitoring for unusual activity. For example, a password change can often be the sign of an account take-over, particularly if it is preceded by a redemption. Automated reporting can help quickly identify these instances by generating alerts to monitoring teams. It is also recommended to protect any profile changes by requiring password authentication as part of the process.

There are numerous tools in the marketplace provided by companies such as Accertify, Forter and Riskified that provide real time monitoring of the signs that an account has been taken over and is compromised.

Outside of personal data, the main value a hacker can access in a member's account is the loyalty currency. The ability for a hacker to fraudulently redeem a member's accumulated points can be reduced and/or blocked by implementing 2FA, as it requires the member to authenticate in a way a hacker may not be able to fulfil. One limitation of this approach is it requires an additional step in the redemption process, which may frustrate members, particularly if they themselves cannot complete the 2FA step (e.g. 'I forgot what my favourite holiday destination is').

If a fraudulent redemption does take place, sending a message to the member's email and phone (e.g. 'We hope you enjoy your new toaster') can act as an alert to the member so they can escalate to customer service and have the incident investigated.

Part of the reason bank accounts are hacked less than loyalty accounts (beyond KYC and better password requirements) is that customers understand that cash is real value. Programs may be able to better engage members to take account security more seriously by communicating that there is real value in the account which needs to be protected.

Hilton Honors

After a 2014 hack of the Hilton Honors program, members reported receiving emails for unauthorised reward redemptions and noticed their points balances were significantly depleted.[490] One member's account was used to pay for six hotel stays at Hilton properties; the corporate credit card associated with the account was then used to buy more reward points for the hacker. Many of the points drained from accounts later appeared for sale online at a fraction of their value. For instance, one vendor sold 240,000 points for US$3.50, another sold off 883,000 points for US$20 worth of Bitcoin; others traded stolen points for US$100 gift cards.

An investigation later identified the points were stolen in a mass brute force attack from multiple hackers permitted by weak security protocols. One user on a forum released a simple code alleged to have been used to breach accounts protected only with a four-digit PIN on the Hilton site.

One positive note for Hilton was that the redemption emails alerted many members to escalate the incident with customer service as soon as it occurred.

Following the attacks, Hilton introduced a more robust sign-in process (including more complex passwords and CAPTCHA codes) as a measure to stop a recurrence of such breaches.

---

490 Pauli, D., 2014, 'Hackers plunder Hilton "HHonors" rewards points, go on shopping spree', The Register, https://www.theregister.co.uk/2014/11/05/hilton_honor_cards_breached/, accessed 20 May 2020.

Misappropriated paper join forms

Risk

Despite living in a digital age, some loyalty programs still require members to fill in a paper form to join. These forms are stored, and at a later stage a staff member is required to manually enter the details into the member database to create the account.

With the forms containing member personal details, fraudsters could gain access to the discarded forms and use them for identity theft and other detrimental activities.

Mitigation

Companies should avoid a join process which requires a member to fill in a paper form. Starting the registration process, then providing the member with a code to compete it online is a safer process, and ensures the member still earns for the specific transaction.

If this is unavoidable, the company should implement a monitoring process which ensures the forms are tracked at all times, and destroyed once the details have been inputted into the member database.

Compromised third-party system links

Risk

Many loyalty platforms communicate with other third-party systems. This includes payment systems such as Point of Sale (POS) and points redemption portals. Each link represents a risk, with an opportunity for a hacker to access the loyalty platform and database if appropriate security protocols are not established.

Mitigation

Periodic audits of system interconnectivity should be conducted to identify weak links. Penetration testing ('pen' testing or ethical hacking) should be conducted to identify security vulnerabilities that a hacker could exploit.

> **British Airways**
>
> In 2018, cyber-criminals stole payment card details from an esti-
> mated 500,000 British Airways passengers who bought flights on the
> www.ba.com website or through the British Airways app, or made
> transactions involving Avios – their loyalty program currency.[491]
>
> Investigations revealed the hack in part involved customers being
> diverted to a fraudulent website, through which their details were
> harvested, including account customer information, payment cards
> and travel booking details. It was identified the security of per-
> sonal data was compromised due to an outdated IT system. British
> Airways were fined £183.4m for the breach, which does not account
> for other costs such as reimbursing affected customers, apology
> advertisement spend and the damage to the brand's reputation.
>
> British Airways appealed the fine, and at the time of writing, the
> appeal is pending.

Join bonus fraud

Risk

A fraudster may join the program multiple times using fake personal details to
access join bonuses.

Mitigation

This is primarily an issue when the join bonus is overly generous and/or the
program allows for points to be transferred. It is recommended to keep the join
bonus relatively low (i.e. start members on the journey to a redemption) and,
in some cases, avoid allowing members the ability to transfer or pool points
altogether.

Limiting one membership to one mobile phone or mobile phone number
can reduce the risk further by making it more difficult and expensive for a
fraudster to take advantage of the join bonus.

---

491 Cellan-Jones, R., 2019, 'British Airways faces record £183m fine for data breach,
BBC, https://www.bbc.com/news/business-48905907, accessed 20 May 2020.

Earn fraud and promotion exploitation

<u>Risk</u>

Fraudsters may identify ways to earn an enormous amount of points in a short time frame. This may be due to known risks or risks which are not obvious to the program operator.

Promotions, such as bonus points campaigns, can act to stimulate member engagement, but they may also provide opportunities for exploitation. Promotions sometimes inadvertently contain loopholes which can allow members to access value in excess of what was planned. In the social media age, these can be shared very quickly with other members, causing an exponential expansion of the impact.

A group may use a single loyalty card for multiple transactions, pooling all the points into one account.

<u>Mitigation</u>

Reporting should be implemented which generates alerts if a single account earns a large number of points, or engages in multiple transactions in a specified period. The identified accounts can then be isolated and frozen pending further investigation.

Program and/or promotion terms and conditions should be constructed in a way which weighs them in favour of the program operator to allow sufficient control in the event an issue is identified.

Social media monitoring should be conducted to identify exploitation of promotions that have spread to the mainstream. Rapid identification can help close the promotion down, thereby curtailing the damage.

Healthy Choice

In 1999, David Phillips, a civil engineer from California, earned 1.2 million airline miles by taking advantage of a Healthy Choice promotion by purchasing large volumes of puddings.[492] The promotion

---

492 Herreria, C. R., 2016, 'Carla, Meet David Phillips, The Guy Who Earned 1.2 Million Airline Miles With Chocolate Pudding', HuffPost, https://www.huffpost.com/entry/david-philipps-pudding-guy-travel-deals_n_577c9397e4b0a629c1ab

rewarded participants with up to 1,000 travel miles for the airline of their choice for every 10 product codes they collected. Recognising the potential, Phillips shopped around for the cheapest products he could find, eventually discovering single pudding cups selling at 25 cents. Purchasing more than 12,000 cups of pudding, he earned 1.2 million miles for just US$3,140, also earning him the nickname 'The Pudding Guy'. Phillips donated the puddings to The Salvation Army, allowing him to claim US$815 in tax deductions.

Starbucks Rewards

Starbucks Rewards ran a promotion which provided members with a free item on their birthday or after accumulating 12 stars. One member took advantage by using their free beverage to create the most expensive Starbucks drink ever.[493] It included 60 espresso shots, protein powder and syrups in a giant Slurpee cup totalling US$54.75, all for free. Restrictions were quickly implemented into the program terms and conditions to prevent other members from replicating the behaviour.

Points transfer/pooling fraud

Risk

The ability to transfer points from one account to another provides opportunities for fraudsters to increase their ability to remain undetected, as it allows them to keep fraudulent earn events small and infrequent, but on a vast scale. Points can then be consolidated into a smaller number of accounts for easy redemption, or even sale. This can lead to vast amounts of fraudulent accounts (often created automatically via bots) which skews reporting.

Frequent flyer and hotel programs often contend with travel agents

---

35a7, accessed 20 May 2020.

493 Northrup, L., 2014, 'New Starbucks Free Drink Record Set With $54 Sexagintuple Vanilla Bean Mocha Frappuccino', Consumerist, https://consumerist.com/2014/05/27/new-starbucks-free-drink-record-set-with-54-sexagintuple-vanilla-bean-mocha-frappuccino/, accessed 21 May 2020.

creating member accounts for travellers without the traveller's knowledge. After the travel is completed, the travel agent transfers all points earned to a single account for their own usage.

eBay and other consumer commerce sites can be used to sell bundles of points or miles, despite this being expressly prohibited by the terms and conditions of the program.

Mitigation

The most effective mitigation is to deny members the ability to transfer or pool points altogether.

If a decision is made to progress with transfers or pooling, then monitoring systems for bot detection and/or where a significant number of accounts are opened either with the same or a similar email address should be implemented, with clear escalation pathways. For example, fraudsters may have emailaddress1@, emailaddress2@, emailaddress3@ and so forth.

Placing limits on transfer activity can minimise the impacts of fraudulent behaviour. This may include only being able to transfer a minimum/maximum number of points at one time, having limits on the number of transfers which can be processed each year, restricting transfer to family members only or charging a transaction fee. An example of this is the Lufthansa Miles & More frequent flyer program which provides a 'Transfer Miles' service allowing members the option to transfer and receive points from another Miles & More member for a transaction fee, with a maximum transfer of 50,000 miles per calendar year.[494]

> **The Travel Agent**
>
> A former travel agent was charged for stealing nearly 3.7 million airline miles from high-end clients, and then using them to buy flight tickets for herself and her family.[495] The travel agent fre-

---

494 Lufthansa, 'Help & Contact', Lufthansa Airlines, https://www.miles-and-more.com/row/en/general-information/help-and-contact.html, accessed 21 May 2020.

495 Airlines IATA, 2019, 'Fraud prevention: Strengthening the defences', International Air Transport Association (IATA), https://www.airlines.iata.org/analysis/fraud-prevention-strengthening-the-defences, accessed 21 May 202.

quently denied her clients access to their airline miles or misled clients into believing that the airlines had imposed restrictions on generating loyalty bonuses.

In truth, the airline miles were misappropriated for the travel agent's own benefit. Some 135 flights for herself and her family worth more than US$109,000 were booked before the fraud was discovered. Policies allowing clients to purchase tickets for other clients and convert frequent flyer miles to other accounts had enabled the travel agent to do the unlawful deed for years.

Though the ability to transfer or pool points is a beneficial feature when used appropriately, without any mitigation or monitoring strategy in place, the potential risks for fraudulent transfers are evident and can go unnoticed. In this case, it was discrepancies in the frequent flyer account of one of the company's top clients which revealed the fraudulent behaviour.

World of Hyatt

Hyatt allows points transfers between any account but only allows this once every 30 days. 'A single member may only participate in a points combining transaction (transferring or receiving points) once every 30 days.'[496] This clause, along with the tedious and manual points combining request form which needs to be submitted, would significantly minimise fraud risks associated with points pooling.

---

496 Hyatt, 'World of Hyatt – Purchase, Share & Gift Points', https://world.hyatt.com/content/gp/en/rewards/purchase-share-gift.html, accessed 29 May 2020

Retro claims fraud

Risk

If the method by which a member can make a retrospective (or retro) claim (e.g. post-purchase entering codes from receipts) does not have appropriate controls, fraudsters may make multiple claims, thereby earning large amounts of points. This will create a secondary issue of increased workload for customer service in processing the claims.

Mitigation

It is recommended to not support retro claims.

If retro claims are introduced, it is recommended to limit claims to a small number per account to minimise fraud exposure and to place time restrictions on when a claim can be made (most airline programs limit the time claim to six months, with QSR's much less).

Referral program fraud

Risk

If the loyalty program is designed to reward members when they successfully invite a new member to join the program, fraudsters can utilise bots to generate multiple new accounts, thereby earning large amounts of bonus points. The program will be filled with fake member accounts, skewing program analytics.

Mitigation

This issue can be resolved if the new member must make at least one transaction for the referral bonus to be released.

Referral tracking reporting can be used to identify accounts which show an unusually large amount of referral activations, with alerts triggered to inform the program operator to investigate.

Limiting the number of referrals an individual member can be rewarded for will help to reduce the magnitude of the risk.

Status matching fraud

<u>Risk</u>

Major loyalty programs which support status tiers sometimes run status matching campaigns. This allows high-status members of other programs to access the same status level without having to earn it via traditional channels such as flights and/or spend.

Depending on the verification processes, it can be possible for fraudsters to create counterfeit membership cards which show they are a high status (e.g. Platinum). They will then receive Platinum with the program. This will then allow them to take advantage of other programs conducting status matching, although this time with a genuine card.

<u>Mitigation</u>

Status matching campaigns should require the member to present more than just a card (or image of a card). They should also be asked to provide evidence of their transaction activity with the program which earned them the status tier. For example, this may be their loyalty program transaction history which proves the accumulation of status credits.

Some airlines have begun collaborating with competitors to verify the status of members seeking status matches as a method to reduce incidences of fraud.

Once the status tier matching has been processed, additional rules can be implemented to further reduce the risk to the program. For example, a member who has received frequent flyer status matching may be required to take two flights within three months or their tier status will be lost.

> **United Airlines**
>
> US airlines have begun collaborating to reduce fraud associated with status matching.[497] One instance involved a member being denied a status match from United Airlines after they were informed their current competitor status was not earned.

497 Leff, G., 2018, 'United Shares Member Info With Other Airlines to Combat Status Match Fraud', https://viewfromthewing.com/

The member had a promotional status generated from an earlier status match. United contacted the competitor airline to research the status, and denied the match on the ground their current status was not earned. Of note, United's status match campaign at the time did not say anything about limitations regarding promotional versus earned.

Redemption fraud

Risk

One example of redemption fraud involves 'double-dipping'. This is where members attempt to conduct a redemption simultaneously via two different channels in an attempt to spend the points twice. For example, a member may attempt to redeem points via a call centre while redeeming online at the same time.

Fraudsters may also attempt to double-dip on single-use digital vouchers. This involves taking a screenshot of the voucher barcode and sharing with friends. The group may then attempt to use the vouchers at the same time via different Point of Sale systems.

Punch cards can be counterfeited, allowing fraudsters to make multiple reward claims without spending with the retailer. This may involve using a fake stamp or creating an entirely fake card.

Another example involves members spending on products to earn points, then redeeming the points on rewards, only to return the products for a refund. The loyalty program wears the cost of the reward, while the business gains no benefit from the transaction.

If the program allows gifting of vouchers, fraudsters may be provided with the opportunity to exploit time zones. For example, one time zone may not have the fraud team actively monitoring suspicious activity, allowing fraudsters to redeem for a voucher which is then sent to another time zone to be spent.

united-shares-member-info-with-other-airlines-to-combat-status-match-fraud/, accessed 21 May 2020.

Mitigation

IT systems should be sufficiently sophisticated to block duplicate redemptions from occurring. If they do occur, the system should trigger an instant alert to enable the reward delivery to be blocked. A short delay in reward delivery may be required to support this process. This is particularly important for redemptions involving digital downloads and for higher value and/or near cash rewards (e.g. gift cards or items like flat screen TVs). From a design perspective, this can be challenging in circumstances where the member base has an expectation of instant gratification, and therefore a balance may be required.

Apps can be configured such that they block the ability for the phone to take a screenshot of the digital voucher barcode. This does not prevent a photo to be taken with another phone, however systems should be high-tech enough to block duplicate redemptions without affecting voucher processing times.

Physical punch cards should only be used for low-value rewards. Redeemed punch cards should be inspected for evidence of fraud. Staff should be trained to be alert for customers making multiple redemptions. Ideally, the program should be transferred from a physical card into a digital card.

The loyalty platform should be configured to deduct points from member accounts in the event of a refund. This can be challenging for coalition programs but is still possible if the program operator is committed. Delays in points being credited to member accounts can help reduce refund fraud. For example, frequent flyer programs can have delays of up to 60 days in points being credited to member accounts, making it more difficult for fraudsters to commit refund fraud.

Systems can be configured so that if the IP address/geolocation where the voucher is created is presented in a different location, it can be blocked.

> **Subway Sub Club**
>
> In 2005, Subway's Sub Club loyalty program rewarded members with free meals every time they filled a punch/stamp card with stamps.[498]

---

498 Ogles, J., 2005, 'Fraud Sinks Subway's Sub Club', Wired, https://www.wired.com/2005/09/fraud-sinks-subways-sub-club/, accessed 21 May 2020.

Advances in computer and laser printer technology allowed fraud-sters to make counterfeit punch cards that were indistinguishable from the real cards. They also sold Subway stamps on eBay.

This led to such extensive levels of fraudulent claims that the pro-gram had to be closed down.

It was later relaunched after taking new technological advances into consideration.

Today's program runs on apps and unique QR codes, making it much more challenging (and ideally impossible) for fraudsters to exploit.

Friendly fraud

Risk

Loyalty programs may be affected by fraud conducted with the complicit acknowledgement of the account holder. For example, they may process a redemption, but then claim the points have been taken without their knowl-edge or consent.

A variation is where the member's family or friends manage to access their account and process redemptions without their knowledge or consent.

Mitigation

Reporting systems (same IP address used, geolocation identifiers, etc.) can help identify some of these instances, and then they can be addressed as cus-tomer service issues. Some loyalty programs, where they have strong grounds to suspect fraud, will suspend the member.

Reporting to monitor for significant abuse is best practice. This includes training call centre staff to write notes detailing the claim, which can be referred to later if the member makes a similar claim. It also includes reporting which details claim activity to support fraud monitoring processes.

The program terms and conditions should ensure the operator has the right to freeze or suspend an account if the correct sign-in details have been used but the account shows signs of suspicious activity. The program should also be covered for member reimbursement claims if a redemption event has taken place.

Staff fraud

Risk

Encouraging frontline staff to participate in a loyalty program can be beneficial because it can help to educate them about the benefits, leading them to promote it to customers. However, it can also lead to fraud issues. For example, frontline staff may choose to scan their own loyalty card when processing a transaction if the customer is not a member, thereby collecting the points. They may process false transactions to generate points earn. Staff may also use multiple accounts to minimise the risk of detection. Staff fraud events may be as simple as the staff member providing a friend with several stamps on a stamp card (instead of one).

With direct access to the loyalty platform, customer service staff can be a major source of fraudulent behaviour. This includes providing bonus points to accounts (their own or family/friends), providing points refunds on vouchers (even though the voucher has been used), secretly creating new promotions with large bonus points offers for their own use, promoting family and friends to high status tiers, and asking the member for their password (so they can later hack the member's account).

Some programs provide staff with incentives to sign new members. This can lead to a situation where customers are registered without them being aware.

Mitigation

Earn monitoring reporting can be used to identify most instances of this type of activity, as it will identify accounts which show consistent earn behaviour throughout the day, a contrast to most member earn activity. If the staff member is using multiple accounts, it may be harder to detect. Limiting one membership to one mobile phone or phone number can reduce the risk further.

An investigation should be conducted to ascertain whether staff can over-ride systems to award extra points to an account by entering false information into the POS.

Some companies ban their own employees from participating in their loyalty program, which may be a consideration for some companies who deem the risk to be too high.

Monitoring and reporting of individual customer service staff is important to identify the amount of points they are crediting to accounts. Any points credited to an account should be supported by notes from the agent justifying the action.

Any accounts which have repeat credits should also be identified as part of the monitoring process. If required, the accounts should be blocked. The ability to do this should be clearly detailed in the terms and conditions.

In instances where members complain that their account has been compromised, any call centre engagement should be included as part of the investigation to determine whether a call centre agent may be involved.

To reduce the incentive for staff to sign new members without the customer being aware, a condition should be implemented whereby the member needs to transact within a specified time period for the staff member to be awarded their bonus.

The Airline Agent

One airline employee accumulated loyalty points from thousands of passengers.[499] The agent put in accurate passenger details, but then used his member details instead of the passengers, which allowed him to accumulate approximately 2.6 million air miles before anyone noticed.

The agent was only caught when a victim customer went into their account to use miles to buy a trip, checked their balance and discovered there was nothing there. When the customer brought this to the attention of the parent company, an investigation ensued,

---

499 Hofmann, S., 2019, 'How to Stop Fraud in Loyalty Programs', Fraud Conference News, https://www.fraudconferencenews.com/home/2019/2/25/how-to-stop-fraud-in-loyalty-programs, accessed 21 May 2020.

and the agent's fraud was discovered. This led to him being sent to prison.

Staff account take-over

<u>Risk</u>

An event even more serious than member account take-over is staff or customer service account take-over. This can provide the fraudster with the ability to credit large amounts of points to multiple accounts, and redeem those points for cash-equivalent rewards (such as gift cards) in sizeable volumes, causing considerable financial damage to the company. Cases of staff account take-over can be exacerbated in circumstances where the compromised account has administrator or high-level security-related rights and privileges, potentially providing fraudsters access to extremely sensitive and valuable data.

<u>Mitigation</u>

Sufficient controls should be established to reduce the likelihood of incidence, such as enforced regular password changes, best-practice password formats, staff training on security protocols and 2FA for login.

Damage minimisation steps can also be introduced, such as a limit on the amount of points which can be credited to an account, and a limit on the number of points credits an agent can process in a set time period.

Marriott

In September 2018, Marriott became aware of a potential security breach after an internal security tool flagged an unusual database query to the Starwood guest reservation database.[500] After engaging with security experts, it was discovered that information on up to 500m guests was compromised. For 327m of these guests, this information included a combination of personal details, travel

---

500 Mitchell, V., 2019, 'Marriott creates new loyalty program following hacking scandal', CMO, https://www.cmo.com.au/article/656393/marriott-creates-new-loyalty-program-following-hacking-scandal/, accessed 21 May 2020.

and reservation transactions, and communication preferences. For several million members, compromised details included passport numbers, payment card numbers and expiration dates.

Investigators uncovered the database query was made by a user with administrator privileges, but revealed the person to whom the account was assigned was not the one who made the query; the hacker had executed a staff account take-over. Clues pointed to a combination of tools, including Remote Access Trojans, to capture user login details. However, the complexity of the breach was greater. It was revealed that unauthorised access had occurred to the Starwood network as early as 2014, and when Marriott acquired Starwood in 2016, they inherited thousands of new hotels and adopted an old reservation system unknowingly infected with malware and compromised by hackers.

Marriott unveiled a new customer loyalty program brand, Marriott Bonvoy the next year and brought together its three legacy loyalty brands under the one banner, presumably discarding antiquated systems in the process.

In February of 2020, Marriott suffered a second breach after a hacker used login credentials of two employees from one of its franchise properties to access customer information from Marriott Bonvoy's backend system.[501] This time, the hacker had direct access to the loyalty data of 5.2 million hotel guests, including personal data, loyalty account information like points balances, partnerships and affiliations (linked airline programs), and preferences (such as room and language preferences).

---

501 Barrett, B., 2020, 'Hack Brief: Marriot Got Hacked. Yes, Again.', Wired, https://www.wired.com/story/marriott-hacked-yes-again-2020/, accessed 21 May 2020.

Key insights

- Loyalty fraud is defined as where deception is used to intentionally secure unfair financial, personal or third-party gains from loyalty programs. Understanding potential risks helps to identify issues early so they can be addressed quickly.

- Different types of security and fraud issues which affect loyalty programs include mass data breaches and account take-overs, misappropriated paper join forms, compromised third-party systems and system Links, join bonus fraud, earn fraud and promotion exploitation, points transfer/pooling fraud, retro claims fraud, referral program fraud, status matching fraud, redemption fraud, friendly fraud, staff fraud and staff account take-over.

- Each security and fraud challenge has at least one mitigation approach, meaning program operators that are proactively managing risk can significantly reduce their exposure to fraudsters, while simultaneously increasing their response time if a security breach or fraudulent act is detected.

Suggested reading

- Pauli, Darren, 2014, 'Hackers plunder Hilton 'HHonors' rewards points, go on shopping spree', The Register, https://www.theregister.co.uk/2014/11/05/hilton_honor_cards_breached/, accessed 20 May 2020.

- Hauser, C., 2020, 'EasyJet Says Cyberattack Stole Data of 9 Million Customers', New York Times, https://www.nytimes.com/2020/05/19/business/easyjet-hacked.html, accessed 15 June 2020.

- Zhong, R., 2018, 'Cathay Pacific Data Breach Exposes 9.4 Million Passengers,' New York Times, https://www.nytimes.com/2018/10/25/business/cathay-pacific-hack.html, accessed 15 June 2020.

- Cellan-Jones, Rory, 2019, 'British Airways faces record £183m fine for data breach⬚, BBC, https://www.bbc.com/news/business-48905907, accessed 20 May 2020.

- Herreria Russo, 2016, 'Carla, Meet David Phillips, The Guy Who Earned 1.2 Million Airline Miles With Chocolate Pudding', HuffPost, https://www.huffpost.com/entry/david-philipps-pudding-guy-travel-deals_n_577c9397e4b0a629c1ab35a7, accessed 20 May 2020.

- Northrup Laura, 2014, 'New Starbucks Free Drink Record Set With $54 Sexagintuple Vanilla Bean Mocha Frappuccino', Consumerist, https://consumerist.com/2014/05/27/new-starbucks-free-drink-record-set-with-54-sexagintuple-vanilla-bean-mocha-frappuccino/, accessed 21 May 2020.

- Ogles, Jacob, 2005, 'Fraud Sinks Subway's Sub Club', Wired, https://www.wired.com/2005/09/fraud-sinks-subways-sub-club/, accessed 21 May 2020.

- Barrett, Brian, 2020, 'Hack Brief: Marriot Got Hacked. Yes, Again.', Wired, https://www.wired.com/story/marriott-hacked-yes-again-2020/, accessed 21 May 2020.

CHAPTER 17

LOYALTY OPERATIONS

'The first rule of any technology used in a business is that automation applied to an efficient operation will magnify the efficiency. The second is that automation applied to an inefficient operation will magnify the inefficiency.'

- Bill Gates

Focus areas

This chapter will address the following questions:

- Should loyalty operations be maintained internally or outsourced?

- What is involved in running the operations of a loyalty program?

- What teams, roles and responsibilities are required to operate a loyalty program?

THE OPERATION OF a best-practice loyalty program involves managing a member database engaging in multi-transaction value accumulation and extensive redemption choices. Many different areas of the business require alignment and investment across both teams and technology to be able to design, implement and operate an effective program. Data analytics support marketing communications and offers, sophisticated accounting rules manage program liabilities, and technology platforms utilise automated capability to optimise lifecycle management. Call centre operations ensure adequate member support is provided, while third-party partners are assisted by commercial teams, and all aspects of the program operations are subject to legal review to minimise litigation exposure.

The complexity of the operation requires a team of experienced and educated professionals to ensure it can run smoothly and profitably. Teams may range in size from one or two people (supported by a wider organisation) to several hundred.

This chapter details the requirements for running the operations of a loyalty program. All programs are different, therefore some of the areas discussed may not be relevant, or the teams may fulfil roles which are variations to the functions detailed.

Insource or outsource

The loyalty industry is highly lucrative. Billions of dollars of points and miles are earned and redeemed each year, while hundreds of millions of dollars is invested in technology to power programs, and significant marketing budgets are devoted to promoting the program benefits.

A company can choose to insource the entire operation (including building their own technology platform), or they can opt to outsource some or all of the operations to service providers.

Outsourcing appears to be increasingly prevalent. *MarketsandMarkets* forecasts the global loyalty management market size to grow from US$7.6 billion in 2020 to US$15.5 billion by 2025, at a Compound Annual Growth Rate (CAGR) of 15.3% during the forecast period.[502]

With outsourcing becoming increasingly prevalent, it is worth exploring the advantages and challenges of outsourcing loyalty operations.

---

502 Loyalty Management Market by Component (Solutions and Services), Organization Size (Large Enterprises and SMEs), Deployment Type, Operator (B2B and B2C), Application (Web and Mobile), Vertical, and Region - Global Forecast to 2025, June 2020 https://www.marketsandmarkets.com/Market-Reports/loyalty-management-market-172873907.html accessed 18 August 2020

Outsourcing advantages

- **Access to expertise**: companies can gain access to expertise from experienced loyalty professionals, with the potential to drive program operational efficiencies and strategic evolution. Good quality loyalty professionals with extensive experience operating across a variety of programs and industries can be difficult to find and costly to hire internally.

- **Independent perspective**: external agencies can apply a fresh, no-nonsense perspective to an existing program, identifying issues which internal management may either be blind to, or not have the appetite to address.

- **Quality existing solutions**: as detailed in Chapter 11, technology platforms are becoming increasingly sophisticated and more affordable, making the idea of building an internal solution less attractive.

- **Time efficiencies**: accessing a large rewards range can take time to develop, while warehousing products may be prohibitively expensive. A single relationship with a reward aggregator can deliver hundreds, thousands or even millions of reward options with no need for the program operator to hold stock.

- **Sophisticated marketing ability**: a loyalty agency may be able to execute marketing campaigns with a level of sophistication which is not possible or viable for the company, delivering personalisation, promotional budget optimisation, and all other associated benefits.

Outsourcing challenges

- **Cost**: the services provided by the agency may come at a higher cost than if the company executed internally.

- **Consistent service**: the company may not receive the consistent level of service expected and required, as the agency may have too many other clients (all with competing priorities) and insufficient resources.

- **Knowledge gap**: there may be a continuous knowledge gap between internal teams and outsource agencies which results in the company being too heavily reliant on the skills of the agency to run day-to-day operations. This may impede the company's ability to directly resolve issues and enquiries which arise.

- **Security and fraud risks**: outsource operations can require member personal data to be held in third-party systems, as well as a need for direct access to member data via third-party staff members.

Outsourcing options

Typically, at least some of the operations associated with larger loyalty programs tend to be outsourced. Within this environment, many service providers have evolved to help companies with the design, implementation and/or operation of their program.

In Chapter 11, four types of loyalty technology solution providers were detailed (full-service loyalty solutions, partial service loyalty solutions, off-the-shelf loyalty solutions and niche loyalty solutions) which can all support loyalty program operations. In addition to this are loyalty consulting agencies which can offer a mix of different services and solutions.

From an ongoing operations perspective, the types of outsource support each provider could provide to a company include:

- **Full-service loyalty solutions**: the entire program can be outsourced by a company which does not wish to be involved in the day-to-day operations of the loyalty program. In these instances, the company relies on the provider for all aspects of program operations, with the costs tending to be quite high.

- **Partial service loyalty solutions**: a company may choose a partial service solution to provide the technology platform, but maintain control of other aspects. For example, the provider may enable rewards supply, but the company maintains control of the communications strategy and execution, as well as customer service support.

- **Off-the-shelf loyalty solutions**: an off-the-shelf solution may be able to provide a company with everything they need to implement and run a loyalty program internally. However, all other elements of the program need to be managed in other ways. This may be insourced, or alternative, they may be outsourced to different agencies (e.g. reward supply could be outsourced to a rewards aggregator, while customer care could be outsourced to an offshore provider).

- **Niche loyalty solutions**: can use their expertise to provide a partial solution solving a specific problem.

- **Loyalty consulting agencies**: specialise in strategically designing and implementing loyalty programs, but may also support post-launch operations and future roadmap evolution. This allows a company to access experienced loyalty professionals as required whilst maintaining the desired level of flexibility and control over loyalty program operations and future strategy.

Operational areas

This section details the role played by different business areas of a company or outsource agency which are likely to be involved in the day-to-day running of a loyalty program.

Strategy

The ambition of a Strategy team is to design, refine and optimise the loyalty program to achieve longer-term company objectives.

The responsibilities of the Strategy team include:

- **Strategic planning**: development of an overall strategic program roadmap supported by analytics (program performance, member segmentation, market research insights, front-line staff interviews, competitor approaches, loyalty trends, loyalty psychology, relevant heuristics and biases, technology advancements, commercial modelling, loyalty fraud risk analysis, legal guidance, program testing and other data points) and lifecycle frameworks. Liaise with senior leaders to translate the strategy into business function plans and work streams.

- **Insights capture**: work with Analytics and Marketing to develop the capability to capture, decipher, understand and apply data-based insights, with a core focus on identifying critical moments that drive delight and build loyalty.

- **Trend monitoring**: proactively identify relevant loyalty trends and translate the future opportunities these trends may unlock for the program.

- **Partner needs**: work with Partner Management to identify opportunities to harness the full potential of the program to support partner customer engagement strategies and company growth.

- **Program benefits**: develop new, or revise existing, program benefits, experiential rewards and the functionality required to increase the program's competitiveness in relevant markets for different segments.

- **Terms and conditions management**: as required, facilitate strategic changes to the program terms and conditions to ensure the program remains on track to deliver to long-term objectives.

The team may also be involved in the wider strategic development of the company, with broader objectives provided at a senior level needing to be incorporated into the more detailed objectives of the loyalty program.

Unless there are highly experienced loyalty professionals within the organisation, a company may consider outsourcing this function. Loyalty strategy and design is very specialised, and becoming increasingly so as new and innovative approaches, technology, trends, data analytics methods and reward options enter the market.

Marketing

A best-practice loyalty program Marketing team will strive to execute communications across multiple channels to deliver hyper-personalised offers targeting the right member with the right message, through the right channel at the right time.

The responsibilities of the Marketing team include:

- **Strategic planning**: development of a marketing communications strategic roadmap supported by analytics (program performance and benchmarking, member segmentation, market research insights, competitor approaches and other data points) and lifecycle frameworks.

- **Marketing execution**: implementation of planned and short-term tactical campaigns designed to achieve the core program objectives by delivering to the strategic roadmap. Communication of past and planned campaign activity to relevant areas of the business to facilitate learnings, member support and enquiries.

- **Campaign tracking**: evaluation of campaign performance and optimisation of subsequent campaigns to increasingly drive member engagement.

- **Agency management**: collaboration with external marketing agencies (as required) by providing strategy, direction and input towards the development of required campaigns that are aligned with the program's brand positioning.

- **Budget management**: development of a detailed plan for management and utilisation of the marketing budget to maximise return on investment.

The team may also be involved in formal projects focused on development of the program, including redesigning, rebranding, strategic formulation and implementation of new technology approaches, changes to the terms and conditions of the program, and other enhancements.

This function is best held within the company. If the program is large, it may be a dedicated loyalty marketing team embedded within the company. For a smaller program, it may sit with the Marketing team of the wider company.

With the rise of AI, some larger programs are outsourcing their marketing operations to specialised AI companies, which could herald a future trend if the operational costs make it a cost-effective option and the results clearly deliver better outcomes. There are data security and control risks associated with this approach as detailed in Chapter 16.

Operations

In the same way that a superior quality product or service experience can play a critical role in building customer loyalty, a quality loyalty program member experience is imperative in maintaining longer-term engagement. The ambition of a best-practice Operations team is to strive to enable an outstanding member experience across all member touchpoints.

The responsibilities of the Operations team include:

- **Member experience improvements**: identification of opportunities to add incremental value to the member experience across multiple touchpoints, then championing and engineering initiatives to facilitate the additions.

- **Irritant resolution**: identification of key member irritants across multiple touchpoints, then championing and engineering neutralisation of the irritants.

- **Operational efficiency development**: review, recommend and implement new methods and procedures to increase the efficiency and effectiveness of daily operations.

- **Reward range management**: procuring reward products or reward suppliers, managing the range, facilitating fulfilment, and acting as an escalation path for order issues.

- **Procurement**: support the procurement of products and services for the operational running of the program via approved vendor-engagement processes.

- **Vendor management**: management of relationships with vendors and virtual teams, including vendor onboarding, system integration support and contract compliance.

- **System configuration**: support the configuration of systems as required to execute on agreed changes.

- **Testing**: design and execution of user acceptance and system integration testing processes for system development and configuration changes.

- **Training**: lead the development and facilitate the implementation of training across front-line staff and other teams (as required) for system and process enhancements, and terms and conditions changes.

Due to the extensive variability in loyalty program designs and company sizes, the Operations team roles may vary widely from what is detailed.

This is a function which can be fully or partially outsourced to access operational or cost efficiencies. For example, the program operator may outsource the rewards range management, but choose to maintain the system configuration function within the program.

Partner Management

It is important that the Partner Management team are supported with the right types of tools to help facilitate partner sourcing and negotiations. This may include professionally crafted presentations, other partner case studies, clear-language contracts and commercial model templates (to help the partner model the benefits of participating in the program). Specific to points-based programs, the Partner Management team should recognise that most individuals outside the loyalty industry are mystified by how programs work, therefore providing a basic education on their structure may be a useful first step.

The responsibilities of the Partner Management team include:

- **Partner strategy**: development and evolution of a partner strategy to identify gaps and growth opportunities for specific companies, categories and industries supported by analytics (local market review, market research, member segmentation, loyalty trends, competitor approaches and other data points) and financial imperatives. Identification of opportunities and innovative strategies to grow the membership base via partnerships.

- **Partner sourcing**: identification and negotiation of new commercial relationships across target categories and industries that deliver to the strategy (e.g. new points earn partners or new offer-provision partners).

- **Partner management**: development and maintenance of positive relationships with program partners. Identification of partner needs and aspirations, and development of initiatives to support their success. Management of any operational or customer issues. Owner of any contractual, program terms and conditions and proposition elements that influence members and operational delivery.

- **Internal collaboration**: work collaboratively with the program team to drive and achieve outcomes focused on partnership delivery and business growth. This may include Marketing (to ensure appropriate promotion of partners to the member base), Finance and Legal (to support contract negotiations and target setting) and Operations (to set-up new partners in the loyalty platform).

- **Financial management**: ownership of partner financial targets and team budgets.

Similar to operations team responsibilities, the Partner Management team scope may vary depending on the type of program design. The size of the company and the program framework chosen will dictate the partner management approach for the program.

A coalition points-based program or an affiliate model will require a business development team to acquire new coalition partners, negotiate contracts and manage relationships, a function which tends to reside within the program. For a member benefits program which focuses more on growing a network of third-party partners that can provide discounts and offers, fully or partially outsourcing to aggregators can deliver some cost-efficiencies. For a smaller retail company program, Partner Management responsibilities may be minimal and be able to be handled by the existing Marketing department.

Analytics

The primary aim of the Analytics team is to understand members and provide insights to engage them effectively across all touch points, thereby translating raw data into commercial action and success. There are many types of analytics, including descriptive, diagnostic, predictive and prescriptive, and each have a role to play in a best-practice loyalty program operation. The team may be supported by a separate team of data scientists.

The responsibilities of the Analytics team include:

- **Strategic planning**: creation and implementation of a member insights strategy to support the achievement of program objectives. Development of data-driven loyalty strategies to maximise customer lifetime value. Identification of trends in member behaviour over time.

- **Data-led forecasting**: estimation of the impact of different strategic scenarios using robust analytical/financial models.

- **Capability expansion**: coordination of technology and process initiatives to further improve the program's ability to understand and engage members.

- **Member segmentation**: development and evolution of member segments based on profiles, preferences, purchase behaviours and the specific elements of member behaviour the program is attempting to influence.

- **Campaign optimisation**: utilisation of analytics and testing methodologies to optimise member targeting and future marketing campaign performance in conjunction with the Marketing team.

- **Insights reporting**: development and production of periodic reporting (daily, weekly, monthly, annually) to support the company in understanding member behaviour and responses to products, services, marketing campaigns, offers and changes in the external environment.

As loyalty programs become more focused on delivering to the needs of members, personalisation of communications and offers will continue to increase in importance. This will place greater focus on the Analytics team and analytical systems, with a recognition they play a critical role.

Large programs tend to have sizeable teams of data scientists and analysts which play a critical role in driving member engagement. Analytics functions can be costly, making it harder for smaller programs to perform effectively in this area. Loyalty platforms can play a role here by providing the program operator with a well-structured data and reporting dashboard enabling easy access to essential member insights. This may be supplemented by a small amount of additional analytics support from the platform provider's team.

Technology

The core focus areas of the Technology team include overseeing technology operations, and evaluating and prioritising them according to established business requirements and goals. The technology department also devises and establishes IT policies and systems to support the implementation, operation and evolution of program strategies.

The responsibilities of the Technology team include:

- **Strategic planning**: analysing the business requirements of all teams to determine their technology needs. Optimising the use of existing systems to deliver to the needs. Identifying and recommending new or upgraded technology solutions when existing systems are inadequate, with a primary focus on automation and configuration capability.

- **Technology operations**: monitoring the use of technology systems and software to ensure functionality, efficiency and interoperability. Ensuring strategic capacity planning. Coordinating IT activities to ensure data availability and network services with as little downtime as necessary. Managing the IT help desk.

- **Policy formulation**: formulation and establishment of IT policies and processes to support the implementation of team strategies.

- **Security management**: identification and elimination of security vulnerabilities.

- **System procurement**: identification and purchase of efficient and cost-effective loyalty systems and software.

- **Vendor management**: building relationships with platform vendors and creating cost-efficient contracts.

- **Budget management**: control budget and report on expenditure.

The future loyalty landscape will include a mix of the technology 'haves' and 'have-nots'. The 'haves' will succeed by utilising loyalty platforms and technology innovations to enable the program operators to deliver a hyper-personalised, omni-channel experience. The 'have-nots' will fail because their ability to innovate will be continually stifled by legacy platforms which are inflexible and expensive to maintain and enhance.

While some companies have built their own loyalty platform solution, this is becoming increasingly rare due to the global availability of high quality, low cost technology. Thus, now and in the future, this is likely to remain an outsourced function.

Customer Service

The role of the Customer Service team is to provide appropriate member support across multiple channels, utilising profile data to personalise the experience as much as possible.

The responsibilities of the Customer Service team include:

- **Strategic planning**: analysing the strategic vision of the program to determine future member support needs. Auditing and identifying system and process needs, and working with IT to identify and recommend new technology solutions when existing systems are inadequate.

- **Contact centre operations**: managing the running of the contact centre, including effective resource planning, reporting analysis, and development of customer service procedures, policies, and standards to exceed agreed service metrics. Ensuring team compliance to all legislation, policies and procedures, and codes of conduct.

- **Irritant resolution**: identification of key member irritants across multiple touchpoints. Resolution of those irritant directly, or via escalation to Operations and other teams.

- **Member experience improvements**: identification of opportunities to add incremental value to the member experience across contact centre touchpoints, then escalation to Operations, Technology, and other teams to own and resolve.

- **Training**: hiring and training of new contact centre agents. Training of agents on new product and service launches, terms and conditions changes, marketing campaigns and other events which may generate contact centre inquiries.

- **Budget management**: control budget and report on expenditure.

Contact centres are increasingly using a range of technologies to provide members with the option to choose how they connect. This includes AI-powered chatbots, apps, social media channels and voice-recognition. Status tier programs may choose to prioritise higher tier members, such that they are moved to the front of the queue during high-volume periods.

The function can just as easily be insourced or outsourced, with the trend to outsourcing continuing globally. Some status tier programs maintain a small team to provide premium tier members with priority service, while other members are directed to an offshore contact centre for support. Some full-service and partial service agencies provide the Customer Service support function as part of their overall product offering.

Finance

The Finance team leads the finance and accounting function, including overseeing statutory reporting, budgeting and forecasting, revenue deferrals and points liability management, compliance, treasury and taxation. Such a team is specifically relevant for large points-based programs which generate sizeable profits from sizeable member bases.

The responsibilities of the Finance team include:

- **Strategic planning support**: working closely with the Strategy team to model the financial impacts of future strategy roadmap scenarios, and provide funding approval. Analysing the financial climate and market trends to assist senior executives in creating strategic plans for the future.

- **Finance operations**: directing financial planning and strategy. Overseeing accounts payable, accounts receivable, tax, treasury, payroll, financial and management accounting functions. Reviewing team budgets.

- **Financial reporting**: managing the financial reporting for the program. This includes monthly financial reporting, budgeting and forecasting, 5-year financial plans and all statutory financial reporting.

- **Risk management**: assessing, managing, and minimising risk, including ensuring that all the program's financial practices are in line with statutory regulations and legislation.

- **Breakage management**: auditing, tracking and managing breakage. Providing recommendations to the Strategy team to adjust terms and conditions to support management of breakage within a pre-defined range.

- **Supplier relationship management**: contract auditing and actuarial services to conduct financial monitoring and modelling. Create and maintain relationships with service providers and contractors, including banking institutions and accountants.

Smaller programs and non-points-based programs can usually access support from the wider company's Finance team, rather than requiring a dedicated loyalty team.

This function tends to be insourced.

Security and Fraud

The Security and Fraud team is involved in oversight and management of all facets of loyalty program security and fraud. This includes ensuring all teams are equipped with the support, knowledge, and solutions required to identify and mitigate any risks.

The responsibilities of the Security and Fraud team include:

- **Strategic development**: investigate best-practice processes and tools required for an effective strategy to appropriately detect and mitigate security risks and safeguard the organisation and program. Ensure preparation and readiness for external and internal threats, and act quickly and decisively when threats and attacks are identified.

- **Security and fraud operations**: manage day-to-day security and fraud monitoring, reporting and advising teams of potential risks, including security breaches of other companies which may cause risks for the program's members. Maintain appropriate structure, processes and documentation at all times. Conduct audits and deliver professional reports in situations of investigation with the appropriate facts and findings. Provide feedback to further develop and improve security and fraud management processes and mitigation strategies.

- **Relationship management**: build strong and trusted relationships across all teams to improve detection performance and mitigate risk. Support teams in implementing and maintaining security monitoring processes and policies, and where necessary, provide further guidance in reporting, incident responses and investigations to limit exposure and liability.

- **Training**: provide regular training across the company to educate teams about risks and risk detection, as appropriate.

Large programs with appropriate security and risk technology and processes may only require a single team member to mitigate risks effectively. Smaller programs may merge this team into the role of another individual or outsource it to the technology platform provider. Platforms are increasingly building security and fraud detection software and reporting into their platforms to assist in this area.

Legal

The Legal team focuses on the legal and commercial issues that need to be addressed as part of the establishment and operation of a loyalty program. In most countries, the laws applicable to loyalty programs and wider member engagement approaches are a disparate bundle of regulations that can create compliance challenges for program operators. Legal expertise in this area is important to ensure the program operations do not unnecessarily expose the company to risks.

The responsibilities of the Legal team include:

- **Strategic planning**: legal review of the strategic plans of teams to ensure compliance. Developing a forward view of regulatory changes which may create future impacts on the program operations (e.g. GDPR).

- **Marketing review**: legal review of advertising and marketing campaigns to ensure due disclosure and compliance with competition and consumer laws. Audit of data capture processes to ensure compliance with privacy regulations.

- **Promotion risk mitigation**: implementation of appropriate terms and conditions to protect the program and company from financial and brand damage in the event a promotion is unexpectedly exploited by members.

- **Partner and supplier contracts**: formulation and review of partner and supplier contracts to support the partner sourcing and product/service procurement processes.

- **Legal representation**: representing the program in instances where legal action has been taken by members, partners, suppliers, government bodies or other parties, or where legal action is being taken by the program against other parties.

- **Training**: assisting in the development of policies, procedures and training for staff on relevant legal issues.

Similar to the Finance team, a large and complex loyalty program may require a dedicated Legal team, while a smaller program may utilise the general counsel of the wider company.

Even larger programs with a dedicated Legal team may from time to time outsource work to a legal firm specialising in loyalty regulations.

Key insights

- The complexity of loyalty program operations requires a team of experienced and educated professionals to ensure it can run smoothly and profitably.

- Loyalty program operations involve teams and/or roles and/or responsibilities which touch many different areas of the business including Strategy, Marketing, Operations, Partner Management, Analytics, Technology, Customer Service, Finance, Security and Fraud, and Legal. The size of the company and the program will influence whether dedicated teams and/or roles are required to manage the program operations, or whether the responsibilities may fall under a broader, existing role within the company.

- A program operator may choose to maintain all the operations within the company, outsource some or outsource all. Outsourcing is becoming increasingly prevalent, however loyalty program operators need to consider both the advantages and challenges of this approach.

THE FUTURE OF LOYALTY

'The best way to predict the future is to create it.'

- Abraham Lincoln

BEST-PRACTICE LOYALTY PROGRAM operators utilise a complex combination of design principles, loyalty psychology and behavioural biases, desirable rewards, appropriate design frameworks, games and gamification, technology, analytics and personalisation, lifecycle management, security and fraud protections, and efficient operations to drive industry-leading member engagement.

There appears to be sufficient academic research and empirical evidence to suggest that loyalty programs, when designed and executed correctly, can work to generate increased visits, spend, brand affinity, advocacy, retention and market share. For this reason, they will continue to attract large amounts of investment and innovation globally which will work to increase their impact and cost-effectiveness.

What does the future for loyalty hold? The conclusion of *Loyalty Programs: The Complete Guide* reviews a collection of innovative developments and emerging challenges which are forecast by the authors to have a material impact on the future of loyalty program design and execution.

Data, machine learning/AI and personalisation

This topic has been covered extensively throughout the book. Improvements in data collection methods and the application of machine learning/AI technology will allow more loyalty programs to deliver personalisation of communications, experiences, and offers at scale. This will eventually manifest in Digital EQ;[503] the ability to anticipate and recognise customer sentiment and deliver a digitally enabled response which optimises the customer experience in real time, serving to build a deeper attitudinal commitment.

Personalisation will not just be limited to digital interactions, but will extend into retail outlets via in-store strategies and phone communications via chatbots. Some retailers will provide the opportunity for members to choose whether they are identified or remain anonymous, while others (such as supermarkets and major retailers) will insist on identification as part of their overall shopping experience.

Machine learning/AI will extend further into contact centre operations, utilising extensive personal data profiles to service member needs, with more complex issues handed over to agents. This will reduce reliance on staff (thereby saving on costs) while allowing for 24-hour service support.

Data challenges

With personalised member experiences powered by data, the capture, analysis, use, and monetisation of member personal data by loyalty programs will become increasingly topical. This will be led by consumers, who will demand better controls over their data, including the right to insist it is deleted from program databases, and government bodies which will legislate more data protections as a counter to the growing dominance of tech giants.

At the same time, digital marketing will suffer the loss of cookies, disrupting current digital targeting and remarketing practices.

Both these developments will increase demand for the capture of zero-party and first-party data. Loyalty programs will be harnessed to play a lead role in the capture of this data, using techniques and tools such as surveys, polls, quizzes, competitions, gamification, and social posts.

---

503 Savransky, M., 2020, 'The Power of Digital EQ', Loyalty & Reward Co, https://www.rewardco.com.au/the-power-of-digital-eq/ accessed 24 June 2020.

This demand will, in turn, stimulate genuine innovation in the loyalty industry, with the added benefit that the importance placed on the member will increase.

Loyalty programs as a product and services brand

With the growth in importance of zero-party and first-party data, the value of the engaged member databases controlled by large loyalty programs will grow. This will enable the loyalty program to harness their brand by developing a range of products and services which they can promote directly to their member base.

This approach will gain traction as co-branded credit card usage diminishes. Many central banks around the world are working to reduce transaction fees payable by merchants, making it harder for banks to fund bonus points.

For a loyalty program, expanding their offering with bespoke clubs, or branded products and services (such as insurance) will help to grow revenues, or at least offset their decline, while growing attitudinal commitment.

Legal trends

It is challenging to predict the approach so many different jurisdictions around the world will take to adjusting regulatory frameworks. That said, loyalty program operators should consider certain trends which point towards a general tightening of consumer protections. Changes to consumer protections could potentially impact program disclosures, communications and operations in the jurisdiction/s in which the program operates.

One area is the collection, use and sharing of data. This includes expanding member personal data definitions (e.g. to include technical data such as IP addresses, device identifiers, location data and other online identifiers), separating out consents for data collection and use (e.g. such as third-party sharing) and seamless deletion of data on the request of a member. The EU's introduction of GDPR provides an interesting template for consideration.

Another area is financial licenses. As large coalition loyalty programs continue to grow, regulators may consider reversing the exemptions enjoyed by loyalty programs. Most laws applicable to financial products (or non-cash payment facilities) do not currently impact loyalty programs, but this could change. In the future, loyalty programs may be treated as financial products and accordingly will be subject to financial product licensing and other conditions.

The third area is disclosure; regulators may increase pressure on loyalty program operators to ensure terms and conditions (and privacy policies) are concise, transparent, intelligible, easily accessible, and written in clear and plain language.

Ever-evolving member expectations

As discussed in Chapter 1, companies such as Netflix, Amazon, Uber and Spotify have redefined what it means to be a service business with a new manifesto;[504] know me, respond quickly, be where I want to be, tell me what you stand for, speak to my pains and passions, give me value for my privacy and reward me for loyalty.

As more companies replicate the customer experience practices of these market-leaders, consumer expectations defined by the new manifesto will be reinforced, increasing the likelihood they will demand the same experience from other brands. If their expectations are not met, brands risk rapid rejection and vocal disapproval. The opportunity for brands is to develop a culture focused on customer experience optimisation and evolution. For some companies, this may start with hiring a customer experience (UX) expert in a senior role in the business to help them commence their journey. Given the accelerating global trends of digital transformation and adoption, the expectations for innovative customer experiences will continue to grow.

Games and gamification

Gamification approaches and techniques will continue to improve, and loyalty platform development will make it easier for program operators to execute campaigns which persuade members to engage in specific behaviours.

While gamification will deliver a significant amount of value, the bigger emerging trend is games. Members of loyalty programs can expect increasing innovation in this area, particularly for programs which centre around an app. As the trend gathers momentum, more sophisticated white-label platforms

---

504 Sawhney, M., n.d., 'Applications of AI in Marketing and Customer Experience Management; Identify use cases in Marketing, Sales and Customer Service - Course 5', accessed 23rd May 2020.

will emerge, supporting the ability for loyalty programs to launch rich gaming experiences at low cost.

Convenience

Gary Vaynerchuk stated that convenience is king. 'In a marketplace of distraction, the company's (sic), products and services that can save you TIME, are going to win. That is why Amazon is a market leader. That is why Prime Now wins. They have simplified the process of buying and selling. They have saved you enormous amounts of time.'[505] Vaynerchuk also mentions Google Now, Siri, text messages, emojis, spell-check and abbreviations as convenience-generating. In particular, he focuses on machine learning/AI as important technology that can save users time by learning and automating processes which would have taken much longer.

There are genuine commercial benefits from focusing on convenience. A US Department of Commerce report[506] identified that stores and offerings focused on convenience have been responsible for an estimated 67 per cent of retail growth. A National Retail Federation report[507] found that 90 per cent of consumers surveyed said they were more likely to choose a retailer based on convenience.

A Deloitte report[508] argued that Covid-19 has accelerated the trend towards consumer desire for convenience, 'with more than 50 per cent of consumers spending more on convenience to get what they need, with 'convenience' increasingly being defined by contactless shopping, on-demand fulfillment, and inventory availability. As such, there has been a surge in

505 Vaynerchuk, G., 2017, 'What start-ups really sell', https://www.garyvaynerchuk.com/startups-really-sell/, accessed 24 June 2020.

506 US Department of Commerce, 'Monthly Retail Trade', https://www.census.gov/retail/index.html, accessed 3 April 2020.

507 National Retail Federation, 2020, 'Consumer View Winter 2020', https://nrf.com/research/consumer-view-winter-2020 accessed 24 June 2020.

508 Lobaugh, K. M., Stephens, B. &Reynolds, C., 2020, 'The future is coming… but still one day at a time', Deloitte Insights, https://www2.deloitte.com/us/en/insights/industry/retail-distribution/retail-and-consumer-products-predictions.html?id=us:2el:3pr:4di6513:5awa:6di:MMDDYY:&pkid=1006899#endnote-sup-4, accessed 24 June 2020.

mobile payment usage, delivery app downloads, and buy-online-pick-up-in-store (BOPIS) adoption.'

Loyalty programs have a clear role to play in the manifestation of convenience. Utilising customer data, marketing channels, machine learning/AI and other opportunities, loyalty program designers and operators will increasingly seek innovative ways to increase the convenience for members in engaging with their brand.

Generation Touch Free

In 2013, Josh Elman coined the term *Generation Touch*,[509] referring to Millennials who grew up tech and device savvy and with the expectation that everything will work by touch.

Covid-19 will completely reset this expectation, with most consumers set to develop an expectation that everything will work *touch free.*

Loyalty programs will play a key role in delivering to the expectations of *Generation Touch Free*. This will include utilising data, technology and psychology to build rich augmented reality experiences (such as virtual try-ons), touch free payment solutions, and a variety of technological innovations which personalise the remote or stay-at-home experience. Any innovation which removes the need for members to touch something that other people have touched will be rapidly embraced.

Payments and convergence

Banks, card schemes and major coalition programs are all investing heavily in converging loyalty and payments. Many start-ups are emerging globally with sophisticated white-label platforms which can enable solutions, allowing a member to link a credit card or bank account to a program which instantly rewards them with cashback, points, or other benefits when they spend. This extends into payment apps which are merging multiple loyalty programs into their offering, allowing them to access valuable member personal data, as well as global players that now offer payments capabilities.

Social media is rushing into this space to ensure they do not miss the

---

509 Elman, J., Sept 2013, 'Generation Touch Will Redraw Consumer Tech', TechCrunch, https://techcrunch.com/2013/09/29/generation-touch-will-redraw-consumer-tech/, accessed 20 July 2020.

opportunity. WhatsApp users can now send and receive money by way of its messaging app, using Facebook Pay, the payments service WhatsApp owner Facebook launched in 2019.[510]

With so much investment in this area, and significant potential in delivering a seamless, instantly rewarding experience, the merging of payments and loyalty is likely to be a mega trend over the next decade.

Security and fraud incidents

With loyalty program operators globally continuing to under-invest in mitigation strategies, one unfortunate trend which is likely to continue is security breaches and fraudulent behaviour. This may be as small as a fraudster exploiting a birthday reward offer to receive it every day, or as big as a database hack accessing the personal data of hundreds of millions of members.

The continuing global proliferation (and digitalisation) of loyalty programs will require loyalty program operators to keep pace with rising loyalty fraud, and related risks and preventative solutions.

The rise of B2B programs

B2B industries have typically been laggards in the loyalty industry, both in implementing programs and in embracing innovative design. As detailed in Chapter 9, B2B programs contain some natural advantages over consumer programs, but also some unique challenges.

As more companies launch attractive programs for their business customers, and the body of knowledge expands regarding what constitutes an effective program, B2B loyalty is already gaining momentum as a significant trend.

Outsourcing

Loyalty technology outsourcing is set to continue for programs both large and small. The industry has evolved sufficiently such that highly sophisticated platforms can be accessed at a low cost, and far cheaper than a company could build internally.

Other outsourcing options, including strategic design and evolution,

---

510 Singh, M. & Lunden, I., 2020, 'WhatsApp finally launches payments, starting in Brazil', https://techcrunch.com/2020/06/15/whatsapp-finally-launches-payments-starting-in-brazil/?guccounter=1, accessed 24 June 2020.

automated marketing, reward supply and call centre operations, will also continue to grow.

Welcome to the Metaverse

The Metaverse is a future iteration of the internet, made up of persistent, shared, 3D virtual spaces linked into a perceived virtual universe. According to a Forbes article,[511] 'Currently, you can only experience the internet when you go to it, but with new connectivity, devices and technologies, we'll be able to experience it all around every single day.' This includes virtual reality and augmented reality merging seamlessly with the real world, and embracing day-to-day social and transactional interactions.

With the evolution of the Metaverse will come promotions, offers, virtual and real goods, and the opportunity to interact with loyalty programs. Virtual currencies as rewards for desired behaviours are a natural fit for this space, including points, miles, cryptocurrencies and tokenised assets.

*

A well-designed loyalty program can work to successfully drive engagement between a brand and members, building deeper attitudinal commitment which manifests in a range of valuable benefits.

Generating sustained, meaningful engagement with members requires a deep understanding of member behaviour and expectations to effectively respond to their needs at each stage of their journey. Loyalty psychology, technology, design frameworks, commercial models, legal requirements, security and fraud risks, and future trends all need to be considered and incorporated for the program to operate as best practice.

The overarching goal of this book has been to provide the definitive guide for loyalty program theory and practice. Future editions will build on this foundation as the authors and contributors continue their research and practise in the loyalty industry. Any feedback on this edition is welcome and encouraged.

With an incredible history, loyalty programs have a bright future.

---

511 Hackl, C. July 2020, 'The Metaverse is coming and it's a very big deal', Forbes, https://www.forbes.com/sites/cathyhackl/2020/07/05/the-metaverse-is-coming--its-a-very-big-deal/#5588c8f9440f accessed 18 August 2020.

KEY LOYALTY PROGRAM METRICS FOR PROGRAM OPERATORS

Member base

<u>Overall</u>

- Total members
- Total active members (typically measured by activity over a time period)
- Total net member growth/decline (typically measured against a previous time period)
- Total net member tier movement (for programs that have status tiers)
- Total net member segment movement (for programs that have well defined segments)

<u>New</u>

- Total new joins
- Total new joins by channel
  - ◦ Website

- Web App
- Native App
- Social media
- In-store
- Kiosk (or any other stand-alone piece of technology located in-store)
- Affiliate partner
- Total new joins by segment
- CPA (cost per acquisition)

Reactivated

- Total reactivated members (typically measured as a % against total inactive)

Churn

- Total actual churned members (lost members, based on inactivity or deregistration from program)
- Total predicted churn (over a pre-determined time frame)
- Churns core rating of existing members

For program operators that value benchmarking analysis, an interesting addition is to measure member activity rates against those of programs within the same industry to see how they compare.

For example, a program operator within supermarkets might find that average activity rates for program members is 60 per cent (vs overall members).

This benchmarking analysis will quickly identify whether a program operator is sitting above or below industry averages, and if any action needs to be taken.

Member marketing and communications

- Total opt-ins by channel
  - Email
  - SMS
  - App
- Total unsubscribes (typically measured as a % against the overall opt-in base)
- Email open rate
- Email click through rate
- Social media followers (split by platform)

Member activity

Onboarding effectiveness

- Average time period from joining for new member to transact:
  - Same day (% of members vs total new joins)
  - Within the first week (% of members vs total new joins)
  - Within the first month (% of members vs total new joins)
- Average per new member:
  - Spend per transaction
  - Frequency of transactions

Overall

- % of members transacting in-store (vs non-members)
- % of members transacting online (vs non-members)

- Average transaction value (typically measured against a previous time period)
- Average purchase frequency (typically measured against a previous time period)
- Average spend per visit (in-store, online, app, etc.)
- Total vouchers / credits earned (over a particular time period)
- Total vouchers / credits redeemed (over a particular time period)
- Total vouchers / credits expired (over a particular time period)
- % of available benefits used by members (provides an indication of how benefits are resonating with members)
- Benefits unused by members (this identifies unused benefits, which a lifecycle strategy might highlight to the member to demonstrate value)
- Average number of referrals by member
- Referral effectiveness (% of referrals that result in the desired action)

For points programs

- Earn

  Programs operators should also measure points earned by type, because these will indicate whether the members are receptive to marketing offers.

  - Total base points earned
  - Total bonus points earned
  - Total non-transactional points earned (these might be for filling in surveys or engaging on social media)
  - Point earn by channel/partner

- Redeem

  - Total amount of points redeemed

- Total $ value of points redeemed

- % of points redeemed, split by category (e.g. gift cards, merchandise, etc.)

- % of members with a redeemable balance (e.g. minimum required for the lowest price reward)

- Expiry

  - % of actual breakage

  - $ of actual breakage

  - % of forecasted breakage (typically measured against a previous time period)

  - $ of forecasted breakage (typically measured against a previous time period)

  If the forecasted breakage is increasing, it is worthwhile to measure this against the net member base movement. If the latter is showing decline, then this is a good indicator of member disengagement and steps will need to be taken to rectify it.

For tier programs

- Total members within each tier (as a % of total members)
- Summary of upward member tier movement (and associated insights related to transaction activity, engagement, etc)
- Summary of downward member tier movement (and associated insights related to transaction activity, engagement, etc)
- Cost of member benefit provision (and points earn, where applicable) per tier
- Analysis of cost per tier vs budget

For member benefits programs

- % of members engaging with any benefit (vs those that don't engage at all)
- Frequency of member engagement with any benefit
- % of members engaging with more than one benefit
- Most popular member benefit categories
- Most popular member benefit products and/or services
- Impact of benefit engagement on member lifetime value
- Impact of benefit engagement on member churn

For cashback / affiliate / card-linked programs

- Total cashback / affiliate revenue earned (over a particular time period)
- Top merchants cashback / affiliate revenue earned at (over a particular time period)
- Top online merchants browsed but not transacted at (over a particular time period)
- Preferred card used
- Average basket size (in-store vs online)

For games / gamification programs

- Total games played (over a particular time period)
- Total game time (over a particular time period)
- Average game time (by game vs overall)
- Impact to member engagement post gameplay (transactions or other engagement metric)
- Impact to ROI (vs comparable time period without gameplay)

Operational areas

<u>Finance</u>

- Annual revenue generated from customer
- Annual general costs of acquiring, serving and retaining the customer
- Total points earned per annum
- Total points redeemed per annum
- Billings per point
- Cost per point forecast
- Cost per point actual
- Annual interest earned on individual's points revenue deferred
- Breakage (total points expired)
- Program costs of acquiring, serving and retaining the customer
- Total cost of earned currency
- Total cost of redemptions
- % of overall revenue contributed by members (typically measured against a previous time period)
- % of revenue contributed by members by channel (typically measured against a previous time period)
- Sales incrementality (member vs non-member)
- Member Lifetime Value by identified segments (typically measured against a previous time period)
- Recency, Frequency, Monetary Value movement by segment (typically measured against a previous time period and look for upwards movements)

Marketing & Analytics

- Member engagement by lifecycle stage (join, onboarding, growth, retention, winback)
- Member engagement by lifecycle (overlaid by persona)
- Churn risk score (by segment and persona)
- Test & learn analysis (campaign based)
- A/B test analysis (campaign based)
- Member communications by channel (eDM, push, SMS, web, social, digital, etc)
- Engagement by channel
- Revenues by channel
- Cost per channel
- % of total budget used per channel
- ROI by channel
- Member benchmarking analysis (by program and/or industry)
- Machine learning and/or AI models and their success in driving sales / incrementality

Call Centre

- % of member enquiries (vs non-member enquiries)
- % of escalated member queries (vs resolved within the first call)
- Irritant summary (by category and # of queries)
- Points earned (by member)
- Total points awarded manually (by member)
- Points redeemed (by member)
- Points expired (by member)

Technology

- Total members in database
- % of active members in database (vs total members)
- Cost per active member (total program revenue divided by total active members)
- % of technology costs vs overall program costs

Security & Fraud

- Member accounts that have earned points more than once per day
- Member accounts that show an earning pattern that's significantly different to previous earn history
- Member accounts with a higher than usual propensity to avail of bonus earn campaigns
- Member accounts that have transferred points more than once per day
- Member accounts that show a transfer pattern that's significantly different to previous transfer history
- Member accounts that have redeemed points more than once per day
- Member accounts that show a redemption pattern that's significantly different to previous redemption history
- Member accounts that have credits applied against them more than once in a week/month
- Member accounts that have credits applied against them more than what is typical over the life of an account
- Member accounts that have credits applied against them over and above the permissible amount
- Member accounts with higher than usual refund activity

- Member accounts with no notes against the profile, even though there is a record of call centre contact
- Member accounts with higher than usual password resetting activity
- Member accounts with higher than usual referral activity
- Creation of a large portion of member accounts within a very short timeframe
- Creation of member accounts with very similar emails
- List of accounts that have been frozen due to suspicious activity
- Staff members accessing member accounts out of standard office hours
- Staff members accessing member accounts more frequently than usual
- Total fraudulent earn transactions (vs overall member transactions)
- % of fraudulent earn transactions by channel
- Total fraudulent redeem transactions (vs overall member transactions)
- % of fraudulent redeem transactions by channel
- % of fraudulent transactions (vs overall member transactions)

Operations / Partner Management

- % of new earn partners (over a particular time period)
- % of members earning with partner (vs overall member base)
- Average member transaction amount with partner (vs other partners)
- Average member frequency of transaction with partner (vs other partners)
- % of new redeem partners (over a particular time period)

INDEX – COMPANY, BRAND AND LOYALTY PROGRAM

Z

Made in the USA
Las Vegas, NV
16 August 2022

53368392R00243